DATE DUE

The Republican Party and American Politics from Hoover to Reagan

During a long period of the twentieth century, stretching from the Great Depression until the Reagan years, defeat generally characterized the electoral record of the Republican Party. Although Republicans achieved some notable victories at the presidential level, a majority of Americans identified with the Democratic Party, not the GOP. This book investigates how Republicans tackled the problem of their party's minority status and why their efforts to boost GOP fortunes usually ended in failure. At the heart of the Republicans' minority puzzle was the profound and persistent popularity of New Deal liberalism. This puzzle was stubbornly resistant to solution. Efforts to develop a Republican version of government activism met little success. The same was true of conservative strategies that stressed a more fundamental rejection of the Democrats' arguments. Technocratic initiatives to improve party organization and communications similarly failed to facilitate an electoral breakthrough. Only the Democratic Party's decline eventually created opportunities for Republican resurgence. The topic of Republicans' engagement with the minority problem is of central importance to understanding modern U.S. political history; this book is the first to scrutinize its long-term evolution.

Robert Mason is senior lecturer in history at the University of Edinburgh. He is the author of *Richard Nixon and the Quest for a New Majority* (2004).

The Republican Party and American Politics from Hoover to Reagan

ROBERT MASON
University of Edinburgh

CAMBRIDGE
UNIVERSITY PRESS

CAMBRIDGE UNIVERSITY PRESS
Cambridge, New York, Melbourne, Madrid, Cape Town,
Singapore, São Paulo, Delhi, Tokyo, Mexico City

Cambridge University Press
32 Avenue of the Americas, New York, NY 10013-2473, USA

www.cambridge.org
Information on this title: www.cambridge.org/9781107007048

First published 2012

Printed in the United States of America

A catalog record for this publication is available from the British Library.

Library of Congress Cataloging in Publication data
Mason, Robert, 1970–
    The Republican Party and American Politics from Hoover to Reagan / Robert Mason.
    p. cm
    ISBN 978-1-107-00704-8 (hardback)
    1. Republican Party (U.S. : 1854–) – History – 20th century.   2. United States – Politics
    and government – 20th century.   I. Title.
    JK2356.M27 2011
    324.273409′04–dc22   2010052381

ISBN 978-1-107-00704-8 Hardback

Supported by the
Arts & Humanities
Research Council

For my teachers

Contents

Acknowledgments   *page* ix

Introduction   1
1   "From Old Home Melodies to Jazz Music": 1928–1933   11
2   "As Maine Goes, So Goes Vermont": 1933–1939   41
3   "The Simple Barefoot Wall Street Lawyer": 1939–1945   79
4   "Liberty versus Socialism": 1945–1953   112
5   "Modern Republicanism": 1953–1961   148
6   "A Choice, Not an Echo": 1960–1968   182
7   "There's a Realignment Going On": 1968–1976   216
8   "You Are Witnessing the Great Realignment": 1977–1989   247
Conclusion   282

Archival Sources   289
Index   293

Acknowledgments

In writing this book, I have been immensely fortunate to benefit from the assistance and support of many individuals and institutions. The book is founded on their generosity, for which I am most grateful.

As the bibliography suggests, it proved especially important for me to have the extremely good fortune to spend an extended spell at the Library of Congress. This chance was thanks to my time as a Fellow at the John W. Kluge Center there. I would like to thank the Center for the award of this fellowship, as well as all the people at the Center who created such an exceptional environment in which to conduct work. During my time at the Kluge Center, and during other visits to Washington, members of staff in the Library of Congress's Manuscript Division offered friendly, professional help that greatly facilitated the task of primary research.

On my return from Washington, the United Kingdom's Arts and Humanities Research Council provided funding to support the writing of the book manuscript. I am very grateful to the AHRC and to the other institutions that provided this project with essential financial support: the British Academy; the Carnegie Trust for the Universities of Scotland; the Eisenhower World Affairs Institute, for the award of an Abilene travel grant; the Gerald R. Ford Presidential Foundation; the Herbert Hoover Presidential Library Association, for the award of a Senator and Mrs. Roman L. Hruska Fellowship; the Lilly Library of Indiana University, Bloomington, for the award of a Ball Brothers Foundation Visiting Fellowship; the Rockefeller Archive Center; and the Roosevelt Study Center, Middelburg, the Netherlands.

The University of Edinburgh's School of History, Classics and Archaeology has not only given me a pleasant academic home; the school has also provided me with all kinds of practical assistance. It is not only my colleagues there who have generously offered help and advice. Students there, too, have contributed much to this project while taking courses relating to my research. At Cambridge University Press, many who participated in the book's development deserve my thanks for their support of this project and for their help – especially the book's editor, Eric Crahan. So do those who worked on the manuscript for the Press.

Along the way, countless other people have given me advice, help, and support in many different ways. I would like to express my thanks in particular to Pertti Ahonen, Tony Badger, Mike Bowen, Tim Boyd, Chris Brown, Gian Mario Cao, Frank Cogliano, Donald Critchlow, Gareth Davies, Alan Day, Owen Dudley Edwards, Fabian Hilfrich, Rhodri Jeffreys-Jones, Jenny Litster, Brett Marston, Paul Martin, John Mason, Sarah Mason, Iwan Morgan, Bent Nielsen, Richard O'Leary, Jacqui Pearse, Allen Pitt, Finn Pollard, Paul Quigley, Mary Lou Reker, Catherine Rymph, Sukhdev Sandhu, Petra Schleiter, Byron Shafer, Rebecca Short, Marc Stears, Balázs Szelényi, and Tim Thurber. Anonymous readers of the manuscript contributed a great deal, too. The same is true of the archivists and librarians at the places where I conducted work on this book. As with all the individuals and institutions who helped me, their advice and assistance were crucially significant; I am very thankful.

Introduction

This book investigates a long period of the twentieth century – from the late 1920s to the 1980s – when fewer Americans identified themselves as Republicans than Democrats, when the Republican Party was the minority party in the United States. *The Republican Party and American Politics from Hoover to Reagan* is about this minority problem. It looks at how leading Republican politicians conceptualized the problem of their party's minority status, the puzzle of why a majority preferred the Democrats. The answers were by no means clear. There was consequently a debate within the party about its problems, a debate that was often fierce. One of this book's goals is to track this debate. Based on their conceptualization of the problem, Republicans took actions to solve it. Another goal is to analyze these efforts to revitalize the party. Their results were often disappointing. Until the party's Reagan era breakthrough – when Republicans nevertheless achieved not majority status but parity with the Democrats – success was short-term at best. The book considers why these plans for party revitalization tended to end in disappointment.

One way to view a political party is as an office-seeking vehicle, working to maximize its candidates' chances of election and thus of power. Within this context, the Republican record from Hoover to Reagan is remarkably, surprisingly weak. Post–World War II Republican administrations dominate perceptions of national politics in their respective years, but their visibility obscures the degree of Democratic success during this period. A "short twentieth century," between the arrival of the Great Depression and the end of the Cold War, was a period when there were almost always more Democrats than Republicans in Congress, in state legislatures, and among governors. More Americans consistently felt a sense of connection and affiliation with the Democratic than Republican Party, considering themselves Democrats, not Republicans. Republican victory was the exception to the rule during this lengthy period of modern U.S. history.

Ideas as well as numbers defined the Democratic era. Support for activist government in pursuit of economic prosperity and welfare guarantees – a liberal agenda that Democrats developed during the New Deal and modified during World War II and afterwards – enjoyed the backing of an electoral majority for decades, and the evolving concerns of this New Deal liberalism were most often at the center of political debate. The challenge facing Republicans was to develop an alternative to the Democrats' agenda that was likely to secure popular support. Within the party there were different policy prescriptions for this alternative, as well as different ideas about the best strategies to win support. The resulting Republican alternative was often reactive, oppositional, and even negative. Leading Republicans struggled, frequently without much success, to develop a more positive, proactive alternative to the Democrats' ideas, only genuinely meeting some success in the 1970s and the 1980s when New Deal liberalism's apparent shortcomings increased a public appetite for conservatism and when the Democratic Party seemed to be running out of ideas. But national debate was not always about New Deal liberalism. Democratic hegemony was far less clear, and even sometimes absent, when politics turned to concerns other than New Deal liberalism – such as, notably, foreign policy and civil rights. Still, these were exceptions to New Deal liberalism's centrality and to an enduring pattern of Democratic rule, Republican failure.

Individuals matter in party politics.[1] The ideas and initiatives that defined the minority debate's contours were often associated with the party's leading figures; this study thus looks extensively at these politicians. Especially prominent among the leading individuals in party politics are those who sought the presidency. Most prominent of all are those who won. As de facto party leader, a presidential candidate and – even more so – a president had a position of unparalleled influence to shape the Republican response to its minority problem, even if the party's largeness and diversity limited the extent of that influence.[2] The limits, indeed, often seemed more extensive than the influence; the party at large not infrequently frustrated its leadership's plans for Republican revitalization. Together with his running mate and vice president, this leader was, moreover, the only officeholder with a nationwide constituency; only at this level did the minority problem crucially become a matter of victory or defeat. The centrality of presidential candidates and presidents to the minority debate means that this book's focus often falls on these leading individuals. It is an approach that rightly invites scholarly wariness; the "presidential synthesis" threatens to conceal more than it reveals.[3] But to a great extent

---

[1] George H. Mayer, *The Republican Party, 1854–1966*, 2nd ed. (New York: Oxford University Press, 1967), vii.

[2] James W. Davis, *The President as Party Leader* (New York: Praeger, 1992); Daniel J. Galvin, *Presidential Party Building: Dwight D. Eisenhower to George W. Bush* (Princeton, N.J.: Princeton University Press, 2010); Sidney M. Milkis, *The President and the Parties: The Transformation of the American Party System since the New Deal* (New York: Oxford University Press, 1993).

[3] Thomas C. Cochran, "The 'Presidential Synthesis' in American History," *American Historical Review* [hereafter *AHR*] 53 (1948), 748–759.

presidential politics gives structure to national party politics. Study of the minority debate demands such a presidency-focused perspective.

Just as the focus of the minority debate was usually personalized and presidential, it usually involved national politics alone – to the exclusion of state and local politics. In institutional terms the party's existence at the national level was weak, strengthening only toward the end of the period that this book considers, still mostly in an organizational rather than ideological sense. The Republican Party was more properly a collection of state parties, together with a conglomeration of other party-related institutions.[4] At the center, the Republican National Committee (RNC) was merely another symbol of the party's loose, decentralized, coalitional nature; RNC members were the choice of the state parties. Exercising relatively little influence, it usually had few duties; a study that was conducted during the 1950s discussed both national committees' "politics without power."[5] The minority problem was by its very nature a concern at the national level, rather than the state and local levels, though personalities and ideas that became nationally important often had state- or local-level origins. Nevertheless, despite its national focus, a key characteristic of this debate was an acute sense of region, reflective of the recognition that it was exceptionally difficult to aggregate successfully the concerns of a diverse, geographically scattered population. At first, the party sought the restoration of a powerful East–West coalition. Later, one of the prominent – and promising – ideas to recapture a majority involved the development of a coalition between South and West.

A paradox of the Republican plight is the strength of conservatism during the minority period. At first sight the decades that began with the New Deal appear to be an era of liberalism, but when examined more closely they are often characterized by conservative success in opposing liberal plans and initiatives. In terms of legislative accomplishment, there were perhaps only two relatively brief moments of far-reaching and successful liberal activism – the mid-1930s "second New Deal" and the mid-1960s "Great Society."[6] Republicans thus secured influence as the minority, normally in collaboration with Democrats skeptical of legislative advance and innovation, though

4 There are few state- or city-level studies of the twentieth-century party. Exceptions include Frank B. Atkinson, *The Dynamic Dominion: Realignment and the Rise of Two-Party Competition in Virginia, 1945–1980*, 2nd ed. (Lanham, Md.: Rowman & Littlefield, 2006); Samuel B. Hand, *The Star that Set: The Vermont Republican Party, 1854–1974* (Lanham, Md.: Lexington, 2002); Roger M. Olien, *From Token to Triumph: The Texas Republicans since 1920* (Dallas: SMU Press, 1982). New work is now appearing: Joseph Crespino, *In Search of Another Country: Mississippi and the Conservative Counterrevolution* (Princeton, N.J.: Princeton University Press, 2007); Sean P. Cunningham, *Cowboy Conservatism: Texas and the Rise of the Modern Right* (Lexington: University Press of Kentucky, 2010).

5 Cornelius P. Cotter and Bernard C. Hennessy. *Politics without Power: The National Party Committees* (New York: Atherton, 1964).

6 James T. Patterson, "American Politics: The Bursts of Reform, 1930s–1970s," in Patterson, ed., *Paths to the Present: Interpretive Essays on American History since 1930* (Minneapolis, Minn.: Burgess, 1975), 57–101.

usually in opposing liberal initiative rather than enacting a conservative alternative. But liberalism's lack of legislative achievement failed to create a favorable climate for Republican growth. It pushed the Democrats toward a moderation that was electorally appealing. Such shortcomings actually reinforced the party's minority status, therefore. By contrast, later in this period, the Great Society's activist flurry of legislation under Lyndon Johnson helped set in motion popular discontent with the Democrats. In pushing forward New Deal liberalism's agenda, the Johnson administration alienated many voters who purportedly supported this agenda.

During this period the Democrats usually managed to articulate the right kind of liberalism for electoral success: one that shrank from policies of economic redistribution; one that developed a welfare state catering to a broad middle class rather than targeted at a smaller constituency of the poor; one that avoided direct engagement with racial inequalities (until a variety of outside pressures forced the party as a whole to do so). Republicans, by contrast, all too often articulated the wrong kind of conservatism – one, at least, that their Democratic opponents managed to characterize as friendly to an economic elite rather than beneficial to Americans more generally. Such a characterization promoted Democratic victory, Republican defeat.

Principled opposition to the Democrats' ideas led many Republicans to articulate the wrong kind of conservatism. Their responses to New Deal liberalism often reveal a fierce conviction that the party's political mission possessed urgent importance to save the nation from activist government's ills. Recognition of the importance of the electoral imperative in practical politics sometimes leads observers to overlook the importance of other factors, notably that of political principle. What is notable about the minority period is that – despite New Deal liberalism's popular strength – some Republicans did not see any conflict between the electoral imperative and political principle. They noticed conservatism's strength and concluded that this signified a non-mobilized rejection of the Democrats' ideas. To these Republicans, the party's puzzle involved a search for the right strategy to activate a hidden majority of disaffection with the Democrats. This view underestimated the extent to which support for programmatic efforts to tackle the nation's problems qualified a conservative preference for smaller government, for individualistic self-reliance. Republicans therefore sometimes articulated the wrong kind of conservatism while believing, inaccurately, that this conservatism – in opposition to New Deal liberalism's programs – was popular. Such misinterpretations exacerbated the minority problem. This is not to suggest, however, that those Republicans who accepted New Deal liberalism's popularity were able to solve the minority problem. Two of the era's presidents, Dwight Eisenhower and Richard Nixon, both recognized this popularity, but neither managed to transform their party's fortunes, despite personal victories and despite thoughtful efforts to do so. The disappointing results of their efforts underscored the profound persistence of Democratic strength, as well as nourishing the argument of those who preferred stauncher opposition to New Deal liberalism.

For many years historians largely neglected the study of post-Depression conservatism, often overlooking the antistatist impulse that coexisted with the trend toward big government.[7] In recent years, however, they have richly analyzed political conservatism's rise since the 1960s. This historiography features some especially insightful explanations for the appeal of traditionalist politics among cosmopolitan, affluent, and forward-looking groups in society and the relationship between racism and opposition to liberalism.[8] Fewer historians have written more specifically about the Republican Party, an institution that has perhaps often suffered from relative scholarly inattention.[9] The chronological focus of this new research has tended to begin with the rise of conservatism surrounding Barry Goldwater's 1964 presidential candidacy; there are fewer works that consider Republicans and conservatives during the tumultuous developments of the Great Depression, the Second World War, and the early years of the Cold War (with the large exception of McCarthyism

[7] Alan Brinkley, "The Problem of American Conservatism," *AHR* 99 (1994), 409–429.

[8] Dan T. Carter, *The Politics of Rage: George Wallace, the Origins of the New Conservatism* (New York: Simon and Schuster, 1995); Lisa McGirr, *Suburban Warriors: The Origins of the New American Right* (Princeton, N.J.: Princeton University Press, 2001); Jonathan M. Schoenwald, *A Time for Choosing: The Rise of Modern American Conservatism* (New York: Oxford University Press, 2001).

[9] Works that analyze the party's history during this period include Donald T. Critchlow, *The Conservative Ascendancy: How the GOP Right Made Political History* (Cambridge, Mass.: Harvard University Press, 2007) and David W. Reinhard, *The Republican Right since 1945* (Lexington: University Press of Kentucky, 1983), which focus on conservative Republicans. Lewis L. Gould, *Grand Old Party: A History of the Republicans* (New York: Random House, 2003) offers a very useful, wide-ranging overview, suggesting that much research about the party remains to be done, especially for the twentieth century. It is surprising that it took many decades for a new alternative to Mayer, *The Republican Party*, and Malcolm Moos, *The Republicans: A History of Their Party* (New York: Random House, 1956) to appear – exemplifying historians' neglect of the party. Important accounts of the party's history during parts of this period are Clyde P. Weed, *The Nemesis of Reform: The Republican Party During the New Deal* (New York: Columbia University Press, 1994); David L. Stebenne, *Modern Republican: Arthur Larson and the Eisenhower Years* (Bloomington: Indiana University Press, 2006); Steven Wagner, *Eisenhower Republicanism: Pursuing the Middle Way* (DeKalb: Northern Illinois University Press, 2006); and Mary C. Brennan, *Turning Right in the Sixties: The Conservative Capture of the GOP* (Chapel Hill: University of North Carolina Press, 1995). Key thematically focused works include Colin Dueck, *Hard Line: The Republican Party and U.S. Foreign Policy since World War II* (Princeton, N.J.: Princeton University Press, 2010); Steven P. Miller, *Billy Graham and the Rise of the Republican South* (Philadelphia: University of Pennsylvania Press, 2009); Nicol C. Rae, *The Decline and Fall of the Liberal Republicans: From 1952 to the Present* (New York: Oxford University Press, 1989); Catherine E. Rymph, *Republican Women: Feminism and Conservatism from Suffrage Through the Rise of the New Right* (Chapel Hill: University of North Carolina Press, 2006); Simon Topping, *Lincoln's Lost Legacy: The Republican Party and the African American Vote, 1928–1952* (Gainesville: University Press of Florida, 2008); and Daniel K. Williams, *God's Own Party: The Making of the Christian Right* (New York: Oxford University Press, 2010). Some biographies offer useful treatment of the Republican Party, notably including James T. Patterson, *Mr. Republican: A Biography of Robert A. Taft* (Boston: Houghton Mifflin, 1972), and Richard Norton Smith, *Thomas E. Dewey and His Times* (1982; New York: Touchstone, 1984).

and anticommunism). Those that do consider this earlier period reveal its
significance for the development of the Republican Party and conservatism;
scholars are now starting to develop a longer-term framework with which to
understand opposition to New Deal liberalism over time.[10]

Where the history of political parties intersects with the scholarship on
modern conservatism's development, its purpose most commonly is to explain
the replacement of the Democratic Party with the Republican Party as the
preferred party among conservative whites in the South.[11] The Republicans'
final lurch away from minority status in large part involved the decay of
the Democrats' "solid South" in favor of increasing success there for the
Grand Old Party, or GOP – first at the presidential level and later, though
very gradually, at other levels of elected office. Scholars have in particular
analyzed race's role in accounting for the distinctiveness of southern party
development.

---

[10] Exceptions include John E. Moser, *Right Turn: John T. Flynn and the Transformation of
American Liberalism* (New York: New York University Press, 2005); Weed, *Nemesis of
Reform*. Books that consider the post-1945 period include Godfrey Hodgson, *The World
Turned Right Side Up: A History of the Conservative Ascendancy in America* (Boston:
Houghton Mifflin, 1996); Michael W. Miles, *The Odyssey of the American Right* (New York:
Oxford University Press, 1980). The new work includes Patrick Allitt, *The Conservatives:
Ideas and Personalities Throughout American History* (New Haven, Conn.: Yale University
Press, 2009); Donald T. Critchlow, *Phyllis Schlafly and Grassroots Conservatism: A
Woman's Crusade* (Princeton, N.J.: Princeton University Press, 2005); David Farber,
The Rise and Fall of Modern American Conservatism: A Short History (Princeton, N.J.:
Princeton University Press, 2010); Allan J. Lichtman, *White Protestant Nation: The Rise of
the American Conservative Movement* (New York: Atlantic Monthly Press, 2008); Joseph E.
Lowndes, *From the New Deal to the New Right: Race and the Southern Origins of Modern
Conservatism* (New Haven, Conn.: Yale University Press, 2008); Kim Phillips-Fein, *Invisible
Hands: The Making of the Conservative Movement from the New Deal to Reagan* (New
York: Norton, 2009); Gregory L. Schneider, *The Conservative Century: From Reaction to
Revolution* (Lanham, Md.: Rowman & Littlefield, 2009).

[11] Exceptions include Critchlow, *Conservative Ascendancy*; Brennan, *Turning Right*; Rymph,
Republican Women. The literature on southern conservatism is extensive, including: Jack
Bass and Walter De Vries, *The Transformation of Southern Politics: Social Change and
Political Consequence since 1945* (New York: Basic, 1976); Earl Black and Merle Black,
The Rise of Southern Republicans (Cambridge, Mass.: Belknap, 2002); Alexander P.
Lamis, *The Two-Party South* (New York: Oxford University Press, 1984); David Lublin,
The Republican South: Democratization and Partisan Change (Princeton, N.J.: Princeton
University Press, 2004); Richard K. Scher, *Politics in the New South: Republicanism, Race,
and Leadership in the Twentieth Century*, 2nd ed. (Armonk, N.Y.: Sharpe, 1997); Byron
E. Shafer and Richard Johnston, *The End of Southern Exceptionalism: Class, Race, and
Partisan Change in the Postwar South* (Cambridge, Mass.: Harvard University Press, 2006).
In this area, work by political scientists remains significant, but the historiography is also
growing. Important contributions include Crespino, *In Search of Another Country*; Kevin
M. Kruse, *White Flight: Atlanta and the Making of Modern Conservatism* (Princeton, N.J.:
Princeton University Press, 2005); Matthew D. Lassiter, *The Silent Majority: Suburban
Politics in the Sunbelt South* (Princeton, N.J.: Princeton University Press, 2006); and William
A. Link, *Righteous Warriors: Jesse Helms and the Rise of Modern Conservatism* (New York:
St. Martin's, 2008).

The minority debate offers a new framework to understand this development. From the early years of Franklin Roosevelt's New Deal coalition, Republicans realized that the conservative South's concerns were in conflict with the evolving agenda of northern urban liberals, often dominant within the Democratic Party. This realization encouraged them to covet southern support as the route to a majority. Especially because southern white hostility to the party of Abraham Lincoln was so deep, at first such defections seemed implausible. Partisanship as well as ideology mattered; conservative southerners remained able to exercise influence within the majority party, and there were often differences between their conservatism and that of most Republicans. By the 1950s, a "new South" of economic development and racial moderation seemed the likeliest source of Republican converts; the 1960s was then a decade of soul-searching conflict as some accepted and even sought support from those against civil rights and others demanded its rejection. Quite glacially, then, congressional strength joined presidential strength for the party, a gradual process that was not really complete until as late as the 1990s.

What this investigation of the minority debate suggests is that – despite the South's electoral importance to the party by the end of the twentieth century – throughout the minority period the South only rarely assumed a position of essential centrality to arguments about how the party might achieve a majority, despite Republican interest in southern support. The solutions that Republicans developed usually involved policy, communication, and organization, rather than the breaking of the solid South as the key priority.

Studies of American political history, especially outside policy history, do not often involve an international dimension. But the history of the minority debate has such a dimension. Because nonliberal parties won more success elsewhere in the world, Republican politicians sometimes looked outside the United States in search of answers to their electoral problems, especially between the 1930s and the 1950s. They usually looked to the United Kingdom, a country with a common language and a party system that had at least some parallels with the American. These lesson-learning efforts were flawed in most cases, however, because the lessons such Republicans promoted reflected their prescription to tackle the party's problems, rather than any objective analysis of the reasons for the U.K. Conservative Party's success. However flawed this activity was, it nevertheless demonstrates that the Republicans' minority debate did not occur within a purely U.S. context.

Party identification – an individual's enduring support for one of the two parties – provides the rationale for the characterization of this period as one of minority status for the Republican Party, even though Republicans controlled the White House for twenty-four of the fifty-six years between 1933 and 1989. Throughout the period, soundings of public opinion usually showed that more Americans were normal supporters of the Democrats than of the Republicans, often by a decisive if not overwhelming degree; one sign of this Democratic-dominated polity is that there were only two years between 1933 and 1989 – the Eisenhower administration's first two years – when Republicans simultaneously controlled the White House, the Senate, and the House of Representatives. Once lost in the 1954 midterms, such control of the federal government was not to return until the twenty-first century.

Political scientists developed the concept of party identification in seeking to explain voting behavior, seeing a sense of affiliation to one of the parties as a form of self-identity among Americans even as fundamental as religious attachment. Family socialization was the usual crucible for the formation of this party attachment, which often then lasted for a lifetime. In elections, party identification was the best predictor of an individual's voting behavior, though it interacted with many other factors, including current evaluation of parties, candidates, and issues – allowing someone to vote for the other party without reconsidering this durable sense of partisan attachment. But this identification helped voters to make sense of political complexities, providing them with a frame through which to view differences between candidates and parties over issues.[12]

Even if it is helpful to observe the transnational dimension that the minority debate acquired occasionally, the concept of party identification is a reminder that the party–citizen relationship in the United States is an internationally unusual one. In one respect, this relationship is unusually distant. American parties lack the mass membership that most of their counterparts elsewhere possess, though the increase since the 1960s in their base of financial contributors muddies this distinction. In another respect, however, active identification with one of the major parties is much more widespread than in most countries; the absence of a mass membership perhaps facilitates such identification. A classic understanding of a political party, developed by political scientist V. O. Key, Jr., uses a three-form framework – the party in government, the party organization, and the party in the electorate – thus stressing the significance of citizens' party attachment as a key element of the party system.[13] An American of this period often considered herself or himself a Republican – rather than simply a supporter of the Republicans – even if lacking formal links with the party. Participation in the nomination process, especially if it involved a formal declaration of affiliation with one of the parties, as it did in some states, doubtless encouraged such self-definition.[14]

If the terminology of party identification suggests that from some perspectives political parties have assumed a particularly significant presence in the nation's life, the history of the party system qualifies the significance of this presence over time. The nineteenth century was a "party period" of deep

---

[12] Kenneth Prewitt and Norman Nie, "Election Studies of the Survey Research Center," *British Journal of Political Science* 1 (1971), 479–502.

[13] V. O. Key, Jr., *Politics, Parties, and Pressure Groups*, 5th ed. (New York: Crowell, 1964).

[14] The concept of party identification raises a problem of terminology because a "Republican" might refer to a supporter as well as to an activist or a leader. This study uses the term in the latter two senses and not the first.

and broad, spirited and enthusiastic engagement in interparty debate and competition; the twentieth century was not. Progressive era challenges to the parties' control over politics marked a turning point toward their decline.[15] During the minority period, most voters did not celebrate democratic participation as their nineteenth-century predecessors had. It was, moreover, a period of further party decline. The way Americans viewed politics increasingly involved candidates rather than parties, largely thanks to the news media's focus on candidates and neglect of parties.[16] But candidates, too, developed strategies that played up their personal claim for office and downplayed their party connection, knowing that such detachment from their party equipped them with greater autonomy to address their own constituency's particular needs. This tendency became especially acute among Republicans, the result of their party's minority status.

Work on party identification is related to the scholarship of electoral realignment. Key pioneered this paradigm in the 1950s with "a theory of critical elections," which University of Michigan scholars soon elaborated in influential work on voting behavior.[17] Realignment then inspired much research in history as well as political science. The idea won popular attention, too; in 1969 Kevin Phillips's *The Emerging Republican Majority*, a book that was much read and much discussed, employed an understanding of cyclical realignments to argue that the era of the Democratic Party's electoral dominance was reaching a close.

This scholarship's starting point was the recognition that durability was a key characteristic of party identification and that this durability allowed one party to maintain dominance within the two-party system for a lengthy period; there was normally a majority party and a minority party. At quite rare times of political upheaval, however, party identification was subject to change. A majority party lost its dominant position to the minority party or even a new political party before stability returned, consolidating this modified situation, often for many decades more. The realignment literature sought to understand such upheaval within the party system and such transformations of voting behavior and party attachment. The precipitation for these breaks with the past was the arrival of new political problems that the existing majority did not satisfactorily address. These new problems undermined the incumbents' electoral dominance, but they also usually encouraged a rearrangement of party coalitions at both elite and mass levels in bringing majority status to one party, minority status to another. The pre–Civil War sectional crisis led to an 1850s realignment, which involved the Whig Party's disintegration and the Republican Party's birth. The Republicans achieved majority status, though

---

[15] Joel H. Silbey, *The American Political Nation, 1838–1893* (Stanford, Calif.: Stanford University Press, 1991), 237–251.

[16] Martin P. Wattenberg, *The Decline of American Political Parties, 1952–1984* (Cambridge, Mass.: Harvard University Press, 1986).

[17] V. O. Key, Jr., "A Theory of Critical Elections," *Journal of Politics* 17 (1955), 3–18.

when the South returned to the Union, Democratic loyalties among whites there created some balance between the parties' fortunes. After the economic crises and Populist challenge of the late nineteenth century, the "system of 1896" involved Republican dominance. But the Great Depression relegated the Republican Party to minority status and allowed the Democratic Party to capture a majority's support.[18] It is the Republicans' post-Depression minority status that is the focus of this book.

In recent years political scientists have questioned realignment theories and thus the concept's utility in understanding electoral history.[19] Whatever realignment's larger utility, the literature valuably calls attention to the Great Depression's political significance – its long-lasting effects, visible in the parties' coalitions and in the durable centrality of New Deal liberalism-related concerns to political conflict. Moreover, the scholarship encourages the perspective that the Republicans' minority problem was resistant to straightforward solutions; this book supports this perspective.

Over time one aspect of the phenomenon of party decline and the emergence of "candidate-centered politics" was a slump in party identification, in the number of Americans who reported a sense of attachment to one of the political parties. From the 1960s, political independence grew in popularity as an alternative to Republican or Democratic attachment. The eventual result is that this book ends not with the Republican Party's final triumph in achieving majority status. Instead, the Democratic Party lost its majority status and joined the Republicans as a second minority party – or Republicans moved from minority to "parity" status. There was no realignment of the kind that Republicans sought; instead there was perhaps what political scientists called a "dealignment." As this book shows, Republicans did not always develop an insightful understanding of the causes of their minority status or a promising strategy to tackle this problem. But they worked hard to deprive their Democratic rivals of the majority prize and to seize it for the Republican Party. The puzzle they tackled was resistant to solution.

---

[18] James L. Sundquist, *Dynamics of the Party System: Alignment and Realignment of Political Parties in the United States*, rev. ed. (Washington, D.C.: Brookings Institution, 1983); Theodore Rosenof, *Realignment: The Theory That Changed the Way We Think about American Politics* (Lanham, Md.: Rowman & Littlefield, 2003).

[19] David R. Mayhew, *Electoral Realignments: A Critique of an American Genre* (New Haven, Conn.: Yale University Press, 2002); Alan Ware, *The Democratic Party Heads North, 1877–1962* (Cambridge: Cambridge University Press, 2006).

"From Old Home Melodies to Jazz Music": 1928–1933

Republican hegemony seemed unassailable in the aftermath of the 1928 elections and Herbert Hoover's presidential victory. John J. Carson, an aide to Senator James Couzens, a Michigan Republican, observed that "my conviction now is that the Democratic party is through forever." Not only did defeat characterize most of the Democratic record in electoral politics since the turn of the twentieth century, but the 1928 presidential nomination of Alfred E. Smith, governor of New York, exposed sharp intraparty differences between North and South. The campaign then deepened those differences. Dependably supportive of the Democratic Party since the Civil War, the white South refused to remain united behind the candidacy of a northern Catholic who opposed Prohibition's suppression of the liquor industry. Carson suspected that the schism was permanent, bringing terminal disarray to a party that even in good health tended to lose American elections. He thought that decades might pass before a new party successfully developed in the ailing Democrats' place.[1]

Confidence among Republicans in their party's future was the result of its own strength as well as the Democrats' weaknesses. Speaking in July 1929 at a Jackson, Michigan, event to mark the party's seventy-fifth anniversary, Republican National Committee chair Hubert Work identified the nation's economic success with Republican leadership. "The unprecedented development of this nation can not, by any mental process, be dissociated from the growth of the Republican Party," Work said. "The public men it has produced have woven the American character into a web of achievements for which the Republican Party has become a symbol." Work insisted that the tariff that protected America's economic output from foreign competition was a cornerstone of this history, and he warned that the key threat to Republican-managed success was the advent of a paternalism that favored government possession "of public necessities," sure to undermine individualistic

[1] John J. Carson to James Couzens, Nov. 8, 1928, box 139, Couzens Papers.

endeavor.² But this reference hinted at one of the party's weaknesses – an intraparty disagreement about utility ownership, one of a larger set of policy disagreements. Though a major exponent of resource development, Hoover disagreed with Senator George W. Norris of Nebraska, who demanded government rather than private distribution of energy generated by federally supported waterways schemes, especially with reference to Muscle Shoals in the Tennessee Valley – a proposal Hoover later described as "the negation of the ideals upon which our civilization has been based."³ Norris, a leading figure in the party's progressive wing, endorsed Smith instead of Hoover in 1928.⁴ But the party's electoral position was secure enough that disagreements between a few dissident progressives and other Republicans posed little danger to presidential success, to its supremacy within the two-party system. The normal national majority of Republicans over Democrats in the 1920s was five million strong.⁵

Hoover's arrival as president opened new opportunities for the party. He was an unconventional Republican and an unconventional politician, one who promised to bring innovation to its relationship with the electorate. At the end of the 1920s, there were signs of complacency and staleness within the party, the result of seemingly effortless dominance of electoral politics. Hoover offered something fresh. But Hoover failed to lead the Republican Party to revitalized success, although he did point it toward a new ideological direction. Instead, he presided over its precipitous decline from majority to minority status, from which the party did not recover for many decades. Hoover became a political symbol of disregard for the economically underprivileged – for the Great Depression's victims – and of attentiveness to the business elite, a symbol that the Democrats would deploy against the Republicans for many decades.⁶ The Depression's onset during the Hoover years meant that the president and party could not escape this electoral decline. But Republican leaders' actions sometimes seemed calculated to encourage rather than alleviate decline, to postpone rather than quicken a comeback. Hoover's response to the Depression was an innovative agenda, but he could not secure prosperity's return, fostering voter disenchantment; the Republican Party's defense of antistatism lastingly aligned it with a set of ideas less popular than those the Democrats would promote after 1932 – New Deal liberalism.

² Hubert Work, speech, July 6, 1929, box 251, Presidential Subject File [hereafter PSF], Hoover Papers.
³ Arthur M. Schlesinger, Jr., *The Age of Roosevelt*, vol. I: *The Crisis of the Old Order, 1919–1933* (Boston: Houghton Mifflin, 1957), 246.
⁴ Ronald L. Feinman, *Twilight of Progressivism: The Western Republican Senators and the New Deal* (Baltimore: Johns Hopkins University Press, 1981), 4–5.
⁵ William Starr Myers, "Looking Toward 1932," *American Political Science Review* [hereafter *APSR*] 25 (1931), 925–926.
⁶ Lou Cannon, *President Reagan: The Role of a Lifetime* (1991; New York: Public Affairs, 2000), 196.

This decline began not long after the party in 1928 achieved its apparently unassailable position. It was a product of the nation's economic crisis that began with the October 1929 stock-market crash. The slump in stock prices was one sign of underlying weaknesses in the economy, and during 1930 output declined and unemployment increased. Although it was still widely believed that these problems amounted to a cyclical correction that Hoover's management would soon help to ease, the first sign of the party's problems at the polls arrived in the 1930 midterms. Republicans suffered major losses – eight in the Senate and more than fifty in the House – leaving both houses of Congress finely balanced between the parties. They maintained a one-seat majority in the Senate, while the Democrats won a one-seat majority in the House. Simeon D. Fess, senator from Ohio and now RNC chair, sought to minimize the scale of the party's problems by asserting that the results were "a crazy quilt." There was at least some truth in Fess's claim that variety characterized the party's fortunes and that local issues helped to account for an individual candidate's success or failure. Nevertheless, the patchwork of results left it clear enough that voters were turning against the Republican Party because of the economic downturn.[7] A. M. Curtis, the Missouri Republican chair, was one of the party leaders who emphasized this factor, in his case noting that it made organizational efforts counterproductive; activists "learned we hauled many voters to the polls that voted the straight Democratic ticket out of protest against conditions," he wrote.[8] This was the last occasion when the new Congress was not due to meet for a year after the election; by the time it met, by-election losses had further eroded Republican totals on Capitol Hill.

The worst of the decline was still to come, however. During 1931 and 1932, economic conditions continued to deteriorate, as did the Republican Party's standing. In the elections of fall 1932, Herbert Hoover secured only 15.8 million votes as opposed to the 22.8 million votes cast for his Democratic opponent, Franklin D. Roosevelt, governor of New York. The states that supported Hoover dwindled to a handful in the Republican bastion of New England (Connecticut, Maine, New Hampshire, and Vermont), along with the middle-Atlantic states of Delaware and Pennsylvania.[9] The party suffered a further congressional setback, too. As a result of the 1932 elections, there were only 117 Republicans in the House, compared to 313 Democrats and 5 representatives of minor parties. In the Senate, the party's contingent fell to thirty-six, who faced fifty-nine Democrats and a Farmer-Laborite.[10]

As Hubert Work noted at the Jackson celebration of the party's anniversary, Republicans at the end of the 1920s were able to look back over a remarkably enduring record of electoral success. Their party had enjoyed a dominant

[7] New York Times [hereafter NYT], Nov. 10, 1930, 7.
[8] A. M. Curtis to Robert H. Lucas, Dec. 20, 1930, box 7, Lucas Papers.
[9] Roy V. Peel and Thomas C. Donnelly, The 1932 Campaign: An Analysis (New York: Farrar & Rinehart, 1935), 230–231.
[10] Mayer, The Republican Party, 424–425.

position in American politics since its emergence during the sectional crisis that led to the Civil War. Between 1860 and 1932 there were only two Democratic presidents, Grover Cleveland and Woodrow Wilson – each serving two terms.[11] Because of their post-Reconstruction political dominance in the South, Democrats achieved more success in Congress. Nevertheless, during this period's thirty-six congressional sessions, Republicans controlled the House of Representatives for twenty-three sessions and the Senate for thirty-one.[12]

As Democratic successes in the 1870s and 1880s demonstrate, interparty competition during the late nineteenth century was often quite evenly matched. The 1896 elections then marked a decisive shift among the electorate toward what was already known as the GOP – Grand Old Party. Over the next three decades, GOP success was interrupted only once: in 1912 Woodrow Wilson, a Democrat, won the election and was reelected in 1916. Wilson achieved his victory when the former Republican president, Theodore Roosevelt, ran as the Progressive or "Bull Moose" candidate in challenging his Republican successor, William Howard Taft, thus fragmenting the party coalition.

Roosevelt's challenge to Taft involved the schism that emerged from the great early-twentieth-century trend of Progressivism, visible in both major parties – but mostly in the governing Republican Party – and in many other aspects of contemporary American life. Concerned about industrialization's impact on society, progressives found much in common with Theodore Roosevelt, who indignantly attacked concentrations of wealth and their ill effects for the nation, while at the state and local levels they similarly pursued reform, often through the Republican Party's structures. Beyond Theodore Roosevelt's third-party candidacy, the progressives remained a dissident faction within the GOP, concentrated in the West, carrying forward a wide-ranging reform agenda with which other Republicans were often uncomfortable, especially those conservatives known as the "Old Guard," concentrated in the East. By no means did all remain dissidents, however; the twists and turns of the party's progressive tradition were complex.

During its years as the nation's majority, the Republicans were the party of the socioeconomic elite – businesspeople, professionals, the wealthy. But the party also enjoyed a diversity of support that accounted for its success in maintaining power. This diverse coalition revealed the significance of sectional and ethnoreligious, as well as socioeconomic, cleavages in understanding the era's politics. As the party associated with the northern cause in the Civil War and Reconstruction, Republicans enjoyed little support in the South but much more in the North; in the post-1896 years, the party achieved a dominant position across much of the Northeast, Midwest, and Far West. As the party of Abraham Lincoln, the Republican coalition attracted African Americans, although in the later nineteenth century Jim Crow laws excluded

[11] The margin of the Democrat's defeat was, however, slim in 1876, 1880, and 1888.
[12] Charles O. Jones, *The Republican Party in American Politics* (New York: Macmillan, 1965), 8.

many from participation in electoral politics across much of the South, where most lived. Among whites outside the South, "old-stock" Protestants of northern European origins were more frequently the party's supporters, while Catholic and Jewish "new immigrants" from southern and eastern Europe were often Democratic adherents. Ethnoreligious controversies formed part of the political context; in addition to being the party of business and national development that Work celebrated in his anniversary address, the Republicans were the party of morality – promoting alcohol's prohibition, for example, and attacking, in the name of good government, the Democratic machines in urban ethnic communities as corrupt. On the Democratic side, the presence in the same party of southern Protestants and northern Catholics fostered tensions that often undermined the effectiveness of the Democrats' opposition to the Republican Party.

These tensions were most evident in 1928, when the Democratic candidacy of New York Governor Al Smith ensured that the Hoover coalition was distinctive in several ways. Smith's eastern urbanism alienated strands of his party's normal coalition, while it also attracted smaller numbers of new voters to the Democratic Party, especially within ethnic communities of northeastern cities. In the traditional Republican stronghold of the Northeast, these gains were substantial enough to peel Massachusetts and Rhode Island away from Hoover. In the South, by sharp contrast, Smith's opposition to Prohibition and his Catholicism shook many voters away from their deeply held Democratic loyalties. Hoover won the states of Florida, North Carolina, Virginia, Tennessee, and Texas, and 48.7 percent of the popular vote in the eleven former Confederate states, though the party made no inroads at other levels of elected office.[13] Within the South, Hoover achieved more success in counties where fewer African Americans lived and in urbanized areas.[14] Despite the southern triumph, there were some danger signs for the GOP in Smith's 1928 coalition. The formidable nature of the Republicans' post-1896 coalition involved its strength among urban workers, but some were now rethinking their Republican loyalty, and in the cities there were new voters at the polls whom Smith was able to mobilize, whereas Hoover was not.[15]

Visible in its politicians' rhetoric, an ideological, as well as demographic, transition took place within the Republican Party during the 1920s. Traditionally, a central theme in this rhetoric was the nation. Compared with contemporary Democrats, they argued in favor of a more energetic government to achieve economic development, and they justified their policies by defining them as American. The cause of free labor had rallied the early Republican coalition

[13] William H. Harbaugh, "The Republican Party, 1893–1932," in Arthur M. Schlesinger, Jr., ed., *History of U.S. Political Parties*, vol. III: *1910–1945: From Square Deal to New Deal* (New York: Chelsea House, 1973), 2118.

[14] V. O. Key, Jr., with Alexander Heard, *Southern Politics in State and Nation* (New York: Knopf, 1950), 318–329.

[15] Kristi Andersen, *The Creation of a Democratic Majority, 1928–1936* (Chicago: University of Chicago Press, 1979).

against slavery's expansion; the party continued to celebrate work, assert a claim to workers' support, and preach capital–labor harmony. The promotion of order against anarchy was another important theme of Republican rhetoric, as was an individualism that stressed the social duties and responsibilities associated with liberty, rather than the opportunities it offered for life choices. The 1920s saw a decline in this Republican embrace of activist government and an increase in its place of antistatist rhetoric. The state, rather than anarchy, began to loom as a threat to liberty. Workers no longer occupied a special place in the Republican appeal, which instead spoke to Americans as a whole, without such recognition of group distinctions. Equal opportunity, the feasibility of which earlier Republicans doubted, became an article of party faith, and Republicans started to rethink individualism as focusing on personal freedom as much as, if not more than, social responsibility.[16] Hoover pioneered many of these new themes initially in response to the challenges of post–World War I economic and social transformations – long before the arrival of the Great Depression's new, more ominous, challenges.

An immensely successful mining engineer, Hoover first gained public attention for philanthropic endeavors, notably the organization of food aid for Belgium during World War I. When the United States entered the war, Hoover worked for the government as food administrator, and afterwards he led food-distribution efforts in war-torn Europe. Hoover was an important adviser on economic matters during Treaty of Versailles negotiations, and in Washington he helped run an industrial conference of government, business, and labor leaders, which presented a progressive set of recommendations, including a minimum wage, a ban on child labor, equal pay for men and women, and mechanisms for collective bargaining. Such activities, associated with progressivism and with the Wilson administration, encouraged both Democratic and Republican interest in Hoover as a 1920 presidential possibility; Hoover indicated that he was interested in the Republican nomination if the party "[adopted] a forward-looking, liberal, constructive platform on the Treaty and on our economic issues" and was "neither reactionary nor radical in its approach to our great domestic questions."[17] Hoover won significant support, but not significant enough. Warren G. Harding was the nominee instead, reflecting the more conservative mood among Republicans, and Harding took the party back to victory. Harding's selection of Hoover as commerce secretary caused some consternation among many in the party because of his progressive associations; the choice of Andrew W. Mellon as treasury secretary was intended as a strongly conservative balance to Hoover's progressivism.[18]

---

[16] John Gerring, *Party Ideologies in America, 1828–1996* (Cambridge: Cambridge University Press, 1998), 57–158.

[17] Martin L. Fausold, *The Presidency of Herbert C. Hoover* (Lawrence: University Press of Kansas, 1985), 14.

[18] Joan Hoff Wilson, *Herbert Hoover: Forgotten Progressive* (Boston: Little, Brown, 1975), 79–80.

At the Department of Commerce, Hoover displayed his political imagination and his promise as a politician able to apply the Republicans' business-oriented concerns to the challenges of a changing economy. Hoover transformed the department's role and size, developing a vehicle to encourage the economy's efficiency and rationalization. A believer in the importance of individual enterprise, he also believed in the need for cooperative mechanisms, informed by expertise, to protect such initiative and maximize its output. The role of government, in Hoover's eyes, was to foster this cooperation and to harness experts' insights through conferences and commissions, but it should never dictate business decisions. The department amassed statistical data to reach a better understanding of the economy, and it developed industrial standards to avoid waste. Hoover responded innovatively to high unemployment in the early 1920s by urging business to maintain wage levels and by advocating government funding for public works. The government's encouragement of voluntary action to achieve cooperative efficiency within the economy was his hallmark.[19] Hoover's mastery of the new consumer-focused economy of the 1920s had some more directly political consequences, too. His 1928 campaign applied modern marketing techniques to the identification and cultivation of interest-group support; it was by no means novel for a presidential candidate to look beyond party and to appeal to the electorate as an array of interest groups with special concerns, but Hoover was especially successful in this regard.[20] He was a new kind of politician in campaigning as well as governing.

Herbert Hoover's unconventional, innovative qualities of leadership offered great promise to a party with a secure grasp on power, one seeking to consolidate and deepen its relationship with the electorate. But Hoover lacked the political skills necessary to respond with enterprise to the party's accumulating electoral difficulties. Despite "a supersensitiveness" to political developments, after the crash Hoover was "not able to interpret vital currents of opinion," according to his friend David Hinshaw.[21] He was, moreover, uneasy in public appearances and a poor speaker – a reflection of his background outside electoral politics. Politicking was something that Hoover did not enjoy.[22] He was, as a journalist put it in 1932, "lacking in political sex appeal" and "as undramatic as a porcelain bathtub, as unspectacular as a cash register, as unmagnetic as a telegraph pole – but, like all of these articles, he is extremely useful and practically inevitable."[23] Extremely successful before 1929, Hoover's political skills would fail the Depression's challenge.

[19] David Burner, *Herbert Hoover: A Public Life* (New York: Knopf, 1979), 159–189.
[20] Brian Balogh, "'Mirrors of Desires': Interest Groups, Elections, and the Targeted Style in Twentieth-Century America," in Meg Jacobs, William J. Novak, and Julian E. Zelizer, eds., *The Democratic Experiment: New Directions in American Political History* (Princeton, N.J.: Princeton University Press, 2003), 222–249.
[21] David Hinshaw to William Allen White, Jan. 18, 1932, box C189, White Papers.
[22] Richard Norton Smith, *An Uncommon Man: The Triumph of Herbert Hoover* (New York: Simon and Schuster, 1984), 30, 33.
[23] *Liberty* clipping, April 23, 1932, box 84, Reprint File, Hoover Papers.

Nevertheless, in the 1932 contest against Franklin D. Roosevelt, some Republicans came to think – wishfully, perhaps – that Hoover was an asset when he revised his earlier intention to avoid much active campaigning and developed a new pugnaciousness to defend his record and attack Roosevelt.[24] Hoover's aides believed that a key speech at Des Moines, Iowa, in early October significantly improved his reelection prospects, and reports from the party's grass roots supported this belief.[25] Henry J. Allen of the RNC called the favorable impact of this and other speeches by Hoover "an unexpected cyclone" that even made victory possible.[26] These reactions are not representative of the wider electorate's reactions to Hoover, however, and instead are suggestive of the ways in which members of the party elite were insulated and removed from public opinion, lacking effective tools to sound opinion. The cyclone of 1932 was one that swept Republicans from power. Although Hoover had again showed innovative thinking in his response to the Depression, his public defense of his policies and his attacks on the Democrats helped to define a path for the Republicans that worsened the cyclone's impact.

At the start of his administration, Hoover's 1928 success in the South seemed particularly promising for party growth. In March 1929 historian J. G. de Roulhac Hamilton – whose research on Reconstruction belonged to the racist, elitist Dunning school that condemned African American participation in politics and attacked radical Republicans' attention to the post–Civil War condition of former slaves – predicted further Republican inroads there due to a wealth of favorable factors: Prohibition; Hoover's popularity; in-migration of northerners and westerners; some loss of confidence in the Democratic Party; and the section's economic development that fostered identification with the party of prosperity. But all depended on the administration's fortunes, according to Hamilton. "Let hard times come, let the administration be a failure, let it attempt to hold the support of negroes [sic] who hold the balance of power in the doubtful States by making the negro an issue in the South, and every tendency here discussed may be crushed out of existence," he observed.[27] Despite such qualifications, Hamilton's remained a highly optimistic view, confident about the Republicans' ability to forge a new relationship with the segregationist South. Another interpretation saw Hoover's success, by contrast, as simply a repudiation of Smith, no indication of any pro-Republican trend.[28]

[24] Theodore G. Joslin diary, Sept. 7 and 11, 1932, box 10, Joslin Papers.
[25] Joslin diary, Oct. 4 and 6, 1932, box 10, Joslin Papers; Henry J. Allen to William Allen White, Oct. 5, 1932, box C187, White Papers; D. W. Davis to Lawrence Richey, Oct. 10, 1932, box 252, PSF, Hoover Papers; William V. Beers to RNC, Oct. 14, 1932, box 34, MacChesney Papers; J. Solis-Cohen, Jr., to Lewis L. Strauss, Oct. 18, 1932, box 33, Strauss Papers; George G. Seaman to Nathan W. MacChesney, Nov. 1, 1932, box 32, MacChesney Papers; James MacLafferty to Lewis L. Strauss, Nov. 6, 1932, box 33, Strauss Papers.
[26] Henry J. Allen to Laird Archer, Nov. 9, 1932, box C1, Allen Papers.
[27] John Hope Franklin, "Mirror for Americans: A Century of Reconstruction History," *AHR* 85 (1980), 4; *NYT*, March 29, 1929, 19.
[28] *Atlanta Independent* clipping, June 12, 1930, box 160, PSF, Hoover Papers.

This was a more realistic analysis of the white South's deep distrust of the Republican Party.

As it was, the party in the South was a highly unusual and ineffective political force. The Civil War and Reconstruction still decisively shaped southern politics. The Republican Party was anathema to most southerners, and a one-party system of politics extended across much of the region, according to which debate about political conflicts occurred within the Democratic Party rather than between the parties. There were no more than small pockets here and there of meaningful Republican support – notably in the Appalachian region of eastern Tennessee, where Union loyalties had been significant during the Civil War. Where African Americans were able to vote, they usually supported the party of Lincoln against the party of segregation, but the segregationist party often excluded them from the polls.

Within such a one-party system, the GOP existed not as an office-seeking institution but as little more than a patronage-distribution body. Critics charged that its leaders had little interest in party growth that was likely to dilute their power, though in many states the obstacles against real growth were great.[29] Active Republicans in the South played a part in the selection of presidential nominees and then in the allocation of federal patronage. They did little else, except in some states engaging in vicious factional battles. In the nomination process, though representative of little but self-interest, they possessed votes that were important to candidates; the votes were often available to the highest bidder. Factional battles were often between segregationist "lily-white" and biracial "black-and-tan" groupings, each seeking official recognition and thus a voice in the processes of presidential nomination and patronage decision-making. During the 1920s support developed in the party for "lily-whitism" as a way to win votes in states where most African Americans were disfranchised, but the approach often involved the creation of racially exclusive organizations.[30]

On becoming president, Hoover was swift to announce a plan to reform the party in the South. In theory, its goal was to attack corruption in patronage matters. In practice, reform encompassed the elevation of lily-white organizations, undermining the influence of black-and-tan African American leaders. A reform-minded dislike for political corruption, rather than racism, informed Hoover's initiative.[31] But much contemporary analysis saw the policy as a strategic choice that favored the electoral cultivation of white southerners at the expense of African Americans. "The Republican party is no longer the party of The People," concluded one African American newspaper, "but the party

[29] Neil R. McMillen, "Perry W. Howard, Boss of Black-and-Tan Republicanism in Mississippi, 1924–1960," *Journal of Southern History* 48 (1982), 209.

[30] Vincent P. De Santis, "Republican Efforts to 'Crack' the Democratic South," *Review of Politics* 14 (1952), 260–262.

[31] Donald J. Lisio, *Hoover, Blacks, and Lily-Whites: A Study of Southern Strategies* (Chapel Hill: University of North Carolina Press, 1985).

of the white people."[32] Charles A. Jonas, a North Carolina RNC member, reported to Hoover that the "prominent" commented supportively that he was "the first President since the Civil War who has shown a sympathetic knowledge of the social and racial problems of the old South."[33]

The plan failed. It reinforced Hoover's already unfavorable image among many African Americans, and it encouraged southern Democrats to mobilize in opposition to this potential threat to their power. In general, the policy fomented conflict rather than progress, immensely difficult in the face of the Democrats' entrenchment in this one-party region. Republican problems were exacerbated, as Hamilton had predicted, by economic woes. Hoover backed away from his reform efforts; in 1932, like Republican presidential candidates before him, he did not visit the South in search of votes.[34]

Prohibition helped to facilitate the largeness and distinctive demographic characteristics of Hoover's 1928 victory as a dry against Smith's wet policy. Even as the Depression began to dominate electoral politics, some Republicans suspected that the wet–dry conflict remained powerful enough to influence voting decisions. In fall 1932 a Missouri Republican commented that "if we lose this State, it will be because Republican St. Louis wants beer and wants it quick and believes that the victory of the Democrats will bring it faster."[35] Some leading Democrats thought similarly. In early 1931, for example, national chair John J. Raskob advocated an emphasis on Prohibition's end as the cornerstone of the Democratic campaign, a reflection of his own wet commitment.[36] The eighteenth amendment's political significance underscored the political role of concerns beyond bread-and-butter matters, of cleavages between different ethnic and religious groups.

Prohibition therefore seemed electorally consequential to the future of the Republican coalition, as well as posing tricky policy questions. In the opinion of Senator William E. Borah of Idaho, an important Republican progressive, the dry contribution to Hoover's election meant a mandate for no change.[37] But public sentiment remained in flux, especially because of the lawlessness associated with Prohibition. Many Republican politicians, including Hoover, came to realize that the trend toward support for repeal was strong.[38] His administration's efforts to improve Prohibition's enforcement tended to underscore its flaws as national policy, rather than solve them.[39] An early signal of the change

[32] *Literary Digest* [hereafter *LD*], April 13, 1929, 5–7 (quotation, 7).
[33] Charles A. Jonas to Herbert Hoover, April 20, 1931, box 166, President's Personal File [hereafter PPF], Hoover Papers.
[34] Peel and Donnelly, *1932 Campaign*, 218.
[35] *NYT* magazine, Oct. 30, 1932, 18.
[36] *Los Angeles Evening Express* clipping, April 8, 1931, box 91, PSF, Hoover Papers; David M. Kennedy, *Freedom from Fear: The American People in Depression and War, 1929–1945* (New York: Oxford University Press, 1999), 62.
[37] William E. Borah to William Allen White, Jan. 13, 1930, box C164, White Papers.
[38] Joslin diary, May 11, 1932, box 10, Joslin Papers.
[39] Fausold, *The Presidency of Herbert C. Hoover*, 125–129.

in opinion was the 1930 primary defeat, linked with Prohibition politics, of two leading dry House members, Louis C. Cramton and Grand M. Hudson, both from Michigan.[40] The midterm contests then provided evidence of the strength of wet sentiment in the urban Northeast, which some argued was powerful enough to deny Hoover a second term, regardless of economic conditions.[41] Even as economic discontent sharpened, some still believed that Prohibition might prove to be the key campaign issue.[42] In July 1932 David Hinshaw noted that six of the seven usually Republican-supporting drivers for the laundry service his family used planned to vote Democratic because they favored repeal.[43]

Passions surrounded discussion of Prohibition. According to Secretary of the Treasury Ogden L. Mills, the issue "divided our Party and well-nigh destroyed it."[44] Reflecting the diversity of public opinion on the subject, Republicans across the country had very different views about Prohibition's electoral salience and the appropriate position for the party to take. In some areas, they insisted that a retreat from resolute dryness spelled disaster for the party. Such views were especially common in the West, Midwest, and South, where some believed that Prohibition remained the party's best hope of election success.[45] The overall calculation was different in the East, where wet sentiment was obvious. But Prohibition advocates there continued to engineer an electoral rationale in support of their position. Dry leaders in New York, for example, argued that, despite a wet majority in the state, their supporters carried the balance of power between the two parties and could therefore throw its electoral college votes to Hoover.[46] The intensity of beliefs surrounding Prohibition made any compromise difficult. In any case, compromise seemed electorally unpromising, too. In the 1930 Illinois contest for the U.S. Senate, sexism was a factor in the defeat of Ruth Hanna McCormick, the first woman to be a major party's Senate candidate, but other Republicans identified her effort to find a compromise on Prohibition as one of her mistakes.[47] "We have nothing to gain by straddling," concluded Senator Arthur Capper of Kansas, because Democratic success among the wets was complete.[48] Maine's Representative Carroll L. Beedy argued in spring 1932 that "any attempt to compromise on the issue of Prohibition would work the party's ruin in the coming elections."[49]

[40] NYT, Oct. 14, 1930, 6.
[41] Outlook and Independent, Nov. 26, 1930, 490–491.
[42] James MacLafferty diary, July 2, 1932, box 1, MacLafferty Papers.
[43] David Hinshaw to William Allen White, July 5, 1932, box C189, White Papers.
[44] Ogden L. Mills to George C. Dyer, Jan. 18, 1933, box 42, Mills Papers.
[45] Oliver D. Street to Robert H. Lucas, Nov. 20, 1930, box 8, Lucas Papers; Richard Lloyd Jones to Norton McGiffin, Dec. 3, 1930, box C75, Allen Papers; E. E. Callaway to Walter H. Newton, box 258, PSF, Hoover Papers.
[46] New York Herald Tribune clipping, Aug. 6, 1932, box 265, PSF, Hoover Papers.
[47] Nathan William MacChesney to Robert H. Lucas, Dec. 22, 1930, box 12, PSF, Hoover Papers.
[48] Arthur Capper to William Allen White, Dec. 30, 1930, box C164, White Papers.
[49] Carroll L. Beedy to William E. Borah, June 1, 1932, box 348, Borah Papers.

These passions fed an intense debate at the national convention in Chicago –
where, by contrast, the delegates paid little attention to Depression policy,
perhaps because they realized their party's difficulty in addressing such issues
persuasively.[50] Despite skepticism about a Prohibition compromise, the convention adopted one, developed by Mills and Secretary of State Henry L.
Stimson, who had finally managed to shake Hoover away from his strongly
dry position. The plank advocated Prohibition's repeal while pledging federal
support for states that wished to remain dry and ruling out the return of the
open saloon.[51] Soundings among congressional Republicans suggested widespread support for the formula, but due to constituency pressures dry politicians resisted an effort, instigated at Hoover's suggestion, to state publicly this
support.[52]

The distinction between the semidry Republicans and the wet Democrats
remained clear-cut, ensuring that the issue retained at least some salience
amid 1932's economic distress. Indeed, a campaign season poll that sought
to explain voters' decisions to switch support from Republicans to Democrats
suggested that Prohibition was especially salient among this group of
switchers.[53] A Colorado Republican reported that his pro-Hoover speeches
met with indifference from most audiences but with enthusiasm from church
and dry groups, encouraging him to conclude "that the President's firm stand
on prohibition is gripping the millions of dry people close to him and they
will go and fight for him loyally."[54] Walter Edge, the ambassador to France
and former senator from New Jersey, believed that Prohibition accounted for
Hoover's marginal loss of his state.[55] In 1933 Prohibition's end would remove
its electoral importance to either party, retreating to complete insignificance
next to the central questions of the nation's response to the Great Depression.
Even in 1932, despite some politicians' suspicions – and hopefulness – otherwise, bread-and-butter concerns were usually closer to the heart of political
debate.[56]

Herbert Hoover's relationship with his party was tense. A former "Bull
Mooser" and a Wilson appointee, Hoover emerged as a leading Republican
in 1920 almost without trace – without any conventional party career before
then. Compounding his background as a party outsider was a disinclination
to take seriously the active cultivation of fellow Republicans, whether inside or
outside Congress. By early 1930 there was even talk of both a third-party challenge to Hoover and the possibility of his predecessor Calvin Coolidge's return

---

[50] Peel and Donnelly, *1932 Campaign*, 90–91.
[51] Fausold, *The Presidency of Herbert C. Hoover*, 195–196.
[52] MacLafferty diary, June 21 and 24, 1932, box 1, MacLafferty Papers.
[53] J. David Houser to Lewis L. Strauss, Oct. 21, 1932, and enclosed report, box 33, Strauss
Papers.
[54] Wayne C. Williams to Walter H. Newton, April 13, 1932, box 257, PSF, Hoover Papers.
[55] Walter E. Edge to Herbert Hoover, Nov. 12, 1932, box 80, PPF, Hoover Papers.
[56] Harold F. Gosnell and Norman N. Gill, "An Analysis of the 1932 Presidential Vote in
Chicago," *APSR* 29 (1935), 977–982.

as the party's next presidential candidate. What encouraged this talk was an array of issue disagreements – over tariff rates, farm policy, Prohibition, and foreign affairs, among others – together with the belief that Hoover did not cater adequately to the party's patronage needs; fear about the Depression's electoral implications was as yet a minor factor.[57] As economic conditions worsened and as Hoover's electoral appeal slipped, this discontent increased. The Republican Party edged away from the president.

Dissatisfaction was strongest among progressive Republicans, whose forces were concentrated in the Senate. Despite his progressive roots and despite the political idiosyncrasies that distanced him from conservatives, Hoover now had little in common with them. It was "a bit of a shock" to William Allen White, editor of Kansas's *Emporia Gazette* and a man with a large presence in national life, especially in Republican circles, when Hoover – a 1912 Bull Mooser like White – told him in 1929 that "every proposal in [the 1912 Progressive Party's platform], viewed in the light of today, was unwise."[58] The arrival of the economic crisis clarified Hoover's differences with the Senate progressives. They attacked his anti-Depression initiatives as inadequate, calling for a larger federal role in alleviating its human impact, including unemployment relief and public works.[59] White considered Hoover's disregard of the progressives a serious mistake. Not only did Hoover lose a group of potential advocates in the Midwest and Mountain states, but he also lost a way to connect with voters there; compared with mainstream conservative Republicans, progressive George Norris, for example, was "nearer the heart and thought of this whole country from Detroit to San Diego," according to White.[60]

White's point was important. To maintain a winning coalition, Republicans needed to achieve strength in both East and West, thus balancing differing economic interests.[61] As 1932 progressed, some Republicans allowed themselves a degree of optimism about trends in the East, encouraging the perception that it was the rural Midwest and West that presented the party's key electoral challenge.[62] Farmers had failed to share the prosperity of the 1920s, and their plight demanded attention well before the Wall Street crash. It was partly in response to the West's Senate progressives that Hoover called a special session of Congress at the start of his administration to develop a solution to the farm crisis. Conflict emerged between Hoover's vision of economic cooperation

[57] *New York World* clipping, Feb. 18, 1930, box 66, Reprint File, Hoover Papers.
[58] Mark Sullivan to William Allen White, Sept. 13, 1929, box C154, White Papers.
[59] Feinman, *Twilight of Progressivism*, 18–32.
[60] William Allen White to Mark Sullivan, Nov. 15, 1932, box C191, White Papers; White to Henry J. Allen, May 23, 1930, box C163, White Papers.
[61] Rosenof, *Realignment*, 15–17; Weed, *Nemesis of Reform*, 85.
[62] Henry J. Allen to W. M. Kiplinger, Aug. 5, 1932, box C5, Allen Papers; William Allen White to Walter H. Newton, Aug. 30, 1932, box C189, White Papers; Joslin diary, Sept. 6 and 18, 1932, box 10, Joslin Papers; A. E. Woodward to Ogden L. Mills, Sept. 12, 1932, box 10, Mills Papers; James G. Strong to Henry J. Allen, Sept. 17, 1932, box C11, Allen Papers; Robert H. Lucas, form letter, n.d. [c. Oct. 4, 1932], box 7, Lucas Papers.

and the progressives' belief in the need for direct federal subsidies, eventually resolved in Congress in favor of the president's formula. Seeing the progressive agenda as too statist, Hoover devised a Farm Board that loaned money to agricultural cooperatives, which aimed to control production and thus avoid damagingly low prices. But the system made relatively little difference to a crisis-beset sector.[63]

George F. Shafer, the North Dakota governor, predicted in early 1932 that wheat prices would determine the election in his strongly Republican state; a 75-cent bushel – itself a very low price – would allow the party to win, whereas a 50-cent bushel would ensure its defeat.[64] The price remained much less than 40 cents in 1932.[65] As the election approached, an Iowa Republican similarly remarked that "with hogs under 3c and corn around 15c and going lower, it is mighty hard to reason with the farmers."[66] In an effort to improve party communications with farmers, the national committee created after the 1930 midterm elections an agricultural division that circulated material to speakers on the Hoover policies' strengths.[67] The task was a difficult one. The idea that Secretary of Agriculture Arthur M. Hyde might make an end-of-campaign tour of the Midwest in 1932 alarmed John D. M. Hamilton, a Kansas Republican. If so, "you can bet your bottom dollar that there is going to be hell a-popping out here again," Hamilton warned.[68]

George Norris, one of the most influential Senate progressives and a Smith supporter in 1928, was also one of Hoover's most hostile critics. This led to a remarkable intervention by the national party in a state party's business – suggesting that Hoover took an expansive view of the president's responsibilities as party leader. Robert H. Lucas, RNC executive director, funded a surreptitious campaign against Norris's 1930 reelection bid, which depicted his support for Smith as an attack on Prohibition and an endorsement of the eastern Democratic agenda.[69] Lucas defended his actions as justified in light of Norris's treachery, which fostered what he called "a growing cancer in the vitals of Republican Party and it must be cut out if the Party is to survive."[70] Although Lucas insisted that he acted independently and spent his own money on the anti-Norris publicity, it was widely and reasonably assumed that he followed Hoover's instructions.[71] During the fall Hoover had certainly encouraged his

---

[63] Fausold, *The Presidency of Herbert C. Hoover*, 49–54, 106–112.

[64] *Devils Lake Journal* clipping, Feb. 12, 1932, box 6, Nye Papers.

[65] Fausold, *The Presidency of Herbert C. Hoover*, 110.

[66] Howard Tedford to Edwin Manning and Nathan W. MacChesney, Oct. 21, 1932, box 33, MacChesney Papers.

[67] Robert H. Lucas, press release, Dec. 5, 1930, box 1188, Press Relations series, Hoover Papers; L. W. Ainsworth to chairs and vice-chairs of agricultural states, Sept. 19, 1932, box 1204, Press Relations series, Hoover Papers.

[68] John D. M. Hamilton to Henry J. Allen, Oct. 29, 1932, box C189, White Papers.

[69] *LD*, Jan. 3, 1931, 5–6; *LD*, Jan. 10, 1931, 5–7.

[70] Robert H. Lucas, press release, Dec. 22, 1930, box 37, Norris Papers.

[71] *Collier's* clipping, Feb. 7, 1931, box 251, PSF, Hoover Papers.

friend Edgar Rickard to take what steps he could to achieve the defeat of a bipartisan group of Senate critics, including Norris.[72] Lucas's intervention did not succeed in undermining Norris, but instead fed intraparty conflict that threatened to jeopardize Republican electoral chances further. In December 1930, economist Paul H. Douglas (later a Democratic senator) predicted that progressive Republicans were likely to join Democratic elements, such as those associated with New York Governor Franklin D. Roosevelt, in creating a new party that would appeal to midwestern farmers and eastern workers.[73]

Claiming that fewer than one in ten Republicans wanted Hoover's renomination and that fewer still were confident of his reelection prospects, leading progressive Harold L. Ickes, a Chicago lawyer, tried to mobilize support for a challenge by Gifford Pinchot, the Pennsylvania governor.[74] "I can see no reason why the Republican Party should deliberately run into a smashing defeat merely to satisfy one man's ambition," Ickes wrote.[75] Ickes soon concluded, however, that responses to his effort were "most unsatisfactory to me and I suppose to Gifford also."[76] Rather than going up against a progressive, Hoover faced minor opposition to his nomination from conservative candidate Joseph I. France, a former senator from Maryland. Though France garnered some support in presidential preference primaries, these results did not dictate the convention vote of the selected delegates, who chose Hoover instead of France, adding their votes to Hoover's overwhelming total for renomination.[77]

Progressive Republicans were never a cohesive bloc. In the Senate, two moderates among them, Oregon's Charles McNary and Kansas's Arthur Capper, actively supported Hoover in fall 1932; four assumed a position of neutrality and six supported Roosevelt.[78] Ickes was one among other progressives beyond Capitol Hill who endorsed the distant cousin of their old political hero, Theodore Roosevelt. The six were responsible for some especially bitter attacks on Hoover. "His theory," wrote Norris, "is that if wealth is made prosperous and that legislation is enacted for the benefit of the millionaires then some of the crumbs of prosperity will be pushed off the mahogany-topped desks of luxury and that the common ordinary people groping around at the feet of wealth will be able to get some substance therefrom."[79] Regretting Hoover's failure to realize some progressives' hopes that he

---

[72] Edgar Rickard diary, Oct. 10 and 11, 1930, box 1, Rickard Collection.

[73] Paul H. Douglas, "The Prospects for a New Political Alignment," *APSR* 25 (1931), 906–914.

[74] Harold L. Ickes to Bronson Cutting, Jan. 30, 1932, box 41, Cutting Papers.

[75] Harold L. Ickes to William Allen White (form letter), March 15, 1932, box C189, White Papers.

[76] Harold L. Ickes to William Allen White, March 18, 1932, box C189, White Papers.

[77] Frank Freidel, "Election of 1932," in Arthur M. Schlesinger, Jr., and Fred L. Israel, eds., *History of American Presidential Elections, 1789–1968*, vol. III (New York: Chelsea House, 1971), 2713.

[78] Feinman, *Twilight of Progressivism*, 41–47.

[79] George W. Norris, "Why I Cannot Support President Hoover For Re-election," n.d., box 2, Norris Papers.

would "liberalize" the party, New Mexico's Bronson Cutting attacked the president as "completely subservient to anti-public interests," and as "doing nothing to relieve the fundamental depression of the country."[80] In light of the administration's "three tragic years" that favored banking and business interests at the people's expense, California's Hiram Johnson called party loyalty "the last refuge of the political moron."[81] One of FDR's last speeches of the campaign wooed disenchanted supporters of the Republican Party. At a meeting organized by the Republicans-for-Roosevelt League, he asked for the support of "Republicans who believe that this country needs the tonic of a new alignment of party loyalties, a new and enlightened support of our national faith."[82]

Hoover faced a softer form of intraparty opposition, too. James MacLafferty, an RNC official, went on two extended trips across the Midwest and the West during 1931 to take the party's grassroots pulse. What he found discouraged him. The Depression fostered defeatism, and he concluded that "many of our republicans have yellow streaks." MacLafferty suspected that the party's long history of electoral success left it ill equipped to meet the challenge of a setback; too many Republican activists seemed unwilling to invest their efforts in a losing cause.[83] MacLafferty's explorations of party sentiment show that the center had an interest in what was on the Republican mind locally; this sentiment was often unenthusiastic about Hoover. During the campaign at the local level, activists often neglected Hoover's presidential candidacy, instead preferring to rescue, if possible, their candidates for congressional and other offices.[84] One Hoover supporter, who believed that this approach damaged the president's campaign, said that candidates were "mistaken" in believing that they could escape connection with Hoover, apart from the progressives whose differences with the administration were clear. "Our fellows will nearly all sink or swim with Hoover," he said.[85]

Hoover's troubled relationship with the party did not only involve other Republicans' eagerness to avoid association with a highly unpopular administration and the progressives' ideological differences with his agenda. Furthermore, his party management was flawed. He earned criticism for his oversight of the national committee and for the quality of his administration's cooperation with Capitol Hill Republicans. One observer concluded that "the Hooverian conception of the Republican party is that every member must work night and day for the honor and glory of Mr. Hoover without

---

[80] Bronson Cutting, "Liberal Leader Appeals To Elect Roosevelt As Only Hope Of The Masses," n.d., box 41, Cutting Papers.
[81] *Chicago Herald & Examiner* clipping, Nov. 5, 1932, box 10, Strother Papers.
[82] *New York Herald Tribune* clipping, Nov. 4, 1932, box 14, Strother Papers.
[83] MacLafferty diary, Nov. 25, 1931, and March 6, 1932, box 1, MacLafferty Papers.
[84] See, for example, H. D. Hatfield to Walter H. Newton, July 15, 1932, box 268, PSF, Hoover Papers.
[85] *NYT* magazine, Oct. 30, 1932, 1–2, 18. Arthur Krock, the article's author, defined this view as that of almost all Hoover Republicans, when speaking in confidence.

establishing any resultant obligation of loyalty on the part of Mr. Hoover."[86] After the 1932 elections, a Republican senator even attributed the defeat to Hoover's willingness to appoint Democrats instead of Republicans – including Attorney General William D. Mitchell, RNC publicity director James L. West, and Reconstruction Finance Corporation (RFC) chair Atlee Pomerene – on the grounds that this demoralized party workers.[87]

Another sign of party disarray, one with significant implications for its political activity, was the difficulty officials experienced in raising funds. The 1932 campaign was consequently short of money, hampering publicity efforts.[88] The party had run so short of funds that it sometimes could not meet its payroll, and stamps for party literature were a commodity in inadequate supply.[89] In fact, the Republican Party remained somewhat better funded than the Democratic Party. But the decline in contributions was problematic for the party, which was used to more money. Having spent about $4 million in 1928, the RNC ran the campaign with funds of less than $3 million; in receiving about $2.5 million during 1932, the RNC achieved less than 40 percent of its 1928 total.[90] In addition to a money problem, the campaign suffered from technical difficulties. The Republicans' campaign organization was usually better than the Democrats', but in 1932 it was inferior.[91] Theodore G. Joslin at the White House described the campaign staff as "about the most worthless I ever saw."[92] This organizational failure was potentially significant in a closely contested race, because a party's electoral fortunes sometimes depended on its success in mobilizing its own vote and minimizing the number of its supporters who stayed at home on election day.[93]

From a Republican perspective, women were the party's potential saviors at the polls.[94] In 1928 the party fielded a special effort to mobilize support among women through a message including the argument that Hoover's record of humanitarianism represented a female set of principles. Some even suspected that women accounted for two-thirds of the Republican vote – certainly an

---

[86] Robert S. Allen, *Why Hoover Faces Defeat* (New York: Brewer, Warren & Putnam, 1932), 58–64 (quotation, 64).

[87] "The 1932 General Election: Press Comment on the President and Comparative Republican Vote," n.d. (no author, no publisher), Herbert Hoover Presidential Library, West Branch, Iowa.

[88] Henry J. Allen to Laird Archer, Aug. 5, 1932, box C1, Allen Papers.

[89] J. R. Nutt to Robert H. Lucas, Sept. 28, 1931, box 7, Lucas Papers; MacLafferty diary, Jan. 28, 1932, box 1, MacLafferty Papers; MacLafferty diary, April 19, 1932, box 1, MacLafferty Papers.

[90] Louise Overacker, "Campaign Funds in a Depression Year," *APSR* 27 (1933), 769–772.

[91] Peel and Donnelly, *1932 Campaign*, 157–159; Edgar Eugene Robinson and Vaughn Davis Bornet, *Herbert Hoover: President of the United States* (Stanford, Calif.: Hoover Institution Press, 1975), 267–268.

[92] Joslin diary, Sept. 25, 1932, box 10, Joslin Papers.

[93] Myers, "Looking Toward 1932," 926.

[94] *NYT* magazine, Oct. 30, 1932, 1–2, 18.

exaggeration of the real total but indicative of the extent of some Republicans' confidence in the party's appeal to women.[95] This confidence survived the Depression's arrival.[96] Hoover himself believed that he was likely to retain support among women – who "did not so easily transfer their affections even politically," he said – even as his support among men ebbed away.[97]

Politicians commonly believed that women's concerns differed from men's, explaining the perceived distinction in voting behavior. As a result, in seeking the support of women, Republicans generally emphasized family issues, such as home ownership and children's welfare.[98] They also argued that their system of tariffs and custody of foreign policy were more likely to protect peace.[99] During the 1932 campaign Hoover delivered a radio address directed at women, in which he presented his anti-Depression efforts as protective of the family, telling his audience that the Depression affected the sexes equally but "on you, the women, falls the full anxiety of the direct effect of the impact of burdens upon the home."[100] Democratic politicians took a similarly family-focused approach to the cultivation of women, together with attacks on Hoover's record on female appointments.[101]

On the day of Hoover's radio talk to American women, Republicans in the East set up events where women would gather together in someone's home for the speech, often also for bridge and other games. (One organizer noted, however, "we have suggested that they occupy themselves at that time in making clothing or knitting sweaters for the children of the unemployed, feeling that this is a better feature than playing cards.")[102] This initiative was a small example of women's extensive organizational activity in support of the party. Despite the 1920 ratification of the nineteenth amendment that granted women the vote, politics remained exceptionally male in key respects. Few women were appointed, and fewer still were elected, to public office. Administration and party discussions about how to salvage Republican electoral prospects in the face of economic disaster very rarely included women, even when they assumed women's centrality as voters to any such rescue. Beyond many levels of male leadership, however, grassroots politics was frequently a female endeavor. The party's hierarchy recognized women as especially important in contributing to organizational work, the door-to-door mobilization of the

[95] Catherine Elaine Rymph, "Forward and Right: The Shaping of Republican Women's Activism, 1920–1967" (Ph.D. dissertation, University of Iowa, 1998), 97–100.

[96] See, for example, Alan Fox to Walter H. Newton, April 15, 1931, box 265, PSF, Hoover Papers; Roy A. Roberts to Theodore G. Joslin, Sept. 5, 1931, box 16, Joslin Papers.

[97] MacLafferty diary, Feb. 16, 1932, box 1, MacLafferty Papers.

[98] *Woman's Journal*, Nov. 1930, 23, 34.

[99] Rhodri Jeffreys-Jones, *Changing Differences: Women and the Shaping of American Foreign Policy, 1917–1994* (New Brunswick, N.J.: Rutgers University Press, 1995).

[100] *NYT*, Oct. 8, 1932, 8.

[101] See, for example, "Three Reasons Why Every Woman Should Vote for Roosevelt and Garner" (handbill), n.d., box 254, PSF, Hoover Papers; Mrs. George W. Sawyer, report, Oct. 29, 1932, box 113, PSF, Hoover Papers.

[102] Henrietta W. Livermore to Lawrence Richey, Sept. 23, 1932, box 14, Strother Papers.

vote.[103] Practical politicians understood such work as vital in maximizing a party's electoral success. Despite women's exclusion from leadership roles, the party's organizational dependence on female activists was open to interpretation as an opportunity; Lenna Lowe Yost, a Republican women's leader, urged other women to participate in campaigns as a way to begin involvement in government.[104] This activity exhibited distinctive features. Republican women's political involvement usually took place in women's political clubs, institutions that were less partisan and more moralistic in their emphasis than male-dominated party organizations.[105] Regardless of Hoover's hopes, women's votes did not save his candidacy. A contemporary estimate suggested that a majority of women, like men, voted in favor of Roosevelt, and that fewer women went to the polls in 1932 than four years before.[106]

African Americans were also important to the party, but they too were neglected. Republican leaders often misunderstood their collective needs. As the 1930 midterms approached, Perry Howard, a Mississippi RNC member and one of the party's leading African Americans, rehearsed the traditional argument that the Democratic history of slavery and segregation ruled out African American support for the rival party, and that "the Republican Party may not have done all for the Negro that it could or should have done, but the fact stands out that all that has been done for the Negro has been done by the Republican Party."[107] This complacent message spelled out the party's problem in issue terms, while Howard himself was a symbol of its organizational problem in mobilizing African Americans. He was an absentee state leader with little interest in party development and much more in yielding power and distributing patronage (though Mississippi was an especially unpromising state to try otherwise). Howard was, in fact, one of the potential victims of the efforts to attack black-and-tan Republicans in favor of lily whites.[108]

When aides brought to Hoover concerns about the party's loss of African American support, he showed no interest in taking real steps to address the problem.[109] His administration similarly neglected race-related concerns, and few African Americans gained appointment to federal office.[110] In 1932 the National Association for the Advancement of Colored People (NAACP) presented a plank to the Republican Party, involving such demands as the termination of the South's lily-white organizations and the introduction of

---

[103] Everett Sanders to Theodore G. Joslin, Sept. 24, 1932, box 251, PSF, Hoover Papers.

[104] *The Guidon*, Oct. 1930, 17, box 196, PPF, Hoover Papers.

[105] Rymph, *Republican Women*, 40–60.

[106] Peel and Donnelly, *1932 Campaign*, 224.

[107] Perry W. Howard, "The Duty of Colored Voters in the Present Congressional and Senatorial Campaign," Oct. 15, 1930, box 251, PSF, Hoover Papers.

[108] McMillen, "Perry W. Howard."

[109] Rickard diary, Aug. 24 and Sept. 4–8, 1931, box 1, Rickard Collection.

[110] Richard B. Sherman, *The Republican Party and Black America: From McKinley to Hoover, 1896–1933* (Charlottesville: University Press of Virginia, 1973), 233–251.

antidiscrimination legislation.[111] In support of the effort to persuade politicians to address civil rights, the NAACP tried to publicize the claim that African Americans possessed the balance of power in a number of states – enough to swing their overall vote toward one of the parties, making a difference in the electoral college's math.[112] The argument was unsuccessful; the platform plank that the party adopted was a disappointment. Walter White, the association's executive secretary, described it as "flapdoodle," condemning the Republicans' record of empty promises on race.[113] However, if Republicans did not listen to the balance-of-power argument, then neither did the Democrats. Democrats offered few reasons for African Americans to reconsider their loyalty to the GOP. For Republicans this was political neglect apparently without electoral consequence.

In explaining his problems, Hoover attached some blame to the news media. He later told Adolph S. Ochs of the *New York Times* that Ochs and William Randolph Hearst "more than any other two agencies turned over the 3,000,000 votes which resulted in my defeat."[114] Their publications symbolized the decline in Hoover's support because in both cases editorial opposition in 1932 followed endorsement in 1928.[115] Both publishers shared many of their readers' disappointment with his record. In Hearst's case, a conservative impulse led him to fear popular unrest and even a threat to democracy if Hoover remained in power.[116]

Hoover's failure with the press was acutely ironic, because during his earlier career he had consistently displayed groundbreaking mastery of public relations – skills that had helped to explain his political success. Paradoxically, however, those skills did not translate successfully to a talent in power for good media relations.[117] In July 1930 A. H. Kirchhofer, a newspaper editor who had worked as a 1928 campaign aide, attributed Hoover's decreasing popularity to his ineffective communications with the public, including a poor relationship with Washington journalists.[118] Those close to Hoover believed that a half of capital correspondents were personally hostile to the administration or

[111] NAACP, "Race Relations Planks in G.O.P. Platform Demanded by Negro Advancement Group," June 14, 1932, box C399, series I, National Association for the Advancement of Colored People Records [hereafter NAACP Records].

[112] Walter White to Herbert A. Turner, June 13, 1932, box C399, series I, NAACP Records.

[113] "G.O.P Plank on Negro 'Flapdoodle,'" June 14, 1932, box C399, series I, NAACP Records.

[114] Herbert Hoover to Adolph S. Ochs, Dec. 13, 1934, box 166, Post-Presidential Individual Correspondence File [hereafter PPICF], Hoover Papers.

[115] Louis W. Liebovich, *Bylines in Despair: Herbert Hoover, the Great Depression, and the U.S. News Media* (Westport, Conn.: Praeger, 1994), 92.

[116] David Nasaw, *The Chief: The Life of William Randolph Hearst* (2000; Boston: Mariner, 2001), 456–457.

[117] Craig Lloyd, *Aggressive Introvert: A Study of Herbert Hoover and Public Relations Management, 1912–1932* (Columbus: Ohio State University Press, 1972).

[118] A. H. Kirchhofer to Herbert Hoover, July 15, 1930, box 180, PPF, Hoover Papers.

worked for hostile newspapers, and that they orchestrated between them their anti-Hoover coverage.[119]

Democratic effectiveness in attacking Hoover compounded the problem. During the Hoover years the Democrats developed a freshly proactive approach to the task of opposition, building the necessary infrastructure to support a constant attack on the incumbents. After his defeat, Al Smith argued that between elections the minority party should promote a constructive alternative to the Republicans, "rather than sit by and adopt a policy of inaction with the hope of profiting solely by the mistakes and failures of the opposition."[120] National chair John Raskob concluded that to function more effectively the Democrats needed a permanent institutional presence; between the 1924 and 1928 campaigns the party had even lacked a national headquarters. He hired on a full-time basis Jouett Shouse as Democratic National Committee (DNC) director and journalist Charles Michelson as publicity director.[121] Michelson orchestrated within his party a program of criticism of Republican actions, representing "a remarkable performance, an illuminating illustration of the amazing power of unopposed propaganda in skilful hands," according to pro-Hoover journalist Frank R. Kent in a magazine exposé as early as 1930.[122] These attacks were first against Republicans in general, especially those in Congress. But in time they focused strongly on Hoover himself, linking all problems with the president.[123]

Some pro-Republican press reaction to the Michelson publicity campaign speculated that its negativity was likely to foster public sympathy rather than hostility toward Hoover. "In short, narrow partisanship and poisonous malice have made Michelson's attacks so vicious as to render them absurd," pronounced an Indiana journalist in August 1930. "The revulsion already has set in."[124] The following spring Kirchhofer similarly counseled Hoover that he "should hope for a continuance of the campaign of abuse and personalities in which the Democrats have been and still are engaged," because its effects were likely to be counterproductive.[125] Republicans tried to develop the line that the administration was the victim of propaganda that misrepresented anti-Depression initiatives, a theme aired during the 1930 campaigns, when this effort included wide circulation of the Kent article about Michelson.[126] In his efforts to mobilize the party rank and file, RNC executive director Robert H. Lucas emphasized the damaging nature of Democratic propaganda and urged local Republicans to stress the point that such opposition

---

[119] Rickard diary, July 29, 1931, box 1, Rickard Collection.

[120] Peel and Donnelly, *1932 Campaign*, 111.

[121] Schlesinger, *Age of Roosevelt*, I: 273–274.

[122] *Scribner's*, Sept. 1930, 290–296.

[123] Fausold, *The Presidency of Herbert C. Hoover*, 85–86, 204.

[124] Lafayette, Indiana, *Journal Courier* clipping, Aug. 29, 1930, box 113, PSF, Hoover Papers.

[125] A. H. Kirchhofer to Herbert Hoover, May 1, 1931, box 180, PPF, Hoover Papers.

[126] Press release, Oct. 28, 1930, box 1189, Press Relations series, Hoover Papers.

was inaccurate and irresponsibly undermined the administration's pursuit of anti-Depression remedies.[127] By the start of 1932, the argument he disseminated within the party insisted that the administration response to an international depression was experiencing success in securing improved economic conditions at home, despite destructive criticism from congressional Democrats and despite a Democratic propaganda campaign to mislead the public.[128] The antipropaganda line did not enjoy adequate success, however. According to the chair of a Republican Party club in California, the weakness and tardiness of the administration's response to Democratic attacks were significant enough to account for the 1932 defeat.[129] But too often Hoover's problem was that the news was bad, rather than that the news was negative. Despite the high-profile defections of the *New York Times* and the Hearst group, an easy majority of the nation's newspapers probably remained supportive of Hoover.[130]

Among the writers sympathetic to Hoover was William Hard. "The definition of Mr. Hoover," Hard wrote perceptively in September 1932, "is that he is an individualist who, in order to preserve all the individualism capable of preservation in our American economic world, has made the Federal Government – beyond all precedent – collectivistic." Although Hoover tended to stress his conservatism – favoring localism and individualism – instead of his actual activism, increasing federal regulation, he was, according to Hard, "a conservative progressively innovating."[131] Hard was thinking of Hoover's Commerce record and pre-Depression presidential agenda, including reform initiatives on child welfare, education, and Native American affairs. But Hard's observation also involved the nature of Hoover's response to the economic crisis, which was activist within a widely shared conception of the federal government's limited powers. During the downturn's early months, when its severity was by no means clear, Hoover urged business leaders to maintain employment levels and wage rates, and he asked Congress and state governments to fund public works. His efforts to maintain economic confidence – which encouraged his description of the problems as a "depression" because it sounded less threatening than the more conventional terms, a "crisis" or a "panic" – were an important element of the strategy, but his opponents later used his expressions of buoyant optimism as examples of failed understanding.[132]

Such measures were inadequate. Seeing the availability of credit and the weakness of the banking system as key problems, Hoover then proposed the creation of the Reconstruction Finance Corporation in legislation passed by Congress in early 1932, after efforts to encourage voluntary action within the

---

[127] Robert H. Lucas to precinct leaders, Dec. 24, 1930, and Feb. 10, 1931, box 6, Lucas Papers.
[128] Robert H. Lucas to precinct leaders, Jan. 14, 1932, box 6, Lucas Papers.
[129] Richard L. Prather to Ogden L. Mills, Nov. 11, 1932, box 10, Mills Papers.
[130] Robinson and Bornet, *Herbert Hoover*, 272.
[131] *Washington, D.C., Sunday Star* clipping, Sept. 18, 1932, box 8, Strother Papers.
[132] Burner, *Herbert Hoover*, 212–253.

banking system proved unsuccessful. The RFC was the most prominent of a number of initiatives to tackle Depression problems; it gave loans to banks, railroads, and some agricultural organizations. The shortcomings of the RFC's efforts, together with charities' and local and state governments' increasing inability to meet the needs of the unemployed, encouraged Hoover in July to sign a relief act plowing money into public works and granting RFC loans to states for direct relief.[133] In seeking to minimize the federal government's role, Hoover feared the consequences in acting otherwise. He thought an expansion of its control over the economy invited business efforts to acquire political power, endangering representative government and leading to fascism or, in the case of labor power, to socialism.[134] There were, moreover, clear signs that Hoover was right to believe in public support for such antistatism. A widespread phenomenon of the early Depression years was a local-level tax revolt, calling for government economy as an anti-Depression remedy – a preference for smaller rather than bigger government.[135] (Fearful of deficits, Hoover offered no such measure, instead increasing income tax in 1932.[136])

Despite Hoover's anti-Depression efforts, the Depression continued to worsen. By fall 1932 gross national product was more than 30 percent lower than the pre-crash level, and declines in industrial output and factory employment were even greater.[137] The initiatives did not, therefore, create a compelling argument in favor of Hoover's reelection. The focus on conservatism instead of activism, as noted by Hard, compounded this problem. Republicans tried to make a number of arguments to shift blame for the economy's travails – arguments that had some substance but lacked electoral force. Believing that it possessed electoral promise, Republicans speedily adopted the line that America's Depression was part of an international economic crisis and that conditions were better at home than elsewhere.[138] In fact, the stress was strong enough to encourage some to suspect that Hoover cared more about Europe than the United States.[139]

As the 1930 elections approached, the RNC's Robert Lucas argued that it was unfair for the Democratic Party to deploy hard times and unemployment in partisan terms, adding the charge that in the hope of political advantage congressional Democrats withheld cooperation from the administration's anti-Depression efforts.[140] The Republican loss of Congress then created a

[133] Fausold, *The Presidency of Herbert C. Hoover*, 151–166.

[134] Burner, *Herbert Hoover*, 273–274.

[135] David T. Beito, *Taxpayers in Revolt: Tax Resistance during the Great Depression* (Chapel Hill: University of North Carolina Press, 1989).

[136] Lichtman, *White Protestant Nation*, 53–54.

[137] Fausold, *The Presidency of Herbert C. Hoover*, 193.

[138] RNC, press release, Sept. 11, 1930, box 1188, Press Relations series, Hoover Papers; Ernest I. Lewis to Will R. Wood, Sept. 19, 1930, box 7, Lewis Papers.

[139] John Callan O'Laughlin to Theodore Roosevelt, Jr., Dec. 2, 1932, box 29, Roosevelt Papers.

[140] *Louisville Courier-Journal* clipping, Aug. 17, 1930, box 7, Lucas Papers; Robert H. Lucas, speech, Aug. 7, 1930, box 8, Lucas Papers.

degree of optimism on the grounds that Democrats now shared the responsibility of government. It was even an outcome for which Hoover had hoped because of this potential advantage.[141] With the Senate still under Republican control after the midterm elections, he suggested that Democrats should be allowed to organize the body, a suggestion that Senate Republicans rejected.[142] In 1932 administration official Ernest Lewis concluded that Democratic control of the House had indeed operated to Hoover's benefit, as both parties now shared responsibility for anti-Depression policy.[143] Also as the 1932 campaign approached, Secretary of the Treasury Ogden Mills – whose privileged background caused an editor to describe him to Hoover as someone who "never said 'Hi, Bill' to a pal in blue jean pants" – similarly hoped for Congress's early adjournment for the country's good, though not the administration's; if Congress stayed in session, "the Democrats will probably succeed in handing us the Election," he wrote.[144] But such views were unrealistic. Regardless of congressional Democrats' actions, the Hoover administration was at the center of political debate. Most perceived the president and his administration as primarily responsible for orchestrating the nation's attack on the Depression. William Allen White noted that a party that claimed responsibility for prosperity during the 1920s should not be surprised to receive the voters' blame for hard times.[145]

Other developments fostered some hope. Notably, Franklin Roosevelt's emergence as a leading presidential prospect for the Democrats kindled a small flame of optimism. Hoover was sure that his chances were best against Roosevelt, worrying when FDR's stock fell within the Democratic Party. "Our salvation lies largely in his nomination," he privately observed during the Democratic national convention.[146] Hoover's low assessment of Roosevelt was a great misjudgment. The Roosevelt selection did not reduce but increased the Republicans' problems. Not only did Roosevelt effectively oppose Hoover during the 1932 campaign, but as president he would prove to be devastatingly effective in confirming the Republican Party as the minority in American politics. But despite these glimmers of misleading optimism, Republicans both inside and outside the White House were usually in little doubt that the electoral outlook was bleak. "We are opposed by 10,000,000 unemployed, 10,000 bonus marchers and 10 cent corn," Hoover remarked in early October, referring to the "Bonus Army" of unemployed World War I veterans who marched to Washington, forming a camp there, to lobby for early payment of a service benefit. "Is it any wonder that the prospects are dark?"[147]

---

[141] Jordan A. Schwarz, *The Interregnum of Despair: Hoover, Congress, and the Depression* (Urbana: University of Illinois Press, 1970), 53.

[142] Kennedy, *Freedom from Fear*, 60.

[143] Ernest I. Lewis to Clyde M. Reed, Aug. 18, 1932, box 5, Lewis Papers.

[144] Richard Lloyd Jones to Herbert Hoover, Sept. 15, 1932, box 166, PPF, Hoover Papers; Ogden L. Mills to Herbert Bayward Swope, April 20, 1932, box 9, Mills Papers.

[145] William Allen White to Lewis L. Strauss, Aug. 30, 1932, box 33, Strauss Papers.

[146] Joslin diary, June 28, 1932, box 10, Joslin Papers.

[147] Joslin diary, Oct. 8, 1932, box 10, Joslin Papers.

Under Speaker John Nance Garner of Texas, the Democratic House had seized its opportunity to obstruct Hoover's plans and to denounce their inadequacy. During the campaign, Republicans then seized their apparent opportunity to characterize Democrats as not only dangerous and irresponsible but also unclear about their own intentions. Garner – the Democrats' vice-presidential nominee – was "a real Republican asset," according to James MacLafferty, and Hoover concluded that Roosevelt was vulnerable both as a "flutter-budget" and as vague.[148] Ogden Mills, a leading administration spokesperson, attacked the Democrats' "vague promises and pronouncements and an utter failure to come to grips with the real problems of the hour." But he also drew a clear line between the parties' view of the federal role in tackling the problems of the Depression – between the Republicans' emphasis on cooperation, voluntary endeavor, and individual initiative, and the Democrats' willingness to create an expanded, wasteful bureaucracy with responsibilities beyond the federal government's capacity.[149] In this way, the campaign developed what would remain the Republican Party's central charge against the Democratic Party for many decades to come; nevertheless, Republicans usually failed to mobilize a majority for antistatism and their party. Mills emphasized a distinction, too, between the administration's respect for sound financial principles and Roosevelt's disregard for them, sure to worsen the state of the economy, he stressed.[150] When Hoover took to the campaign trail, he followed a similar path. He said that Roosevelt's was "the dreadful position of the chameleon on the Scotch plaid."[151] Roosevelt's anti-Depression proposals were indeed often vague and contradictory, but Roosevelt nevertheless managed to communicate his determination to get to grips with the economy's troubles in a new way.

The promise of a "New Deal" substantiated the other element of Hoover's attack on the Democrats, which in the end stressed their proposals' perilous radicalism. On October 31 Hoover said that these proposals "represent a profound change in American life" and "a radical departure from the foundations of 150 years which have made this the greatest nation in the world."[152] In identifying the Democrats as radical, Republicans believed they had identified an electoral vulnerability. They also believed the danger was real. From the Philippines, where he was governor-general, Theodore Roosevelt, Jr., observed that "We are in sober truth struggling for the very existence of the social order to which we were brought up."[153] An eastern Republican told Hoover that the opposition was "a radical form of socialism."[154]

This was a belief often evident in the campaign, which Republicans sometimes discussed more dramatically than Hoover and top administration

[148] MacLafferty diary, July 11, and Aug. 9, 1932, box 1, MacLafferty Papers.
[149] Ogden L. Mills, speech, Sept. 30, 1932, box 153, Mills Papers.
[150] *NYT* clipping, July 12, 1932, box 11, Strother Papers.
[151] Freidel, "Election of 1932," 2735.
[152] Robinson and Bornet, *Herbert Hoover*, 274.
[153] Theodore Roosevelt, Jr., to Charles D. Hilles, July 4, 1932, box 28, Roosevelt Papers.
[154] Frederic C. Wolcott to Herbert Hoover, Oct. 10, 1932, box 257, PSF, Hoover Papers.

spokespeople such as Mills did. In a speech at Parkersburg, West Virginia, Phil Campbell, a former congressperson, said that "the same appeal to the radical element and to the socialist mind" characterized all Roosevelt's speeches, and Campbell condemned the big-spending response to the Depression they suggested, comparing his proposals with policies in the Soviet Union, and contrasting them with Hoover's American principles.[155] Although he believed that the Hoover administration had drifted dangerously toward excessive regulation, Representative James M. Beck of Massachusetts saw the choice facing voters as clear-cut between conservatism and Soviet-like radicalism, accused Roosevelt of stirring class hatred, and warned that the implications of his victory were dangerous. "The forces of radicalism will have triumphed and the possible result will be, if these radical forces control this government for four or eight years, to convert this proud republic into a bastard imitation of the soviet regime at Moscow," he warned.[156] Borah, campaigning as a "neutral" – pro-Roosevelt – Republican, suspected insightfully that a strategy emphasizing an attack impetus was unlikely to be effective, because the campaign involved a turn against the incumbents rather than a turn toward FDR; Republicans instead needed to offer positive reasons for their reelection. "I may be all wrong, but I think it a shame that the Republican campaign managers should insist upon electing Roosevelt," he wrote. "They ought at least to permit him to do that himself."[157]

The theme that Republicans were holding the line against the threat of "a Democratic-Radical coalition" was one that predated the campaign. It was a theme that Robert Lucas programmed for party speakers in 1931, together with the claim that "Internationalists and Communists" were helping Democrats "to discredit the President of the United States and to destroy the Republican Party."[158] The nation's turbulence seemed to create an opportunity for such dark warnings. This turbulence was especially evident in Washington, D.C., during June and July when the Bonus Army protesters convened; many saw the violence that characterized the army's eviction of the demonstrators as a final blow to any reelection chances Hoover might still have retained.[159] It was also evident in the despair that was growing among farmers, some of whom in the summer joined a strike to protest prices below the cost of production.[160] Nevertheless, these expressions of antiadministration sentiment did not amount to a radical challenge to the government; nor were the Democrats harbingers of radicalism. It was with little difficulty that Roosevelt managed to shrug off such accusations. "My policy is as radical as American liberty; as radical as the Constitution of the United States," he remarked.[161]

[155] Phil Campbell, "Roosevelt the Radical," Oct. 8, 1932, box 272, PSF, Hoover Papers.
[156] Schlesinger, *Age of Roosevelt*, I: 178, 246; *Boston Herald* clipping, Oct. 28, 1932, box 254, PSF, Hoover Papers.
[157] William E. Borah to Harry J. Brown, Oct. 8, 1932, box 347, Borah Papers.
[158] Robert H. Lucas to Republican speakers, May 8 and June 20, 1931, box 7, Lucas Papers.
[159] Burner, *Herbert Hoover*, 309–312.
[160] Schlesinger, *Age of Roosevelt*, I: 265–268.
[161] Peel and Donnelly, *1932 Campaign*, 178.

Leading Republicans sometimes conceived the electorate as divided between the "thinking" and the "unthinking," a conception that revealed a certain wariness about mass democracy. The distinction involved the self-serving belief that members of the former group appreciated the wisdom of Hoover's policies, together with the defeatist conclusion that so-called unthinking voters were beyond the reach of rational debate. The terminology was not new; a *New York Times* editorial noted that the Republican Party had "boasted and believed for years that it was the principal repository of political virtue and intelligence."[162] During his difficult 1930 reelection struggle, Arthur Capper, the progressively inclined U.S. Senator from Kansas, identified discontent with the administration's farm program as his key obstacle because, he wrote, "There are a good many of the unthinking voters blaming the administration for the hard times we are going through."[163] Capper's fellow Kansas progressive, William Allen White, worried about "the moron mind at the bottom, the mind that makes lynching mobs and elects demagogues in the South and follows quacks in the West, and the various Tammanies in our cities." However, he was anxious, too, about middle-class political apathy and about a lack of leadership capacity within the nation's elite.[164] As 1932 progressed, White concluded that Hoover enjoyed some success in building support among "the upper reaches of political intelligence," but not among "[t]he moronic underworld."[165] Others agreed with the White thesis that the thinking understood the merits of Hoover's Depression remedies better than the unthinking, with some wondering whether key figures in a community who supported the Republican Party might successfully lead wider public opinion in its direction.[166] Hoover himself distrusted emotion-based appeals as demagogic, preferring a high-minded approach to political communication, a preference that hindered his message's effective dissemination.[167]

These discussions reveal the persistence of beliefs more usually associated with an earlier era, when anxieties about voters' inattentiveness to issues and their unquestioning sense of party loyalty encouraged Gilded Age reform schemes of voter education.[168] They are a partisan version of a belief that political participation was the prerogative of a white, middle-class elite, assumed to be well educated and informed; during the early decades of the twentieth century, reformers' "get-out-the-vote" efforts did not seek to mobilize the less socioeconomically privileged, but only this elite.[169] Roy V. Peel and Thomas

---

[162] *NYT* clipping, April 12, 1931, box 37, Norris Papers.

[163] Arthur Capper to Walter H. Newton, Oct. 27, 1930, box 261, PSF, Hoover Papers.

[164] William Allen White to Glenn Frank, Jan. 22, 1931, box C176, White Papers.

[165] William Allen White to Henry J. Allen, March 4, 1932, box C187, White Papers.

[166] Homer Hoch to William Allen White, May 24, 1932, box C189, White Papers.

[167] Donald A. Ritchie, *Electing FDR: The New Deal Campaign of 1932* (Lawrence: University Press of Kansas, 2007), 33.

[168] Glenn C. Altschuler and Stuart M. Blumin, *Rude Republic: Americans and Their Politics in the Nineteenth Century* (Princeton, N.J.: Princeton University Press, 2000), 267–268.

[169] Liette Gidlow, *The Big Vote: Gender, Consumer Culture, and the Politics of Exclusion, 1890s–1920s* (Baltimore: Johns Hopkins University Press, 2004).

C. Donnelly, who wrote a contemporary analysis of the 1932 campaign, posited a distinction between how "educated people" and the "masses" viewed the campaign, arguing that the educated did not perceive a real difference between the parties on the issues and that the masses did, and therefore suggesting – misleadingly – that the Hoover–Roosevelt conflict was little more than rhetorical.[170] Within the Republican Party a significantly different view was that of William E. Borah, who offered a progressive critique of such elitism. Borah found fault not in the public's ignorance but in the Republican elite's failure to understand the electorate's concerns. He observed that "the masses had come to believe that the party no longer spoke to them." Although the party's rank and file was in tune with those concerns, "a few gentlemen whose conception of the nation and its policies did not extend far beyond Manhattan Island" were responsible for the creation of a platform that brought defeat, according to Borah.[171] He saw the party as out of step with most Americans.

The contemptuous view of the average voter informed a variety of campaign prescriptions. One was defeatist. David Hinshaw, who organized a network of clubs in support of Hoover's reelection, concluded in July that the party had a chance only if army intelligence tests of World War I were wrong in finding that no more than one in five Americans was "above 14 years old mentally."[172] Another was more positive, thanks to its identification of a way to reach the mass electorate. A Newark, New Jersey, lawyer, active in Republican politics, urged the party to develop a strategy recognizing the decisiveness not of "reason and logic" but of "the emotions arising in the breasts of the discontented, the despairing, the unemployed, the man whose wages have been cut, who resents the reduction in his fortunes, whose home has been lost, whose savings have been depleted or destroyed, who has not paid and is not able to pay his excessive taxes or the interest on his mortgage."[173] Simplification of the Republican message would facilitate its communication with "the ordinary listener, who averages a ten-year old mind," newspaper publisher Frank E. Gannett told Henry J. Allen, who was in charge of RNC publicity.[174] The campaign made explicit use of the point that worried Republicans in private. An advertisement, designed for the voluntary use of GOP-supportive newspapers, encouraged voters to think, telling them that Roosevelt's "appeal is made to the UN-THINKING."[175]

A concomitance of Republican contempt for voters was voter contempt for the party. When Borah reached the conclusion that a popular belief in the party's elitist concerns accounted for its downfall, he reflected the results of soundings among leading Idaho citizens. "The republican party has suffered much because it is regarded as a rich man's party and poor men have shied

[170] Peel and Donnelly, *1932 Campaign*, 124.
[171] William E. Borah to J. H. Peterson, Nov. 11, 1932, box 347, Borah Papers.
[172] David Hinshaw to William Allen White, July 5, 1932, box C189, White Papers.
[173] Fred G. Stickel, Jr., to Mark Sullivan, Sept. 23, 1932, box 210, PPF, Hoover Papers.
[174] Frank E. Gannett to Henry J. Allen, Oct. 17, 1932, box C76, Allen Papers.
[175] Charles A. Segner to Henry J. Allen, Oct. 26, 1932, box C76, Allen Papers.

away from it," a journalist observed. "We are practically all poor now and the party that wins must appeal to the poor people."[176] Supported by the Michelson campaign that spoke of the economic crisis as the "Hoover Depression" and of shanty towns for the homeless as "Hoovervilles," the image of the president and, by extension, the party as loftily unconcerned about the plight of ordinary Americans, as interested instead in the fortunes of banks and large corporations, was damaging. It contrasted sharply with Franklin Roosevelt's appeal to what he called the "forgotten man." A Democratic leaflet bluntly distinguished "the party of the people" from the Republican Party's protection of "the rich and the powerful."[177] Already known as the party of business, the GOP was deeply vulnerable to such attacks as soon as prosperity ended, especially because it was all too easy for Democratic speakers to characterize the administration's record in this way. Hoover's elevated rhetoric did little to challenge such a characterization.

The paradigm of the thinking voter influenced some analyses of the defeat. Frank Knox, the *Chicago Daily News* publisher, told Hoover that "the thinking people of the United States, the people who used their brains, voted for you," while "[t]hose who were controlled by their emotions, and of course this is always a great majority, voted against you."[178] More pithily, Representative U. S. Guyer of Kansas observed, "An empty stomach has no brains."[179] The dominant analysis among Republicans of the defeat minimized the responsibility of the administration and the party, seen as powerless against the anti-incumbent tide of hard times. "The Archangel Gabriel could not have won on the Republican ticket after the last four years of depression," Theodore Roosevelt, Jr., remarked.[180] Searching for a shred of consolation in the landslide, some in the Hoover White House took some satisfaction in the overwhelming nature of the defeat on the grounds that a smaller margin was likelier to foster recriminations about campaign mistakes.[181]

Although the paradigm of the thinking voter smugly suggested that Republican success should be greater among the more socioeconomically advantaged, the key feature of these anti-incumbent elections was a generalized turn away from the party. All groups signaled dissatisfaction with its record and a desire for an alternative, and intensifications of anti-Republican sentiment occurred where the Depression's effects were severest.[182]

---

[176] John L. Brady to R. P. Parry, Nov. 29, 1932, box 369, Borah Papers.

[177] Democratic National Campaign Committee Labor Bureau, leaflet, n.d., box 254, PSF, Hoover Papers.

[178] Frank Knox to Herbert Hoover, Nov. 11, 1932, box 167, PPF, Hoover Papers.

[179] U. S. Guyer to Ogden L. Mills, Nov. 13, 1932, box 10, Mills Papers.

[180] Theodore Roosevelt, Jr., to Charles D. Hilles, Dec. 2, 1932, box 28, Roosevelt Papers.

[181] Joslin diary, Nov. 9, 1932, box 10, Joslin Papers; Walter H. Newton to Nathan W. MacChesney, Nov. 10, 1932, box 14, MacChesney Papers.

[182] Gosnell and Gill, "Analysis of the 1932 Presidential Vote," 983–984; Harold F. Gosnell and William G. Colman, "Political Trends in Industrial America: Pennsylvania an Example,"

As Hoover approached the end of his time as president and as Roosevelt prepared the launch of the New Deal, the United States was on the verge of great political upheaval. "Well, I should say it will be a change from old Home Melodies to jazz music," Hoover remarked, according to a journalist who asked him about the implications of his departure from the White House. "This is a jazz age, and people are jazz crazy. They wanted a change, and that's what they're getting."[183] The crucial question for the Republican Party involved its response to this new politics, its shape as yet unknown. Never a party insider and now a rejected candidate, Hoover seemed unlikely to play a large part in developing this response. But Hoover was making plans to ensure that he would retain influence within the party in order to help determine the response, as well as protect his legacy. He saw his role as likely to be important in preventing Old Guard conservatives, who posed a threat to more forward-thinking ideas about party politics such as his, from party domination.[184] This was not to be the shape of the Republican debate in a jazz-crazy era, however. Hoover secured influence in the debate about the party's response to its descent to minority status, but his struggle to defend the ideas developed in his campaign against Franklin Roosevelt helped to confirm the Republicans' new electoral problems.[185]

Public Opinion Quarterly [hereafter *POQ*] 4 (1940), 476–482; W. Phillips Shively, "A Reinterpretation of the New Deal Realignment," *POQ* 35 (1971–72), 621–624.

[183] Henry L. Misselwitz to Raymond Clapper, n.d., box 7, Clapper Papers.

[184] Joslin diary, Dec. 10, 1932, and Jan. 31, Feb. 3, and Feb. 19, 1933, box 10, Joslin Papers.

[185] Thomas M. Slopnick, "In the Shadow of Herbert Hoover: The Republican Party and the Politics of Defeat, 1932–1936" (Ph.D. dissertation, University of Connecticut, 2006).

"As Maine Goes, So Goes Vermont": 1933–1939

The New Deal produced a sustained period of electoral disaster for the Republican Party. In the Roosevelt administration's first major test at the polls, in 1934, Democrats confounded normal expectations of a midterm slump for the White House party by making gains, leaving Republicans with only 25 U.S. senators, 103 representatives in the House, and 7 governors. The 1936 elections then offered further disappointments. Alfred M. Landon, Kansas's governor and one of the few 1934 victors, suffered a resounding defeat in the presidential contest, winning fewer than seventeen million votes to Franklin Roosevelt's total of more than twenty-seven million. The Republican share of the electoral college dwindled to a northern New England rump of just two states – Maine and Vermont. Republican representation on Capitol Hill declined still further – to sixteen in the Senate and eighty-nine in the House. These devastating results caused some to wonder whether the party had any future at all.

The future looked brighter before long. Frustrations with Roosevelt's second term allowed Republicans to win back some of these losses in 1938, picking up eight Senate seats, eighty-one House seats, and thirteen governorships. These gains were substantial but fell far short of Democratic totals, thus confirming the GOP's status as the nation's minority; even a good year was not good enough. Still, the gains rekindled optimism in the party. Many Republicans started to conclude that public opinion was moving in favor of their argument that the New Deal was a flawed approach to government. In fact, this qualified comeback for the party was the product of voter frustration with the New Deal's flawed execution; it did not mark a rejection of New Deal principles. Republican optimism was therefore sometimes a misinterpretation of the midterms' meaning.

Disenchantment with the Republican Party reflected a decisive majority's endorsement of the New Deal – an immensely diverse collection of initiatives designed to alleviate the Depression's human suffering, achieve economic recovery, and construct a system providing social-insurance protections against future downturns. Questions of government activism became central to politics, and Republican answers to those questions found less public favor than those of their Democratic opponents. Most Republicans emphasized their commitment to tackling the Depression's economic and human problems, but disagreed with the Roosevelt administration about the extent of government activism necessary to solve them, arguing variously that the New Deal formula was ineffective, unconstitutional, or dangerous to individual freedom. They also argued that New Deal programs suppressed business confidence, thus postponing a recovery.

Roosevelt's first term created a Democratic coalition that was based, most importantly, on the less socioeconomically privileged, those most in need of the New Deal's help – the "forgotten man" to whom FDR had pledged his efforts during the 1932 campaign. This differed from his 1932 vote, which represented a rejection of the Hoover administration and the Republican Party among all sections of the population. In some respects, the new coalition of the "forgotten" resembled previous patterns of support for the Democratic Party; Catholic and other ethnic communities of "new-immigrant" backgrounds in the cities were among the coalition's most loyal elements. The white South, moreover, retained its overwhelming affiliation to the Democratic Party, delivering a dependable block of votes in the electoral college and a constant group of officeholders on Capitol Hill. Other groups were newcomers to the party's coalition. African Americans were also among the forgotten people who supported the Democrats. Often the victim of discrimination in New Deal programs' local implementation, African Americans nevertheless began to reconsider their support for the party of Abraham Lincoln.[1]

Roosevelt himself played an especially important role in the New Deal coalition's creation. An enormously popular politician, he harnessed this popularity to secure the enactment of his anti-Depression policies and to boost his party's fortunes, as well as to secure personal triumphs at the polls. He was also an unusually skillful behind-the-scenes strategist.[2] In 1936 one journalist likened FDR to a St. Louis Cardinals star in calling him "a political Dizzy Dean, [who] has the bleachers with him, is a hero of the previous World's Series, has an expert assortment of curved balls which he shoots, first on the left and then on the right, now a high one and then a low one."[3] Republicans

[1] John M. Allswang, *The New Deal and American Politics: A Study in Political Change* (New York: Wiley, 1978).

[2] Alonzo L. Hamby, "High Tide: Roosevelt, Truman, and the Democratic Party, 1932–1952," in William H. Chafe, ed., *The Achievement of American Liberalism: The New Deal and Its Legacies* (New York: Columbia University Press, 2003), 21–61; Marc Landy, "Presidential Party Leadership and Party Realignment: FDR and the Making of the New Deal Democratic Party," in Sidney M. Milkis and Jerome M. Mileur, eds., *The New Deal and the Triumph of Liberalism* (Amherst: University of Massachusetts Press, 2002), 73–85; Jerome M. Mileur, "The 'Boss': Franklin Roosevelt, the Democratic Party, and the Reconstruction of American Politics," in Sidney M. Milkis and Jerome M. Mileur, eds., *The New Deal and the Triumph of Liberalism* (Amherst: University of Massachusetts Press, 2002), 86–134; Sean J. Savage, *Roosevelt the Party Leader, 1932–1945* (Lexington: University Press of Kentucky, 1991).

[3] *Review of Reviews*, June 1936, 33.

sometimes took comfort in the personal foundation of the Democratic Party's popularity. One, for example, interpreted the party's disastrous 1934 showing as "an expression of confidence in President Roosevelt and not an approbation of all of his policies."[4] Once Roosevelt was gone, Republican fortunes would surely change, some thought – a complacent view that sometimes discouraged serious contemplation of the New Deal's popular strength, beyond Roosevelt's personal support.[5] But they could not at first know that Roosevelt would uniquely and successfully seek third and then fourth terms as president, thus long postponing their post-FDR opportunity. Much more significantly, this view failed to recognize that the New Deal's electoral success involved ideas as well as a leader. An urgent appetite for respite from Depression ills became a longer-term embrace of activist government to ensure a return to prosperity and then its maintenance, and to insure people against the vicissitudes of individual economic misfortune. This activism – New Deal liberalism – became the bedrock of the Democrats' majority status and the Republicans' minority status.

As the New Deal unfolded and as the Democratic Party developed new and formidable strength, leading Republicans responded in a variety of ways. Especially at the start of the Roosevelt administration, inaction frequently characterized their response – the reflection of bewilderment at the fast-moving political scene and a desire to take stock of this change. But feverish action, both intellectual and organizational, infected the GOP at other times, as Republicans sought to update party principles, remind the electorate of their merits, and ensure that the party's structures were effective in mobilizing support.

A cauldron of anxiety about the nation's future overwhelmed many Republicans, compelling them to challenge staunchly New Deal liberalism's emergence. Viewing the New Deal with great alarm, they believed that the administration's initiatives amounted to an assault on individual liberty and that the expansion of presidential powers was an unconstitutional attack on democratic structures. Such beliefs caused some to see the New Deal as a step toward socialism and regard Franklin Roosevelt as a would-be dictator. Others more swiftly, more calmly accepted the need for government to take an enlarged role in guiding the economy and offering welfare protections, though they often shared concerns about the dictatorial drift of a political approach that embraced an expanded executive in pursuit of its goals, together with doubts about its effectiveness. Alarm about the federal government's growth thus informed the response to New Deal liberalism among most Republicans, whether more or less conservative in outlook. As this party debate developed during the 1930s, action was not much more successful than inaction in halting their Democratic opponents' capture of a majority, however. The Republicans'

[4] Charles D. Hilles to Mrs. Paul FitzSimons, Nov. 13, 1934, box 87, PPICF, Hoover Papers.
[5] Karl A. Lamb, "Republican Strategy and the Congressional Election of 1938" (D.Phil. thesis, University of Oxford, 1957), 39–40.

antigovernment agenda found support among a minority of Americans – a group insignificant in electoral terms by contrast with the impressive new Democratic coalition.

Republican progressives advocated a more sympathetic response. Those in Congress often voted for New Deal measures; at election time – as in 1932 – many either remained neutral or even actively supported FDR. But their intra-party influence was limited. These dissidents were poorly organized and prone to internal division. A high tide of influence occurred in 1936, when the party sought a synthesis between the conservative East and the less conservative, more progressive West in forlorn search of victory against Roosevelt, though this search was not complete enough to embrace the progressives' agenda. Their faction then declined. Some moved across to the Democrats. Others shared the general Republican anxiety that New Deal liberalism involved excessive executive authority; this identification of common interest subsumed the old contrast between progressives and regulars.

Republicans believed that the antistatist concerns at the heart of their New Deal response were not fundamentally out of step with public opinion. They were right to do so, and it was therefore by no means unreasonable for them to conclude that this response had electoral promise. At the state level through-out the 1930s, Democrats as well as Republicans often enjoyed success by promoting retrenchment rather than expansive government, policy-making caution rather than experimentation.[6] Furthermore, a preference for local-ism persisted, despite the federal government's growth, as did a preference for individualistic self-reliance, despite the emergence of a welfare state. This antistatism nevertheless coexisted, paradoxically, with a desire for assertive anti-Depression action. Among Roosevelt's achievements in guiding the New Deal was to craft anti-Depression remedies that, on the whole, were prudent enough to maintain popular support and sap the potential of any Republican counterattack. As defined by Roosevelt, New Deal liberalism did not pose a threat to the principles that Republicans defended as under threat from administration initiatives.

During the "Hundred Days" of energetic anti-Depression initiative that began the New Deal, Maine's Senator Wallace H. White, Jr., counseled cau-tion for Republicans because of the president's huge popularity: "I suppose prudence dictates that one should not attempt to swim against the tide."[7] This caution, together with an awareness that political developments were moving fast, encouraged Republican politicians to avoid much public discus-sion about their party's future. Of course, this all-important topic absorbed their private attention. Republicans recognized the significance of the New

[6] James T. Patterson, *The New Deal and the States: Federalism in Transition* (Princeton, N.J.: Princeton University Press, 1969); John Braeman, Robert H. Bremner, and David Brody, eds., *The New Deal*, vol. 2: *The State and Local Levels* (Columbus: Ohio State University Press, 1975).

[7] Wallace H. White to Wingate F. Cram, March 20, 1933, box 1, Wallace White Papers.

Deal's innovations and realized that the old foundations of the party's pre-Depression success were probably obsolete. Some among them preferred a response of outright conservatism, steadfastly opposing the New Deal almost in its entirety, whereas others, often from the party's progressive tradition, believed that some or even many elements of the New Deal – such as wage and hour controls and the self-regulation of industry – deserved measured support. But silence united them, reflecting both an uncertainty about how the new politics would evolve and an expedient desire to allow the administration to make mistakes.[8]

Congressional votes on New Deal initiatives indicate the contours of GOP opposition. The Glass-Steagall Banking Act and the Economy Act, fairly conservative measures to reform the financial system and cut government spending, secured widespread Republican support, though also some opposition among progressives. The business-friendly elements of the National Industrial Recovery Act fomented Republican disagreement about this legislation's merits, while the Agricultural Adjustment Act secured some farm-state support among Republicans. The early New Deal's more liberal initiatives – such as the Federal Emergency Relief Act and the creation of the Tennessee Valley Authority – won some support among progressives; most Republicans, however, displayed their conservative opposition.[9]

Silence did not last long. Anger and outrage about the New Deal within the GOP came to the surface in early 1934 in a way that revealed concern about the new doctrine of government activism. Three of the party's leading figures signaled antigovernment alarm. Former Secretary of the Treasury Ogden L. Mills attacked the concentration of power in Roosevelt's hands, calling the development unparalleled since "the days of absolute autocrats," condemning the growth of government control over the economy as unconstitutional. "The whole conception of a planned and directed national economy is destructive of the most fundamental principles upon which the American system rests," Mills said. "It cannot be carried out unless the central government be vested with complete and arbitrary authority over the actions of individuals and the right to regiment them."[10] Theodore Roosevelt, Jr., also placed a concern about democracy at the center of his attack on the New Deal, which, he said, "is reactionary and unAmerican because it carries as its logical conclusion some type of autocratic government." He sounded similar anxieties about bureaucracy, regulation, regimentation, and their adverse impact on individual liberty.[11] Placing greater emphasis than Mills and Roosevelt on common ground with the New Deal's goals to secure recovery, Michigan's Senator Arthur H. Vandenberg nevertheless said that the nation was "living under political

---

[8] *Collier's*, Nov. 25, 1933, 13, 50; Roland N. Stromberg, *Republicanism Reappraised* (Washington, D.C.: Public Affairs, 1952), 44–45.

[9] Weed, *Nemesis of Reform*, 119–149.

[10] Ogden L. Mills, "Where Do We Go From Here?" Jan. 29, 1934, box 207, Clapper Papers.

[11] Theodore Roosevelt, Jr., speech, April 18, 1934, box 207, Clapper Papers.

dictatorship." For Vandenberg – who unlike Mills and Roosevelt grappled with the detail of New Deal initiatives on Capitol Hill – the economic emergency justified such an approach to government in the shorter term, but he warned his party to be watchful of bureaucracy and presidential power, potentially dangerous to individual liberty.[12]

Mills, Roosevelt, and – more so – Vandenberg all sought to identify elements of the New Deal with which they agreed; all supported its goals to ease human suffering and solve the nation's economic problems, and Vandenberg was even ready to accept emergency use of unconventional approaches to government. But the more conspicuous element of their varying messages was a fundamental opposition to the New Deal's methods, rooted especially in an understanding of individual liberty as fragile under the weighty expansions of the federal government, particularly of the executive through an array of new agencies. A progressive perspective encouraged a different conclusion, however. William Allen White was skeptical of this emerging emphasis on freedom's protection: "The bill of rights, I fear, in the bright lexicon of Young Teddy is to be the bulwark of privilege rather than a defense of democracy."[13]

The electoral challenge for Republicans was the construction of a persuasive case for the antistatist critique when the New Deal was popular. Angry, passionate opposition to the New Deal did not easily accommodate any dilution of this critique. Some thought in any case that any such dilution was unnecessary and unproductive; a stress on difference was more promising. Herbert Hoover took this view. Defense of his administration's record pushed him toward anti–New Deal hostility, but he insisted that this approach made electoral sense, too. According to Hoover, voters would choose a Democrat wholeheartedly in favor of the New Deal in preference to a Republican selectively supportive of its goals and initiatives. "The only people the Republicans have to appeal to are the ones opposed to the fundamental principles involved in it," he wrote in early 1934.[14] Believing an anti–New Deal turn inevitable if not imminent, Representative James W. Wadsworth of upstate New York advocated staunch opposition to resist dangerous radicalism, but also to maintain electoral support. In May 1935 he wrote that "if we pussyfoot and offer compromises we shall lose the respect of all thinking men and as a party we shall perish, to be succeeded in the years to come by some other group which will have the guts to make the big fight."[15]

At first the Republican National Committee adopted a no-compromise line. Shortly after the 1932 defeat, national chair Everett Sanders insisted that the millions who voted for Hoover vindicated his anti-Depression policies, claiming that this support "constituted not only an approval of the record of the party while in control of the government, but it also constituted a

[12] Arthur H. Vandenberg, speech, Feb. 17, 1934, box 207, Clapper Papers.
[13] William Allen White to Herbert Hoover, April 11, [1934], box C215, White Papers.
[14] Herbert Hoover to John Callan O'Laughlin, Jan. 29, 1934, box 167, PPICF, Hoover Papers.
[15] James W. Wadsworth to Dennis T. Flynn, May 15, 1935, box 28, Wadsworth Papers.

mandate to the party to 'carry on'."[16] He was eager to develop an offensive against the New Deal and criticized fall 1933 campaigns that downplayed Democratic–Republican differences.[17] His eagerness precipitated a party crisis in early 1934 when the national committee issued a pamphlet accusing the administration of using Civil Works Administration (CWA) relief funds in search of votes.[18] At the time of the pamphlet's publication, CWA spending was under debate in Congress, and Republicans there objected to the RNC's untimely intervention. The party's House and Senate campaign committees announced their independence from the RNC.[19] Institutional jealousies thus compounded strategic disagreements. The conflict was also a reminder of the different incentives and motivations that informed the actions of different elements within the party. Congressional Republicans needed to respond to each legislative initiative; extracongressional Republicans faced no such obligation. The election cycle subjected those in Congress to the need – remorseless in the House – to be attentive to constituency concerns. Elections were important, too, to extracongressional Republicans, but the importance was less personal, less direct.

Moving away from Sanders's no-compromise formula, the RNC then sought a balance between accommodation and attack. In June 1934 it issued a statement on party policy, characterizing the United States as "backward in legislation dealing with social questions," and advocating engagement with Depression problems "in a broad, liberal and progressive spirit, unhampered by dead formulas or too obstinately clinging to the past." But alarm about New Deal methods qualified this sympathy with its goals; the nation faced a choice between democracy and "an all-powerful central government." A political system of democratic institutions, a constitutional system of protected liberties, and an economic system grounded in individual initiative were all in danger, the statement emphasized.[20] The balance between accommodation and attack was therefore an uneasy one and did not satisfy all; not all favored such qualifications of attack. One RNC member instead advocated a strategy to "[expose] the methods of the New Deal as tending to lead to Socialism and Communism," to emphasize "that these New Deal policies found their inspiration in the Socialism of Marx and Engel."[21]

Sanders's successor, Henry P. Fletcher – associated primarily with party conservatives but with a history of Progressive era insurgency – resolved the balance in favor of attack, not accommodation. He privately acknowledged

---

[16] Everett Sanders, radio speech, Nov. 9, 1932, box 4, Sanders Papers; *The League of Republican Women Magazine, District of Columbia*, Dec. 1932, 6, 19, box 205, PPF, Hoover Papers.

[17] Everett Sanders to John Callan O'Laughlin, Oct. 23, 1933, box 60, O'Laughlin Papers.

[18] RNC, "C. W. A. Scandals! What Could You Expect?" box 207, Clapper Papers.

[19] John Callan O'Laughlin to Herbert Hoover, Feb. 27, 1934, box 167, PPICF, Hoover Papers.

[20] "Statement of Party Policy," June 6, 1934, box C251, White Papers.

[21] Transcript of RNC executive session, June 5, 1934, reel 4, *Papers of the Republican Party, part I: Meetings of the Republican National Committee, 1911–1980*, series A: *1911–1960* (Bethesda, Md.: University Publications of America, 1986).

the need for a more constructive accent but worried that a lack of attack would boost Roosevelt's ability to move in the statist direction that he feared.[22] This was a fight important in policy terms, but it was also sure to secure popular endorsement eventually, he believed.[23] At celebrations of the party's eightieth anniversary, Fletcher compared powers delegated to the president by Congress with those of Adolf Hitler and Benito Mussolini, saying that Roosevelt had "in turn delegated the control of the livelihood, business and property of the individual American citizen to a vast maze of theorizing, meddling, directing, spending, lending and borrowing agencies, lettered on the Russian model." He promised expert study of the Depression's problems to develop a GOP alternative to the New Deal – an inadequate acknowledgment that the party's anti-Depression alternative was often as vague as its condemnation of administration methods was harsh.[24]

Perhaps partly because of the difficulty in developing a Republican alternative, it was attack, not accommodation, that largely characterized the party's message during the 1934 campaigns – though there were significant exceptions, notably among party progressives.[25] Roosevelt tackled Republican criticisms directly, asking Americans whether they had suffered any loss of liberty and whether conditions were better than in 1932; downplaying party politics, he reached out to Republican supporters.[26] Maine's September election results were sobering; an anti–New Deal strategy warning of socialism and dictatorship sent the party's support plummeting, defeating Representative Carroll Beedy and nearly defeating Senator Frederick Hale.[27] There was nevertheless little evidence that the strategy of most office-seeking Republicans changed significantly after Maine. While they seemed readier to praise the New Deal's goals, they remained as likely to assail its methods not only as ineffective but as dangerously unconstitutional, too.[28] Principle encouraged such a strategy, as did the insight that this position had longer-term promise.[29] Some sensed that a turn against the New Deal might not be so distant; also in September a *Literary Digest* pilot poll suggesting a marginal anti–New Deal majority attracted attention in party circles.[30] More realistically, Ogden Mills noted a pro-Republican trend only within the business community, whereas the "great mass of the people are whole-heartedly for the Administration."[31]

[22] *LD*, June 16, 1934, 12; Henry P. Fletcher to William Allen White, June 25, 1934, box C215, White Papers; Fletcher to Mark Sullivan, Feb. 28, 1934, box 16, Fletcher Papers.
[23] Henry P. Fletcher to Frederick Hale, Sept. 13, 1934, box 16, Fletcher Papers.
[24] Henry P. Fletcher, speech, July 7, 1934, box 16, Fletcher Papers.
[25] *NYT*, Sept. 30, 1934, 25.
[26] Schlesinger, *Age of Roosevelt*, I: 489–490, 503–505.
[27] *NYT*, Sept. 10, 1934, 12.
[28] *Washington Post* [hereafter *WP*], Sept. 15, 1934, 9; *WP*, Sept. 30, 1934, M3; *NYT*, Oct. 5, 1934, 2.
[29] Henry P. Fletcher to Frederick Hale, Sept. 13, 1934, box 16, Fletcher Papers.
[30] Lewis L. Strauss to Herbert Hoover, Sept. 17, 1934, box 33, Strauss Papers.
[31] Ogden L. Mills to John Sweeney, Oct. 18, 1934, box 11, Mills Papers.

Republican rhetoric reinforced, rather than challenged, this disadvantageous situation. "The party, and its candidates, with few exceptions, were trying to tear down, and were offering nothing in the place of that which they wanted to destroy," Senator George W. Norris wrote shortly after the 1934 midterm elections, reflecting his progressive perspective of discomfort with the GOP at large. "The people have very rightly condemned such a course."[32]

Fletcher analyzed the results very differently from Norris. Echoing Sanders's earlier attacks on the CWA, Fletcher instead blamed fall 1934's setbacks primarily on "the most cynical and shameless use of public money to influence votes," a point he had also made during the campaign itself.[33] Many Republicans agreed, explaining Democratic victories during the New Deal as reliant on the "bought vote" – spending programs' direct beneficiaries.

The argument had at least some substance. Relief recipients, as Depression victims and New Deal beneficiaries, were likely to agree with administration policies; a March 1936 Gallup poll placed their support for Roosevelt's reelection at nearly eight in ten.[34] "What Civil War pensions and protective tariff favors have been to the Republican party for many years, relief is coming to be for the Democratic party," wrote journalist Raymond Clapper in spring 1936, further arguing that welfare spending was a source of potential corruption to which some local politicians had already succumbed and which would be difficult for the administration to resist.[35] Many Republicans believed the administration had failed to resist the temptation, distributing relief funds according to political as well as human needs.[36]

Harry Hopkins sought to avoid manipulation of the Works Progress Administration (WPA) spending he administered, as did Harold Ickes in directing the Public Works Administration. However, relief's local implementation created an opportunity for political favoritism – despite Washington's efforts to eliminate such misconduct. Administration investigations revealed that Pennsylvania Democrats used the WPA to raise money and seek votes.[37] Some Democrats in GOP-controlled localities similarly complained that Republicans engaged in such political manipulation of WPA spending.[38] Even Washington's decisions were not immune from sensitivity to political factors, which seemed more important than relative levels of need in explaining state-by-state differences in the allocation of relief money.[39]

[32] George W. Norris to Ray Tucker, Nov. 10, 1934, box 1, Norris Papers.
[33] Henry P. Fletcher, statement, Nov. 11, 1934, and Fletcher, "Campaign Issues," Oct. 30, 1934, box 207, Clapper Papers.
[34] *Philadelphia Inquirer* clipping, March 15, 1936, box 1328, Pinchot Papers.
[35] *Review of Reviews*, April 1936, 35–36, 69–71.
[36] John Callan O'Laughlin to Herbert Hoover, Nov. 3, 1934, box 167, PPICF, Hoover Papers.
[37] Searle F. Charles, *Minister of Relief: Harry Hopkins and the Depression* (Syracuse, N.Y.: Syracuse University Press, 1963), 166–205.
[38] Paul R. Connery to James A. Farley, Sept. 11, 1936, box 55, Farley Papers; Andrew J. May to Farley, Aug. 8, 1936, box 55, Farley Papers.
[39] Richard Jensen, "The Last Party System: Decay of Consensus, 1932–1980," in Paul Kleppner et al., *The Evolution of American Electoral Systems* (Westport, Conn.: Greenwood, 1981), 205–206.

Nevertheless, conceptions of the bought vote tended to exaggerate its significance. More importantly for the development of the party's response to New Deal liberalism, the bought vote was a dangerous explanation for GOP travails. This analysis encouraged a complacent acceptance of electoral decline and discouraged serious contemplation of the deeper reasons for New Deal liberalism's popularity.[40] Still, despite its dangers, the belief was widespread, especially among the more conservative people in the party.[41] Distrust of mass democracy sometimes informed the thesis. A Philadelphia lawyer and party activist observed that "our situation is that 90% of those on relief and the millions in Federal and State jobs are for Roosevelt, and 90% and more – I would almost say 99 44/100% – of the intelligent people are against Roosevelt."[42]

One of the first to observe the bought vote, Arthur Vandenberg detected a local decline in Michiganders' support for the administration during fall 1933 until Civil Works Administration payments began. He soon concluded that 1934 spending plans were "calculated virtually to Tammanyize the whole United States – the good old theory that those who get money out of a Government will vote for the Party which sponsored the payments."[43] Hoover similarly interpreted a slump in Republican registration figures as revealing an anxiety that government agencies assisted only registered Democrats.[44] Few Republicans defeated during the early New Deal did not blame the bought vote.[45] After his 1934 defeat, Pennsylvania's Senator David A. Reed was among them, claiming that the administration invested $186,000 in his home county shortly before the election, and that Democratic workers in Erie sought campaign contributions from relief recipients.[46] According to John Callan O'Laughlin, publisher of the *Army and Navy Journal* who was spending a short stint at the RNC, "the voting strength of the beneficiaries" was "part of a gigantic political machine, the biggest the country has ever known."[47]

But not all Republicans believed in the bought vote's power. Some viewed the idea with skepticism. This skepticism sometimes involved a different misunderstanding of Democratic strength – that popular support for the New Deal was an illusion. During a 1935 trip across the West, a Cincinnati businessperson concluded, "It's my sincere opinion, based upon recent observations, that the dear people benefited, will take the money and use part of it to purchase gasoline upon which to ride to the nearest voting booth, there to repudiate the present administration and all of its economic insanities."[48] Another Cincinnatian,

[40] Glenn Frank, speech, Feb. 13, 1939, box 116, Strauss Papers.
[41] Weed, *Nemesis of Reform*, 46–47.
[42] Ira Jewell Williams to Frank Altschul, Sept. 27, 1938, folder 31, Political Files, Altschul Papers.
[43] Arthur H. Vandenberg to Herbert Hoover, Jan. 13, 1934, box 242, PPICF, Hoover Papers.
[44] Herbert Hoover to Henry P. Fletcher, Aug. 25, 1934, box 16, Fletcher Papers.
[45] Weed, *Nemesis of Reform*, 47.
[46] *Review of Reviews*, April 1936, 35–36, 69–71.
[47] John Callan O'Laughlin to Herbert Hoover, Jan. 27, 1934, box 167, PPICF, Hoover Papers.
[48] Unsigned to George B. Chandler, Aug. 15, 1935, box 103, Taft Papers.

Charles P. Taft – William Howard Taft's son – thought differently, identifying relief as a potentially pro-Republican issue, because both beneficiaries and those in favor of help for the unemployed did not like the programs' bad management.[49] John Hamilton, a Kansas Republican, thought the bought vote explained poor opinion-poll results – because of "terrorism … practiced by Roosevelt agents" on WPA beneficiaries and union members – but the voting booth's privacy allowed someone to cast a GOP vote even if afraid to voice this support openly.[50] Still another argument dwelled on the high expectations the administration generated by taking such an activist approach to Depression problems. The inescapable disappointment of such expectations reduced the bought vote's danger, according to James Wadsworth.[51]

The 1936 landslide's overwhelming nature meant that the bought vote could not be seen as decisive in securing Republican defeat. "No one can say the election was bought," wrote O'Laughlin. "The relief vote, the colored vote, the labor vote, joined the moderately well to do in rolling up the staggering ten million plurality the President received."[52] But Republicans still widely emphasized the bought vote as a key explanation for defeat.[53] An analysis of the results that Hoover circulated, assumed to be his work, discussed the bought vote ("[t]he enormous government pay rolls") second only to 1936's economic upturn.[54] Also influenced by the bought-vote paradigm, Joseph B. Ely, an anti–New Deal Democrat and Massachusetts governor between 1931 and 1935, argued that the Roosevelt landslide was actually a poor result for his party, because the reelection bid secured – according to his calculation – no more than five or six million votes from people who did not receive government money, as opposed to Landon's seventeen million.[55] Landon himself believed that even members of Republican precinct committees in Kansas and other states supported Roosevelt "because of jobs that were being handed out."[56] "The really amazing thing," he later observed, "is that I did get seventeen million votes, in the face of a rising business index and the political relief organization."[57]

The concept of the bought vote became a normalized aspect of the way many Republicans understood the New Deal's electoral power, if a less central strand of their analysis of the minority problem, and an accepted phenomenon

49 Charles P. Taft, *You and I – and Roosevelt* (New York: Farrar & Rinehart, 1936), 9; see also George H. Sibley to Alf M. Landon, Oct. 27, 1936, box 58, Landon Papers.

50 "Hamilton Sees Landon Landslide Exceeding 'Digest' Poll's Peak," Oct. 31, 1936, box 147, Clapper Papers.

51 James W. Wadsworth to Herbert L. Satterlee, July 24, 1935, box 27, Wadsworth Papers.

52 John Callan O'Laughlin to Herbert Hoover, Nov. 7, 1936, box 168, PPICF, Hoover Papers.

53 Henry O. Evjen, "The Republican Strategy in the Presidential Campaigns of 1936 and 1940" (Ph.D. dissertation, Western Reserve University, 1950), 194.

54 "Forces in the Campaign," n.d. ("Sent me by Hoover 1936"), box 168, PPICF, Hoover Papers.

55 Henry Breckenridge to Alf M. Landon, Nov. 18, 1936, box 83, Landon Papers.

56 Alf M. Landon to E. S. [sic] Bennett, Nov. 29, 1937, box 83, Landon Papers.

57 Alf M. Landon to James L. Wright (draft), March 11, 1940, box 102, Landon Papers.

that usually induced less anxiety and alarm than it did when the idea first emerged.[58] The late 1930s work of Rogers C. Dunn, an analyst of public opinion, reflected and helped sustain this belief.[59] Dunn claimed that he could explain election results by counting four Democratic voters for each relief recipient and WPA beneficiary (though he did not clarify his methodology for doing so). On this basis the "WPA vote" in 1938, for example, remained as high as 31 percent.[60] Republicans expressed concern about the electoral impact of government spending through support for the 1939 Hatch Act, which banned federal employees, including workers on federal relief projects, from involvement in political campaigns.[61] In sum, the idea of the bought vote during the 1930s exercised an anesthetic effect on the Republican Party, discouraging many from acknowledging the appeal of New Deal liberalism as more than a pragmatic, selfish calculation of personal financial benefits. It also encouraged a defeatism that expected no victory during the New Deal.

Fear of political corruption informed the bought-vote thesis. A broader belief about corruption, rooted in the progressive tradition, animated another Republican view of party problems – also catalyzed by the 1934 results. This involved the political influence of the socioeconomically powerful. According to William E. Borah, the party's key problem was that it was "associated too closely with the predatory interests of this country," though he sometimes suspected, too, that "that those now in control of the party and the organization have a suicidal bent."[62] George Norris, another Republican in the progressive bloc, provided a more substantial criticism by faulting the party's failure to advocate a constructive alternative to the New Deal, its reliance instead on negative attack.[63] Regretting the antistatist emphasis, Oregon's Senator Charles McNary said that the party "should quit its abstractions and alarms and get down to the level of human sympathy of human understanding." The party did not speak to the electorate's concerns, he charged: "'Regimentation' is a fine, mouth-filling word, but it fills no empty stomachs" – echoing Borah's pithier remark that "You can't eat the Constitution."[64] This critique of the New Deal – and the dominant Republican response to the New Deal – formed a promising foundation for an alternative vision of the party's future. The progressives' political approach involved a determination that the party should cut away from any business connections to assert its commitment to the people's interests.[65]

---

[58] Steve Neal, *Dark Horse: A Biography of Wendell Willkie* (1984; Lawrence: University Press of Kansas, 1989), 166.

[59] "Notes on the Republican Party," n.d., box 43, Davenport Papers.

[60] Rogers C. Dunn to Carter Glass, Feb. 1, 1939, box 1, Dunn Papers.

[61] Kennedy, *Freedom from Fear*, 349.

[62] William E. Borah to James E. Shepard, Jan. 19, 1934, box 398, Borah Papers; Borah to William Allen White, Sept. 26, 1935, box 428, Borah Papers.

[63] George W. Norris to Ray Tucker, Nov. 10, 1934, box 1, Norris Papers.

[64] *New York Herald Tribune* clipping, Dec. 2, 1934, box 207, Clapper Papers.

[65] E. E. Johnston to Henry P. Fletcher, Dec. 21, 1935, box 400, Borah Papers.

Progressive Republicans had not helped the party much during the 1934 campaign. During his few appearances, Senator James Couzens declined to endorse the entire Republican ticket and failed to issue a statement in support of fellow Michigander Arthur Vandenberg (despite Vandenberg's pleas), but always praised Roosevelt. Dependably to supportive applause, Couzens said that of the four presidents who were in office during his time in Washington Roosevelt was "the only one who has indicated a keen interest in the common people whom Lincoln pleaded for" – thus condemning Roosevelt's recent Republican predecessors as well as lauding the president (and connecting him with the GOP's history).[66] Other progressives not facing reelection, including McNary and Senator Arthur Capper of Kansas, stayed inactive.[67] Such disaffection encouraged FDR to contemplate a realignment in which the Democratic Party would become cohesively liberal and the Republican Party, its conservative counterpart; progressives would thus join with Democrats. The goal led him to downplay his Democratic identity and cultivate progressives.[68]

The 1934 results lent support to the progressive argument; among Republican candidates, the more conservative fared worse than the less conservative.[69] The conservative counterargument, by contrast, strained credulity. Hoover privately remarked after the midterm elections, "It would seem to me that when 44% of the voters have sufficient emotion on the subject to vote against the New Deal, they have given a fairly definite indication that the vast majority occupy a place in the social spectrum somewhere to the 'Right.'"[70] The progressives still in the party did not influence the construction of Republican strategy much, however. They could not harness extensive party support; idiosyncratic shortcomings undermined the effectiveness of William E. Borah, the leading figure among them; and they did not work well together.[71] When in late 1934 Borah attacked conservative domination of the party, Couzens observed that "for 40 years Senator Borah has had nothing but words and I can not understand why anyone should take him seriously."[72]

Opposition to monopoly formed the heart of Borah's concerns, as was the case for many fellow progressives. Skeptical of the electoral power of the emphasis on the Constitution's defense – against the expanding role of the federal government and especially of the executive – that was developing in the party, Borah believed that antimonopoly politics should inform an emphasis instead on ordinary Americans' bread-and-butter concerns. "It stirs my blood," he wrote to Theodore Roosevelt, Jr., "to have men talk about the preservation of constitutional government who are the liveried servants of

[66] James Couzens to Charles L. McNary, Oct. 5 and 29, 1934, box 5, McNary Papers.
[67] Charles L. McNary to James Couzens, Oct. 16, 1934, box 5, McNary Papers.
[68] Arthur M. Schlesinger, Jr., The Age of Roosevelt, vol. II: The Coming of the New Deal (Boston: Houghton Mifflin, 1959), 503–505.
[69] Schlesinger, Age of Roosevelt, II: 507.
[70] Herbert Hoover to John Callan O'Laughlin, Nov. 17, 1934, box 167, PPICF, Hoover Papers.
[71] Feinman, Twilight of Progressivism.
[72] WP, Dec. 5, 1934, 2.

those artificially combined economic forces, monopolies which are now fixing prices and levying tolls on millions of distressed people."[73] TR, Jr., replied for many Republicans in dismissing monopoly's significance as a campaign issue.[74] In fact, concern about the Constitution created the possibility of common ground between Borah and the party's nonprogressive elements. Although Borah doubted the Constitution's power as an electoral issue, he worried that liberty was in peril due to disregard for democratic principles – just as most other Republicans did.

Distrust of the powerful, then, informed Borah's diagnosis of party problems. Confidence in youth shaped his prescription for party revitalization, and he correctly saw young Republicans as a supply of support for his agenda.[75] During intensely contested discussions in late 1934 about the party's way forward, he even threatened the creation of a new youth-based party to challenge the Republican Party's entrenched conservatism.[76] Others outside progressive ranks shared Borah's conviction that the party needed to boost its support among younger Americans; this was a priority for several party organizations.[77] George Olmsted, a Young Republican activist, stressed youth's importance both by observing that four in ten voters were under the age of thirty-seven and by suggesting that the party in many states relied on the work of younger activists, the "shock troops available to do the lowly political chores on a volunteer basis."[78] Borah and Olmsted were right about youth's political importance. In fact, an important element of the New Deal's pro-Democratic earthquake was a pronounced Republican failure among young Americans and new voters; polls soon suggested such a connection between age and party attachment.[79] A New Deal generation would help to account for the Democrats' majority status for decades to come. Republican efforts to suppress this surge proved unsuccessful.

Borah's political idiosyncrasies encouraged some to believe that he alone among leading Republicans could corral an electoral college majority, perhaps invading the South as well as winning the West and maintaining the support of orthodox Republicans.[80] Borah, moreover, enjoyed potential support outside the major parties – from Francis E. Townsend, for example, who claimed that his organization, which was calling for old-age pensions of $200 each month, had a membership of ten million. Townsend urged Borah to create a

[73] William E. Borah to Theodore Roosevelt, Oct. 2, 1935, box 27, Roosevelt Papers.
[74] Theodore Roosevelt to William E. Borah, Oct. 13, 1935, box 27, Roosevelt Papers.
[75] Weed, *Nemesis of Reform*, 48.
[76] Theodore C. Wallen, "Borah Threat Of New Party Made in Reply to Hilles Call," Dec. 1, 1934, box 207, Clapper Papers.
[77] Theodore Roosevelt to Hanford "Jack" MacNider, April 3, 1934, box 29, Roosevelt Papers; Republican Builders, "Political Preparedness: Citizenship in Action," [1934], box 207, Clapper Papers.
[78] George Olmsted to RNC, Sept. 25, 1935, reel 4, *Papers of the Republican Party*, part I, series A.
[79] *Philadelphia Inquirer* clipping, Sept. 27, 1936, box 1328, Pinchot Papers.
[80] *Philadelphia Inquirer* clipping, Dec. 8, 1935, box 1328, Pinchot Papers.

third party, a suggestion that Borah rejected.[81] If Borah's idiosyncrasies helped increase his electoral promise, they also made him an implausible presidential prospect; the GOP at large was not willing to support his candidacy. The progressive vision was, instead, increasingly marginal to Republican analysis of the minority problem.

"Black Monday," May 27, 1935, was a bright day for the Republican Party. The Supreme Court handed down three unanimous decisions – including the National Industrial Recovery Act's invalidation – which challenged the expansive interpretation of government powers at the heart of much of the New Deal. "We have been relegated to the horse-and-buggy definition of interstate commerce," Roosevelt said, a comment Vandenberg described as an unintended echo of Mussolini, Hitler, or Stalin.[82] The decisions limited the New Deal in a way Republicans could not. They also seemed to create a strategic opportunity for the party. A journalist told one leading Republican that "I think there is a ready made issue for the next campaign, the question of fitting the Constitution around the New Deal."[83] "It seems to me," rejoiced Wadsworth, "that we have him on the great fundamental issue – our form of government."[84] Henry Fletcher soon went on the attack, branding the New Deal a failure and charging the administration with efforts to depict the Constitution as a scapegoat for this failure, while accusing it of intending to remove "Constitutional barriers to 'planned economy' ... [b]ecause they stand in the way of a centralized, socialistic state, governed without restraint or limit, by a President and a subservient Congress."[85]

The issue of the Constitution seemed powerful enough to redraw the lines of conflict between the parties, likely to encourage dissenting Democrats and Republicans to switch allegiance in what John Callan O'Laughlin predicted would be "an era of political strife such as the country has not seen since prior to the Civil War."[86] Later that year, the final session at the annual conference of the Women's National Republican Club included "a speaking tableau, the signing of the Constitution, in which appeared in costume, the leading figures of that historical occasion" – emphasizing the issue's centrality to the outlook of many Republicans.[87] Republican optimism was returning.[88] Other developments of 1935 assisted this return. With the arrival of the "second New Deal," which featured the Social Security Act and National Labor Relations Act (or Wagner Act) among its accomplishments, Roosevelt cast aside his

[81] *NYT*, May 28, 1936, 2.
[82] William E. Leuchtenburg, *The Supreme Court Reborn: The Constitutional Revolution in the Age of Roosevelt* (New York: Oxford University Press, 1995), 89–90.
[83] Clarence H. Judd to Henry J. Allen, June 4, 1935, box C5, Allen Papers.
[84] James W. Wadsworth to Herbert L. Satterlee, July 24, 1935, box 27, Wadsworth Papers.
[85] Henry P. Fletcher, "Fundamental Issues in the Making," July 29, 1935, box 18, Fletcher Papers.
[86] John Callan O'Laughlin to Herbert Hoover, June 1, 1935, box 167, PPICF, Hoover Papers.
[87] *The Guidon*, Oct. 1935, box 18, Fletcher Papers.
[88] *LD*, April 6, 1935, 5.

former stress on national unity to tackle the economic crisis. Legislation such as the Public Utility Holding Company Act and the Revenue Act encouraged business funding for the party to increase.[89] Still, it was the arrival of the Constitution's defense as an issue that especially revitalized Republican spirits. Serious concern about constitutional issues also created an imperative for such an emphasis.

Not all Republicans agreed that the Constitution's defense created such an electoral opportunity. On the one hand, Frank Knox declared that the 1936 campaign would involve "the most crucial test of the permanence and stability of American institutions since the campaign of 1860."[90] On the other, although Alf Landon identified a connection between a decline in Roosevelt's popularity and his "horse-and-buggy" remarks (together with his tax policy), Black Monday did not alter his belief that the key anti–New Deal issue was the dollar's stability.[91] Landon thus privately echoed Borah's insight – superficially obvious but not so to many Republicans – that bread-and-butter anxieties were sure to trump niceties of constitutional doctrine.

Landon's stress on the pugnacious element in Roosevelt's response to the Supreme Court decisions was an important recognition that Republicans could not place a threat to the Constitution at the center of its anti–New Deal campaign unless the nature of that threat, as articulated by leading Democrats, was clear. Instead, Roosevelt avoided any repetition of charges similar to the "horse-and-buggy" comments until after the 1936 elections. He remained almost entirely silent on the Supreme Court despite its further invalidation of New Deal legislation, including the Agricultural Adjustment Act. He was determined to minimize the Republicans' apparent strategic opportunity.[92]

Concern about the Constitution was the rallying point at the Grassroots Republican Conference, a gathering of midwestern Republicans in June 1935 at Springfield, Illinois, a location chosen, as Iowa Republican Harrison E. Spangler put it, to "give it the thought of a pilgrimage to the shrine of Lincoln."[93] The party leaders who planned the meeting – the most prominent in a 1935 series of regional meetings – set as its goal the party's revitalization through the creation of a statement of principles and the establishment of a headquarters in the Midwest to aid campaigns, together with consideration of how to finance and implement these initiatives.[94] The meeting's announcement typified many Republicans' melodramatic anxiety about the New Deal, assailing Roosevelt's "vast and dangerous power" and speaking of a party

---

[89] Weed, *Nemesis of Reform*, 73–87.

[90] *Chicago Daily News* clipping, June 20, 1935, box 7, Knox Papers.

[91] Alf M. Landon to John McGrath, June 27, 1935, box 22, Landon Papers; Landon to W. M. Kiplinger, Aug. 16, 1935, box 78, Landon Papers.

[92] William E. Leuchtenburg, "When the People Spoke, What Did They Say?: The Election of 1936 and the Ackerman Thesis," *Yale Law Journal* 108 (1999), 2081–2087.

[93] Harrison E. Spangler to Theodore Roosevelt, April 3, 1935, box 30, Roosevelt Papers.

[94] *NYT*, April 28, 1935, E10; unsigned, "Memorandum of Conference Held at Kansas City, February 17, 1935," box 1, Hamilton Papers.

mission "not only to end the depression but also preserve our very institutions." It spoke of the disappearance of the traditional Democratic Party; in its place, a "new group, without a mandate from the people, seek to impose upon us 'a new and economic and social order' which is alien to American institutions and is as reactionary as the Middle Ages. To them individual initiative should be suppressed and we are to become mere wards and pawns in a bureaucratic state."[95]

At this time of growing party optimism, Springfield's midwestern Republicans believed that victory was possible through a conservative emphasis. In their view, the 1934 midterms revealed the existence of a party base of thirteen and a half million people. This figure was much smaller than Roosevelt's twenty-two million of 1932, but they thought dissatisfactions with the New Deal were wide-ranging enough to cause former Republican voters to return to the fold and disaffected Democratic voters to switch party in numbers great enough to create a Republican majority.[96] The 6,000-strong meeting helped to reinforce the new optimism – "a hypodermic needle in the sluggish Republican arm," according to one journalist.[97]

Underlining the meeting's strong emphasis on the Constitution as the principal anti–New Deal issue, there was some talk there of adopting the "Constitutional Party" or the "Constitution Party" as a new name, which, among other benefits, might attract southern support, which was otherwise wary of the Republicans. Party traditions were too important to nurture such an idea, however.[98] As well as optimistic, the general tenor was conservative. Although some conservatives griped about the resolutions' shortcomings – former Secretary of Agriculture Arthur Hyde said that the position on agriculture "was born of cheap politics" – the meeting provided much for critics to interpret as conservative strength in the party.[99] According to the *Philadelphia Record*, the meeting's stress on sound money demonstrated "that the King of Money has his loyal lackeys in the Middle West as well as in the rest of the country," and that the party had little interest in the human problems of the Depression. But sympathetic press comment suggested that the party was managing not only to recover its fighting spirit, but also to identify the administration's weaknesses.[100] A Virginia newspaper, for example, speculated that a successful emphasis on the Constitution and states' rights "would be the answer to a three-year Republican prayer."[101]

Concern about the Constitution occurred within a broader climate of concern about democracy's future. In late 1935, comparing the New Deal with

[95] Press release, May 6, 1935, box 1, Hamilton Papers.

[96] Raymond Clapper, *Watching the World* (New York: McGraw-Hill, 1944), 142.

[97] *LD*, June 20, 1936, 5.

[98] *NYT*, June 8, 1935, 1–2; *WP*, June 10, 1935, 1, 3.

[99] Nathan William MacChesney to Lawrence Richey, July 5, 1936, box 131, PPICF, Hoover Papers; Arthur M. Hyde to Herbert Hoover, June 13, 1936, box 98, PPICF, Hoover Papers.

[100] *LD*, June 22, 1935, 11–13.

[101] *WP*, June 16, 1935, B7.

"the early phase of Nazism" in Germany, columnist Mark Sullivan wrote that the following year might see "the last presidential election America will have."[102] On the Democratic side, some associated the Republican Party with such danger. John Nance Garner, the vice president, spoke privately in 1935 of his fear that a reactionary Republican would defeat Roosevelt in 1936, and a fascist or communist government was then probable, a revolution possible.[103] Seeking to harness the climate's electoral benefit, in early 1936 the RNC broadcast a radio program, *Liberty at the Cross Roads*, which dramatized the New Deal's impact on daily life, warning of regimentation and excessive taxation through martial music and skits.[104]

Some Republicans believed that the assertion of connections between the New Deal and communism was a potent issue – accusations that infuriated Roosevelt, who saw himself as saving and not sacrificing capitalism.[105] In doing so, they followed the noisier anticommunism of others, including business groups and notably the American Liberty League, an organization of anti–New Deal Democrats – together with American Nazis, members of the American Legion, and William Randolph Hearst's publications.[106]

Many harbored fears about democracy's future. According to a 1936 Gallup poll, 45 percent of respondents believed "that the acts and policies of the Roosevelt administration may lead to dictatorship." More than eight in ten Republican supporters agreed, but nine in ten Democratic supporters did not.[107] Opinion about the Constitution was similarly divided along party lines. Eight in ten Democrats believed that the Supreme Court should be "more liberal in reviewing New Deal measures"; about the same proportion of Republicans believed that it should not.[108] Such concerns thus amounted to a powerful response to the New Deal, but their close relation to larger evaluations of the administration's record equipped them with little capacity for the development of a Republican advantage – even though many in the party suspected otherwise. When leading Republicans warned of the New Deal's dictatorial and anticonstitutional nature, they therefore reinforced the party attachment of existing supporters, rather than winning over new ones.

There were also calmer voices in the Republican Party – voices that advocated an emphasis not on attack but accommodation, voices that won some influence as 1936's electoral test approached. In *You and I – and Roosevelt* Charles P. Taft outlined a strategy for the recapture of some four million who

[102] Arthur M. Schlesinger, Jr., *The Age of Roosevelt*, vol. III: *The Politics of Upheaval* (Boston: Houghton Mifflin, 1960), 500.
[103] Harold L. Ickes diary, March 12, 1935, reel 1, Ickes Papers.
[104] *NYT*, Jan. 15, 1936, 1, 13; *WP*, Jan. 15, 1936, 9.
[105] John Callan O'Laughlin to Herbert Hoover, Oct. 10, 1936, box 168, PPICF, Hoover Papers.
[106] M. J. Heale, *American Anticommunism: Combating the Enemy Within, 1830–1970* (Baltimore: Johns Hopkins University Press, 1990), 105–113.
[107] *Philadelphia Inquirer* clipping, Aug. 2, 1936, box 1328, Pinchot Papers.
[108] Leuchtenburg, "When the People Spoke, What Did They Say?" 2109.

supported Roosevelt in 1932, as a way to secure victory in 1936. Taft saw the electorate as comprising three groups, each of roughly thirteen million voters: Republicans, Democrats, independents. According to this view, then, the Democrats did not straightforwardly dominate the electorate, because both parties had a similarly sized bedrock of support; interparty competition was quite evenly matched. For victory, the crucial group was the last – the independents – and it was Roosevelt's ability to secure ten million of them in 1932 that accounted for Hoover's defeat.

Taft argued that the four million the Republicans needed to win back "must be moderates and they probably fit the ancient definition of mugwumps" (good-government advocates of the late nineteenth century); the platform must therefore appeal to these moderates. He acknowledged that this was unlikely to satisfy some, but for conservatives the alternative in Roosevelt was much less ideologically congenial. "If the bitter enders win out and manufacture a platform from a miscellaneous assortment of political lumber glued together by the spittle of hate," Taft warned, "the Republicans are beaten before they begin."[109] Less compelling than Taft's identification of the party's opportunity was his discussion of policy. Often thin and sometimes admitting an ignorance of key issues, it betrayed his background in municipal politics, failing to map out convincingly the route to the independents' cultivation. The vague quality of his alternative to the New Deal was not only Taft's shortcoming, but a feature of many party moderates.[110]

Significantly, Taft shared key concerns about the New Deal with more conservative Republicans. He did not like the administration's disregard of sound economics in developing its initiatives and of democratic processes in implementing them. But his analysis lacked the shrillness that infected some Republicans. Moreover, he downplayed the potential of the Constitution's protection as a winning issue. Landon, who thought that the book contained "a lot of good stuff," recruited Taft for his presidential campaign after Taft sent him a copy inscribed "[t]o the man who fits the blueprint set forth in this little book."[111] As a campaign aide, Taft still struggled with practical application of his thesis. Consulted by Taft about labor, Cornelia Bryce Pinchot, a Pennsylvania labor reformer, appreciated his "effort to formulate a liberal policy" on the subject, but found this effort "hopelessly out of date – at least ten years behind the times."[112]

A different form of electoral calculation, involving region, helped inform the party's selection of Landon as presidential nominee. The Kansan's western identity was not the least among his qualifications for the nomination.

[109] Taft, *You and I – and Roosevelt*, 8.
[110] George H. Mayer, "The Republican Party, 1932–1952," in Arthur M. Schlesinger, Jr., ed., *History of U.S. Political Parties*, vol. III: *1910–1945: From Square Deal to New Deal* (New York: Chelsea House, 1973), 2270.
[111] Alf M. Landon to Raymond Clapper, April 1, 1936, box 78, Landon Papers; *Newsweek*, July 25, 1936, 12–14.
[112] Cornelia Bryce Pinchot to Raymond Clapper, July 19, 1937, box 8, Clapper Papers.

Contemporary understandings of the electoral college's logic, rooted in the long years of Republican success between the Civil War and the Great Depression's advent, divided the nation into three regions, each with its own dominant concerns: the industrial East, the agricultural West, and the Democrats' solid South. Needing the support of two regions to secure presidential victory, the GOP had successfully balanced the concerns of East and West; it could not normally expect southern support. The nomination of a westerner in 1936, many Republicans believed, would facilitate the reincarnation of the winning coalition. As famed public relations expert and author Bruce Barton noted in fall 1935, "I am sure that everyone in the East recognizes that the only hope of success is to find a candidate in the Middle West."[113] The argument reflected the assumption that the party was strongest in the East, that the problems of the agricultural West and the New Deal's positive impact in rural areas posed a special challenge.[114] In Congress, many New Deal measures had secured support among western Republicans while usually meeting opposition among easterners.[115] However, this sectional analysis overlooked New Deal success in the East, especially among city dwellers and industrial workers. Still, the perception of the party's electoral needs encouraged a shift in its internal balance of power. Traditionally, eastern Republicans dominated the national party and the choice of presidential candidates, while westerners enjoyed congressional influence thanks to common ground with Democrats from the agricultural South.[116] Now, the West seemed to offer something that the East needed.

Landon's appeal within the party involved his policy ideas and electoral record, too. Republicans saw him, among thin ranks of potential candidates, as a proven vote winner – the only GOP governor elected in 1932 and reelected in 1934. His position on issues suggested success in the precarious task of balancing accommodation with attack in responding to the New Deal. Landon stressed fiscal discipline but also saw benefits for Kansas in cooperation with New Deal initiatives, and he tackled the Depression through such steps as a mortgage moratorium for penniless farmers, the regulation of public utilities, the introduction of an income tax, and the abolition of the poll tax.[117] Despite fiscal discipline's importance to Landon, this approach meant that he became known rather derisively as a "me-too" candidate among those conservatives who discounted the electoral importance of any such balance; it was a term that would for several decades dominate intraparty discourse as a conservative charge against a moderate strategy that opponents saw as sure to fail. Sidestepping the feverish embrace of the Constitution's defense, Landon instead identified more mundanely the electoral promise of New Deal waste.[118] The me-too balance involved support for the New Deal's anti-Depression goals

---

[113] Bruce Barton to Richard E. Berlin, Nov. 2, 1935, box 52, Landon Papers.
[114] *Philadelphia Inquirer* clipping, Sept. 26, 1935, box 1329, Pinchot Papers.
[115] Weed, *Nemesis of Reform*, 117–168.
[116] Clapper, *Watching the World*, 136.
[117] Patterson, *New Deal and the States*, 140–141.
[118] Alf M. Landon to John D. M. Hamilton, June 12, 1935, box 78, Landon Papers.

but attacks on its methods as inefficient, rather than dangerously unconstitutional. It also involved the assertion of distance from Republicans associated with the Harding, Coolidge, or Hoover administrations, with the Old Guard, or with big business.[119]

Many Democrats saw the me-too strategy as their biggest threat. In 1936 most were confident about their party's prospects but often agreed that a Charles P. Taft–like attack on the New Deal's inefficiencies was more dangerous than a more profound denunciation of its unconstitutional and dictatorial nature.[120] Connecticut's Senator Francis Maloney thought his party had little to fear from charges connected with the Constitution and dictatorship, but he identified "heavy expenditures, bureaucracy and extravagance" as a vulnerability.[121] FDR himself thought that Landon should begin by repudiating elite media and business support – associated with a deeper-seated rejection of the administration as well as a disconnection from ordinary Americans – and then emphasize his support for New Deal programs while condemning their poor administration and inefficiencies.[122] Similarly recognizing the strategy's danger, national chair James Farley attempted to defuse the threat by challenging its sincerity and reminding voters that this me-too approach was far from characteristic of many Republicans, arguing that their focus on states' rights and business orientation created fundamental differences between the parties. Republican victory would, in sum, "deliver the fate of the people ... to the very selfish interests which wrought the ruin from which Roosevelt has delivered us," he said.[123]

Landon later concluded that his party's congressional record, involving strenuous opposition to the New Deal overall, limited his ability to move away from conservatism.[124] But his New Deal response embraced anxieties that created common ground with more conservative Republicans. What helped to precipitate his nomination candidacy was his belief that the New Deal's direction was perilous, even if pre-1933 conservatism was now obsolete. "I think four more years of the same policies that we have had will wreck our parliamentary government," he wrote in 1935, "and four more years of the old policies will do the same job also."[125] Concern about White House economic policies informed this gloomy outlook in particular.[126] When, toward the end of the campaign, journalist Raymond Clapper insisted to Landon that,

[119] An exception was fellow Kansan Henry J. Allen. *NYT* clipping, Aug. 19, 1936, box 1329, Pinchot Papers.

[120] Frank M. McHale to James A. Farley, Sept. 16, 1936; Wayne Coy to Farley, Oct. 1, 1936; R. B. Louden to Farley, Sept. 10, 1936; and J. Don Kerlin to Farley, Oct. 14, 1936, box 55, Farley Papers.

[121] Francis Maloney to James A. Farley, Aug. 15, 1936, box 55, Farley Papers.

[122] Samuel I. Rosenman, *Working with Roosevelt* (London: Rupert Hart-Davis, 1952), 131.

[123] *The Political Issues Which America Faces in 1936, as presented at the New York Herald Tribune Forum, September 23, 1936* (New York: New York Herald Tribune, 1936), 28–29.

[124] Alf M. Landon to George Rothwell Brown, Nov. 2, 1942, box 117, Landon Papers.

[125] Alf M. Landon to Raymond Clapper, Nov. 2, 1935, box 78, Landon Papers.

[126] Alf M. Landon to Stanley High, Nov. 4, 1935, box 52, Landon Papers.

contrary to Republican alarmism, FDR was no communist, Landon replied that "his policies [were] leading to dictatorship" through the concentration of control in the president's hands over financial matters.[127] Such private concerns informed his public rhetoric in ways that some saw as validating Farley's questioning of me-too politics. Novelist Upton Sinclair, for example, observed that at the convention Landon "sounded to me like a regular conservative making an effort to sound liberal."[128]

Clapper's words of caution to Landon suggest that his campaign was a flawed implementation of the me-too thesis. This was not entirely Landon's responsibility. Many in the party reinforced a strongly anti–New Deal message, rather than Landon's qualified criticisms of administration initiatives. Among them were John Hamilton, the new national chair, and Frank Knox, the vice-presidential candidate, programmed as the campaign's two most prominent speakers after Landon.[129] Hamilton went on a postconvention tour to enthuse party workers, winning some praise for his success in organizational revitalization.[130] He did so with a rather shrill message. Rallying Wisconsin county chairs, for example, Hamilton promised to expose parallels between Roosevelt on the one hand and Hitler, Mussolini, and Stalin on the other. "The trend of the Roosevelt administration," he told them, "is toward dictatorship."[131] The aggressiveness of Hamilton's rhetoric partly stemmed from his desire to promote grassroots activism, but also reflected his approach to electoral politics more generally. Speaking to party activists in 1935, Hamilton blamed Hoover's defeat on "four years of vicious, dirty, low propaganda" that the Democrats inflicted on the Republicans, saying that "being nice" did not bring victory. "Those Republicans who say we should talk on constructive issues don't know their politics. You beat men in office, you don't elect men," he explained. "People vote their dislikes."[132]

Hamilton had less prominence in the fall, but in late October he again dramatized the anti–New Deal message by claiming that the newly formed Social Security Administration intended to issue metal tags to all workers that its scheme covered, creating "two groups of citizens in this nation – those who are numbered and those who are not numbered."[133] Still, Knox stayed on the attack during Hamilton's quiet period, emphasizing the New Deal's threat to the Constitution and, more prosaically, inflation's threat to insurance policies.[134] He spoke, too, of the New Deal as "un-American," seeking

[127] Raymond Clapper diary, Oct. 27, 1936, box 8, Clapper Papers.
[128] Upton Sinclair to William Allen White, July 10, 1936, box C250, White Papers.
[129] Donald R. McCoy, *Landon of Kansas* (Lincoln: University of Nebraska Press, 1966), 325.
[130] David Lawrence, "Hamilton Pep Tour Brings Results," Aug. 19, 1936, box 147, Clapper Papers.
[131] John D. M. Hamilton, speech résumé, July 9, 1936, box 19, Hamilton Papers.
[132] *Time*, Sept. 21, 1936, 14–16.
[133] "New Deal Plans To Tag Toilers, Hamilton Says," [Nov. 1?,] 1936, box 147, Clapper Papers.
[134] Lamb, "Republican Strategy," 44–45.

support for the GOP as "the American way." "The New Deal candidate," Knox said, "has been leading us toward Moscow."[135]

Charles Taft recognized that the Landon campaign failed to communicate its me-too message effectively – "the headline writers and the speakers down the line turned the material [on the Constitution] into regular Liberty League stuff." He also regretted Landon's failure to emphasize better the issue of government efficiency, which *You and I – and Roosevelt* had identified as a promising way to increase the Republican vote.[136] The strategy's poor implementation also gained the attention of Gifford Pinchot, a leading progressive and Pennsylvania governor until 1935. When he spoke at a Landon–Knox event, he noted that the other political speeches there were "full of cursings of the New Deal," but little that offered a positive alternative or discussed Landon's strengths.[137] According to one Republican, his party's candidates deserved defeat because they "did everything they could to help the Democrats to convince the electorate that the Republicans represent the economic royalists and the forces of selfishness."[138] One example was a party meeting in Santa Maria, California, where an Iowa legislator said that the country was "already under a dictatorship" and a local activist spoke of the administration's "tendency to work with Communists."[139]

But Landon himself was not the most effective proponent of me-too politics, especially as the campaign progressed. In its early weeks, he seemed to achieve a careful balance between support for popular goals and opposition to unpopular failings. "Landon, endeavoring to coagulate the various elements opposed to the Administration, is denouncing waste and extravagance, but is for relief," noted John Callan O'Laughlin, rather skeptically. As a result of this search for balance, the Republican presidential candidate was, for example, "endorsing the unionization of Labor and its right to bargain collectively, which constitutes approval of the Roosevelt policy, but objecting to the Administration's method of enforcing the principle," he added.[140] O'Laughlin's critical observations are suggestive of the strategy's shortcomings – its potential lack of clarity and coherence, the fuzziness and weakness of its New Deal alternative.

In time, however, the Landon campaign changed. Landon called on Roosevelt to indicate "whether he intends to change the form of our government – whether labor, agriculture, and business are to be dominated and managed by government," warning also of an "attack on our freedom … from

[135] Schlesinger, *Age of Roosevelt*, III: 606.
[136] Charles P. Taft to E. Ross Bartley, Dec. 21, 1936, box C250, White Papers.
[137] Gifford Pinchot to Roy Roberts, Sept. 21, 1936, box 1329, Pinchot Papers.
[138] Richard B. Scandrett, Jr., to James P. Goodrich, Dec. 1, 1936, box 2, Goodrich Papers.
[139] Santa Barbara, Calif., *Morning Press* clipping, n.d., box 11, series 1, Hickenlooper Papers.
[140] John Callan O'Laughlin to Herbert Hoover, Sept. 26, 1936, box 168, PPICF, Hoover Papers.

within."[141] Taking up the argument that through economic planning Roosevelt was leading America toward dictatorship, he said, "No nation can continue half regimented and half free."[142] Rhetoric along these lines caused Pinchot to warn Landon that it was important "to show the people on relief and their families that you are their friend."[143] But like Hamilton, Landon attacked the Social Security Act; intending to attack its methods and shortcomings while accepting its principle, his criticisms sometimes sounded like an attack on its popular underlying concept of social insurance.[144] "The country thus got the impression that the Republican party was still as thoroughly reactionary as it had been under Coolidge and Hoover," concluded one progressively inclined Republican.[145]

Politicians lacked reliable data on public opinion when developing strategy, which sometimes encouraged them to reach inaccurate conclusions about the strategically promising ways to oppose Roosevelt.[146] For example, during the summer Henry J. Allen privately forecast the possibility of "a landslide resulting from the psychology of the protest vote."[147] The highest-profile source of misinformation was the opinion poll conducted by *Literary Digest* magazine, which used poor techniques in predicting easy victory for Landon.[148] Some contemporaries were aware of its shortcomings, but it nevertheless provided useful evidence for the Landon campaign to insist that its chances were greater than most assumed. In some cases, it offered support to a genuine Republican belief that public sympathy was with the party – despite most indications suggesting otherwise – encouraging the idea of a "silent vote" in their favor.[149] The extent of misperceptions should not be exaggerated, however. Most expected a defeat (even though its overwhelming scale, a widespread repudiation of the party, was often a surprise).[150]

Lincoln's memory was important for this era's Republicans. Lincoln Day was a landmark of the GOP year, a time of speeches about the present-day implications of the party's founding ideals. Such contemplation rarely dwelled much on race, but a legacy of the party's early years was African Americans' loyal support for "the party of Lincoln." During the 1930s African Americans started to move this loyalty toward the party of Roosevelt instead, recognizing New Deal help for the economically deprived – despite the racial

[141] McCoy, *Landon*, 319, 321.
[142] Schlesinger, *Age of Roosevelt*, III: 623.
[143] Gifford Pinchot to Alf M. Landon, Sept. 16, 1936, box 1329, Pinchot Papers.
[144] Schlesinger, *Age of Roosevelt*, III: 613, 635–636.
[145] Bronson Batchelor to Gifford Pinchot, Nov. 17, 1936, box 1328, Pinchot Papers.
[146] John G. Geer, "Critical Realignments and the Public Opinion Poll," *Journal of Politics* 53 (1991), 434–453; Weed, *Nemesis of Reform*.
[147] Henry J. Allen to Richard H. Waldo, July 20, 1936, box C11, Allen Papers.
[148] Peverill Squire, "Why the 1936 *Literary Digest* Poll Failed," *POQ* 52 (1988), 125–133.
[149] *Philadelphia Record* clipping, Oct. 4, 1936, box 1328, Pinchot Papers; *NYT*, Nov. 1, 1936, E4.
[150] Clapper diary, Oct. 27 and Nov. 19, 1936, box 8, Clapper Papers.

discrimination endemic to many programs' local implementation. The difference between the 1932 and 1936 voting decisions of African Americans was dramatic. In Philadelphia's black districts, for example, seven in ten voters voted for Hoover, but only three in ten voted for Landon.[151] For a Chicago activist, the reason was straightforward. The parties' history was now much less important than "the knowledge that their only sustenance came from the Democratic Party," he said in 1939.[152] But as the GOP lost African American support, it did little to prevent the loss. Even though Republicans emphasized individual liberty in response to government's growth, they much less frequently thought about freedom in the context of race.[153]

In 1936 Republican speakers appealed to African Americans by discussing the party's Lincolnian heritage and attacking the New Deal. Landon stressed his commitment to equality and his appointment of African Americans in Kansas. The attacks included the charge that government programs were relegating African Americans to permanent dependence on such largesse.[154] William S. Bennet, the party's Harlem congressional candidate, commended to Landon this emphasis on "the apparent determination of the present administration to keep the colored people on relief and give jobs to white people."[155] Pledging equal treatment in relief and government employment, and promising jobs, Landon spoke of relief as "modern reservation[s] on which the great colored race is to be confined forever as a ward of the federal government." This statement was, according to RNC publicity, "a new 'emancipation proclamation.'"[156] Such rhetoric was not persuasive enough to arrest the Democratic trend among African Americans, however.

The slippage of black support needed attention. It was potentially consequential; there was some talk that in eight states of the urban Northeast and Midwest, together with West Virginia, the vote of African Americans was large enough to hold a balance of power between the parties.[157] A Landon aide blamed the impact of federal spending and black leaders' attacks on Landon, despite his "sympathetic understanding of [African Americans'] problems."[158] Others identified black-and-tan southerners as an obstacle to the development of a successful appeal to African Americans.[159] But there was often a clear-cut contrast between a history of Republican neglect and New

[151] Nancy J. Weiss, *Farewell to the Party of Lincoln: Black Politics in the Age of FDR* (Princeton, N.J.: Princeton University Press, 1983), 205–207.
[152] Elmer W. Henderson, "Political Changes among Negroes in Chicago during the Depression," *Social Forces* 19 (1941), 542.
[153] Clapper, *Watching the World*, 144–145.
[154] Weiss, *Farewell to the Party of Lincoln*, 195–197; unsigned, "Alfred M. Landon has done the following for the colored people of Kansas," n.d., box 79, Landon Papers.
[155] William S. Bennet to Alf M. Landon, Oct. 5, 1936, box 54, Landon Papers.
[156] McCoy, *Landon*, 312.
[157] Schlesinger, *History of U.S. Political Parties*, III: 2912.
[158] Willard Mayberry to Edward Lowber Stokes, Oct. 15, 1936, box 58, Landon Papers.
[159] Transcript, RNC executive session, Dec. 17, 1936, reel 5, *Papers of the Republican Party*, part I, series A; James E. Shepard to Ogden L. Mills, Nov. 6, 1936, box 12, Mills Papers.

Deal concern for the underprivileged, however racially unfair in implementation.[160] In Cincinnati, for example, a party activist explained the Democrats' success among African Americans by pointing to their record of help for and cultivation of the black community. Local Republicans, by contrast, offered nothing.[161] Complacency or misunderstanding compounded the problem; despite such testimony, Robert Taft – Charles P. Taft's brother, who would later become one of the era's most prominent Republicans – subsequently concluded that in Cincinnati "on the whole, we handled the colored people as well as we could have done."[162]

A 1939 report by Howard University political scientist Ralph J. Bunche showed that views such as Robert Taft's were wrong. Commissioned by the RNC to advise the Republican Program Committee – charged with formulating a new statement of party principles – the report emphasized the New Deal's importance to African Americans in explaining their pro-Democratic trend. The report also criticized Republican interest in cultivating the white South, as well as weak and "self-seeking" African American leaders within the party. Instead of "the old slogans," Republicans needed to demonstrate "concrete evidence … of a determination to fully integrate the Negro in American life," Bunche wrote. Such ideas were too bold for the party, however. The committee largely ignored the report, instead returning to attacks on the New Deal in order to seek African American support.[163]

During the Hoover years, many assumed that women, like African Americans, were more dependably loyal to the Republicans. Now there were signs in polls that women were readier to leave the party than men.[164] Noting such trends, aide Agnes E. Meyer urged Landon to give women prominence in his campaign.[165] In a campaign statement to women, Landon spoke to traditional notions of their role by emphasizing the nation's need for "better housekeeping" in place of the Democrats' spending.[166] On the Democratic side, DNC Women's Division director Molly Dewson's organizational innovations, which discouraged any distinctive focus on issues supposedly of special interest to women, overshadowed Republican efforts, and 1932's apparent gender gap in Hoover's favor disappeared. In 1936 there was no difference between the votes of men and women, though Republican-supporting women were perhaps a little more likely to vote than Democratic-supporting women.[167] But in light of the belief that until 1932 women were more Republican than men

---

[160] Weiss, *Farewell to the Party of Lincoln*, 89–95, 216–218.

[161] Henry W. Ferguson to Robert A. Taft, Nov. 5, 1936, box 104, Taft Papers.

[162] Robert A. Taft to John W. Bricker, Dec. 22, 1936, box 104, Taft Papers.

[163] Weiss, *Farewell to the Party of Lincoln*, 268–270 (quotations, 269).

[164] *Philadelphia Inquirer* clipping, March 15, 1936, box 1328, Pinchot Papers.

[165] Agnes E. Meyer to Alf M. Landon, April 17, 1936, box 78, Landon Papers; McCoy, *Landon*, 278.

[166] Carl A. Rott to Emma Finley, n.d., box 55, Landon Papers.

[167] Jo Freeman, *A Room at a Time: How Women Entered Party Politics* (Lanham, Md.: Rowman & Littlefield, 2000), 193–196.

were, this result suggested that, because of the Democrats' revitalization, the party base was perhaps becoming more male as well as more white.

The 1936 elections revealed the party coalitions' new shape – to the GOP's disadvantage. They exposed the redundancy of the sectional thinking that had informed enthusiasm for Landon's candidacy. No longer was the East a stronghold for the Republican Party. The South remained safely solid for the Democrats, but outside the South class now characterized the interparty cleavage more persuasively than region. Poorer Americans supported Roosevelt and the Democrats; wealthier Americans supported Landon and the Republicans.

The Democrats' new strength was especially visible in the cities.[168] In encouraging the emergence of a new, powerful Democratic coalition, New Deal politics caused many to vote for the first time, usually for the Democrats; there was a surge in voter turnout. The Democratic coalition – both urban and working class – was also distinctive in the higher level of support the party achieved among Catholic Americans, Jewish Americans, and African Americans. Not only was the Republican Party less urban and more socioeconomically privileged, it was also more white and more Protestant.[169] Organized labor helped consolidate the New Deal coalition's strength. Founded in late 1935 because of the American Federation of Labor's inadequacies in organizing mass production industries, the Committee for Industrial Organization, later the Congress of Industrial Organizations, or CIO, created the Labor Non-Partisan League in 1936 to assist Roosevelt, contributing a tenth of Democratic campaign funds.[170]

The defeat encouraged doubts about the party's capacity to survive, but Republican optimism soon supplanted despair. Democratic mistakes and setbacks created opportunities for the GOP that its own politicians were unable to manufacture. The first misstep was particularly significant. Roosevelt unveiled a Supreme Court reform plan, to add a new justice for each over the age of seventy who did not retire. He justified the plan as an effort to help the justices manage an expanding workload, but its widely recognized rationale involved Court opposition to key New Deal measures, which endangered the achievement of his larger agenda. The proposal apparently provided evidence of Roosevelt's disregard for the Constitution and his desire to dismantle obstacles to the exercise of his presidential powers, thus confirming Republican fears. While Republicans' attacks on New Deal initiatives as constitutionally dangerous had failed to seize the imagination of people beyond their shrinking party base, the "court-packing" plan was a tangible example of an innovation that was too far-reaching, even for many FDR supporters. Popular opposition

---

[168] Samuel J. Eldersveld, "The Influence of Metropolitan Party Pluralities in Presidential Elections Since 1920: A Study of Twelve Key Cities," *APSR* 43 (1949), 1189–1206.

[169] Sundquist, *Dynamics of the Party System*, 229–239, 219.

[170] Anthony J. Badger, *The New Deal: The Depression Years, 1933–1940* (Basingstoke, U.K.: Macmillan, 1989), 123, 250–251.

to the plan encouraged Landon to suspect that "losing the election, we have apparently won our fight to save America."[171] Against the proposal, the party embraced a strategy of silence, allowing disappointed Democrats to lead the successful campaign of opposition.[172]

The episode renewed Republican confidence and boosted support for the party. At the elite level it helped cement the progressives' decline as a dissident wing. By 1937 three deaths had reduced the Senate bloc to nine, including three who voted for Republican organization but adopted a non-Republican label. Of the nine, only Robert La Follette, Jr., of Wisconsin supported the plan; concern about executive power informed the progressives' critique, though remaining individualistic in its detail. The administration's plan for government reorganization then reinforced these concerns. As its agenda assumed an increasingly urban emphasis, only Norris and La Follette remained with the New Deal.[173]

Similar factors – opposition to court reform and government reorganization, dislike for the emergence of an urban liberal agenda, and a desire to signal independence from the New Deal – fostered conservative Democratic criticisms of the administration, too. Among southerners, hostility to the New Deal's increasingly city-oriented outlook reflected the belief that it paid too much attention to African Americans, as well as too little to their sectional and rural concerns. The result was the emergence in Congress of an informal conservative coalition between anti–New Deal Democrats and Republicans. Acting together, in 1938 they enjoyed some success in challenging the New Deal's liberalizing trajectory on government reorganization and taxation, though not on relief spending and fair labor standards.[174]

As the speculation at the Springfield meeting about a "Constitution Party" revealed, coalition talk was not new in 1937. Back in 1934, Theodore Roosevelt, Jr., had hoped that conservative southerners would join Republicans "under the same tent" while appreciating the practical obstacles to such a move.[175] The party's electoral setbacks later that year encouraged the argument that only through a formal association with conservatives could Republicans secure a stable political future, generating by early 1935 what one journalist described as "vague and undercover" discussions about such association.[176] Anti–New Deal Democrats who joined the Liberty League, supportive of the Republican Party, were among the most avid exponents of the argument; Jouett Shouse, one of its leaders, even suggested that their preferred route to coalition involved the Republicans' selection of a conservative Democrat as

---

[171] Alf M. Landon to J. A. Meckstroth, June 22, 1937, box 86, Landon Papers.
[172] James T. Patterson, *Congressional Conservatism and the New Deal: The Growth of the Conservative Coalition in Congress, 1933–1939* (Lexington: University of Kentucky Press, 1967), 85–124.
[173] Feinman, *Twilight of Progressivism*, 117–156.
[174] Patterson, *Congressional Conservatism*, 125–249.
[175] Theodore Roosevelt to Gary I. Crockett, July 27, 1934, box 27, Roosevelt Papers.
[176] *North American Review*, March 1935, 250–256; WP, Feb. 2, 1935, 2.

their 1936 presidential candidate, though a Democrat for the vice presidency would be an acceptable compromise.[177] In December 1935 the RNC adopted a resolution inviting the support of Jeffersonian Democrats in opposition to New Deal disregard for states' rights and individual liberty.[178] During the 1936 campaign, Landon said that as president he would include Democrats in his cabinet, though he devoted little emphasis to the commitment; Hamilton urged speakers to downplay partisanship to facilitate conservative Democrats' support.[179] That August some anti-FDR Democrats met in Detroit, but the meeting disappointed Republicans who hoped that it might signal the start of high-profile, attention-grabbing conservative defections. The group did not include prominent Democrats, and the participants' focus was criticism of their own party rather than endorsement of Republican candidates.[180] All this amounted to little before Roosevelt's plan for court reform.

In 1938 Franklin Roosevelt tried, unsuccessfully, to "purge" a number of conservative congressional Democrats. His effort to defeat five Senate opponents and John J. O'Connor, chair of the House Rules Committee, encouraged some to contemplate Republican backing for conservative Democrats at the polls – an electoral alliance, supplementing the congressional coalition. Mark Sullivan, for example, advised Republican voters to support conservative Democrats in primaries.[181] There are signs that such intervention by Republican voters might have taken place in Idaho where Senator James O. Pope, a liberal, lost to the more conservative Representative D. Worth Clark.[182] But this was an exception. On the whole, Republicans defended their partisanship – as did Democrats, however conservative. Although he privately acknowledged the possibility of a coalition ticket for the 1940 presidency, John Hamilton steadfastly opposed any such support in 1938. He argued that even conservative Democrats were indeed Democrats who assisted their party in many ways and were never ready to help Republicans.[183] Only in the South, where congressional Republican prospects were hopeless, did Hamilton signal support for conservative Democrats; in this case, these congressional Democrats did not embrace and even sometimes rejected such support.[184]

Closer Republican cooperation with southern Democrats led to questions about the party's relationship with African Americans, already in trouble due to New Deal liberalism's help for the needy. The NAACP's Walter White

177 James W. Wadsworth to Charles D. Hilles, May 15, 1935, box 28, Wadsworth Papers.
178 Transcript, RNC meeting, Dec. 16, 1935, reel 4, *Papers of the Republican Party*, part I, series A.
179 John Callan O'Laughlin to Herbert Hoover, July 25, 1936, box 167, PPICF, Hoover Papers; George H. Sibley to Alf M. Landon, Oct. 27, 1936, box 58, Landon Papers; Fred S. Purnell to speakers, Sept. 30, 1936, box 1329, Pinchot Papers.
180 *NYT*, Aug. 10, 1936, 18; John Callan O'Laughlin to Herbert Hoover, July 31 and Aug. 15, 1936, box 167, PPICF, Hoover Papers.
181 *LD*, May 15, 1937, 12–13.
182 Patterson, *Congressional Conservatism*, 269–270.
183 Clapper diary, June 8, 1938, box 8, Clapper Papers.
184 Patterson, *Congressional Conservatism*, 282–283.

heard talk of an emerging consensus among Republicans that they now had no hope of black support and that the party was determined to seek southern support, considering the party's connection with African Americans as the key obstacle to breaking the solid South.[185] Hamilton denied as "absolutely nonsense" that this was the implication of congressional cooperation between conservative Democrats and Republicans.[186] Other Republicans' thinking gave good reason for White's fears, however. For example, in private Landon coolly acknowledged that any new party "would have to be a Lily-white party to get anywhere in the South."[187] Ralph Bunche was right, then, to conclude that Republican interest in the white South – however tentative and insubstantial – was an obstacle to rebuilding party support among African Americans.

Events of 1937 and 1938 would improve party fortunes, but the aftermath of the 1936 catastrophe saw Republicans searching for ideas to craft a successful comeback. Some of these efforts called for improvements in party organization to tackle perceived campaign shortcomings. Others looked for new ways to articulate the party's antigovernment response to New Deal liberalism. In spring 1937 Ogden Mills delivered a lecture series, subsequently published as *The Seventeen Million*, on the party's future.[188] "The present, we suppose, is too sad to talk about," one journalist wrote.[189] Mills insisted that the defense of the individual against the New Deal's collectivistic drift promised to restore the party to dominance.[190] In support of the claim, he noted that just a 12 percent swing against FDR was enough to defeat him, "and there are millions who voted for Mr. Roosevelt because of recovery and their faith in him who have no intention to become the subject of a collectivist state."[191] The prediction that conflict between individualism and collectivism was likely to determine the alignment between the parties bred hope among Republicans; if their party secured the support of all conservatives, victory looked probable.[192]

Such a perspective encouraged a clear statement of the party's antistatism. Hoover was the most prominent among a number of Republicans advocating a midterm convention to state party principles. Among other Hoover opponents, Landon attacked the idea, fearing an effort to reestablish party control.[193] Differences about policy and strategy were genuine. So were personal animosities. Endemic to politics, ambition had the potential to spark an actively contested, productive debate about the party's future; in the

[185] Walter White to John D. M. Hamilton, Nov. 11, 1938, box L27, series II, NAACP Records.
[186] John D. M. Hamilton to Walter White, Dec. 5, 1938, box L27, series II, NAACP Records.
[187] Alf M. Landon to R. C. Garland, Feb. 6, 1937, box 84, Landon Papers.
[188] Ogden L. Mills, *The Seventeen Million* (New York: Macmillan, 1937).
[189] Jamaica, N.Y., *Long Island Press* clipping, June 8, 1937, box 209, Mills Papers.
[190] *NYT* clipping, April 22, 1937, box 209, Mills Papers.
[191] Fort Wayne, Ind., *News-Sentinel* clipping, April 23, 1937, box 209, Mills Papers.
[192] Beverly, Mass., *Times* clipping, June 5, 1937, box 209, Mills Papers.
[193] Alf M. Landon to Richard Lloyd Jones, Jan. 30, 1937, box 85, Landon Papers.

1936 defeat's aftermath, ambition instead seemed to impede it. Despite the anti-Roosevelt tide of 1937, Frank Altschul, a New York Republican, reported difficulties in raising money for the party, which he attributed to confusion about the Republican agenda and to personal conflicts. He complained that "the clash of personalities over perfectly trivial issues," instead of concern about substance, dominated public perceptions of the party.[194] Landon agreed that personal ambitions posed an obstacle to party growth, singling out Hoover.[195] For Hoover supporters, by contrast, Landon was the chief culprit. "Everything I have learned," O'Laughlin told Hoover, "indicates that Landon is more interested in his effort to pull you down than he is to build up the Republican Party."[196]

Out of disagreement came compromise. The RNC established a Program Committee under Glenn Frank, former president of the University of Wisconsin.[197] Considered a perceptive critic of the New Deal, Frank had soon replaced an early acceptance of the need for strong leadership to tackle Depression problems with concern about its dictatorial nature, developing the argument that the administration's economic management stifled production.[198] The committee was an elaborate, ambitious operation, prompting one participant to describe its inaugural session as "the most remarkable political meeting since the Constitutional Convention of 1787." Seeking to develop what Frank called "an utterly honest and objective audit of the New Deal" and apply Republican principles to contemporary problems, it involved several hundred members (disproportionately representative of business), who met as regional subcommittees on a variety of topics, before sharing their findings to generate an overall report.[199] The committee's productivity did not match its energy, however. The report did not appear until early 1940, and its influence on the 1940 party platform was minimal.[200]

The Frank committee's proceedings did not change the party's direction, but these discussions did reflect the renewed spirit of Republican optimism. The "Roosevelt recession's" arrival was a crucial event. In 1937 unemployment neared 20 percent as production in key industries suffered a sharp decline, a development that encouraged Roosevelt to edge toward a Keynesian acceptance of government spending to compensate for economic downturns. It also encouraged many New Dealers to perceive the possibility that the nation had

[194] Frank Altschul to Alf M. Landon, Oct. 16, 1937, box 83, Landon Papers.
[195] Alf M. Landon to Raymond Clapper, Sept. 9, 1938, box 89, Landon Papers; Landon to Don Berry, Oct. 14, 1937, box 83, Landon Papers.
[196] John Callan O'Laughlin to Herbert Hoover, Dec. 13, 1937, box 168, PPICF, Hoover Papers.
[197] Cotter and Hennessy, *Politics without Power*, 193–194.
[198] Lawrence H. Larsen, *The President Wore Spats: A Biography of Glenn Frank* (Madison: State Historical Society of Wisconsin, 1965), 153–159.
[199] Ronald Bridges, "The Republican Program Committee," *POQ* 3 (1939), 299–306 (quotation, 301); Lamb, "Republican Strategy," 88–89.
[200] Lamb, "Republican Strategy," 96; William J. Donovan, memo, Oct. 24, 1946, box 28, series 2, Dewey Papers.

reached an economic maturity, involving permanently high levels of unemployment and demanding the permanently extensive management of the economy by the government. The recession's causes included excessive spending cuts that the administration initiated in response to 1936's improved conditions, the Federal Reserve Board's high interest rates, and the collection of Social Security taxes (without the payment yet of old-age benefits).[201] For Republicans, the picture was more straightforward. The New Deal had at last openly proved itself a failure.

While the committee's discussions about the party's future course included much disagreement, belief in the New Deal's failure provided a degree of unity and fresh hope. Even before the Frank committee first met, a New Yorker caught the mood in writing to fellow members of a contrast between the long decades of Republican prosperity and the failed New Deal. "The situation arising from [Roosevelt's] lack of definite policies, efforts to create class consciousness, class hatreds, executive inefficiency, vacillation of purpose, lack of sound planning, waste, denunciation of bankers, business and industry, has become a menacing one of paralysis of business and industry through lack of confidence and fear," he wrote.[202] During the 1938 campaign, Frank echoed such sentiments both in assaulting the New Deal as a failure and in branding the administration's pluralistic approach to politics as the agent of class conflict. There was "an ill-tempered warfare of group against group from which nothing but political confusion, economic paralysis, and national decline can possibly come," he said.[203] Particularly influential among the Frank committee's papers was an attack on the thesis of the "vanquished frontier" as a "hoax" and on the "economics of scarcity" that such beliefs encouraged. Science and industry offered a new frontier for growth that business could exploit, Republicans insisted.[204] The perception of Democratic failure thus fostered belief in a Republican opportunity.

In search of lessons for the Republican Party, John Hamilton visited the headquarters of the United Kingdom's Conservative Party in 1937, believing that the British Conservatives had successfully tackled problems similar to his own party's.[205] The lessons Hamilton looked for involved the contribution of good organization to electoral success. The permanence of key Conservative institutions, sustained by paid constituency agents across the country as well as by party officials in London, ensured that campaigns did not begin with the time-consuming diversion of essential organizational arrangements, which had absorbed Hamilton the previous summer. At the grass roots was a broad base of volunteers working for the cause; Hamilton noted the Conservatives'

---

[201] Badger, *New Deal*, 112–115.
[202] William S. Bennet to committee members, Feb. 1, 1938, box 116, Strauss Papers.
[203] Glenn Frank, speech excerpts, Sept. 14, [1938], box 366, Burton Papers.
[204] Lamb, "Republican Strategy," 95.
[205] John D. M. Hamilton to Frank Altschul, Aug. 20, 1937, folder 37, Political Files, Altschul Papers.

recognition that "often the dry and uninteresting field of politics" did not maintain the volunteers' necessary interest, leading to a stress on social as well as political activities.[206]

In thinking about the GOP within the context of this transatlantic comparison, Hamilton was not alone.[207] The common language facilitated the comparison, but more significantly, British Commonwealth nations were rare examples of countries with a two-party system that resembled that of the United States at least in some respects.[208] Most importantly, perhaps, Conservative success in winning power during the United Kingdom's depression years encouraged envious enquiry. Even though it was the party of privilege, the Conservative Party nevertheless managed to articulate concern with the depression's human impact.[209] It was this aspect of the Conservatives' record, rather than their organizational structures, that struck some as instructive. Thomas E. Dewey, the party's New York gubernatorial candidate, said that the Conservatives were "years ahead of us in what they are doing"; Raymond Clapper noted that "the British conservatives have shown infinitely more intelligence than our conservatives."[210] According to a British friend, Bronson Cutting's progressivism – which caused great difficulty for him in the Republican Party – placed him within the Conservative Party's mainstream and "would cause not a moment's alarm in England, save perhaps among a few 'die-hards' in the House of Lords."[211] Indeed, the policy contrast between the two parties was so sharp that Hamilton found his welcome in London lacked warmth, and all the officials he met but one declared support for Roosevelt.[212]

Still, it was the question of organization that concerned Hamilton as national chair. Recognizing the party's inferiority in this regard, he told his counterpart James Farley that the Democratic Party, by contrast, was "a masterpiece of effective organization."[213] Other Republicans agreed that electoral problems were partly related to a lack of organizational capacity. Landon thought the party's "disorganized condition ... in so many states" contributed to his campaign's ills, noting that his postelection mail often made a similar point.[214]

[206] John Hamilton, "Memorandum on English Conservative Party Organization," June 1937, box 22, Hamilton Papers.

[207] See, for example, Ogden L. Mills to George E. Sokolsky, June 15, 1934, box 11, Mills Papers; Alf M. Landon to E. G. Bennett, Nov. 29, 1937, box 83, Landon Papers; and Joseph Newton Pew, Jr., to Frank Altschul, Sept. 28, 1938, folder 31, Political Files, Altschul Papers.

[208] Taft, You and I – and Roosevelt, 10–11.

[209] Robert Blake, The Conservative Party from Peel to Major (London: Heinemann, 1997), 235–246.

[210] Clapper diary, Oct. 12, 1938, box 8, Clapper Papers; Raymond Clapper to Roy W. Howard, Nov. 22, 1937, box 133, Howard Papers.

[211] Gordon Gardiner, remarks, May 6, 1936, box 92, Cutting Papers.

[212] Clapper diary, Jan. 10, 1938, box 8, Clapper Papers.

[213] John D. M. Hamilton to James A. Farley, Nov. 10, 1936, box 1, Hamilton Papers.

[214] Kansas City Times clipping, Nov. 13, 1936, box 1, Hamilton Papers; Alf M. Landon to Orie L. Phillips, Dec. 26, 1936, box 53, Landon Papers.

Hamilton's investigation of the Conservative Party helped equip him with ideas to tackle the problem, and he made good progress in improving the party's operations between campaigns. He established a program of sustaining memberships, which provided the party with continuing funds. His recognition that volunteers, especially among women, were important to political success encouraged him to offer support to the National Federation of Republican Women's launch in 1938. Organizational efforts also included the creation of an RNC office dealing with African American matters and the development of the national committee's research division, previously active only during campaigns.[215] Despite such successes, Hamilton believed that his project also experienced failure. He saw the nature of his departure from the RNC as exemplifying this failure. Hamilton decided to retire from full-time politics in 1940 when Wendell L. Willkie, the newly nominated presidential candidate, replaced him as national chair. Willkie offered him the RNC executive directorship, but Hamilton declined. The problem was not the reassignment itself. Instead, in Hamilton's eyes, this demotion provided evidence "that the party would not accept the English theory of permanency of personnel in organizational activities."[216]

Other organizational efforts to revitalize the party took place outside its existing institutions. These efforts had first emerged at the start of the Roosevelt administration. Not long after Hoover left office, Ogden Mills helped to establish Republican Federal Associates, intended to be a group of former administration officials loyal to the outgoing president (extending to include postmasters), all working for a 1934 comeback. In what would prove to be a common response to outside organizations of this kind, Senator David Reed spurned membership, saying he did not wish "to join any clique or faction within the party.[217] Mills insisted that the goal was not to promote a particular individual or faction, but instead to tackle the problem of the party's lack of organizational capacity between elections. But there was an ideological dimension to his goal, too, because he wished to discourage the party's "disintegration into groups and advocating many different forms of political philosophy."[218] The connection with Hoover did not help, and the initiative achieved little progress; during its first eight months of operation the organization raised less than $5,000, not nearly enough to support its work.[219]

Mills soon tried again. He launched Republican Builders, a broader-based New York organization.[220] He hoped that its activities would act as a pilot for a community-based organization across the nation, "prepared

[215] Lamb, "Republican Strategy," 62–79.
[216] Neal, *Dark Horse*, 184.
[217] *NYT* clipping, April 24, 1933, box 207, Clapper Papers.
[218] Ogden L. Mills to Lloyd Griscom, June 6, 1933, box 11, Mills Papers.
[219] Gary Dean Best, *Herbert Hoover: The Postpresidential Years, 1933–1964* (Stanford, Calif.: Hoover Institution Press, 1983), I: 10–12, 17; Arch Coleman to Herbert Hoover, Nov. 11, 1933, box 38, PPICF, Hoover Papers.
[220] Julian S. Mason to governing members, March 9, 1934, box 80-A, Mills Papers.

to fight in defense of American institutions by carrying on a campaign of education, and by serving as a rallying point for sound public opinion." Its success outside New York was even more limited than within that state, however.[221] An exception was a Cincinnati fundraising drive by Robert Taft, which indicated "that there is underneath the surface a latent and powerful opposition to much that is going on in Washington; that this opposition comes from the rank and file and awaits only organized leaders," according to David Hinshaw, an official of Republican Builders.[222] Builders met various problems in mobilizing this support. One involved the recruitment of volunteer energies on which it depended and which represented one of its rationales. May Davie, a Builders leader, reported that she could recruit such support among women, "because of course women are much less busy and almost always available for Organization work," but men were less responsive. "I am completely exhausted with trying to make busy and tired men (who by the time I see them usually have had the extra cocktail that entirely dulls their brains) work for the Builders," she wrote.[223] Like the Republican Federal Associates, Republican Builders faded away, suffering financial difficulties; by the end of summer 1934 its bank account held only $50.[224] The disappointing experience of such clubs sharply contrasted with their aspirations, which often encompassed democracy's improvement as well as party revitalization.[225]

Another outside organization, operating at the end of the 1930s, was less high-minded, promoting an individual politician's candidacy. Although Herbert Hoover labeled the Republican Circles as "the only satisfactory form of Republican organization to fight the New Deal in 1940 that I have seen," the groups were actually a factional effort to mobilize Hoover loyalty. The groups successfully spread across the West in 1939 via local elites; each circle had a small membership of community leaders, who each created new circles. By year's end it reportedly had a membership of 85,000. These efforts did not secure much convention support for Hoover in 1940, however. At his peak in the multiballot convention voting, he secured just thirty-two votes, with a maximum of thirteen from California and, elsewhere in the West, a handful from Colorado and Utah.[226] Although the Republican Circles claimed a goal of party revitalization similar to Republican Builders, the organization was dedicated to a candidate's rather than the party's cause. But neither group had much success in developing persuasive answers to the minority problem.

[221] Ogden L. Mills to Walter Frew, May 10, 1934, and Lloyd E. Meyer to Helen V. Logan, Nov. 23, 1934, box 80-A, Mills Papers.

[222] David Hinshaw to William Allen White, March 7, 1934, box C215, White Papers.

[223] May Davie to Ogden L. Mills, March 15, 1934, box 80-A, Mills Papers.

[224] Helen V. Logan to Ogden L. Mills, Aug. 31, 1934, and Mills to May Davie, Oct. 2, 1934, box 80-A, Mills Papers.

[225] The Republican Woman, March 1932, 10, box 16, Strother Papers.

[226] Best, Herbert Hoover, I: 121, 123, 146, 164 (quotation, 123); Clapper diary, Nov. 8, 1938, box 8, Clapper Papers.

The party at last made a comeback in 1938. An RNC analysis referred to the "truly spectacular nature of Republican gains," with 50.7 percent of the vote in House races outside the South. The report claimed that the party had developed a base of twenty-one states, providing 221 safe electoral votes for a Republican presidential candidate against 259 votes for a Democrat.[227] Victory did not provide straightforward or uncontested answers to the minority problem, however. It was the result not so much of Republican achievement in selling party proposals as dissatisfaction with the Democratic record. Disappointing economic developments, including the 1937 "Roosevelt recession," challenged the electorate's confidence in the administration. Opposition to Roosevelt's perceived excesses – the court-packing plan and the attempted purge of conservatives – also created the context for Republican attacks on the Democrats. But Republican candidates responded differently to the administration's decline, and salient issues varied from race to race.[228] Republicans often merely stressed Democratic failures without their own solutions of any specificity.[229] The Republican comeback was mostly an anti-incumbent tide that different politicians sought to interpret as a pro-Republican surge, but their analyses took different paths.

Two Republicans immediately identified as potential candidates for the presidency personified the uncertain meaning of the 1938 results. One was New York County district attorney Thomas E. Dewey. Dewey narrowly lost his gubernatorial race against Herbert Lehman, the popular Democratic incumbent; this achievement was nevertheless impressive enough to elevate him to the party's leading ranks, so that, according to Gallup, a third of Republicans preferred Dewey, in a crowded field, as the presidential candidate. Dewey's campaign focused mostly on state-level issues, but he called himself a "New Deal Republican," while offering some criticisms of the administration's economic record and its centralizing tendencies.[230] He commented that 1938's Republican gains did not signify a desire for any pause in progress toward Roosevelt's social goals, but instead designated a desire for continued progress of a sound nature.[231] Dewey's expressions of sympathy with the New Deal sometimes startled other Republicans. He told Frank Altschul of his belief "that nine-tenths of the New Deal legislation was sound and proper"; Altschul wondered whether Dewey was "so far on the left wing of the Republican Party as to require constant watching."[232] When John Hamilton told Dewey

[227] "Republican Gains in the 1938 Elections," Dec. 1938, reel 1, *Papers of the Republican Party*, part II: *Reports and Memoranda of the Research Division of the Headquarters of the Republican National Committee, 1938–1980* (Bethesda, Md.: University Publications of America, 1986).

[228] Milton Plesur, "The Republican Congressional Comeback of 1938," *Review of Politics* 24 (1962), 525–562.

[229] Lamb, "Republican Strategy."

[230] Smith, *Thomas E. Dewey*, 265–274.

[231] Clapper diary, Dec. 17, 1938, box 8, Clapper Papers.

[232] Frank Altschul, "Tom Dewey," Sept. 14, no year, folder 22, Political Files, Altschul Papers.

of his hope that Roosevelt would seek a third term in order to create state socialism as a clear-cut issue between the parties, Dewey disagreed, much preferring a more conservative Democrat. According to Hamilton, he said that with Roosevelt as candidate "it would be impossible to out-promise him and that was what people had to do today in order to win office."[233] Dewey identified conservative Republicans' influence in the party as the key obstacle to its success.[234]

The view of Robert A. Taft, the new senator from Ohio, was different. Taft interpreted his victory as a repudiation of the New Deal. He qualified this interpretation, however, by distinguishing between his sympathy for "the earlier humanitarian measures," such as assistance for the elderly and unemployed, and his opposition to "the basic principles, which the New Deal has adopted during the last two years; the principles of planned economy and government regulation of commerce, agriculture and industry, and the arbitrary power demanded to carry out such a program."[235] The antiadministration tide of 1938 meant that both Dewey and Taft – among others – enjoyed success at the polls, though with different messages. The difference reflected the emergence of a new regional cleavage within the party. No longer was the key cleavage between western progressives and eastern conservatives. Instead, a new breed of eastern Republicans articulated greater sympathy with the New Deal; a new breed from the Midwest and West offered a more conservative emphasis.[236]

Differences between the Republican campaigns in New York and Ohio meant that Dewey and Taft were both able to claim electoral support for their interpretation of the party's necessary direction. These differences assumed importance within the party, but the ideological gap was not necessarily so significant. One observer characterized the intraparty debate as between "no, but" Republicans and "yes, but" Republicans, the former starting with a denunciation of the New Deal before outlining areas of agreement and the latter beginning with praise of liberalism's goals before condemning its shortcomings. Political rhetoric and policy emphasis, rather than ideology, were more significant in separating them.[237] The common ground of anti–New Deal, antistatist sentiment caused the New Republic columnist T.R.B. to interpret Dewey's nonconservative reputation as misleading. Dewey was "as comfortably Republican as the elephant's trunk," he observed in spring 1940. "To date, he hasn't used the word 'normalcy,' but Harding would understand and approve everything he has said."[238] Certainly on Capitol Hill the party's unity in conservatism was noteworthy. After the 1938 elections in Congress,

[233] John D. M. Hamilton diary, June 9, 1939, box 2, Hamilton Papers.
[234] Altschul, "Tom Dewey"; Clapper diary, Oct. 12, 1938, box 8, Clapper Papers.
[235] Robert A. Taft, statement, Jan. 3, 1939, in Clarence E. Wunderlin, Jr., ed., The Papers of Robert A. Taft, vol. II: 1939–1944 (Kent, Ohio: Kent State University Press, 2001), 4.
[236] Weed, Nemesis of Reform.
[237] American Mercury, March 1940, 263–272.
[238] New Republic, April 22, 1940, 534.

Republicans acted with a remarkable degree of agreement in opposing any extension of the New Deal, especially in the House.[239] Outside Congress there was some more variety; the party's governors were likelier to accept elements of the New Deal in carrying out their executive duties.[240] But soon the response to World War II's approach, rather than to New Deal liberalism, would assume special importance in national politics.

---

[239] Patterson, *Congressional Conservatism*, 288–324; *New Republic*, Oct. 7, 1940, 492–495.
[240] Patterson, *New Deal and the States*, 139–143.

3

"The Simple Barefoot Wall Street Lawyer": 1939–1945

In the early fall of 1939, not long after the outbreak of World War II in Europe, Herbert Hoover gave Thomas E. Dewey some advice about how to pursue his 1940 presidential ambition. The advice addressed the difficulty of establishing a position on foreign policy, as war erupted in Europe, at a time when there was much division within the party – and among the electorate – about how to respond, and when the geopolitical future held so much uncertainty. Hoover told Dewey to avoid discussion of national issues as much as possible, to concentrate instead on state and city matters. This was because events in foreign policy were moving so rapidly that any statements at that point potentially endangered his intended quest for the nomination and then, if successful, for the presidency. Such statements might create policy commitments that later became unwise or unpopular in light of subsequent developments, Hoover explained. Conveniently for Dewey, his position as New York County district attorney provided him with an excuse to evade questions of foreign policy and stress another issue instead, connected with his current duties, one of broad appeal. "Everybody's against crime and all applaud the man who is doing such a great job as [Dewey] is in catching up with evildoers," according to Hoover.[1] The strategic advice was good. Foreign policy was a difficult subject and a dangerous issue, especially for Republicans when anti-interventionism remained widespread within the party yet the tide of neutrality, strong during the 1930s, was starting to retreat.

Hoover's advice was not good enough, however, to save Dewey. Unable to escape entirely the discussion of foreign policy with the world at war, Dewey revealed his inexperience. Moreover, he voiced both internationalist and anti-interventionist sympathies.[2] After France's fall to Nazi Germany in May 1940 – a development that confronted the United States with the prospect of

[1] [Burton Heath,] "Report of conversation with H. on Thursday, Oct. 5, 1939," box 20, series 10, Dewey Papers; Neal, *Dark Horse*, 60.
[2] Robert A. Divine, *Foreign Policy and U.S. Presidential Elections, 1940–1948* (New York: New Viewpoints, 1974), 13–15.

an entirely hostile, totalitarian Europe, in addition to similarly threatening Japanese domination of east Asia – Dewey's candidacy seemed increasingly implausible. The nation did not need a novice in foreign policy as president, and many Americans were concluding that a lack of realism about the total-itarian threat had clouded the anti-interventionist view of global affairs, the perspective identified with the GOP.

It was, indeed, soon after the European war arrived in September 1939 that Republican prospects started to fall away. Washington correspondents who by two to one that spring had predicted a Republican victory – a reflec-tion of administration problems at home – were soon in similar agreement that a Democratic presidential success was now likelier – the result of crises overseas.[3] It was not only Dewey's chances that international developments dashed. Robert A. Taft, the other key Republican celebrity that the 1938 comeback created and another presidential aspirant, also discovered that his hostility to the nation's participation in World War II became a handicap. The same was true for dark-horse candidate Arthur H. Vandenberg.[4] Republican ranks looked thin.

Collectively bewildered by the challenge of fast-changing events overseas, the party turned to a charismatic outsider, Wendell L. Willkie, as presidential candidate. New to electoral politics and a registered Democrat until 1939, Willkie found his opportunity because events overseas destroyed the main candidacies.[5] He was not a prisoner of obsolescent commitments on foreign policy. But he had gained prominence in public life not because of his for-eign policy views, but thanks to his attacks on New Deal regulation of the utilities sector; he was a leading utilities executive and among business's best defenders during the 1930s.[6] Although he would soon gain a reputation as a me-too supporter of New Deal liberalism, this was misleading. It is true that Willkie sympathized with New Deal welfare protections, but this repu-tation failed to recognize his stinging criticisms of the New Deal's approach to economic management. The originator of the phrase "Big Government" to demonize the ills of excessive Washington activism – a response to crit-ics of "Big Business" – Willkie was a creative exponent of the view that the New Deal was a failure.[7] He was an especially harsh critic of the belief asso-ciated with New Deal thinkers such as Thurman Arnold and Stuart Chase that the American economy had reached a stage of maturity where extensive

---

[3] *Newsweek*, Dec. 4, 1939, 12.

[4] Divine, *Foreign Policy*, 16–17.

[5] John Morton Blum, *V Was for Victory: Politics and American Culture during World War II* (New York: Harcourt Brace Jovanovich, 1976), 264.

[6] Mark H. Leff, "Strange Bedfellows: The Utility Magnate as Politician," in James H. Madison, ed., *Wendell Willkie: Hoosier Internationalist* (Bloomington: Indiana University Press, 1992), 22–46.

[7] Geoffrey Nunberg, *Talking Right: How Conservatives Turned Liberalism into a Tax-Raising, Latte-Drinking, Sushi-Eating, Volvo-Driving, New York Times–Reading, Body-Piercing, Hollywood-Loving, Left-Wing Freak Show* (New York: Public Affairs, 2006), 123.

management by the government was necessary and where past expectations of economic growth were unsustainable. Central to his campaign was the claim that his leadership would reinvigorate the economy, thus restoring prosperity and conquering unemployment. His business background exposed him to Democratic attack that his agenda catered for elites. "[A]ll of his thinking and all of his interests have been in conformity with those of our monied gentry," noted Secretary of the Interior Harold Ickes.[8]

Willkie, nevertheless, enjoyed a degree of popularity that made him an especially promising critic of New Deal liberalism. He possessed an appeal that seemingly extended far beyond the 1936 coalition. Shortly before the convention, Sterling Morton, a friend of Alf Landon, who had led efforts to mobilize business in 1936, discounted Willkie's ability to appeal "to the so-called 'lower third'" – the Democrats' stronghold – but considered him potentially strong among "the small business man, ... the savings bank depositor, the insurance policyholder, etc., and people of that type – the so-called 'middle third.'" Willkie was, therefore, "almost irresistible."[9] With this support from the "middle third," Willkie would win. Another Republican wrote of "an amazing undercurrent in his favor – not from Wall Street and State Street, but from the common people who realize that we need an executive of no mean proportions to pull this country together."[10] Such enthusiasm secured him the nomination. According to columnist Walter Lippmann, "Mr. Willkie's title comes directly from the people who, despite the strategems [sic] and tricks of politicians, in the end were truly represented by the delegates," over whose conservatism "a great tide of popular opinion" in Willkie's favor surged.[11] In other words, the party's heart was not with Willkie, but a Republican desire to win propelled him toward the nomination.

But although Willkie promised greater success in mobilizing public opinion against New Deal liberalism, it was his position on foreign policy that was notably distinctive – the reason why an outsider was able to win the 1940 nomination. Willkie was determined to push the party away from isolationism and clarify its commitment to internationalism. During the 1940 campaign, this internationalism involved predominantly an agreement with the administration about the need to revise neutrality legislation in order to offer more active support to the Allies in their struggle against Nazi Germany, though Willkie also vigorously criticized the administration's record and the detail of its policies in this regard. Afterward, Willkie pursued his mission more stridently, determined to use his leadership position to quash Republican isolationism during the tumultuous debate in 1941 about the nation's response to World War II. The attack on Pearl Harbor terminated that debate, but Willkie continued his battle to eradicate any isolationist traces within the

[8] Ickes diary, May 19, 1940, reel 3, Ickes Papers.
[9] Sterling Morton to Alf M. Landon, June 5, 1940, box 96, Landon Papers.
[10] Gaspar G. Bacon to Alf M. Landon, June 10, 1940, box 98, Landon Papers.
[11] *New York Herald Tribune* clipping, June 29, 1940, box 1323, Pinchot Papers.

party, especially with respect to the creation of postwar structures of international cooperation – a permanent embrace of internationalism. His desire to reshape the party did not dwell on foreign policy alone, however; it also extended to the domestic arena. He insisted that the party should redefine its conservatism in order to achieve relevance to ordinary Americans. In these ways, Willkie sought to transform the party and the way it engaged with the minority problem.

Willkie and his supporters could claim that their interventionism involved a Republican tradition of interest in the wider world.[12] The party was historically an advocate of expansionism. In the nineteenth century Republicans were responsible for the purchase of Alaska, the incorporation of Hawaii, and the negotiation of trade agreements with foreign countries, together with the decision to fight the 1898 Spanish-American War that led to a further acquisition of overseas territories. After William McKinley's embrace of an American imperialism, Theodore Roosevelt and William Howard Taft followed an internationalist path. Subsequently, even after World War I Republican administrations undertook such initiatives as the Washington disarmament conference, the creation of antiwar treaties with other nations, and active opposition to the Japanese invasion of Manchuria.

But isolationism had strong party roots, too. An especially notable manifestation of this uneasiness about international connections was the Republican role in defeating Woodrow Wilson's plan for American membership in the League of Nations after World War I. Later, during the 1930s, North Dakota's Gerald P. Nye led a Senate investigation of active support among bankers and businesspeople for U.S. involvement in that war, an investigation that helped to inform neutrality legislation, which passed with wide Republican backing.[13]

Indeed, it is more accurate to see the Republican tradition in foreign policy as involving not internationalism but an assertive nationalism; the interpretation of the nation's interest sometimes led Republican politicians toward expansionism and engagement with the wider world, whereas after World War I it more frequently encouraged them to avoid such engagement.[14] The strength of the latter sentiment engendered much Republican opposition to Franklin Roosevelt's efforts, as war arrived in both Asia and Europe, to modify American isolationism in order to voice opposition to Japanese aggression and to provide help to the Allies against Germany. The challenge that Willkie undertook in transforming the party's approach to foreign policy was therefore great. His understanding of the nation's mission overseas was drastically different from his Republican opponents'.

[12] Wendell L. Willkie to Mark Sullivan, April 8, 1941, Willkie Papers; *Des Moines Register* clipping, Sept. 17, 1941, Willkie Papers.
[13] Richard E. Darilek, *A Loyal Opposition in Time of War: The Republican Party and the Politics of Foreign Policy from Pearl Harbor to Yalta* (Westport, Conn.: Greenwood, 1976), 7–10.
[14] Mayer, *The Republican Party*, 450.

Willkie's struggle against the anti-interventionists earned him many party enemies. Even though during World War II the GOP at large edged toward a permanent internationalism (if wary of the *One World* idealism that Willkie projected in his best-selling 1943 book of that title), Willkie's 1944 effort to regain the nomination was hopeless. As a result, his final contribution to the minority debate was indirect, one that extended for decades beyond his death during the 1944 fall campaign. He became a symbol, demonized by conservatives, of what they perceived as the error of a me-too response to the Democrats – seen as wrong strategically as well as ideologically. The conspiratorially minded among them were sure that a cabal of eastern financial and publishing interests secured Willkie's nomination against the desires of most Republican activists. Such a suspicion informed some Republican reactions to his candidacy from the start. Just before the party met, Iowa's Harrison Spangler wrote that "a certain group of extreme internationalists centered in the lower part of New York City are pulling all strings and bringing all pressure possible to stampede the convention for Mr. Willkie."[15] Supportive coverage by New York–based media outlets and assistance from other elements of an "eastern establishment" certainly helped Willkie. Skillful strategies employed by leaders of the Willkie effort maximized their candidate's chances by fostering the surge of pro-Willkie support and by magnifying popular perceptions of its significance. But over time this perspective lost sight of the genuine enthusiasm that Willkie supporters mobilized for their candidate, at a time when the crisis overseas had fomented disarray in Republican ranks.

On his nomination, Willkie's charisma and the enthusiasm he unlocked were clear. So was his distinctive approach to foreign policy, which after the German advances in Europe seemed more relevant than the anti-interventionism of other leading Republicans. Even so, his rise was spectacular and unexpected. "Nothing so extraordinary has ever happened in American politics," Harold Ickes noted. "Here was a utility man – a big utility man – a Morgan man – a Director of Morgan's First National Bank of New York – a man who has never held public office or been a candidate for public office – a democrat until a couple of years ago – who, without any organization, went into a republican national convention and ran away with the nomination for President." (Ickes understated Willkie's extraparty organizational strength.) Because of his political skills, Willkie was, Ickes thought, "no easy candidate to defeat," especially because the Republicans balanced the ticket with the vice-presidential choice of Oregon's Charles L. McNary, the Senate minority leader.[16] McNary balanced Willkie not only as a westerner and senior party insider. He was, moreover, a prominent supporter of public power, thus able to alleviate any political damage stemming from Willkie's protection of private

[15] Harrison E. Spangler to Lawrence Richey, May 27, 1940, box 97, Post-Presidential Subject File [hereafter PPSF], Hoover Papers.
[16] Ickes diary, June 29, 1940, reel 3, Ickes Papers.

utilities.[17] Still, the Democrats were determined not to allow Willkie to depict himself as something new, instead linking him with a reactionary rejection of the New Deal. Franklin Roosevelt soon decided to elevate the theme "of corporate, entrenched wealth against the great mass of the people," according to Ickes, thus exploiting New Deal liberalism's electoral benefits. "I believe that this will be more clearcut than at any time in the past," Ickes wrote, "and I believe that on this issue we can win; certainly on no other issue can we win."[18]

The paradigm of electoral politics that shaped the Willkie candidacy, as well as informing the perspective of many other contemporary Republicans, did not accept that the Democratic majority was safe and dependable. According to this view – supported by poll data – the Democrats lost their majority soon after the 1936 elections. Republicans made some gains at the Democrats' expense, but it was independent voters who became the crucial factor in electoral politics – loyal supporters of neither party, ready to vote for either. The Gallup organization reported that in March 1937 one in two Americans was a supporter of the Democrats, compared with one in three on the Republican side; 15 percent of the electorate was independent. By July 1940, the Democrats' share had slipped to 41 percent and the Republicans' had increased to 38 percent. One in five was an independent.[19] The New Deal coalition thus no longer seemed so formidable, and the key to victory was success among the independents. The perspective resembled that of Charles P. Taft's 1936 book, *You and I – and Roosevelt*, though the number of independents was smaller than Taft's one-third. It similarly led to an emphasis on moderation as the party's way ahead, on the need to communicate the party's message with uncommitted voters who were susceptible to both parties' cultivation.

Central to the Willkie campaign was a special organization to win over these independents, along with disaffected Democrats – another way in which the Willkie phenomenon sought to build the party and seek a majority. The Willkie clubs, which first emerged to secure the nomination for their candidate, remained in operation after the convention to complement party efforts that focused on the mobilization of Republican supporters. According to Oren Root, Jr., a founder of the clubs organization, "a Willkie Club to every 2,500 population would be sure to enlist all the independent voters of each state."[20] The mission was ambitious. Raymond Moley, a journalist and former FDR aide, increasingly disillusioned with liberalism, later wrote that the party and the Willkie clubs were in theory together able to organize an electoral majority, but that the "professionals'" suspicions and the "amateurs'" impetuosity meant that such a productive relationship was impossible.[21]

---

[17] Steve Neal, *McNary of Oregon: A Political Biography* (Portland: Western Imprints – The Press of the Oregon Historical Society, 1985), 183–188.

[18] Ickes diary, June 29, 1940, reel 3, Ickes Papers.

[19] Mildred Strunk, *Public Opinion, 1935–1946* (Princeton, N.J.: Princeton University Press, 1951), 576.

[20] Oren Root, Jr., to John Curby, Aug. 9, 1940, box 13, Willkie Clubs Papers.

[21] Raymond Moley, *27 Masters of Politics* (New York: Funk & Wagnalls, 1949), 51.

The Willkie clubs did indeed foster intraparty animosities and jealousies, limiting their majority-building contribution. Endemic to most political endeavor, such factional conflict found a new outlet with the amateurs' ascendancy.[22] Some Republicans argued that the clubs' centrality to the Willkie effort was counterproductive – a blow to the morale of longer-established activists, who therefore lacked the necessary enthusiasm to work hard for the cause, but whose contribution was essential to any party victory.[23] One reporter noticed "the faintly superior attitude which too many of the volunteers adopted with respect to the party faithful," whose "ruffled feelings ... lost votes."[24] John Hamilton, who was national chair until shortly after Willkie's nomination, tried to quantify the impact of low morale on activists' energy, estimating that as a result Willkie would lose perhaps five to seven votes in each precinct – enough to lose the election.[25] Such a perspective revealed a very different approach to the minority problem from that of the Willkie paradigm. Rather than moderation to attract independent voters, it called for fidelity to party principles in order to enthuse those most committed already to the GOP. This approach also downplayed New Deal liberalism's electoral power, assuming that the inadequate mobilization of Republican support accounted for Democratic success. The clash of paradigms was evident in an exchange between Raymond L. Buell, a leading Willkie aide, and David Hinshaw, the former Hoover aide. Supporting the view that Willkie needed to enthuse rank-and-file Republicans to achieve victory, Hinshaw told Buell that "most of the independent voters of the nation are Republicans on the loose."[26]

With victory in mind, grassroots activists sometimes concluded that party unity and a degree of synthesis between the two approaches were necessary.[27] A clubs activist in Arizona concluded that cooperation with the party and with a Democrats' Willkie organization was "one of the hardest phases of our work," favoring "a policy of doing most the giving, which, of course, is hard on one's disposition, but very good for the cause," and reporting that relations were consequently "friendly and mutually helpful."[28] In one Illinois county, it was active Republicans who launched a Willkie club to secure non-Republican support, thus avoiding conflict but also potentially stifling new activism.[29] But tensions were more common than cooperation, mirroring national-level conflicts – not just the result of personal rivalries and ideological differences, but also of different approaches to political engagement between the professionals and the amateurs. One GOP state chair later advanced the fundamental critique that extraparty organizations were inimical to the nation's two-party

[22] *Time* clipping, Sept. 9, 1940, box 46, Buell Papers.
[23] David Hinshaw to Raymond L. Buell, Sept. 11, 1940, box 46, Buell Papers; Monte Appel to Nathan William MacChesney, Oct. 16, 1940, box 15, MacChesney Papers.
[24] Walter T. Bonney to Raymond L. Buell, Nov. 11, 1940, box 2, Buell Papers.
[25] Mary Earhart Dillon, *Wendell Willkie 1892–1944* (Philadelphia: Lippincott, 1952), 211.
[26] David Hinshaw to Raymond L. Buell, Sept. 11, 1940, box 41, Davenport Papers.
[27] John E. Curby to Richard M. Egan, Sept. 13, 1940, box 13, Willkie Clubs Papers.
[28] Frank C. Brophy to Oren Root, Jr., Nov. 4, 1940, box 11, Willkie Clubs Papers.
[29] Pence B. Orr to Wendell L. Willkie, July 13, 1940, box 12, Willkie Clubs Papers.

system, seeing a candidate-centered approach that did not involve activism for the entire slate as illegitimate, likely to breed a European form of multiparty politics and instability.[30]

The Willkie clubs achieved remarkable success in creating branches and recruiting members. In Iowa, Willkie supporters did not nearly reach their over-ambitious goal of 1,100 clubs; they nevertheless established 400 groups across the state, with an estimated total membership of 150,000.[31] In neighboring Illinois the number of clubs was about 2,200, and in lightly populated Arizona it was 75.[32] The clubs' national headquarters distributed the "Willkie Worker Kit," claiming to receive as many as 25,000 requests for the kit weekly.[33] Such efforts boosted the party's grassroots effectiveness; despite their minority status, Republicans flexed their organizational muscle in 1940 across the country. According to a late October poll, more Americans received Republican than Democratic literature and more were contacted by Republican than Democratic workers.[34] "The Willkie clubs were a tonic that the Republican organization needed," Joseph W. Martin, Jr., the Massachusetts congressperson whom Willkie chose to replace John Hamilton as RNC chair, later wrote. "They brought enthusiasm, aggressiveness, and color into the campaign – and they raised a great deal of money."[35]

Martin's point about money was important. New regulation of campaign finance, known as Hatch Act II, limited a "political committee's" annual spending to $3 million and an individual's or association's campaign contribution to $5,000, though the restrictions did not apply to state or local committees. The limits were significant; in 1936 the Republican Party spent almost $9 million. It was therefore in the parties' interests to encourage the decentralization of fundraising and the creation of extraparty political organizations. Although Willkie ill-advisedly announced his intention to run a campaign that cost no more than $3 million in total, its need for more money meant that the Associated Willkie Clubs' separate identity from the party was financially as well as organizationally beneficial.[36]

Although the clubs helped revitalize the party, at least in the short term, they did not necessarily transform its base socioeconomically or even ideologically, though these activists were perhaps younger than most Republicans.[37] A key motivation for GOP enthusiasm for Willkie was his effectiveness as free

[30] Transcript, state chairs' meeting, June 21, 1941, box 6, Stassen Papers.
[31] Willard D. Archie to Alf M. Landon, Sept. 11, [1940,] box 96, Landon Papers; Archie to Oren Root, Jr., Oct. 30, 1940, box 12, Willkie Clubs Papers.
[32] Associated Willkie Clubs of America, meeting transcript, Dec. 14, 1940, box 1, Willkie Clubs Papers; Frank C. Brophy to Oren Root, Jr., Nov. 4, 1940, box 11, Willkie Clubs Papers.
[33] *Current History and Forum*, Oct. 22, 1940, 32.
[34] Strunk, *Public Opinion*, 579.
[35] Joseph W. Martin, Jr., *My First Fifty Years in Politics*, as told to Robert J. Donovan (New York: McGraw-Hill, 1960), 109.
[36] Louise Overacker, "Campaign Finance in the Presidential Election of 1940," *APSR* 35 (1941), 701–727.
[37] Moley, *27 Masters*, 51.

enterprise's defender, an effectiveness that seemed much greater than that of his party rivals.[38] At first impressed by the pro-Willkie movement, Alf Landon later saw its grassroots leadership as a problem because "in too many places the local 'economic royalists' rushed in to head these clubs."[39] When these leaders met after the election to discuss the movement's future, some spoke of good-government goals and the need to make the Republican Party more moderate. But others railed against the New Deal in ways scarcely distinguishable from those of party conservatives.[40]

This was consequential for the campaign. In late August, a Portland, Oregon, activist warned Root that "too much attention is being centered among the upper crust where you are already just about 100% established," overlooking lower-income voters whose support was critical. There was "too much Ritz in this campaign."[41] Sometimes conscious of this elitism, clubs attempted outreach. This concern was evident in the organization of the "Back-to-Work-With-Willkie Dance Week," part of a youth effort, involving dances at the lowest cost possible in order to facilitate participation by people of all income groups.[42] In the industrial community of New London, Connecticut, the club's target member was one earning between $900 and $1,800 annually – someone not poor but far from wealthy.[43] But such efforts lacked larger success. John B. Hollister, a former congressperson from Ohio who advised Root on questions involving liaison with the regular party, concluded "that their activity was largely confined to a social group which did not include many of the class which has to be reached if we are to change things."[44]

One of Willkie's most compelling strengths as a candidate was the extent of his potential support among disaffected Democrats.[45] "Thousands of hard-shell Democrats who have been increasingly disillusioned and disgusted with the New Deal find in Mr. Willkie the excuse they needed to vote the Republican ticket," Landon wrote in July.[46] Eager to maximize such support, Willkie stressed the development of a Democrats-For-Willkie organization – another extraparty group, separate from the Willkie clubs. This

[38] Norman Hulbert Strouse, "Reminscences of Willkie 1940 campaign in Ca.," March 1976, U.S. History Manuscripts, The Lilly Library, Indiana University.

[39] Alf M. Landon to Allen E. Walker, July 17, 1940, box 96, Landon Papers; Landon to Raymond Clapper, Nov. 30, 1940, box 101, Landon Papers.

[40] Associated Willkie Clubs of America, meeting transcript, Dec. 14, 1940, box 1, Willkie Clubs Papers.

[41] Kenneth L. Cooper to Oren Root, Jr., Aug. 24, 1940, box 14, Willkie Clubs Papers.

[42] Richard B. Kay to F. W. Dearborn, Oct. 16, 1940, box 13, Willkie Clubs Papers.

[43] Stacy K. Beebe to Oren Root, Jr., Aug. 2, 1940, box 11, Willkie Clubs Papers; Ellsworth Barnard, *Wendell Willkie: Fighter for Freedom* (Marquette: Northern Michigan University Press), 265.

[44] Donald Bruce Johnson, *The Republican Party and Wendell Willkie* (Urbana: University of Illinois Press, 1960), 120; John B. Hollister to Wendell L. Willkie, Dec. 5, 1940, Willkie Papers.

[45] Frank L. Fetzer to Herbert Hoover, June 18, 1940, box 58, PPICF, Hoover Papers.

[46] Alf M. Landon to Charles L. McNary, July 11, 1940, box 101, Landon Papers.

allowed sectional outreach, providing a chance for southerners to vote for a Republican without supporting the party.[47] In Richmond, the Democrats-For-Willkie campaign emphasized that the president was not a real Democrat; Willkie was.[48] The group did not challenge its supporters' Democratic affiliation, though Republicans sometimes spoke of Willkie support as a step toward their party.[49] "If it is understood by the electorate of these States that a vote will promote the prestige and political influence of the members of these Republican organizations, then the people, even though they are in full sympathy with Mr. Willkie, will vote against him," warned one clubs activist, who even claimed – unpersuasively – that two-thirds of southerners supported Willkie over Roosevelt and the right strategy might secure a majority of states there for him.[50] Despite its focus on whites, this activity did not necessarily neglect African Americans – in Charlottesville, Virginia, Willkie campaigners claimed to be the first activists in many years to seek black support.[51] Still, the idea of southern white support for a Republican was rather implausible. Complaining about clubs investment in the South, a Maryland leader observed that "with the millions, yes billions, that the Roosevelt Administration has thrown and continues to throw into the South, it is ridiculous to think that anything would move the people to exchange FDR."[52] But the legacy of the Civil War and Reconstruction, as well as the impact of New Deal liberalism, remained strong in discouraging southern white GOP support.

The Willkie choice was a sign of Republican desperation, its difficulty in finding a leading insider to respond effectively to fast-moving and troubling events overseas. But there was another kind of desperation among Republicans, too, about American democracy's future. When Franklin Roosevelt broke precedent to seek a third term, many in the party believed this was an excellent way to dramatize what they saw as the New Deal's dictatorial drift, thus placing it at the campaign's heart. An RNC leaflet warned, "Vote Against a Third Term and Dictatorship or You May Never Go to the Polls Again in a Free Election," and Republicans declared October 23 "National No Third Term Day."[53] It was therefore an emotion-laden campaign.[54] The concern was often not expedient but genuine; William Allen White, for example, feared that "four more

[47] Ruth Hanna Simms to Thomas E. Dewey, July 16, 1940, box 48, series 1, Dewey Papers.
[48] Henry S. Hotchkiss to John Read Burr, Aug. 5, 1940, box 15, Willkie Clubs Papers.
[49] Johnson, *Republican Party and Wendell Willkie*, 116–117; Jennings C. Wise to Richard M. Egan, July 27, 1940, box 15, Willkie Clubs Papers.
[50] Unsigned to Oren Root, Jr., and Russell W. Davenport, July 12, 1940, Democrats-For-Willkie Papers.
[51] Augusta M. Jarman to Mrs. Henry Breckenridge, Oct. 7, 1940, box 15, Willkie Clubs Papers.
[52] Kirk A. Landon to Carl Touhey, Sept. 23, 1940, box 13, Willkie Clubs Papers.
[53] RNC, "No Third Term" (flyer), n.d., box 148, Taft Papers; Johnson, *Republican Party and Wendell Willkie*, 151.
[54] Moley, *27 Masters*, 51.

years of Democratic control of our government would so weaken the opposition that we might slide into the one party system which is terrible."[55]

Willkie – described by one journalist as engaged in politics to save democracy – pursued the theme.[56] "An irresponsible government in Washington during the next four years will result in the downfall of democracy here and its destruction elsewhere," he said in Boston.[57] In Coffeyville, Kansas, he accused Roosevelt of "[straining] our democratic institutions to the breaking point," warning that "if, because of some fine speeches about humanity, you return this Administration to office, you will be serving under an American totalitarian government before the long third-term is finished."[58] But the theme's power against that of New Deal liberalism was limited at best. After the election Buell concluded that it enjoyed some success in boosting Republican fortunes among midwestern farmers and Catholics, but economic concerns remained more important in the cities – to the Democrats' benefit.[59]

On the Republican side, emotion also erupted around the allegation that communist sympathies suffused the administration and the Democratic Party. House committee hearings on communist activity in organized labor, education, and federal agencies – under Representative Martin Dies, a Texas anti–New Deal Democrat – helped fuel the allegation. Representative Kent Ellsworth Keller, an Illinois Democrat, argued that appropriations to support the committee amounted to "a Republican campaign fund" and that Dies sought "to aid the Republican at the expense of the Democratic Party."[60] The allegation of communist infiltration certainly seemed electorally promising. "This is one issue they are vulnerable on and it would be foolish if we didn't use it," thought Representative Frank Carlson of Kansas.[61]

The RNC circulated literature accusing the administration of fifth-column activity, beginning with the official recognition of the Soviet Union in 1933, and emphasizing the presence of fellow travelers and radicals in appointive office.[62] Missouri Republicans issued a leaflet stating that Henry A. Wallace, Roosevelt's running mate (as John Nance Garner's replacement) and a former progressive Republican, "once praised Dictators Lenin, Stalin, and Mussolini, and repeated religious criticisms which are certain to horrify many good Christian Americans."[63] Republicans sometimes moved beyond the claim that the New Deal sympathized with communism and toward the argument

[55] William Allen White to Judson King, Aug. 30, 1940, box C344, White Papers.

[56] *This Week*, Aug. 18, 1940, 7, 11.

[57] Unsigned notes, n.d., box 46, Buell Papers.

[58] "1940 Campaign Speeches by Wendell Willkie on Keeping Out of War," box 50, Nye Papers.

[59] *Berkshire Eagle* clipping, Dec. 4, 1940, box 46, Buell Papers.

[60] William Gellerman, *Martin Dies* (1944; New York: Da Capo, 1972), 175, 191.

[61] Frank Carlson to Alf M. Landon, June 12, 1940, box 101, Landon Papers.

[62] RNC, "Our Own Fifth Column," box 1323, Pinchot Papers.

[63] Hugh A. Bone, *"Smear" Politics: An Analysis of 1940 Campaign Literature* (Washington, D.C.: American Council on Public Affairs, 1941), 10.

that New Deal liberalism was a form of totalitarian politics. At a California meeting of Republicans, one speaker argued that yet more threatening than any fifth column was the New Deal's socialistic drift. "Either we are to maintain a Constitutional Republic and all that Constitutional Republic *stands for* – or we are to have frozen upon us forever a government by officialdom as arbitrary as that of the Hammer and Sickle or the Swastika," she warned.[64] If Republicans sometimes saw socialism or communism among Democrats, Democrats sometimes sensed a different strand of totalitarianism among Republicans. At the time of Willkie's nomination, Harold Ickes predicted "that fascist elements, which are rapidly forming in this country, will rally behind him and that Willkie will represent their point of view."[65] When he took to the campaign trail, Roosevelt spoke of extremists, skeptical of democracy, who supported Willkie.[66]

But the key strand of the Democrats' attack on Willkie challenged the view that he represented something new. They used his big-business background and defense of private enterprise to characterize him as a typical Republican, wedded to corporate interests, concerned about business and not ordinary Americans. Ickes most famously called Willkie "the simple barefoot Wall Street lawyer," also describing him more comprehensively as "an utterly inexperienced public-utility lawyer whose only claim to consideration is that he has successfully represented, and won the gratitude of, some of the biggest interests in Wall Street."[67] Along similar lines, Attorney General Robert H. Jackson characterized his role at the Department of Justice as involving efforts "to stop the increasing concentration in this country of great aggregations of other people's money in the hands of lawless, irresponsible and ruthless men like Wendell Willkie."[68]

Although Democratic campaigners effectively attacked his business connections, Willkie did not develop his message about the New Deal's failure with anything approaching a similar effectiveness. Raymond Buell concluded that Willkie failed to explain clearly the key charge that the New Deal was responsible for persistently high unemployment. Voters, he thought, were likely to believe that Willkie's difference with Roosevelt over the New Deal did not involve such important substance but was simply a matter of effective management.[69] In the middle of October, one Republican activist – presumably following the campaign more closely than most Americans – reported that voters frequently asked him about Willkie's plans to solve joblessness; he

---

[64] Ferne Mattei, speech excerpts, July 25, 1940, box 148, Taft Papers.

[65] Ickes diary, June 29, 1940, reel 3, Ickes Papers.

[66] Robert E. Sherwood, *Roosevelt and Hopkins: An Intimate History* (New York: Harper, 1948), 193–194.

[67] *Liberty*, Oct. 19, 1940, 14.

[68] *Time*, Nov. 4, 1940, 12–13.

[69] Raymond L. Buell to Russell W. Davenport, Aug. 7, 1940, and Buell to Francis W. Coker, Dec. 29, 1940, box 46, Buell Papers.

was himself uncertain about the proposals because "in none of the speeches that I have read or heard has this specific question been covered."[70]

This failure was unfortunate because there were signs that Willkie's position had potential strength. An end-of-campaign poll suggested that, among those who did perceive a difference between the candidates' solutions to unemployment, more preferred Willkie's ideas to Roosevelt's. In the same survey, Willkie enjoyed a similar edge on the restoration of business confidence and the control of government spending.[71] A pioneering academic study of voting behavior, based on survey research in Erie County, Ohio, found that some less affluent voters moved from Roosevelt to Willkie on such grounds – but the numbers were small, not enough to weaken the Democratic Party's hold on the electorate.[72]

Willkie found much to praise as well as condemn in New Deal liberalism – earning him the me-too tag among Republicans as well as muddying the distinction between his ideas and Roosevelt's. Although he attacked not only the administration's management of the economy but also the concepts underpinning its economic policy, Willkie endorsed collective bargaining, minimum wage and maximum hour standards, banking and utilities regulation, Social Security, and assistance to farmers, among other key New Deal achievements. He thus worried less about big government than many other, more conservative, Republicans did; he concentrated his concern on the waste and inefficiency that he said blighted New Deal programs' implementation. Nevertheless, central to this endorsement of many New Deal goals was the critique of New Deal economics, leading to the argument that the administration's achievements were meaningless in view of prosperity's absence.[73] Conservative Republicans' dissatisfaction with Willkie's support for New Deal reforms sometimes led them to overlook the significance of his fundamental attack on the administration's economic policy.[74] Willkie, therefore, not only failed to develop an anti–New Deal message that won majority support for the Republican Party. He also managed to infuriate many in his own party.

Initial campaign plans sidelined the U.S. response to World War II as an issue. On the one hand, Roosevelt clearly sought to derive electoral benefit from his institutional prestige as commander-in-chief, and discussion of the war was likely to reinforce this advantage. On the other hand, the domestic record seemed vulnerable to attack.[75] "Because the New Deal has made such an abject failure in its handling of domestic issues," Landon remarked in April,

---

[70] Howard A. Sommer to Charles A. Halleck, Oct. 15, 1940, box 6, Halleck Papers.

[71] Strunk, *Public Opinion*, 619–620.

[72] Paul F. Lazarsfeld, Bernard Berelson, and Hazel Gaudet, *The People's Choice: How the Voter Makes Up His Mind in a Presidential Campaign*, 3rd ed. (New York: Columbia University Press, 1968), 98–99 (quotation, 99).

[73] Barnard, *Wendell Willkie*, 206–207.

[74] Mark Sullivan to Wendell L. Willkie, April 9, 1941, Willkie Papers.

[75] Raymond L. Buell to Wendell Willkie, May 15, 1940, box 46, Buell Papers; William Allen White to Frank Knox, May 17, 1940, box C344, White Papers.

"it is obviously seeking to make the issues of the 1940 election those of foreign policy."[76] Willkie certainly saw no electoral benefit in anti-interventionism, just as he saw no policy advantage; anti-interventionists were firmly in the Republican camp, and a majority of Americans were in favor of assistance to the Allies, though against active involvement in the war – the formula that the Roosevelt administration pursued through strong defense and through aid to aggression's victims. On officially accepting the nomination, Willkie emphasized his agreement with this approach, saying that he was "glad to pledge my wholehearted support to the President in whatever action he may take in accordance with these principles." But he also attacked FDR's implementation of his foreign policy as clouded by "inflammatory statements and manufactured panics," as well as a lack of candor with the public.[77] In discussing foreign policy, Willkie tried to strike a balance between support and criticism. He helped secure Republican support for the nation's first peacetime draft.[78] He also supported the destroyers-for-bases agreement to aid the United Kingdom, while attacking its extracongressional, secretive negotiation as "the most dictatorial and arbitrary act of any President in the history of the United States."[79]

Democrats sought to link Willkie with Republican anti-interventionism, branding him an appeaser – encouraging him to modify his strategy and take to the offensive on foreign policy.[80] He now emphasized defense as his presidential priority because of administration failings. "As a matter of fact, we are totally unprepared to defend ourselves," he commented during an October radio address.[81] Adding the charge that FDR was a warmonger to the attack on the inadequacy of defense preparations, he thus often echoed the anti-interventionists, disappointing some supporters.[82] Willkie referred to two of Roosevelt's most famous campaign pledges – one of 1932 and one of 1940 – in saying, "If his promise to keep our boys out of foreign wars is no better than his promise to balance the budget, they're almost on the transports!"[83]

Despite the campaign's shortcomings, Willkie's appeal was strong enough to shake the loyalty of key groups within the Democratic coalition that Roosevelt had assembled in 1936. There were even signs of his capacity to reach out to the "forgotten man" to whom Roosevelt had dedicated his New Deal efforts. A Boise, Idaho, Willkie club dispatched "a rough appearing individual" to

[76] Alf M. Landon, speech, April 4, 1940, box 6, Stassen Papers.

[77] Divine, *Foreign Policy*, 42–48 (quotations, 47–48).

[78] Neal, *Dark Horse*, 138–139.

[79] Joseph Barnes, *Willkie: The Events He Was Part Of, The Ideas He Fought For* (New York: Simon and Schuster, 1952), 203.

[80] Raymond L. Buell to Harry N. Howard, Oct. 8, 1940, box 41, Davenport Papers.

[81] "Willkie Pledges Strong Defense as 'First Job,'" clipping, datelined Oct. 9, 1940, box 50, Nye Papers.

[82] Neal, *Dark Horse*, 159–160. The drift of Willkie's earlier rhetoric criticized Roosevelt as an appeaser rather than a warmonger. Barnes, *Willkie*, 225.

[83] Johnson, *Republican Party and Wendell Willkie*, 153.

canvass opinion among the community's poorer members, discovering that Roosevelt's edge was much narrower than in the FDR–Landon contest – thanks to sentiment against the New Deal and a third term. The canvasser added the unsurprising observation that "the majority of pool hall loafers are indifferent as to who should be President."[84]

Most strikingly, organized labor's support for the administration suffered some slippage. John L. Lewis, president of the United Mine Workers of America and the Congress of Industrial Organizations, believed that Roosevelt was taking labor support for granted, generating frustrations that personal tensions between the two men aggravated. He was critical of the administration's domestic record – particularly the persistence of high unemployment – and of its foreign policy, which he saw as leading the nation to a foreign war.[85] Lewis was not alone within labor ranks in contemplating support for Willkie, despite the movement's significant gains under the New Deal. According to Sumner H. Slichter, a Harvard economist advising the Willkie campaign, there was a Republican opportunity among labor leaders who feared the loss of their organizations' autonomy with increased government control of the economy during wartime.[86] Slichter predicted that up to one-third of labor members were prepared to vote for Willkie due to unemployment's persistence, as well as these apprehensions about labor's future.[87] According to a report on labor sentiment, "from Portland, Maine to Portland, Oregon you would hear the same criticism of the New Deal from the workers: they would say the labor laws are all right, but would add 'they are being administered by a bunch of intellectual nuts'."[88]

But the campaign achieved little of this promise. A Pennsylvania labor leader, in supporting Willkie, spoke of "the right of the common man against the forces which would deprive him of his democratic rights."[89] Lewis also endorsed Willkie, but few leaders of CIO unions shared the endorsement, which seemed to have little impact on rank-and-file unionists – with the exception of mining communities where there was evidence of some significant gains for Willkie. In general, FDR's support among CIO workers fell by no greater a proportion than it did among the electorate at large between 1936 and 1940.[90]

Similarly wishing to exploit the politics of interest-group pluralism, the NAACP's Walter White argued that African Americans decisively held the balance of power in any fairly close election. It was an argument that Raymond

---

[84] Oscar W. Worthwine to Oren Root, Jr., Aug. 23, 1940, box 12, Willkie Clubs Papers.

[85] Melvyn Dubofsky and Warren Van Tine, *John L. Lewis: A Biography* (New York: Quadrangle/ New York Times, 1977).

[86] Sumner H. Slichter to Raymond L. Buell, Sept. 14, 1940, box 46, Buell Papers.

[87] Raymond L. Buell to Russell W. Davenport, July 17, 1940, box 46, Buell Papers.

[88] Raymond L. Buell to Russell W. Davenport, July 26, 1940, box 46, Buell Papers.

[89] B. C. Clarke to Lewis G. Hines, Oct. 12, 1940, box 16, Hines Papers.

[90] Irving Bernstein, "John L. Lewis and the Voting Behavior of the C.I.O.," *POQ* 5 (1941), 233–249.

Buell, at least, on the Willkie campaign accepted.[91] White claimed that their ballots were important in seventeen states, amounting to 281 votes in the electoral college – more than enough to elect a president – and that they were ready to use the vote as "a potent weapon" against discrimination.[92] It was crucial to White's argument that both parties actively cultivate African American support, thereby promoting the cause of racial justice. But White himself was skeptical of Republican sincerity in this regard, rejecting the Willkie campaign's efforts to recruit his support on the grounds that the party only developed interest in African American matters as elections approached.[93]

The Willkie campaign recognized that the New Deal's record of concern for society's underprivileged made it difficult to win back minority support. As an alternative to this record, Willkie could offer only promises, hoping for African Americans' trust. Such promises were unlikely, by contrast, to cost support among white southerners, used to hearing politicians make civil rights commitments that they then abandoned.[94] Thus, when Willkie spoke to African Americans, he emphasized his antidiscrimination commitment.[95] The RNC's Francis E. Rivers repeated the 1936 argument that the New Deal sought to relegate African Americans to the status of "'an unemployable', whom it will treat like the American Indian was treated, and confine the colored man on modern reservations of relief."[96] But promises were not enough. Compared with Landon, Willkie secured increased support among African Americans, but the Republican share still amounted to barely one in three.[97]

One convention innovation was the platform's endorsement of the Equal Rights Amendment. The issue confused some; some California delegates reportedly believed the amendment's goal was the promotion of equality for men.[98] Intended to appeal to women, this endorsement enthused some, but it alienated others, who opposed the amendment because they feared it would outlaw legislation protective of women, especially in the workplace.[99] Marguerite M. Wells, president of the National League of Women Voters, therefore attributed GOP support for the amendment to the absence of women from the convention's resolutions committee, insisting that the Democrats were friendlier to women's interests than the Republicans.[100] Even those who favored the amendment did not necessarily support the Republican cause on these grounds. One member of the National Women's Party – a proponent of

[91] Raymond L. Buell to Russell W. Davenport, July 19, 1940, box 46, Buell Papers.
[92] *Liberty*, Oct. 12, 1940, 35–36.
[93] Walter White to C. Fulton Oursler, Nov. 7, 1940, box A78, series II, NAACP Records.
[94] Raymond L. Buell to Charlton MacVeagh, Sept. 6, 1940, box 41, Davenport Papers.
[95] Barnard, *Wendell Willkie*, 232.
[96] Francis W. Rivers, "Final Appeal to the Colored Voters," [1940,] box 43, series 9, Dewey Papers.
[97] Everett Carll Ladd and Charles D. Hadley, *Transformations of the American Party System: Political Coalitions from the New Deal to the 1970s* (New York: Norton, 1975), 60.
[98] *Philadelphia Evening Bulletin* clipping, June 27, 1940, box 16, Hines Papers.
[99] Rymph, *Republican Women*, 81–82.
[100] Raymond L. Buell to Russell W. Davenport, July 26, 1940, box 46, Buell Papers.

the amendment – criticized what she saw as Willkie's equivocal support for equality, undermining the plank's effectiveness. She also noted that the GOP problem was to offer merely promises when the administration had developed a record of some egalitarianism.[101]

A commonly assumed political distinction between men and women concerned war; women were considered warier of war. To some Willkie activists, attacks on the administration's drift to war were sure to build support among women.[102] To others, the picture was more complicated. A Boston activist agreed about the issue's pro-Willkie potential, but she also noted that women among whom she campaigned were often responsive to the pro-Roosevelt argument against a change of administration at a time of such international danger.[103] Nevertheless, in a campaign broadcast, Willkie defined what he attacked as the administration's lack of preparedness for war as a matter of special concern to women.[104] Some anecdotal evidence suggested that women were more ready to support Willkie than were men.[105] Gallup pollsters did not use gender, however, as a category to dissect the electorate until fall 1943, when mass military service had feminized the electorate. The results then showed women modestly more supportive of the Democratic Party than men were.[106] If women were likelier to support Willkie, what qualified their impact on the Republican coalition was the smaller likelihood of women than men to vote. One survey suggested that this difference was dramatic, that almost seven in ten men voted in 1940 but only one in two women did.[107]

The New Deal coalition held, and Roosevelt won his third term. Republican results were open to an interpretation of qualified optimism, however. Rallying party loyalists early the following year, national chair Joe Martin revealed the persistence of belief in the bought vote's negative implications for the party by describing Willkie's 22 million as "a good majority of the free votes in the country," also noting that the party won over half of the vote outside the South.[108]

It was important for Martin to remind Republicans of their electoral progress because a sour mood of mutual recrimination overwhelmed much analysis of Willkie's defeat. Tensions between pro- and anti-Willkie Republicans were marked. On the anti-Willkie side, Hoover was quick to notice the statistic that supported his more conservative vision for the party. Willkie apparently ran behind Republican gubernatorial and congressional candidates – a vote

[101] Helena Hill Weed to Alf M. Landon, Oct. 29, 1940, box 102, Landon Papers.
[102] Marlin S. Casey to Oren Root, Jr., Oct. 19, 1940, box 12, Willkie Clubs Papers.
[103] Margot A. Ketchum to Oren Root, Jr., Oct. 24, 1940, box 13, Willkie Clubs Papers.
[104] "Willkie Pledges Strong Defense as 'First Job.'"
[105] Raymond L. Buell to Russell W. Davenport, Oct. 8, 1940, box 46, Buell Papers.
[106] Strunk, *Public Opinion*, 600–621, 626.
[107] Louis Harris, *Is There a Republican Majority? Political Trends, 1952–1956* (New York: Harper, 1954), 108.
[108] Minutes of RNC meeting, March 24, 1941, reel 7, *Papers of the Republican Party*, part I, series A.

deficit of between one million and two million according to his calculations. He concluded that Willkie had lost the election because he did not secure the support of regular GOP voters; Willkie's mistake was his departure from traditional Republican themes, Hoover claimed.[109] In fact, Hoover's math was questionable. A comparison between votes for U.S. senators and votes for president suggested that Willkie only sometimes, not always, ran behind Senate candidates.[110] Among Willkie supporters, factional conflicts helped explain the defeat. Such views were not even unique to the Willkie camp. To explain the same phenomenon that Hoover noted, Ruth Simms, who had managed Dewey's nomination campaign, emphasized a lack of organizational effort, underpinned by the perceived self-interest of activists. Such activists did not work hard for Willkie and, she suspected, did not even vote for him, telling Dewey, "Party workers in the big industrial cities prefer to control a defeated organization rather than to turn it over to a leader in whom they have no confidence."[111] On the day after his defeat, Samuel F. Pryor, a Connecticut RNC member, offered Willkie himself similar analysis – that "you could have been President if you had worked with the party organization."[112]

Central to this analysis was disagreement about the club movement's impact. It was alternatively seen as the party's savior through the recruitment of new, forward-looking enthusiasts and as the party's destructor, because those enthusiasts had different goals and ambitions by comparison with existing Republican loyalists. The clubs' future was therefore controversial. For some Willkie advocates, integration was an attractive goal, to harness the new activists' energies and to move the party in their direction.[113] "I think we have got to get into the Republican party, rededicate the Republican party, revivify it, and in order to do that we have got to work locally," a Detroit activist told fellow clubs leaders. Most agreed, though one thought the task hopeless, because the party organization "as it is constituted today is not going to reach the fellow down in the grassroots."[114] Outside the party, some Willkie supporters banded together in an effort to establish a nonpartisan good-government organization, pledged to support better candidates for office.[115] But this vestige of the clubs did not last long. By then rather inactive anyway, the national office closed down soon after Pearl Harbor.[116] The extent to which Willkie activists decided to join the regular Republican organization is unclear. Much clearer is the instability of an organization dedicated to the promotion of an individual candidate in the absence of this candidacy.

[109] Herbert Hoover to Mark Sullivan, Nov. 9, 1940, box 97, PPSF, Hoover Papers.
[110] Barnard, *Wendell Willkie*, 264.
[111] Ruth Hanna McCormick Simms to Thomas E. Dewey, Dec. 2, 1940, box 48, series 1, Dewey Papers.
[112] Dillon, *Wendell Willkie*, 227
[113] [Raymond L. Buell] to Wendell L. Willkie, Nov. 27, 1940, box 46, Buell Papers.
[114] Meeting minutes, Dec. 14, 1940, box 1, Willkie Clubs Papers.
[115] John L. Underhill to Charles Dillingham, July 21, 1941, box 21, Willkie Clubs Papers.
[116] Oren Root, Jr., to Russell W. Davenport, Dec. 12, 1941, Willkie Papers.

War's approach had made a difference to the presidential election's outcome, just as it had influenced convention delegates' selection of the GOP nominee. Some Republicans believed that the troubled global situation explained FDR's victory, thus arguing that it represented no mandate for New Deal liberalism.[117] Poll analyst Claude Robinson offered some support to this contention, concluding that the international crisis might have been decisive in Roosevelt's favor – that in the absence of any such crisis Willkie might have won. But he also emphasized that the results contained a sterner message for the party, about New Deal liberalism's continuing electoral power. "Somehow the Republican party has allowed itself to become stigmatized as the party that is against the workingman, against union labor, against social security and generally against the 'good life,'" he wrote, advocating urgent attention to the problem for the party to achieve any realistic chance of winning a majority.[118]

Poll-informed logic such as Robinson's met some resistance in the party, however. Like his candidate, Russell Davenport, *Fortune* magazine's managing editor and an advisor to Willkie, was a newcomer to party politics; his campaign dealings with Republicans caused him to note "a peculiar vein of sentimentality and lack of realism" within the party, encompassing a disinclination to believe poll results.[119] Indeed, Robert Taft attributed the 1940 defeat to excessive deference to the perceived dictates of public opinion, instead insisting that the path to success involved loyalty to Republican principles and their effective communication.[120] Thomas Dewey, by contrast, advised fellow Republicans that they should "never argue with the Gallup Poll."[121]

There was disagreement, too, about the contribution of Willkie's interventionism to the outcome. Anti-interventionists often concluded that "if we had been more definite and decided in our opposition to involvement in foreign wars, the result would have been different," in the words of one Republican.[122] Another believed "that if Mr. Willkie had taken a stand, at least, for delay in conscription and thereby put the administration in the position of the war party, he could have swept the country from Ohio west."[123] Willkie's supporters saw things differently. Raymond Buell saw the popular perception of Roosevelt as the more skilled in foreign policy as a contributory factor to Willkie's defeat. The party's isolationism, especially in Congress, prevented Willkie from better challenging this perception,

[117] See, for example: Robert P. Burroughs to New Hampshire Republican leaders, Jan. 16, 1941, Willkie Papers; Clarence Budington Kelland, speech, Sept. 22, 1941, box 784, Taft Papers.

[118] Claude Robinson, "The Roosevelt-Willkie Campaign: A Study of the Primary Social and Economic Determinants of the 1940 Presidential Election," Feb. 6, 1941, box 6, series 1, Hickenlooper Papers.

[119] [Russell W. Davenport,] "Notes on the Republican Party," n.d., box 43, Davenport Papers.

[120] Robert A. Taft to Colby Chester, Aug. 12, 1942, box 162, Taft Papers.

[121] Thomas E. Dewey to E. G. Bennett, Sept. 10, 1940, box 4, series 10, Dewey Papers.

[122] Frank O. Lowden to Ruth Simmons, Nov. 22, 1940, box 108, Hanna–McCormick Family Papers.

[123] Charles T. Wishart to Thomas A. O'Hara, Dec. 4, 1940, Willkie Papers.

according to Buell.[124] The stage was thus set for an intensification of the party debate about World War II.

Already a controversial figure in the party, Willkie became yet more divisive after his defeat. He was determined to transform the party, but the nature of its response to New Deal liberalism was not this project's main feature. His focus was instead foreign policy – to cut the party away from isolationism and ensure its commitment to internationalism. Willkie was not strongly situated to do so, however. As a failed presidential candidate, he had no official position; he thus had independence but no institutional authority. Many in the party saw his presidential campaign as flawed, and some saw his failure to assume an anti-interventionist position as a key flaw – sapping his informal authority.[125] Such Republicans had little inclination to follow Willkie's lead. But, for Willkie, their views constituted the problem he needed to solve.

Factional and personal jealousies overlaid ideological differences, intensifying the resistance to the Willkie project. His methods, too, encouraged conflict. Impatient with anti-interventionism's strength in the party – which he privately attributed to the influence of leading businesspeople who feared the wartime increase in government regulation of the economy and in taxation – he invested little energy in seeking compromise with his Republican opponents.[126] Alf Landon soon complained that Willkie apparently thought "that it's sound strategy to build up a reputation for sturdy independence by slapping some other Republican leader, or ignoring them."[127]

In encouraging the party to embrace internationalism, Willkie did not employ an argument that this was a way for the minority party to unlock the support of a majority. Instead, he argued that a failure to abandon anti-interventionism was likely to jeopardize the party's very existence. In support of such reasoning, a *New Republic* editorial posited that, in view of public support for aid to Britain, isolationist success in controlling the party would lead to Republican victory in only four or five states of the Midwest in 1944.[128] But this argument did not help Willkie to carry the party with him. Instead, he faced more and more opposition. "It is just like the Republican Party," wrote columnist Raymond Clapper in February 1941. "After these lean years it stumbles accidentally upon a man with real political sex appeal and promptly proceeds to toss him down the chute."[129]

Willkie's belief in the need to revitalize the party caused him to start action straight after his defeat. On November 11 he outlined a conception of "loyal

[124] *Berkshire Eagle* clipping, Dec. 4, 1940, box 46, Buell Papers.
[125] Frank O. Lowden to Ruth Simms, Nov. 22, 1940, box 108, Hanna–McCormick Family Papers; Charles T. Wishart to Thomas A. O'Hara, Dec. 4, 1940, Willkie Papers.
[126] Unsigned, Jan. 16, 1941, reel 45, *President Franklin D. Roosevelt's Office Files, 1933–1945*, part 4: *Subject Files* (Bethesda, Md.: University Publications of America, 1994).
[127] Alf M. Landon to Raymond Capper, Jan. 29, 1941, box 117, Landon Papers.
[128] *New Republic*, Jan. 27, 1941, 99.
[129] Clapper, *Watching the World*, 166–167.

opposition," involving constructive criticism of the administration. It was a vision that many Republicans rejected as a call for excessive cooperation with the administration.[130] Loyal opposition in practice then created more disquiet. Willkie fomented party strife when in early 1941 he announced support for the administration's lend-lease proposal, which undercut neutrality legislation by offering assistance to belligerents considered important to national security. Soon afterwards he visited the United Kingdom to see the war's impact there, on his return giving strong testimony in favor of the bill in Senate committee. Republican politicians were almost in unanimity against lend-lease, and key figures among them insisted that Willkie's actions, which helped secure the bill's passage, sacrificed his leadership position. Landon privately grumbled about Willkie's willingness to be "constantly running interference for the president," which "an opposition leader should never do."[131] Willkie saw a different imperative for the party. Before he left for London, Willkie had told a party group that "if the Republican party in this year of 1941 makes a blind opposition to this bill and allows itself to be presented to the American people as the isolationist party, it will never again gain control of the American government."[132] Later that year, historian Arthur M. Schlesinger, Jr., made a similar observation in comparing intraparty debate with party politics during the pre–Civil War sectional crisis, suggesting that the GOP was in danger of collapse as irrelevant to the nation's needs.[133]

Willkie won over few leading Republicans, but he achieved support elsewhere. A poll suggested that two in five people who had voted for Roosevelt in November now said that Willkie would be a good president – but one in four of his own voters viewed his actions with disappointment.[134] Such findings nevertheless suggested that most Republican voters supported lend-lease, strongly implying that Willkie was closer to the party's supporters than his Republican critics were.[135] The criticism he encountered – Representative William P. Lambertson of Kansas assaulted him as "America's No. 1 warmonger," for example – did not deflect Willkie from his advocacy of the administration's assistance for the Allies, though he continued to make some attacks on its inadequate preparedness for war.[136]

The Pearl Harbor attack and American entry in World War II in December 1941 collapsed anti-interventionism. That debate was over, but another began. Although controversy no longer surrounded war participation, the question of postwar involvement in structures of international cooperation became

[130] Johnson, *Republican Party and Wendell Willkie*, 165–167 (quotation, 166).

[131] Alf M. Landon to Arthur C. Smith, Sept. 25, 1941, box 111, Landon Papers.

[132] Neal, *Dark Horse*, 186–207 (quotation, 190–191).

[133] *The Nation*, Dec. 6, 1941, 561–564 (quotation, 564).

[134] George Gallup, "Willkie's Action Wins Nation-Wide Support," clipping, [March 1, 1941,] box 46, Buell Papers.

[135] Johnson, *Republican Party and Wendell Willkie*, 173.

[136] Neal, *Dark Horse*, 207–216; William P. Lambertson, speech, Oct. 23, 1941, box 50, Nye Papers.

important, and Willkie thought the need for the party to repudiate isolationism remained as urgent as ever. He urged the RNC to issue such a repudiation,
then choosing to interpret a compromise resolution affirming a commitment to
postwar international cooperation as a success for his cause. His next step was
to ensure that party candidates embraced this internationalism.[137] Suspicious
of Dewey's tardy conversion to internationalism, Willkie encouraged opposition to his quest for the 1942 New York gubernatorial nomination. "Wendell
is going around the State offering the nomination to everybody over the age of
21 who has been in the Republican Party any length of time," Dewey wrote.[138]
Neither this effort nor a short-lived draft-Willkie operation impeded Dewey's
nomination victory, however; that fall Dewey would win the governorship,
strengthening his position as a presidential aspirant, gaining influence as
Willkie's ebbed. Ready to speak out against the renomination of officeholding Republicans – an unusual and controversial action for a party's titular
leader – Willkie nevertheless limited such active opposition to the nationally
notorious case of Representative Hamilton Fish of New York. He declined to
assist other internationalist candidates "even though I were stuffy enough to
think I ought to," citing insufficient time, and remembering FDR's failed 1938
purge of conservative Democrats.[139]

Though insubstantial, these activities unsurprisingly earned Willkie considerable enmity within the party. A spring 1943 poll of leading activists in Indiana,
Willkie's childhood state, found nine in ten opposed to his candidacy for the
1944 presidential nomination. "We need no Willkies," wrote one. "He con-
curs with this Administration's internationalist and interventionist program too
much. What we need is a President who will first minister unto his own house-
hold, for his that does not, the Scripture tells us, is worse than an infidel."[140]

Hoping to foster party unity on foreign policy, leading Republicans
convened a September 1943 conference at Mackinac Island, Michigan, to
discuss the postwar outlook domestically as well as internationally. Willkie
did not receive an invitation. Republicans there adopted a commitment to
"[r]esponsible participation by the U.S. in postwar cooperative organization among sovereign nations to prevent military aggression and to attain
permanent peace with organized justice in a free world." The Mackinac
declarations won praise for success in moving beyond the party's anti-interventionist past, but there was skepticism, too, about the depth of the new-
found unity and the genuineness of the apparent transcendence of significant
differences about foreign policy.[141] The Mackinac statement was "something

---

[137] Robert A. Taft to Hulbert Taft, April 27, 1942, box 785, Taft Papers.
[138] Thomas E. Dewey to Ruth Hanna McCormick Simms, May 8, 1942, box 48, series 1, Dewey
    Papers.
[139] Wendell L. Willkie to Bartley C. Crum, Aug. 11, 1942, Willkie Papers.
[140] Harrison E. Spangler to B. B. Hickenlooper, April 5, 1943, box 10, series 2, Hickenlooper
    Papers.
[141] *Boston Herald* clipping, Sept. 8, 1943; Cleveland, Ohio, *Plain Dealer* clipping, Sept 8, 1943.
    both in box 4, series 2, Hickenlooper Papers.

out of Alice in Wonderland," according to one journalist.[142] Another noted
that it was "so shrewdly drawn that it won the indorsement of the most
advanced internationalists and the most rabid isolationists who took part in
the project."[143]

By the time of the Mackinac meeting, the demands of 1944 electoral politics were on the minds of Republicans. Some intraparty unity on the vex-
ing question of postwar international organization was not the only prize
that participating Republicans sought. They also looked for an absence of
significant conflict in this regard between the parties, because this allowed
campaign debate to shift to the home front and to what they considered an
advantageous emphasis on liberty against the Democratic agenda's socializing
drift.[144] On foreign policy, Mackinac placed the party closer to the center of
public opinion, now decisively different from the interwar mood that had been
friendly to neutrality. In 1943, three in four poll respondents said the nation
should take a larger role in world affairs after than before World War II and
four in five supported wartime steps toward a postwar plan "to set up with
our Allies a world organization to maintain the future peace of our world."[145]
The party's turn toward internationalism was often an acceptance of geopolitical as well as electoral reality; many Republicans reached the conclusion
that the old emphasis on neutrality was obsolete, though differences remained
about the best way to promote peace. They did not need Willkie to help them
in reaching this conclusion.[146]

When Willkie turned his attention to domestic matters, he returned to his
1940 theme that the New Deal was an economic failure but its social goals
deserved protection and development. He now placed yet more emphasis on
the latter than the former. His critique of the obstacles facing free enterprise
now stressed the inadequacies of business leadership as well as the stifling
impact of government regulation. "Some of the talk we hear about 'free enterprise' or 'private enterprise' is just propaganda on the part of powerful groups
who have not practiced real enterprise in a generation, and have no intention
of doing so," he wrote, calling for greater worker involvement in the enterprise system.[147] He also questioned the defense of states' rights by arguing that
economic and government efficiency depended on federal power; in Willkie's
eyes, Republican antistatism should be revised to insist on the federal government's proper use, rather than boosting state and local governments at
its expense.[148] Such statements intensified party disquietude about his me-
too agenda; his opponents within the party encouraged and exploited this

[142] *Washington Daily News* clipping, Sept. 8, 1943, box 4, series 2, Hickenlooper Papers.

[143] *Baltimore Sun* clipping, Sept. 8, 1943, box 4, series 2, Hickenlooper Papers.

[144] *Saturday Evening Post*, Dec. 11, 1943, 17, 50–52, 57.

[145] Jerome S. Bruner, *Mandate From the People* (New York: Duell, Sloan and Pearce, 1944), 233–235 (quotation, 234).

[146] Blum, *V Was for Victory*, 271–275.

[147] Barnard, *Wendell Willkie*, 429.

[148] Johnson, *Republican Party and Wendell Willkie*, 287.

characterization of his views in order to discredit them and him.[149] Some discontented club activists launched the Associated Ex-Willkie Workers Against Willkie; its chair attacked Willkie for "simply opposing the New Deal for not being New-Dealish enough."[150]

Especially notable was Willkie's position on civil liberties and civil rights. Willkie displayed his credentials as a civil libertarian in ways scarcely less remarkable than his internationalist project. In private law practice, he successfully represented the secretary of the California Communist Party in the Supreme Court, a Russian American appealing his citizenship's revocation on the grounds that he had concealed his party membership when seeking naturalization.[151] But it was the cause of racial equality that absorbed his special attention.[152] He developed a friendship with Walter White, who entirely revised his earlier skepticism about Willkie's commitment to civil rights, on Willkie's death commenting that "Negroes have lost one of the truest friends they have ever had."[153] He later stated that a second Willkie presidential candidacy might have attracted the support of three in four African Americans, while Roosevelt was sure to achieve a similar majority in competition with any other Republican.[154] Doubtless an exaggeration, White's estimate nevertheless reveals Willkie's success in articulating his concern about racial inequality.

Willkie pursued his agenda to transform the party by seeking its 1944 nomination; "his aim was no less than the political, moral, and social regeneration of the Republican Party," an aide later noted.[155] But consolidation of the Willkie agenda – support for the administration's socioeconomic goals but opposition to its methods as wasteful, ineffective, dictatorial – faced strategic, constituency-based obstacles that an Indiana Republican perceptively identified. On the one hand, Representative Charles M. LaFollette found it difficult to persuade businesspeople that the goals were worthy. For them, the nature of Willkie's challenge to the New Deal was too weak. On the other hand, it was no easier to convince workers of administration shortcomings. "They refuse to see, or don't understand, the dangers inherent in the Rooseveltian method," LaFollette explained to Willkie.[156] This was an insightful analysis of the difficulties in crafting an alternative to New Deal liberalism likely to win mass support. The prospect of intraparty enthusiasm for such an agenda was even more unlikely; Willkie's effort to revitalize the party by discussing the shortcomings of its message and messengers did not easily garner widespread Republican support. Willkie set himself an especially challenging task

[149] *Des Moines Register* clipping, June 21, 1944, box 10, series 2, Hickenlooper Papers; Adelaide Walker to Russell W. Davenport, April 13, 1944, box 42, Davenport Papers.
[150] Robert Paterson to Carroll Reece (form letter), n.d., Willkie Papers.
[151] Neal, *Dark Horse*, 267–271.
[152] *Look*, Oct. 5, 1943, 25–27.
[153] Walter White to Metz Lochard, Oct. 8, 1944, box A673, series II, NAACP Records.
[154] Walter White, "Will the Negro Elect Our Next President?" n.d., box A83, series II, NAACP Records.
[155] Adelaide Walker to Russell W. Davenport, April 13, 1944, box 42, Davenport Papers.
[156] Charles M. LaFollette to Wendell L. Willkie, Sept. 24, 1943, Willkie Papers.

by actively waging a primary campaign in Wisconsin, where the isolationist tradition was particularly strong. It was a challenge he failed. Gaining no delegates at all, Willkie proved the party's refusal to accept his ideas' wisdom.[157] He withdrew from the nomination contest, a defeat that Democrats sometimes employed as proof of their opponents' deep conservatism, out of tune with the people. "The Willkie of 1944 was a John the Baptist crying in the wilderness of a Republican reaction," commented one.[158]

Willkie's efforts to recast the GOP reflected his discomfort with the existing lines of conflict between and within the parties. After the collapse of his nomination quest, he developed a new political interest, which Gifford Pinchot reported to FDR. Willkie contemplated the desirability of a more coherent party system, one that concentrated liberals in the Democratic Party and conservatives in the Republican Party. The idea was also attractive to Roosevelt, who, frustrated by conservative Democrats' opposition, sought a more progressively focused party. Despite the New Deal coalition's electoral strength, its diversity undermined its utility as a vehicle for liberalism. "From the liberals of both parties Willkie and I together can form a new, really liberal party in America," Roosevelt told aide Samuel I. Rosenman. Although no such development was possible in the shorter term, he invited Willkie to a meeting that Willkie postponed until after the elections. Because Willkie died in early October 1944, the meeting never took place.[159]

One reason why many Republicans were disinclined to listen to Willkie was a growing confidence in conservatism's electoral strength. War mobilization's demands seemed to expose the shortcomings of the administration's economic management; there was ample evidence of waste and inefficiency – the inescapable result of war's challenges, but in Republican eyes the product of New Deal liberalism's deficiencies. But this confidence was misplaced because there was no real sign during the war of a rightward shift. "Gradually the slogan of 'As Little Government as Possible' is coming to read 'As Much Government as Necessary,'" commented Jerome S. Bruner, an analyst of public opinion, in 1944.[160] Still, the war's electoral impact favored the GOP for practical reasons; wartime dislocations were likelier to prevent Democratic than Republican supporters from voting.

The nation's adjustment to war was unquestionably difficult, leading to a decline in the incumbent Democrats' support, fostering this new Republican optimism. In 1942 military setbacks compounded apparent shortcomings in the home front's mobilization to meet the needs of war, encouraging a perception of poor management.[161] As in the late 1930s, many Republicans concluded

---

157 Barnard, *Wendell Willkie*, 444–469.
158 Mark Ethridge, "For What the Hell Should We Apologize?" (DNC leaflet), May 15, 1944, box 100, PPSF, Hoover Papers.
159 Rosenman, *Working with Roosevelt*, 423–429 (quotation, 423).
160 Bruner, *Mandate From the People*, 153–222 (quotation, 209).
161 Richard N. Chapman, *Contours of Public Policy, 1939–1945* (New York: Garland, 1981), 187–190.

that there was a reasserction of conservatism when, at best, there was simply disappointment with the Democrats' record – rather than any larger rejection of New Deal liberalism.[162] In late September, Frank E. Gannett, RNC assistant chair, told congressional Republicans that Americans were "disgusted with the bungling, confusion and inefficiency that we witness every day." Still, the current midterm campaign involved larger concerns because of the wartime expansion of executive powers. Commending the protection of democracy as a winning issue, Gannett said that "victory on all continents and the Seven Seas will amount to nothing if the New Deal and other left wing groups succeed in destroying our Constitution."[163] Not all Republicans took such a confrontational approach. Dewey perceived public recognition of "what a confused, inadequate and bad job is being done in Washington," but preferred "to let these incompetent New Dealers stew in their own juice and discuss merely state issues."[164] He more calmly spoke to wartime frustrations by calling for better government, as well as New York tax reform and fair reapportionment that was likely to tackle rural overrepresentation usually in the Republicans' favor.[165] But in fall 1942 it was more common for Republicans to sense the decline of public confidence in New Deal liberalism.[166]

Willkie made a hundred-dollar bet in May 1942 that Republicans were likely to suffer further significant congressional losses that fall because their organizational efforts could not match the Democrats' machine strength and because the political impact of federal spending also disfavored them.[167] Willkie was wrong. Republicans made spectacular gains. The results were good enough to allow the RNC to issue a press release entitled, "The Republican Party Is Now Supported By The Majority Of The Voters" – pointing out that in 1942 there was a combined vote of 53.9 percent for the party's House of Representatives candidates and 57.7 percent for its gubernatorial candidates.[168] Willkie was right, however, that a party's successful mobilization of supporters was a significant determinant of its prospects. Wartime dislocations of military service and migration hit the Democratic Party harder, and its voters were less likely to go to the polls than Republican supporters.[169] A similar pattern was subsequently evident in local elections in 1943, causing a White House pollster to conclude that there was no Republican trend, that the Democratic coalition remained strong; Democrats simply needed to tackle their problem of participation.[170]

[162] Raymond L. Buell to Henry R. Luce, Nov. 5, 1942, Willkie Papers.
[163] RNC press release, Sept. 30, 1942, box 366, Burton Papers.
[164] Thomas E. Dewey to Alf M. Landon, Aug. 5, 1942, box 24, series 10, Dewey Papers.
[165] Smith, *Thomas E. Dewey*, 349–350.
[166] Blum, *V Was for Victory*, 221–234.
[167] John B. Hollister, "Memorandum of Bet Made with Wendell Willkie on May 27, 1942," Willkie Papers.
[168] RNC, news release, July 19, 1943, box 162, Taft Papers.
[169] Hadley Cantril and John Harding, "The 1942 Elections: A Case Study in Political Psychology," *POQ* 7 (1943), 230–233.
[170] Louis H. Bean to Isador Lubin and Harry Hopkins, Feb. 4, 1944, reel 32, *President Franklin D. Roosevelt's Office Files*, part 4.

Republicans did not always recognize this advantage, and from his New York perspective Dewey suspected that the Democratic coalition's urban nature facilitated mobilization. "Our difficulty, of course, is that it is easier to walk a block and cast a Democratic vote in New York City than it is to get out the Ford and drive ten miles to cast a Republican vote upstate," he observed in September 1943.[171] It is true that the GOP coalition was more rural and the Democratic coalition was more urban, but turnout actually helped Republicans. War boosted this advantage.

The special wartime case of weak turnout among soldiers – a group more supportive of the Democrats – assisted the Republicans. Very few filed an absentee ballot in 1942. A "war ballot" established by Congress in September as an alternative to state ballots exempted soldiers from the registration and poll-tax laws in the individual states, though not from other suffrage requirements. The lateness of its creation contributed to the war ballot's ineffectiveness as a way of boosting the vote. An effort therefore began in 1943 to improve the war ballot in an administration-supported proposal to establish stronger federal regulation. The battle over voter qualifications became an important one. The stakes were high for Republicans; as congressional debate developed, polls suggested that three in five servicepeople intended to vote for FDR, enough to ensure Republican defeat. The stakes were high, too, for southern segregationists, who saw that any federal legislation attacked their states' ability to exclude African Americans from voting. Republicans therefore found common ground with conservative Democrats in opposing the bill, advocating an alternative that was more deferential to state voting laws. This antiliberal version of the war ballot triumphed, and in 1944 – as in 1942 – few servicepeople used it; only twenty states certified the federal ballot. The debate nevertheless encouraged thirty-eight states to improve their own laws in order to facilitate absentee voting by military personnel. However, soldier turnout in 1944 remained low – marginally lower than one in two.[172]

Wartime conditions seemed to remove any rationale for belief in the bought vote. Relief rolls greatly declined, and many who had experienced economic hardship were now enjoying plentiful work and higher wages – if also shortages and rising prices.[173] Indeed, one analyst attributed the Republicans' 1942 gains primarily to the drastic reduction of the WPA, finding little change of party choice among other groups but noting that between 1938 and 1942 the number of WPA workers, mostly supportive of the Democrats, became much smaller.[174] Belief in the bought vote nonetheless persisted. An article in the 1944 national convention's official program revealed Republicans' acceptance that the bought vote remained a factor in electoral politics, suggesting

[171] Thomas E. Dewey to Bourke B. Hickenlooper, Sept. 24, 1943, box 10, series 2, Hickenlooper Papers.
[172] Boyd S. Martin, "The Service Vote in the Elections of 1944," *APSR* 39 (1945), 720–732.
[173] Blum, *V Was for Victory*, 222.
[174] John Harding, "The 1942 Congressional Elections," *APSR* 38 (1944), 56–58.

the influence of Rogers Dunn's analysis: "If the rule of thumb ratio of four votes to every payroller is applied, this means the Republican candidate, who is almost certain to be pledged to reduce Federal civilian employment drastically, will start out by spotting his opponent some 12,000,000 votes."[175]

More significantly, despite the WPA's disappearance, Republicans developed a more sophisticated version of the bought-vote thesis to see the Democratic Party's politics of interest-group pluralism as vote-buying behavior, placing the administration's friendliness to labor and African Americans within this framework.[176] This was an understanding of electoral politics that Republican speakers used as a way to attack their opponents. At a 1944 campaign rally, vice-presidential candidate John W. Bricker said that "there would be no question in the mind of any person here about the outcome of the election if the free judgment of the American people divorced from selfish interests were to be registered." Still another administration use of money for electoral gain, Bricker argued, was funding for government publicity, intended to change public opinion in its favor.[177] The sense that Democratic largesse stacked the odds against Republican prospects thus remained.

In policy terms, Republicans were securing more influence. The defeat of the liberal bill to improve soldiers' access to the polls was just one example of the conservative coalition's wartime success. Between 1942 and 1945 southern Democrats joined with Republicans in opposition to nonsouthern Democrats in 23 percent of important Senate votes. The conservative coalition there was more visible, cohesive, and successful than it had been during the New Deal.[178] "For the past two years," observed Senator Carl A. Hatch, a New Mexico Democrat, in summer 1944, "the Republican minority, aided by certain elements among the Democrats, has controlled the United States Senate."[179] On many occasions Republicans thus achieved their goal to check New Deal liberalism across such diverse areas as business regulation, agriculture, social welfare, labor, education, and civil rights.[180]

One of the conservative coalition's achievements was the 1943 Smith-Connally Act, intended to attack labor, placing wartime restrictions on strike action and restricting the contributions of labor organizations and corporations to political parties. Its passage intensified labor concerns about the conservative drift in Washington and about the 1942 campaign, which revealed the Democratic Party's shortcomings of voter mobilization. These concerns led CIO leaders to create the Political Action Committee (PAC), designed to

---

[175] C. M. Oehler, "Elephant Faces Stirring Campaign," "The Republican 23rd National Convention, Chicago, Illinois, June 1944: Official Program," 24–25, 58, box 101, PPSF, Hoover Papers.

[176] Alf M. Landon to William K. Hutchinson, Oct. 12, 1944, box 125, Landon Papers.

[177] RNC, "It's Time to Change," n.d., box 12, series 2, Hickenlooper Papers.

[178] John Robert Moore, "The Conservative Coalition in the United States Senate, 1942–1945," *Journal of Southern History* 33 (1967), 372–373.

[179] Allen Drury, *A Senate Journal, 1943–1945* (New York: McGraw-Hill, 1963), 241.

[180] Moore, "Conservative Coalition," 374–375.

promote the participation in elections not only of union members but of other sympathetic groups too, to apply the unions' organizational skills to the electoral arena. Under Sidney Hillman of the Amalgamated Clothing Workers of America, the PAC was ready to support friendly Republican candidates for Congress while operating primarily for the Democrats' benefit through an extensive grassroots network.

Labor soon claimed some successes during the 1944 primary season in aiding some challengers to conservative Democratic incumbents; Martin Dies, who was starting a congressional investigation of the PAC, withdrew from his renomination campaign when an organization drive substantially increased voter registration in his district. After FDR's renomination – when the president acknowledged labor's importance to his party by consulting Hillman over the selection of Harry S. Truman as his running mate in Henry Wallace's place – Hillman formed the National Citizens Political Action Committee (NC-PAC) to pursue a progressively focused education and registration drive as a way to comply with Smith-Connally restrictions on labor activity. NC-PAC's liberalism attracted some key figures of old Republican progressivism; George Norris was honorary chair, and Gifford Pinchot served on its executive committee.[181] The Hatch Acts' regulation of campaign finance made such outside organizations, now actively encouraged by both parties, all the more important.[182]

Though many congressional Republicans feared it, some in the party insisted that labor's political power was an opportunity, not a threat. National chair Harrison E. Spangler said that the PAC's political muscle was likely to drive American Federation of Labor (AFL) unions toward the Republicans and that strikes at home won votes for the party among soldiers overseas.[183] Right-leaning columnist Frank R. Kent advised Dewey to prioritize opposition to labor radicalism in his campaign, "because the full story of this New Deal–C.I.O.–Communist fourth term combination is as sinister and cynical a one as our political history contains."[184]

Thomas E. Dewey, the Republican presidential candidate, made campaign use of anticommunism, but he was confident in a broader domestic agenda as likely to bring victory. In June he observed that "every day of successful war brings us closer to the time when our people will be thinking of the domestic future of the United States. Certainly, if they can give their full attention to domestic problems, they will vote Roosevelt out unanimously."[185] A White House poll of March supported the view that war decisively shaped electoral politics, reporting a majority for FDR over Dewey by 51 to 32 percent if war persisted, but a majority for Dewey by 51 to 30 percent if peace

---

[181] Matthew Josephson, *Sidney Hillman: Statesman of American Labor* (Garden City, N.Y.: Doubleday, 1952), 590–627.
[182] Louise Overacker, "Presidential Campaign Funds, 1944," *APSR* 39 (1945), 899–925.
[183] *Collier's*, July 29, 1944, 21, 29–30.
[184] *Des Moines Register* clipping, July 14, 1944, box 10, series 2, Hickenlooper Papers.
[185] Thomas E. Dewey to Alf M. Landon, June 6, 1944, box 24, series 10, Dewey Papers.

returned.[186] Reconversion issues thus favored Dewey, even though confidence in Roosevelt's liberalism stayed strong, according to other White House polls – social security, as well as national security, was a strength for the president.[187]

At the start of the 1944 campaign, domestic problems were uppermost for three in four Americans, anxious first about reconversion and jobs, and then about a durable peace.[188] Dewey aimed to elevate reconversion's salience as an issue. In a September speech, he asked, "Shall we expose our country to a return of the seven years of New Deal depression because my opponent is indispensable to the ill-assorted, power-hungry conglomeration of city bosses, Communists and career bureaucrats which now compose the New Deal?"[189] But, in time, reconversion played less significantly to the Republicans' advantage. According to polls, voters accepted the Republican argument that the party was capable of better government management than the Democrats. The Republican association with depression remained powerful, however; many saw the Democrats as likelier to secure prosperity.[190] Dewey was, therefore, wrong to suspect that domestic issues unequivocally pushed voters toward his party. But he was right to see that many considered a change at the White House as likely to impede the war's end.

Roosevelt won again. Some interpretations of his fourth-term victory attributed critical credit to PAC activity in mobilizing the Democratic vote, especially in big cities.[191] In response to PAC success, Republicans rediscovered the wisdom of John Hamilton's emphasis on the importance of organization and the party's need to construct a permanent bureaucracy. This was the campaign's key lesson, Dewey and national chair Herbert Brownell, Jr., both emphasized.[192] One attraction of this analysis was its avoidance of policy questions that might encourage intraparty division. Another attraction was its popularity among rank-and-file party workers, for whom weak organization made sense as an explanation for defeat.[193] Another factor that Republicans discussed was the need for better publicity (especially between campaigns because current research in public opinion suggested campaigns

---

[186] Hadley Cantril and Gerald B. Lambert, poll report, March 17, 1944, reel 32, *President Franklin D. Roosevelt's Office Files*, part 4.

[187] Hadley Cantril and Gerald B. Lambert, poll report, Jan. 4, 1944, reel 32, *President Franklin D. Roosevelt's Office Files*, part 4; Opinion Research Corporation, report, Aug. 21, 1944, box 11, series 2, Hickenlooper Papers. About one in three respondents to the administration poll said that Roosevelt was too liberal.

[188] Hadley Cantril, poll report, Sept. 7, 1944, reel 32, *President Franklin D. Roosevelt's Office Files*, part 4; "Election Forecast," Oct. 30, 1944, box 366, Burton Papers.

[189] Thomas E. Dewey, speech, Sept. 25, 1944, box 12, series 2, Hickenlooper Papers.

[190] Strunk, *Public Opinion*, 621–643.

[191] *Newsweek*, Nov. 13, 1944, 2–5.

[192] Thomas E. Dewey to Katharine Kennedy Brown, Jan. 8, 1945, box 24, series 4, Dewey Papers; Herbert Brownell, Jr., "The Republicans' Future Role," Jan. 21, 1945, box 38, series 2, Dewey Papers.

[193] *Saturday Evening Post*, Oct. 27, 1945, 14–15, 37.

made relatively little difference to voter evaluations of the parties).[194] In principle neutral in ideological terms, the publicity explanation for defeat was more popular among conservatives because it suggested that the party's message did not need to change, but only the effectiveness of its communication needed to change.[195]

The concern about organization led to the creation of an RNC division for liaison with African American and ethnic communities and a section on candidate recruitment.[196] The urban interest that these efforts reflected was important. As one observer noted in 1942, "Problem Number One for the GOP is to rebuild its power in America's big cities."[197] It remained so in 1944. Huge Democratic pluralities in the cities were responsible for overturning Republican extraurban success in the party's pre-Depression Northeast and Midwest strongholds. Indeed, in many highly populated states, important in the electoral college, the cities were largely if not overwhelmingly responsible for Democratic victory.[198]

But Republicans often viewed their urban challenge with unease, many preferring to assail the power of PAC and big-city bosses in attacks that sometimes revealed discomfort with the mass electorate. Walter S. Hallanan, an RNC member from West Virginia, told Dewey that he "would far rather be a member of a united and virile minority under the inspiring leadership of solid and upstanding Americans like yourself and John Bricker than to be identified with a decadent majority which finds its leadership and strength in political and economic groups whose philosophy of government is alien."[199] Arizona's Clarence Budington Kelland similarly condemned the electorate's "decadence" in explaining Dewey's defeat, seeing the New Deal as corrosive of "the ultimate integrity of of [sic] our citizens" and bemoaning the impact of recent decades' immigration. Kelland wrote that "the American as we have always understood him, exists now only in a small minority."[200] Such thinking suggested obstacles of understanding and imagination to serious efforts to confront the GOP's urban problem. Though not all shared this unease, the party's constituency and its officeholding base gave its leaders a greater degree of affinity with rural and small-town America.

---

194 Opinion Research Corporation, report, Nov. 11, 1944, box 100, PPSF, Hoover Papers; Lazarsfeld et al., *The People's Choice.*
195 See, for example, Clarence Budington Kelland to Thomas E. Dewey, Nov. 9, 1944, box 94, series 4, Dewey Papers; Katharine Kennedy Brown to Thomas E. Dewey, Dec. 28, 1944, box 24, series 4, Dewey Papers; Robert A. Taft to Charles D. Hilles, May 21, 1945, box 786, Taft Papers.
196 Herbert Brownell with John P. Burke, *Advising Ike: The Memoirs of Attorney General Herbert Brownell* (Lawrence: University Press of Kansas, 1993), 69.
197 *The Republican*, July 1942, 29.
198 Eldersveld, "Influence of Metropolitan Party Pluralities."
199 Walter S. Hallanan to Thomas E. Dewey, Jan. 20, 1945, box 74, series 4, Dewey Papers.
200 Clarence Budington Kelland to Thomas E. Dewey, Nov. 9, 1944, box 94, series 4, Dewey Papers.

Republicans differed about the 1944 results' policy implications. A journalist working in the Senate noted that some Republicans there concluded that they indicated a need for the party to liberalize its domestic and foreign policies. The response of others, more commonly, was quite different: "With twenty-two million votes? Why should we liberalize? What do you mean, *liberalize*? We're doing all right."[201] The view that things were "all right" – or even better – still insisted that the 1938 and 1942 gains provided evidence of a pro-Republican drift. According to this view, the 1940 and 1944 disappointments were not testimony of the New Deal coalition's enduring power, but occasions when war saved FDR from otherwise likely defeat.[202] The president, Hoover-era RNC publicity director Henry J. Allen told Dewey, "used his Commander-in-Chief badge with great cunning and effectiveness" to win.[203]

Such analysis suggested that "the simple barefoot Wall Street lawyer's" impact on the party's understanding of its minority problem was slender at best. At worst, his 1940 defeat merely fed the argument that moderation was not the right strategy to maximize the party's vote. In terms of domestic policy, there were few signs of more Republican enthusiasm for the emphasis on engagement with human problems that Willkie counseled. Willkie's impact on the development of Republican ideas about foreign policy is also open to question. There is no doubt that his noisy charisma and commitment to the internationalist cause ensured that he had prominence in the debate between internationalists and anti-interventionists. But other Republicans embraced the need to rethink anti-interventionist ideas with World War II's arrival. Moreover, as conflicts over Cold War bipartisanship would reveal, a modified form of the debate persisted within the party beyond Willkie.

Willkie retained symbolic importance in the party for decades to come. His posthumous reputation was not informed by his ability to attack New Deal liberalism in ways that garnered new support for the party, but by his Wall Street connections. His candidacy consolidated a new form of regional conflict among Republicans. No longer was a schism with western progressives the party's key sectional division. Instead, many noneasterners in the party now identified the East as dissident, disruptive, divisive. They saw the East's financial and business interests as exercising influence within the party to support an internationalist and me-too agenda, also noting the role of media conglomerates in promoting Willkie and internationalism. *Fortune*'s role in publicizing Willkie's political ideas and in providing his campaign with personnel was especially evident, but Henry R. Luce and his Time–Life publications made a more wide-ranging contribution to the moderate, anti-isolationist cause within the party. Another Willkie enthusiast in the media world, though not based in the East, was Gardner Cowles, Jr., of *Look* magazine and the *Des Moines Register and Tribune*; Cowles's brother, John, who ran Minneapolis newspapers, also

[201] Drury, *Senate Journal*, 294.
[202] *Fortune*, April 1947, 77–85, 213–228.
[203] Henry J. Allen to Thomas E. Dewey, n.d., box 3, series 4, Dewey Papers.

engaged in GOP politics. Such support amounted to an unfair advantage, Willkie's Republican opponents thought. The Willkie episode convinced them that money and the media were against them.

The perception that Willkie blurred policy differences with the Democrats for electoral advantage, but lost, encouraged the belief among conservative Republicans that they should remain true to principle in pursuit of victory.[204] In losing his battles both to topple Roosevelt and to reshape the Republican Party, Willkie thus undermined his argument about the party's future and bolstered his Republican opponents' analysis of the minority problem.

[204] Gould, *Grand Old Party*, 265–287.

4

"Liberty versus Socialism": 1945–1953

Both pessimism and optimism characterized the GOP outlook on peace's return. On the one hand, the Democrats' policy ambitions kindled Republican pessimism. Many in the party had a dark view of the liberal agenda that Harry S. Truman pursued as president; Truman assumed the presidency on Franklin Roosevelt's death in April 1945, not long before the end of World War II in Europe. According to Senator Robert A. Taft, writing in 1949, "the Truman program contains a series of police-state measures to attain Utopia, which, taken together, would completely destroy liberty in the United States, impair justice and equality and subject every American family to the dictates of an all-powerful state."[1] On the other hand, a climate of electoral optimism accompanied the gloom-laden policy outlook. This optimism reflected the belief that the administration's pursuit of what Truman called the "Fair Deal" was sure to alienate a majority of Americans; its return to the concerns of New Deal liberalism encouraged many Republicans to conclude that their victory was certain. In 1950, Republican politicians made the point explicit by adopting the theme of "liberty versus socialism" for their midterm campaign.

Republican confidence was misplaced, however. The party did make gains during this period, but not because of a generalized turn away from New Deal liberalism. In 1946, the problems of postwar reconversion created discontent with the incumbent Democrats. The subsequent success of the early 1950s was thanks to the arrival of fresh concerns that targeted different dissatisfactions with the in-party, summarized in 1952 as "Korea, Communism, and Corruption." It was thanks, too, to the arrival of a newcomer to electoral politics as the Republicans' presidential candidate, Dwight D. Eisenhower, who restored the party at last to the White House.

The implications of a World War II hero's political malaise overseas helped inform the new alarm that infected the party. Winston Churchill's Conservative Party suffered a landslide defeat in the United Kingdom's 1945 general election. In government, the victorious Labour Party vigorously pursued the

---

[1] *Look*, May 10, 1949, 23–25.

construction of a welfare state, the National Health Service at its vanguard, and the nationalization of key industries. Parallels between Labour's policies and the administration's Fair Deal agenda became a central strand of how many Republicans perceived the Democrats' goals and an element of how they attacked Democratic proposals. The Fair Deal was, according to Senator Hugh Butler of Nebraska, for example, socialist in intent because of its resemblance to Labour's explicitly socialist policies.[2] More broadly, Republicans characterized their concerns as American by contrast with their opponents' affinity with foreign socialism and even communism. Taft exemplified this argument in 1952 by referring to the New Deal as "a program imported from Europe."[3] Urging fellow southerners to turn to the GOP, journalist William Bradford Huie condemned the Roosevelt and Truman administrations' "Russia-worshippers" who "have labored to convert America into the monolithic, one-party, socialistic state – one member of a world organization of monolithic, one-party, socialistic states."[4] The parallels were not new, but – nurtured by the early Cold War's climate of concern about communism, as well as by the tide of welfarism in other countries – they became more numerous and vehement.

These attacks achieved some success in challenging the Democratic Party's liberalizing trajectory. Republicans and conservative Democrats defeated many Fair Deal proposals; there was no significant expansion of New Deal reform during the Truman years. As the Fair Deal's fortunes languished in legislative torpor and as Republicans assailed Democrats for harboring dangerously socialistic designs for the nation, the goals and ambitions of the Democratic Party as a whole became more modest, more moderate.[5] Truman even sought to preempt Republican proposals in some key areas, including labor relations, wage and price controls, the federal budget, and anticommunism.[6] In this sense, the period was one of progress for the minority party's concerns. The Democrats' modification of their party's policy agenda helped them to maintain the support of a majority, however.

The 1946 elections gave Republicans their first taste of federal-level power since the New Deal's arrival. Voters signaled dissatisfaction with the Democratic record in handling the inescapably difficult transition from war to peace, characterized by economic woes of unemployment, inflation, and

[2] "Statement submitted by Senator Hugh Butler," n.d. [c. early 1950], box 787, Taft Papers.
[3] Robert A. Taft, speech, April 22, 1948, in Clarence E. Wunderlin, Jr., ed., *The Papers of Robert A. Taft*, vol. III: *1945–1948* (Kent, Ohio: Kent State University Press, 2003), 424.
[4] *American Mercury*, Oct. 1951, 3–11.
[5] Jonathan Bell, *The Liberal State on Trial: The Cold War and American Politics in the Truman Years* (New York: Columbia University Press, 2004); Alonzo L. Hamby, "The Clash of Perspectives and the Need for a New Synthesis," in Richard S. Kirkendall, ed., *The Truman Period as a Research Field: A Reappraisal* (Columbia: University of Missouri Press, 1974), 113–148.
[6] Anthony Badger, "Republican Rule in the 80th Congress," in Dean McSweeney and John E. Owens, eds., *The Republican Takeover of Congress* (Basingstoke, U.K.: Macmillan, 1998), 176–177.

shortages. Catching the spirit of protest, the party's principal midterm slogan asked voters, "Had enough?"[7] Republicans made net gains of twelve seats in the Senate and fifty-four in the House of Representatives to secure control of both bodies, with a 54.3 percent share of the two-party vote in House contests. The RNC analysis of the results emphasized success in eroding the New Deal coalition, claiming major progress among urbanites, African Americans, foreign-born voters, and young people. It also celebrated party success among veterans, women, and members of organized labor. Labor's political power, a Republican concern in 1944, no longer seemed so formidable; most candidates endorsed by the CIO Political Action Committee and the National Citizens PAC experienced defeat.[8]

But often those who switched to the Republican Party were dissatisfied with the shorter-term problems of reconversion, and they had not had enough of New Deal liberalism more generally. The urban, rather than rural, nature of the Republican resurgence reflected the cities' greater susceptibility to the impact of price rises, while low turnout suggested that the failure of Democratic supporters to cast a vote – their abstention rather than their defection, let alone conversion – helped account for Republican victories. These abstentions, according to analyst Louis Bean, totaled as many as nine million, numbering seven million on the Democratic side but just two million on the Republican.[9] The Republican National Committee's own analysis of public opinion suggested that the theme of "stabilization" was especially salient, a reflection of insecurities about the future, anxieties about rising prices, and the threat of unemployment. One finding was suggestive of New Deal liberalism's power in a way surprising to staffer Zach Taylor. The poll reported "85% who rank [Roosevelt] next to Lincoln and above Washington," he told Alf Landon. "That is quite shocking to me and I don't ask you to believe it either, but there it is."[10]

When leading Republicans discussed the victory at a December RNC meeting, they recognized its protest nature and the consequent need to use their governing opportunity to fashion a more positive set of reasons to retain the support of disaffected Democratic voters.[11] But they also sensed that this protest involved a larger rejection of New Deal liberalism in favor of Republican antistatism.[12] Privately, Taft remarked that his party won "because the

[7] *NYT*, Nov. 10, 1946, 99.

[8] "The 1946 Elections: A Statistical Analysis," April 1947, reel 1, *Papers of the Republican Party*, part II; *NYT*, Nov. 11, 1946, 1, 28.

[9] Louis H. Bean, "The Republican 'Mandate' and '48," in Richard M. Dalfiume, ed., *American Politics Since 1945* (Chicago: Quadrangle, 1969), 40–46.

[10] Zach Taylor to Alf M. Landon, Oct. 14, 1946, box 126, Landon Papers.

[11] Transcript, RNC meeting, Dec. 5, 1946, reel 8, *Papers of the Republican Party*, part I, series A.

[12] Gary Donaldson, *Truman Defeats Dewey* (Lexington: University Press of Kentucky, 1999), 18, 34–35, 217; Reinhard, *Republican Right*, 36; George S. Roukis, *American Labor and the Conservative Republicans, 1946–1948: A Study in Economic and Political Conflict* (New York: Garland, 1988); Gould, *Grand Old Party*, 310–311; Mayer, "Republican Party, 1932–1952," 2285.

people finally were brought to realize what the New Deal was trying to do in regulating their daily lives."[13] This analysis amounted to an overestimate of mandate; shorter-term problems that encouraged an anti-incumbent vote, rather than any longer-term turn to conservatism, were at the heart of Republican gains.

But such beliefs were unsurprising in view of the tendency of many Republican candidates in 1946 to unleash stark, if not strident, attacks on liberal claims, as well as posing the question, "Had enough?" – exemplified by a number of contributions to a series of RNC campaign broadcasts, *Listen, America!* National chair Representative B. Carroll Reece of Tennessee said that "a comparatively small group of persons beholden to the political ideology of Moscow have insinuated themselves into positions of great influence within the Government." Its members "call the tune to which the Administration dances, and the tune is strangely like the Internationale."[14] An Ohio colleague in the House of Representatives, Clarence J. Brown, called the campaign "a battle between forces working to destroy the American system and those determined to save it from destruction."[15] "The philosophy of regimentation, centralization of power in Washington, and expansion of bureaucracy is leading the nation rapidly down the road to State Socialism which, unless it is reversed, will eventually rob the people of our freedom and liberty," said Representative Charles W. Vursell of Illinois in his *Listen, America!* broadcast.[16] In other campaign appearances, Vursell attacked the Roosevelt and Truman administrations' foreign as well as domestic policies for the inadequacy of the Democratic Party's defense against communism, singling out the Yalta agreement as a sell-out to the Soviet Union. This was not the emphasis of most Republican politicians, however, who usually reserved criticisms of their Democratic rivals to the domestic arena.[17]

Locally, Republican candidates often made similar points to those of the *Listen, America!* broadcasts. In California, in his House campaign against Democratic incumbent Jerry Voorhis, Richard M. Nixon – one among many returning veterans making a debut in politics – told voters that no election since 1860 was more significant. "We must decide whether we are to continue down the road to a socialist planned economy, or whether we are going to give the American system of free enterprise a chance to operate," he said on election eve.[18] Later considered an especially enthusiastic exponent of the anticommunist assault on Democrats, in 1946 Nixon was within the party's mainstream in presenting the election as a high-stakes choice between

---

[13] Robert A. Taft to Howard Elliott, Dec. 26, 1946, box 879, Taft Papers.

[14] Reece, "Listen America! True Liberalism," n.d., box 42, Stassen Papers.

[15] Brown, "Listen America! Let's Preserve the Republic," n.d., box 42, Stassen Papers.

[16] Vursell, "Listen America! The Stakes are High," n.d., box 42, Stassen Papers.

[17] Athan G. Theoharis, *The Yalta Myths: An Issue in U.S. Politics, 1945–1955* (Columbia: University of Missouri Press, 1970), 52–55.

[18] Richard M. Nixon, radio talk, Nov. 4, 1946, PPS 208.36, Nixon Pre-Presidential Speech File.

statism and liberty.[19] Those clearly on the party's moderate wing joined the attack. Seeking to represent New York in the Senate, Irving M. Ives spoke of a similar choice, one between free enterprise and dictatorially inclined centralization.[20]

The perception of mandate that the campaign fostered was not entirely a matter of overconfidence. There was a selective appetite for the Republicans' conservatism in preference to the Democrats' liberalism. Strikes and high prices encouraged hostility toward labor. A May poll, for example, reported that two in three respondents were more likely to support a candidate in favor of union regulation, three in five were less likely to support a candidate supported by the CIO-PAC, and only one in four thought well of the CIO.[21]

Despite many Republicans' excessive optimism about the emergence of a new conservatism – their misinterpretation of mandate – in power they did not pursue this mandate with excessive zeal. Their congressional record posed little threat to the post–New Deal status quo as a whole. Although congressional Republicans did not in general support extensions to New Deal innovations, they did not fundamentally challenge such achievements as Social Security, fair labor standards, and farm subsidies. There were two important areas of conservative initiative. First, in both 1947 and 1948 Congress passed a tax cut, though only in the latter year managing to override a Truman veto. Second, the 1947 Taft-Hartley Act also overcame a presidential veto to outlaw a variety of "unfair labor practices" by unions, restrict union shops, and allow federal government injunctions against strikes that "imperiled the national health or safety."[22] The tax cut and regulation of organized labor amounted to significant challenges to New Deal liberalism. Moreover, in developing these policies, Republicans successfully identified areas where conservative initiative was likeliest to win public support because there was widespread concern about government's cost and labor's power. Still, what the Republicans left unchanged among New Deal achievements was more significant than those revisions.

Although the 80th Congress posed little threat to the New Deal's reform legacy as a whole, the rhetoric of many Republicans sounded otherwise.[23] This defense became especially intense in response to Democratic attacks as the 1948 elections approached. At an Indiana Republican rally, Representative Joseph W. Martin, Jr., House speaker, characterized critics of "this American Congress" as "left wing radicals who were frustrated in their effort to firmly establish State Socialism."[24]

---

[19] Irwin F. Gellman, *The Contender: Richard Nixon – The Congress Years, 1946–1952* (New York: Free Press, 1999).

[20] *NYT* clipping, Oct. 11, 1946, box 101, PPSF, Hoover Papers.

[21] Psychological Corporation, poll report, May 1946, box 39, series 2, Dewey Papers.

[22] Badger, "Republican Rule," 167–171; Susan M. Hartmann, *Truman and the 80th Congress* (Columbia: University of Missouri Press, 1971), 213–214.

[23] Mayer, "Republican Party, 1932–1952," 2285.

[24] Joseph W. Martin, Jr., speech, Oct. 7, 1948, box 10, accretion 10200-ab, Scott Papers.

The long years of minority status had sapped the Republicans' capacity to deal creatively with the ascent to congressional majority. Some journalists reported that congressional Republicans viewed the responsibilities of power with unease, preferring the more familiarly comfortable role of opposition.[25] According to Senator Raymond E. Baldwin, a Connecticut Republican, the formal and informal biases in favor of seniority, which increased the influence of long-serving officeholders at the expense of newcomers such as Baldwin, meant that the party's dominant voices on Capitol Hill were usually those from safe Republican constituencies. Neglected newcomers were likely to be experienced in winning votes among those without long-standing Republican loyalties – experience that the party at large needed to consider in search of enduring electoral success.[26] As academic D. W. Brogan noted, senior Republicans – those who had survived the Democratic tide of the 1930s – were from "exactly those areas of the country most out of touch with average American opinion," and it was "quite natural that people who represented unchanging districts should ignore the fact that most of the United States was, and is, profoundly affected by the New Deal."[27]

Opposition to New Deal liberalism brought much unity to the GOP.[28] During the 80th Congress, party discipline reached an impressively high level, especially in the House.[29] When congressional Republicans had discussed leadership positions and committee chairs, it was rivalry between supporters of presidential contenders Thomas E. Dewey and Robert A. Taft that mostly accounted for disagreements, not significant differences of ideas.[30] A *Nation* editorial noted that policy disagreements accounted for clashes among Democrats, "whereas the current Republican squabbling is in large part merely the consequence of personal rivalries sparked by Presidential ambitions."[31] Policy disagreements among congressional Republicans did erupt. There were arguments in 1947 about the extent to which the Truman budget should be cut; in 1948 a housing bill that Taft cosponsored with two Democrats met defeat in the House, and an education bill he developed experienced the same fate.[32] Still, throughout this period differences among congressional Republicans on domestic policy were relatively insignificant; those from the Northeast were becoming less hostile toward the agenda of New Deal liberalism and those from the Midwest more so, but agreement remained much more common than disagreement. The key exception involved

[25] *Nation*, Nov. 23, 1946, 574–575.

[26] *American Magazine*, Sept. 1947, 24–25, 130–133.

[27] D. W. Brogan, "Trends in American Policy," *International Affairs* 25 (1949), 126–127 (quotation, 127).

[28] Brownell, *Advising Ike*, 70.

[29] Badger, "Republican Rule," 170–171.

[30] *NYT*, Dec. 29, 1946, 73.

[31] *Nation*, March 22, 1947, 319–320.

[32] Donaldson, *Truman Defeats Dewey*, 40, 146–147.

farm policy, where Republicans representing agricultural areas moved away from their conservatism to support federal assistance to farmers and other Republicans did not.[33]

Ideology was similarly marginal to the 1948 choice between Dewey and Taft. When the party selected Dewey, the belief that he was a stronger candidate, better able to beat Truman, was especially important; the disappointing margin of Taft's 1944 Senate reelection labeled him electorally unskilled – a setback to his presidential ambitions. It also reflected the Dewey team's superior ability to manage an effective delegate operation.[34] Ideas were less important. When Republicans met for the 1948 convention, a preponderance of unity was again evident. Only a limited number of issues fostered some disagreement, notably housing policy and social security.[35]

This background of unity helped create a Republican attack on the Democrats as incoherent. The Democrats were, in Dewey's words, "a congeries of elements which are absolutely and utterly inconsistent, ranging from the Southern Negro-hating Democrat to some Negro supporters in the North and from the big city bosses to the CIO."[36] The criticism, which acknowledged the existence of conservatism as well as liberalism among Democrats, did not undermine the key theme of "creeping socialism"; in his 1946 speeches Taft, for example, stressed Democratic factionalism while arguing "that the legislative program of the Party is dominated by the PAC with a program for complete regulation of the lives of all American citizens."[37] The Democratic Party's inclusiveness was actually an important element of its success in maintaining majority status. But the Republican Party's coherence was a strength in mounting a successful attack on the Democrats.

Leading Republicans did much to squander the advantage of party coherence, however. Conflict between the moderately conservative "Deweyites" and the more assertively conservative "Taftites" defined this period for the party. The party succumbed to factional disputes to an extent that far outstripped the significance of ideological difference. Dewey and Taft, the chief rivals for the presidential nomination and party leadership, distrusted each other. Many of their supporters believed that there was much at stake – personal if not ideological – in the battle's outcome, and behaved accordingly.[38] "The rule or ruin type of party workers has split our party since Theodore Roosevelt days,"

[33] Barbara Sinclair, *Congressional Realignment, 1925–1978* (Austin: University of Texas Press, 1982), 51–72.

[34] Richard S. Kirkendall, "Election of 1948," in Arthur M. Schlesinger, Jr., and Fred L. Israel, eds., *History of American Presidential Elections, 1789–1968*, vol. IV (New York: Chelsea House, 1971), 3114–3116.

[35] *Business Week*, June 26, 1948, 15–16.

[36] Thomas E. Dewey to John Burton and Elliott V. Bell, July 25, 1946, box 3, series 10, Dewey Papers.

[37] Robert A. Taft to J. D. Fisher, Nov. 4, 1946, box 879, Taft Papers.

[38] Michael D. Bowen, "Fight for the Right: The Quest for Republican Identity in the Postwar Period" (Ph.D. dissertation, University of Florida, 2006).

observed one activist in 1949, "and the Republican party can stand very little of it in the remnant that is left."[39]

Underlying the Dewey–Taft differences were regional tensions. Taft – distrustful of the East as inimical to his political principles – worried, as he noted in 1944, that Dewey approached issues "from the New York standpoint."[40] Understanding such animosities, Ruth Hanna McCormick Simms, Dewey's 1940 campaign manager, urged him to develop a broader understanding of public opinion across the country, which his "small group of very intelligent New York men," none of whom had ever lived outside the East, was unable to grasp.[41] Robert R. McCormick, the father of Simms's deceased husband and the idiosyncratically conservative publisher of the *Chicago Tribune*, expressed these tensions with perhaps the most exuberance – exuberance of a conspiratorially minded kind. Dismissing Dewey as "no American" but "a New Yorker," during the 1946 campaign McCormick observed, "Everybody knows that the Democratic party is the party of the Russian-loving Communists in this country, just as the Eastern wing of the Republican party is controlled by the international bankers of New York who are determined to perpetuate British imperialism through the power and influence of the United States."[42] It was indeed an advantage for Dewey, as journalists Stephen Hess and David Broder later pointed out, that he "commanded the most effective political force in the G.O.P., that combination of big money, mass-media influence and organizational skill in nominating conventions that is called the 'Eastern Establishment'" – even if McCormick misrepresented its internationalist agenda.[43]

McCormick viewed the East with hyperbole and even hysteria, but a reality of policy disagreement underpinned his factional animosity. Although the Republicans' response to New Deal liberalism had much in common, the difference on Capitol Hill between Republicans from the coasts and those from the interior remained sharp when the subject was foreign policy (especially visible when the issue was foreign aid).[44] "Republicans as a Party are still pseudo isolationists," wrote Minnesota's Representative Edward J. Devitt in 1947.[45]

---

[39] Gladys E. Heinrich Knowles to Hugh Scott, July 21, 1949, box 6, Scott Papers.

[40] Robert A. Taft to Alf M. Landon, Aug. 11, 1944, box 162, Taft Papers; Robert W. Merry, "Robert A. Taft: A Study in the Accumulation of Legislative Power," in Richard A. Baker and Roger H. Davidson, eds., *First Among Equals: Outstanding Senate Leaders of the Twentieth Century* (Washington, D.C.: Congressional Quarterly, 1991), 167.

[41] Ruth Simms to Thomas E. Dewey, June 5, 1944, box 108, Hanna–McCormick Family Papers.

[42] *NYT* clipping, Sept. 22, 1946, box 101, PPSF, Hoover Papers.

[43] Stephen Hess and David S. Broder, *The Republican Establishment: The Present and Future of the G.O.P.* (New York: Harper & Row, 1967), 16.

[44] Sinclair, *Congressional Realignment*, 42–48; H. Bradford Westerfield, *Foreign Policy and Party Politics: Pearl Harbor to Korea* (New Haven, Conn.: Yale University Press, 1955), 21–79.

[45] Edward J. Devitt to Bernhard LeVander, May 15, 1947, box 2, Minnesota Republican State Central Committee Records [hereafter MRSCC Records].

What Devitt criticized as "pseudo-isolationism" was a wariness of a new internationalist consensus – not entirely out of step with public sentiment, which seemed to accept the need for active American involvement in global affairs but also still reflected a desire to be aloof from the world's intractable problems. By spring 1947, for example, polls suggested that a majority of Americans, never enthusiastic about the organization, were dissatisfied with the progress of the United Nations (UN), the key institution of international cooperation.[46]

But if the party retained pseudo-isolationism within its ranks, it nevertheless played an important role in the construction of early Cold War policy, operating within a framework of bipartisan cooperation. Although there were congressional critics of Truman's foreign policy, Republicans of the 80th Congress supplied vital votes to secure the enactment of aid to Greece and Turkey, the passage of relief aid elsewhere in Europe, and later the creation of the Marshall Plan of wider-ranging support for European reconstruction. Similarly, many congressional Republicans supported preparations for the North Atlantic Treaty Organization (NATO), the cornerstone of mutual-security policy, and the institution of a temporary draft.[47]

A further intraparty difference was institutional. The party's 1948 ticket of Dewey and California's Earl Warren emerged from gubernatorial, not congressional, politics, where executive responsibilities encouraged them to develop a different kind of record, one that stressed initiative rather than opposition. On Capitol Hill, Republicans seemed uncertain how to translate their anti–New Deal liberalism into an affirmative legislative agenda when they gained power, but many Republican governors had not betrayed similar uncertainty in tackling executive duties. Discussions about domestic policy at Mackinac Island in 1943 had drawn attention to the distinctive Republicanism demonstrated by the growing group of the party's governors.[48] At Mackinac the governors successfully lobbied for a bolder statement of domestic policy; while criticizing Democratic custody of the economy as severely flawed, the governors – many of whom harbored presidential ambitions – also embraced a reform-minded approach to welfare expansions.[49] In encouraging Dewey to rely heavily on the twenty-six Republican governors during his 1944 campaign, David Hinshaw wrote that they "embody and symbolize the resurgent growth and the attractive new vitality and strength of the party," displaying impressive abilities in leadership, public relations, and administration.[50] In his keynote at that year's national convention, Warren commended the Republican gubernatorial record as "progressive, enlightened and in the public interest," attentive to

[46] Gabriel A. Almond, *The American People and Foreign Policy* (1950; New York: Praeger, 1960), 67–115.

[47] Hartmann, *Truman and the 80th Congress*, 47–70, 104–120, 159–185.

[48] *Nation's Business*, May 1948, 29.

[49] *Kansas City Star* clipping, Sept. 8, 1943, and *Washington Daily News* clipping, Sept. 8, 1943, both in box 4, series 2, Hickenlooper Papers; Walter Lippmann, "Today and Tomorrow: Republican Strategy," clipping, n.d. [1943], box 162, Taft Papers.

[50] David Hinshaw to Thomas E. Dewey, May 3, 1944, box 80, series 4, Dewey Papers.

health, education, and care of the needy.[51] Warren himself assembled a formidable record in this regard and in other areas, including pensions, highways,
prisons, labor relations, and race. The policies involved a focus on social progress that Warren connected with the party's Lincolnian inheritance.[52] But the
contrast between governors and congressional Republicans was not only one
of policy record. Governors with larger ambitions also often had the chance to
sidestep nationally controversial issues. Mindful that it was beneficial to keep
options open for the presidential year of 1948, Dewey had often responded to
1947's tumultuous developments by declining to comment.[53]

The gubernatorial formula apparently made electoral sense; the minority
problem seemed less acute at the executive than legislative level. The Republican
Party enjoyed more success in competition for the nation's statehouses than
for other political bodies.[54] There were eighteen Republican governors after
the 1938 elections, then twenty in 1940, twenty-four in 1942, twenty-three in
1944, and twenty-five in 1946.[55] In the run-up to the 1944 elections, the number reached a peak, with a Republican as governor in twenty-six states cov-
ering 70 percent of the nation's population.[56] In this sense, then, the nation's
minority party had succeeded in mobilizing the support of a majority even
before the 1946 breakthrough, thanks to a policy agenda more affirmative
and moderate than the congressional stress on oppositional antistatism, even
while maintaining an emphasis on New Deal liberalism's shortcomings. This
success naturally led to an argument that gubernatorial Republicanism possessed special electoral power. Warren, for example, insisted that the party
should craft positions between extremes of left and right in order "to appeal
to the great mass of voters who demand that progress be made in the solution
of their individual problems which in the aggregate constitute the problems of
our day."[57] It was by no means an argument that all were prepared to accept.
Indiana Republicans, for example, interpreted election returns quite differently in order to emphasize the importance of the Midwest – and hence a more
conservative approach to policy – to any strategy to capture a majority.[58]

Differences about strategy – the way to build a majority – encouraged Dewey
to embrace a moderate image and Taft, a conservative image. Dewey's background in New York politics, as well as his experience of presidential defeat
in 1944, persuaded him that the Republican Party needed to woo potential
defectors from the Democratic Party by minimizing disagreements with New

[51] Earl Warren, speech, June 26, 1944, box 162, Taft Papers.
[52] Richard B. Harvey, *Earl Warren: Governor of California* (New York: Exposition Press, 1969), 119–163.
[53] *Harper's*, April 1948, 293.
[54] Ware, *Democratic Party Heads North*.
[55] *Nation's Business*, May 1948, 29.
[56] *Collier's*, July 29, 1944, 21, 29–30.
[57] Harvey, *Earl Warren*, 165.
[58] Department of Research, Indiana Republican State Committee, "Midwest Republican Conference in Indiana," May 10, 1947, box 2, MRSCC Records.

Deal liberalism. Taft, by contrast, reached an opposite conclusion about the way to beat the Democrats; he wanted to emphasize difference. There were also policy disagreements between the two, notably on race and labor. But the perception of disagreement was greater than the reality.[59]

Still, tensions within the Republican Party – whether personal, regional, institutional, strategic, or issue-based – seemed negligible by contrast with the Democratic Party's fractures, which fissured in 1948. Henry Wallace, the former vice president, headed the ticket of the Progressive Party, critical of Cold War policy as anti-Soviet and attractive to fellow travelers, and J. Strom Thurmond, the South Carolina governor, was the candidate of the States' Rights Democratic Party, or "Dixiecrats," critical of civil rights policy as inimical to white supremacy and thus attractive to white segregationists. These divisions nurtured Republican complacency. Local- and state-level factional disputes had often helped Republicans achieve breakthroughs where there was Democratic strength otherwise.[60] But in 1948 Democratic weaknesses were not the only causes of the widespread belief that a comeback landslide was all but certain. Some Republicans thought instead that their own strengths, as indicated by the gradual increase in their party's fortunes since the 1938 midterms, accounted for this likely outcome.[61] Moreover, when the White House party lost Congress in the midterms, it was expected to lose the presidency, too, in the ensuing elections.

The climate of optimism encouraged Dewey to adopt "the utterly stupid spirit of a sweetness and like [sic] campaign," according to the retrospective analysis of Hugh Scott, a former Pennsylvania congressperson and Dewey's choice as national chair. This was an inappropriate strategy "against a manure spreader like brother Truman," Scott later concluded.[62] Dewey spoke little of congressional Republicans' achievements, confident that victory was likely and that a quiet campaign was the best way to promote party fortunes. In response to the fraying of the Democratic Party, the Truman campaign sought to mobilize the powerful New Deal coalition through a reassertion of the reasons for the Republicans' minority status. Truman started by calling the party's bluff in challenging congressional Republicans to take action on housing and inflation, among other promises in a platform that embraced gubernatorial affirmativeness. The results allowed Truman to condemn a "do-nothing" session.[63] He then assaulted the party as representative of a socioeconomic elite and as responsible for the Great Depression. His September speech at the national plowing contest in Dexter, Iowa, exemplifies the assault. There he

---

[59] Bowen, "Fight for the Right," 3–17, 113–114, 151–152.

[60] John Braeman, Robert H. Bremner, and David Brody, "Introduction," in Braeman, Bremner, and Brody, eds., *The New Deal*, vol. 2: *The State and Local Levels* (Columbus: Ohio State University Press, 1975), xiv.

[61] *Nation's Business*, May 1948, 29.

[62] Hugh D. Scott, Jr., to Leroy Johnson, July 21, 1949, box 10, accretion 10200-ab, Scott Papers.

[63] Hartmann, *Truman and the 80th Congress*, 194, 202.

called Republican leaders "cold and cunning men," who wanted "a return of the Wall Street economic dictatorship," with "low prices for farmers, cheap wages for labor, and high profits for big corporations." A Republican administration, Truman said, "[would] listen to the gluttons of privilege first, and the people not at all."[64] This "give-'em-hell" campaign invited a reconsideration of the Dewey strategy, but a canvass of leading Republicans brought a widespread endorsement.[65]

Absent from the campaign was much discussion of foreign policy, despite the Cold War's arrival and despite the finding of pollsters that foreign policy was more important to more voters than domestic policy.[66] Polls also suggested that Americans had more confidence in the Republicans than the Democrats to run the nation's foreign policy, though the difference was marginal. Looking for anti-Truman arguments, Dewey had contemplated attacks on the shortcomings of administration policy toward both Asia and Europe as part of his campaign. Senator Arthur Vandenberg, however, persuaded him that an embrace of bipartisanship was politically advantageous. According to Vandenberg, who led the party in the Senate on foreign policy while Taft took that role on domestic policy, this was because it allowed the party to take credit for achievements such as the Marshall Plan and because it avoided the aggravation of conflict with Democrats that might impede the successful development of a Dewey administration's foreign policy.[67] Such advice proved more persuasive than that of some within the party's isolationist tradition – now stressing anticommunism – who even advocated a total focus on foreign policy against Truman and an attack on the Democrats as mounting an inadequate defense against the Soviet Union.[68] Dewey consequently supported the administration's approach to foreign policy and limited his criticisms to minor points about its implementation's effectiveness. As Dewey's representative, John Foster Dulles worked closely with Secretary of State George C. Marshall, attending the September meeting of the UN General Assembly, where foreign ministers treated him as Marshall's near-term successor.

It was Truman, toward the end of the campaign, who elevated foreign policy's prominence. Anxious about Henry Wallace's threat in the big cities of the North, he started to defend his overseas record in a more outspoken way, assailing the "isolationist forces in the Republican party." The new tone arrived too late to make much difference, however.[69] The overall climate on foreign policy was one of silent consensus. Public responses to the campaign

[64] NYT, Sept. 19, 1948, 1, 2.
[65] Brownell, *Advising Ike*, 83–84; Hugh Scott, *Come to the Party* (Englewood Cliffs, N.J.: Prentice-Hall, 1968), 52; Smith, *Thomas E. Dewey*, 535–536.
[66] RNC Research Division, poll report, Sept. 7, 1948, reel 1, *Papers of the Republican Party*, part II.
[67] Divine, *Foreign Policy*, 200–201, 206–208, 223–226, 245–247; Hartmann, *Truman and the 80th Congress*, 13–14.
[68] Theoharis, *Yalta Myths*, 63–64.
[69] Westerfield, *Foreign Policy and Party Politics*, 296–324.

reflected this mood, and the arrival of the Cold War failed to create a cleavage between the party coalitions. Whereas there were clear differences on domestic policy between the greater conservatism of Dewey voters and the greater liberalism of Truman voters, there was no similar distinction in views on foreign policy.[70]

Dewey was a politician enthusiastic about polling as a way to understand the electorate. It is thus a supreme incongruity that poll problems characterized his campaign. The polls were certainly encouraging; in predicting easy victory for Dewey, they suggested that the New Deal coalition's decay, which most Republicans perceived, was real. An Elmo Roper poll in September, for example, reported that only one in three lower-middle-income voters – a crucial element of the Democratic coalition – intended to vote for Truman, compared with the majority within this group that preferred Roosevelt in 1944. A similar slump was seen among big-city and younger voters.[71] The polls also suggested that the Republican record was popular with respect to topics such as labor reform and congressional investigations of communism.[72] The way Roper discussed his poll findings, however, should have sounded a warning signal, though it did not. Roper identified not a conservative turn to Dewey but a no-confidence vote in Truman, whom he saw as unable to replicate Franklin Roosevelt's skill in holding together the Democratic coalition. Praising Dewey for maintaining distance from the 80th Congress's conservatism, he noted "that the people have not foresaken [sic] the liberalism they grew to know so well under Roosevelt."[73] In other words, New Deal liberalism retained its popularity beyond FDR. Truman would prove to be its beneficiary; Dewey, its victim.

Like many contemporaries, Roper underestimated Truman. Truman achieved a victory that was, in the words of the RNC report on the results, "one of the most astonishing upsets in political history." Dewey won twenty-two million votes to Truman's twenty-four million; Wallace and Thurmond won little more than a million each. Congressionally, Republicans suffered a major setback, losing nine Senate seats (one-half of those defended) and a net total of seventy-five House seats. There was also a net loss of five governors, and Republicans maintained control of both houses in only fifteen states, compared with twenty-five states after the 1946 midterms. The national committee's research division acknowledged labor's importance in electing Truman but stressed rural and particularly agricultural defections as crucial in ensuring Dewey's defeat. This analysis emphasized labor's responsibility, by contrast, for overturning the Republican majority in the House – especially

---

[70] George Belknap and Angus Campbell. "Political Party Identification and Attitudes Toward Foreign Policy," *POQ* 15 (1951–1952), 602–603.

[71] RNC Research Division, poll report, Sept. 20, 1948, reel 1, *Papers of the Republican Party*, part II.

[72] RNC Research Division, poll report, Sept. 7, 1948, reel 1, *Papers of the Republican Party*, part II.

[73] Elmo Roper, radio talk, Sept. 19, 1948, box 52, series 5, Dewey Papers.

due to the work of the CIO-PAC and Labor's League for Political Education of the AFL in targeting Taft-Hartley supporters.[74] An Iowa farmer told Samuel Lubell, a journalist who specialized in the exploration of public opinion, that he voted for Truman rather than making a long-contemplated switch to vote Republican because "I remembered the depression and all the good things that had come to me under the Democrats."[75] One scholar concluded that "unless the Republicans can adapt themselves better to changes of public sentiment, they stand a good chance of going the way of the Federalists and the Whigs."[76]

The 1948 defeat was traumatic for the party. The preelection assumption of certain victory compounded the disappointment that Republicans experienced. Disappointment ignited a vicious bout of soul-searching and blame apportionment. It deepened factional conflict in what one RNC leader called an episode of "self-immolation."[77] Hosting a national committee meeting in January 1949, Omaha, Nebraska, briefly became a center of the debate. An editorial in the city's *World-Herald* newspaper embraced a conservative interpretation of the party's shortcomings by greeting RNC members with the message that their party was a "moral coward" for its failure to stand up for antistatist convictions. According to the newspaper – with a reference to the Democratic machine in Truman's home state of Missouri – Americans "will accept a brave and fighting leadership tainted even with Pendergastism and absolutism rather than a leadership that crawls – and trails its flag."[78] Though hostile, the message was in accordance with the views of many at the meeting, where the lack of fight in 1948 was a common explanation for the defeat. Hugh Scott, who as national chair was the object of much criticism, joined them in emphasizing this point, but his embrace of the criticism failed to undermine the vehemence of the protest against his leadership.

Beyond agreement about the adverse impact of the campaign's lackluster nature, there was disagreement about 1948's mistakes – disagreements that the responses of Nebraska's own Republican politicians exemplified. Deploring a me-too strategy that led to defeat at a time when the Democrats' agenda jeopardized American liberties, Senator Kenneth S. Wherry said that "if the legislative enactments of the Eightieth Congress had been taught and the people had been educated to its advantages in fourth grade school language so they understood it, we would have a Republican Congress today and a Republican president." By contrast, Val Peterson, the state's governor, dwelled on the party's image problem – its association with hard times, with opposition to

[74] RNC Research Division, "The 1948 Election: A Statistical Analysis," May 1949, reel 1, *Papers of the Republican Party*, part II.
[75] Samuel Lubell, *The Future of American Politics*, 2nd ed. (1952; Garden City, N.Y.: Doubleday Anchor, 1956), 171.
[76] *Harvard Alumni Bulletin*, Nov. 20, 1948, 213–216, box 5, Nash Papers.
[77] Jane H. Macauley to Bernhard LeVander, Feb. 18, 1949, box 2, MRSCC Records.
[78] *Omaha World-Herald* reprint, Jan. 26, 1949, box 7, Scott Papers.

reform and regulation, with society's "haves" rather than "have nots."[79] Both Wherry and Peterson differed from the postelection conclusion of Joseph S. Wishart, the state party's acting chair, who more prosaically identified farm policy as key to Republican fortunes in Nebraska.[80] At the RNC meeting, Wherry's interpretation was more common than Peterson's or Wishart's.[81] The implications of such analysis encouraged a reassertion of conservatism. While Dewey shared Republican opposition to Fair Deal proposals and support for a balanced budget, he privately deplored the new tone as backward-looking and counterproductive. He wrote that "if they believe they are going to stop farm price supports, pensions, unemployment insurance, and social advances, they are crazy and they are likely to lose our freedom for us ... by leading the country into a one-party system."[82]

Inviting the party's some 180,000 precinct workers to report their views, Scott uncovered a tetchy, frustrated conservatism at the grass roots. A Nebraskan wrote, "Why don't you me-too guys who are running the party try dropping dead?" Together with criticism of the campaign as smugly overconfident and poorly organized, such opposition to me-tooism was widespread. "We tried Landon, Willkie and Dewey, and each got licked because of me-tooism and One World bunk," wrote an Oregon Republican. "There's not much difference between 'me' and 'me-too' except that 'me' is in the White House." But some respondents blamed the 80th Congress's record as unhelpful to the mobilization of support for the party.[83]

As in 1944, poor organization was one explanation for defeat.[84] "The humble but essential task of ringing doorbells must be revived by the Republican Party if we are once again to assume our rightful place as the majority party," argued Scott.[85] Labor's support for the Democrats often animated this concern. "There is only one good party organization in the country today and that is Organized Labor," Dewey told Landon. "So long as the Democrats stay with Labor they do not need one of their own."[86] The stress on organization as an explanation for defeat was less likely to foster intraparty conflict than talk of issues. It was a concern that often encouraged innovation and hard work. At the party's center, new services were initiated in support of candidates, such as courses on campaigning and the production of radio messages, while many state and local parties paid renewed attention to precinct-level mobilization of the vote. The administration's healthcare proposals provided

---

[79] Transcript, RNC meeting, Jan. 26, 1949, box 6, Scott Papers.

[80] Joseph S. Wishart to A. T. Howard and Nebraska RSCC members, n.d., box 42, series 2, Dewey Papers.

[81] Transcript, RNC meeting, Jan. 26, 1949, box 6, Scott Papers.

[82] Smith, *Thomas E. Dewey*, 553.

[83] *Collier's*, June 18, 1949, 28, 32–36.

[84] RNC, "Minutes of Meeting of Representatives of the Republican State Central Committees," March 13, 1949, box 7, Scott Papers.

[85] Hugh D. Scott, Jr., to Bernhard LeVander, Dec. 23, 1948, box 2, MRSCC Records.

[86] Thomas E. Dewey to Alf M. Landon, Jan. 19, 1949, box 24, series 10, Dewey Papers.

a rationale for the special organization of medical professionals in support of the GOP cause.[87] The RNC identified marginal Senate and House seats and concentrated its resources on aiding Republican chances there.[88]

Another explanation for the defeat – the fuzzy, vague quality of the Dewey campaign – spurred concern about the quality of the party's public communications, a concern also revealing the view many Republicans held that their approach to politics was more elevated than the Democrats'. "We Republicans are the world's worst salesmen!" said Senator Homer E. Capehart of Indiana.[89] The concern led House Republicans to create a policy committee, aiming to publicize the party's record better, although minority leader Joe Martin failed to exploit it in this way with any enterprise or productivity.[90] It was also the subject of a study by the RNC's research division. The resulting report contended that a gulf existed between the parties' tactics. Ever since Charles Michelson's orchestration of anti-Hoover rhetoric at the start of the Depression, Democrats readily resorted to misrepresenting the Republican Party, according to the report. It was a more difficult task, by contrast, to communicate the merits of the Republican agenda. "Unfortunately, Republicans are at a keen disadvantage in the promotion of their program when it necessarily encompasses the unpleasant but hard facts of life with respect to sound economy," the report observed. "We rebel at adopting the cheap and deceitful tactics of our political opposition which cynically and without conscience promotes a 'Pie in the Sky' campaign of redistribution of other people's wealth." It advocated a sharper program of attack on the opposition – more aggressive, less high-minded.[91] Such criticisms reflected party anger with the low-key nature of the Dewey campaign, but they did not acknowledge the abrasive rhetoric that many Republican politicians often used already.

The perception that the Dewey campaign lacked a clear message not only led to a desire for better publicity but also encouraged the belief among some Republicans that the party needed to present a more distinctive – more conservative – alternative to New Deal liberalism. This belief that the 1948 campaign's fuzziness was a strategic mistake led to support for a new statement of party principles.[92] The nature of those principles seemed clear to most; their core amounted to the defense of "liberty against socialism." Arthur E. Summerfield, chair of the RNC's strategy committee, observed that "the

[87] *NYT*, Nov. 1, 1950, 39.
[88] Minutes of RNC executive meetings, May 19 and July 31–Aug. 1, 1950, reel 10, *Papers of the Republican Party*, part I, series A.
[89] *Nation's Business*, March 1949, 25.
[90] Jones, *Republican Party*, 101.
[91] RNC Research Division, "The Use of Words in Selling the Republican Party to the American Voter," Feb. 1949, box 786, Taft Papers.
[92] Minutes of Republican Strategy Committee meeting, Dec. 13, 1949, reel 9, *Papers of the Republican Party*, part I, series A; Karl E. Mundt to Robert A. Taft, Dec. 26, 1949, box 787, Taft Papers; Harrison E. Spangler to Taft, Jan. 10, 1950, box 787, Taft Papers; transcript of RNC Policy Committee, Jan. 18, 1950, reel 9, *Papers of the Republican Party*, part I, series A.

difference between the Roosevelt and Truman Administration is that with Roosevelt we were drifting toward socialism but with Truman there is no drift – it's a headlong rush."[93] Although its exponents viewed the theme of liberty against socialism as a positive effort to mobilize voters in support of principles central to the party, critics interpreted its oppositional element as the more important and the theme therefore as another example of Republican negativity.[94] Another criticism was that an articulation of principle was not a promising way to reach out to new voters; Senator Margaret Chase Smith of Maine advocated "the 'dollars and cents' language of the common man," about the impact of taxation on "the working man's pocket," rather than talk of principle. "Talking about saving billions of dollars and about the threat of our Government going socialistic or communistic isn't the 'average next door neighbor' talk and it isn't going to attract the attention of the average, common man," she told Taft.[95] The release of the principles statement at the launch of the 1950 campaign revealed an awareness of the party's need to shed its image of elitism; it took place at a dollar-per-box chicken lunch that Republicans contrasted favorably with a hundred-dollar Democratic fundraising dinner. Still, Smith's concerns were sound. The document was, according to one journalist, "about as stimulating as the manifesto of a garden club denouncing communism."[96]

Disappointments with the 1948 campaign also encouraged a turn away from bipartisanship. So did other factors, including an increase in Democratic interest in autonomous action on foreign policy and the reduced influence of both Vandenberg (a result of illness) and Dulles (a consequence of his failed 1949 Senate bid). Although interparty disagreements were at first limited to marginal questions over spending levels, they soon became more serious.[97] In 1949, the Soviet Union's successful test of an atomic bomb and Alger Hiss's two perjury trials in connection with espionage accusations made the Democrats more vulnerable to Republican attack.[98] For many Republicans, the accusations against Hiss – a former New Deal bureaucrat and State Department official who had served as an adviser at Yalta – substantiated the existence of disloyalty in government. Hiss, moreover, symbolized the liberalism they opposed.[99] Most of all, communist successes under Mao Zedong in the Chinese civil war against Chiang Kai-shek's nationalists facilitated a Republican charge of Democratic failure in foreign policy. As Republican politicians emphasized, no bipartisan discussion of any substance occurred on China until it was too late to save Chiang, a background that left them free to pursue their attack.[100] In 1946,

[93] *NYT*, Dec. 14, 1949, 1.
[94] *Collier's*, May 6, 1950, 74.
[95] Margaret Chase Smith to Robert A. Taft, Jan. 14, 1950, box 787, Taft Papers.
[96] *Commonweal*, Feb. 17, 1950, 500–501.
[97] Westerfield, *Foreign Policy and Party Politics*, 325–342.
[98] Theoharis, *Yalta Myths*, 87–98.
[99] Robert Griffith, *The Politics of Fear: Joseph R. McCarthy and the Senate* (Lexington: University Press of Kentucky, 1970), 43–45.
[100] Westerfield, *Foreign Policy and Party Politics*, 343–369.

only those of relatively extreme views joined Charles Vursell in attacking the Yalta agreement; now most Republicans did.[101] North Korea's invasion of South Korea in June 1950 – soon followed by U.S. intervention in the South's support under a UN resolution – hugely elevated foreign policy's salience to electoral politics. Although Republicans usually supported the administration's initial response to the war's outbreak, they soon developed the thesis that the war was a demonstration of its inadequacies, the flawed nature of its defense against communism, especially in Asia. The replacement of bipartisanship with conflict over foreign policy encouraged Republican politicians to develop a new appeal for the 1950 midterm contests.[102]

As always, local variation characterized the congressional elections, but their pro-Republican feature in 1950 was often not so much the power of liberty versus socialism as the appearance of new anti-incumbent issues. Republicans criticized the Democratic record on communist subversion in government, corrupt practices in government, and especially the war in Korea.[103] Guy George Gabrielson, the national chair and an enthusiastic exponent of assaulting the administration as socialistic, reflected the shift in telling RNC members as campaign season began that the political climate had changed, and "the predominant issue today is the incompetence of the Party in power to achieve peace or provide an adequate national defense."[104] Herbert Hoover similarly noted, "Our old issues of economy and reduction of Government expenditures are practically lost in this mass of military operations." Although Hoover clearly regretted this loss and saw his party's fortunes as consequently dependent on overseas disappointment, the campaign emphasis had promise.[105]

Candidates in two neighboring Minneapolis–St. Paul districts pursued very different campaigns in ways that suggested the relative electoral appeal of anti-statist and anti–Korean War politics. In one, Republican incumbent Walter Judd, a leading critic of the Democrats' foreign policy, emphasized the war, a focus assisted by his opponent Marcella Killen. Killen attacked Judd's opposition to bipartisanship as well as defending the Fair Deal agenda. In the other, Republican challenger Alfred D. Lindley assailed Roy Wier, the Democratic congressperson, as leftist, drawing parallels between Wier's voting record and that of Vito Marcantonio, an American Labor Party representative from New York – a favored way among many Republicans to demonize an opponent. Wier in turn accused Lindley of hostility to labor within his wider defense of New Deal liberalism's goals. Surveys suggested that public opinion about the

[101] Theoharis, *Yalta Myths*, 97–98.
[102] Ronald J. Caridi, *The Korean War and American Politics: The Republican Party as a Case Study* (Philadelphia: University of Pennsylvania Press, 1968), 25–93.
[103] William A. Glaser, "Hindsight and Significance," in William N. McPhee and Glaser, eds., *Public Opinion and Congressional Elections* (New York: Free Press of Glencoe, 1962), 277–278, 281.
[104] Minutes of RNC meeting, Sept. 14–15, 1950, reel 10, *Papers of the Republican Party*, part I, series A.
[105] Herbert Hoover to Edgar Rickard, Oct. 13, 1950, box 191, PPICF, Hoover Papers.

issues and evaluations of the parties were very similar in the two districts, but the emphasis on foreign policy proved much more successful in activating a Republican majority, helping Judd to achieve reelection. Lindley's antistatist message managed to maximize the vote against him, leading to his defeat.[106]

A successful UN offensive under General Douglas MacArthur in late September, which led to Seoul's recapture, perhaps undermined the Republicans' attack on the administration over the war and the issue's electoral effectiveness for their cause. The attacks nevertheless continued. In a national election-eve radio address, Harold Stassen, former Minnesota governor and a presidential aspirant, charged "the blinded, blundering American-Asiatic policy under the present national Administration" with responsibility for the Korean War. "It has been five years of coddling Chinese Communists, five years of undermining General MacArthur, five years of snubbing friendly freedom-loving Asiatics, and five years of appeasing the arch-Communist, Mao-Tse-tung." The war helped Republicans to make gains, but it was not as unambiguously an antiadministration issue as it had appeared at the start of the campaign. Although the party won twenty-eight more seats in the House of Representatives and five in the Senate, these gains were smaller than those in the three previous midterm contests of 1938, 1942, and 1946.[107]

If the 1948 elections seemed to repudiate Dewey's answer to the minority problem, one of the highest-profile 1950 contests apparently – but misleadingly – lent support to an approach that instead stressed a conservative alternative to the Democrats' liberalism. It also boosted the presidential prospects of Dewey's principal rival. In Ohio Robert Taft won reelection by a comfortable, though far from effortless, margin, a victory that he deployed to challenge his reputation as a poor campaigner. He also used his victory to promote the argument that a liberty-versus-socialism emphasis was the way to defeat the Democrats. As the architect of labor regulation, Taft was a chief target of CIO-PAC leaders in 1950. His reelection bid emphasized that outsiders to Ohio were responsible for the anti-Taft campaign. "Senator Taft's defeat would mean the beginning of a union boss-controlled government in America," charged campaign manager Willis D. Gradison, arguing that the stakes extended beyond his candidate's reelection to embrace "[t]he whole philosophy of our government and the individual enterprise system."[108] There were indeed signs that this emphasis helped Taft win support among union members and that, bolstered by good organization, it maximized turnout in Republican areas. But the weakness of Taft's opponent, Joseph Ferguson, whom Frank Lausche, Ohio's governor and a fellow Democrat, declined to endorse, was also a factor that contributed to the outcome, together with the

---

[106] Philip H. Ennis, "The Contextual Dimension in Voting," in William N. McPhee and William A. Glaser, eds., *Public Opinion and Congressional Elections* (New York: Free Press of Glencoe, 1962), 197–210.

[107] Caridi, *Korean War*, 79–103 (quotation, 95).

[108] Citizens Committee for the Re-election of Taft, "Buckeye Bulletin," n.d., box 2, Starzinger Papers. The quoted text is underlined in the original.

generalized anti-Democratic trends of 1950. The victory was, according to Samuel Lubell, "largely a vote for moderation" – often a desire to hold the gains of New Deal liberalism – rather than an embrace of conservatism.[109] It therefore did not provide a case study of a conservative emphasis as a way to win, though this was the conclusion that Taft encouraged.

The outcome of the 1950 elections suggested that anticommunism, a long-time salvo of some Republicans in the battle against the Democratic Party, was at last starting to hit some targets. Senator Joseph R. McCarthy of Wisconsin was at the forefront of the new attack barrage, launching his Red hunt that February. The post–World War II years had witnessed a stream of espionage revelations that fed anxiety about domestic communism. The January 1950 guilty verdict in Alger Hiss's second perjury trial convinced many Republicans that the case of government disloyalty was now proved.[110] The clamor to denounce Democrats as soft on communism involved an anxiety about the majority party's ideological drift as well as its custody of national security. Former RNC official Robert H. Lucas in early 1945 wrote of an imperative for Republican action "to defeat the purposes of the New Deal-Communist set-up," for example.[111] Republicans also recognized the electoral promise of anticommunism and the charge that Democrats had failed to secure the nation against subversion's threat. The upsurge in anticommunist rhetoric and activity thus expressed frustrations over their difficulty in achieving power.[112]

Dewey made little use of anticommunism as a political issue in 1948.[113] Not only was this decision consistent with his above-the-fray tactics, but it also reflected a regretful awareness of his 1944 excesses.[114] But the larger campaign involved an anticommunist component. Asked in a radio interview for his opinion of the top issue, national chair Hugh Scott said that it was a desire for "a real house cleaning in Washington to get the Communist fellow-travelers and subversives out of the government departments." This was especially important "because it involves not only the integrity of our American system of constitutional government, but also because it touches the very heart of our National security and National survival."[115] In his newsletter, Scott's efforts to enthuse fellow Republicans depicted the campaign in terms very different from Dewey's blandness – "as a crusade for fundamental Americanism,"

---

[109] *Saturday Evening Post*, Feb. 10, 1951, 32–33, 142–148 (quotation, 148).

[110] Richard M. Fried, *Nightmare in Red: The McCarthy Era in Perspective* (New York: Oxford University Press, 1990), 21–22, 92–93.

[111] Robert H. Lucas to Robert A. Taft, Feb. 20, 1945, box 6, Lucas Papers.

[112] Earl Latham, *The Communist Controversy in Washington: From the New Deal to McCarthy* (Cambridge, Mass.: Harvard University Press, 1966), 398–399, 422–423.

[113] Richard M. Fried, "Voting Against the Hammer and Sickle: Communism as an Issue in American Politics," in William H. Chafe, ed., *The Achievements of American Liberalism: The New Deal and Its Legacies* (New York: Columbia University Press, 2003), 108–109.

[114] Smith, *Thomas E. Dewey*, 507.

[115] Transcript, radio interview with Hugh Scott, Sept. 16, 1948, box 10, addition 10200-ab, Scott Papers; Hugh D. Scott, Jr., "The Chairman's Letter," Sept. 1, 1948, box 6, Scott Papers.

fought in order to elect their party's politicians so that "the malignant cells of world Communism will no longer find sheltered haven in Washington."[116]

It was an issue that often pulled Republicans together. In Pennsylvania, for example, strident anticommunism was a unifying feature among Republicans otherwise riven by factional conflict between moderate and conservative wings.[117] McCarthy's emergence, however, encouraged some disagreements to surface because of doubts about his bullying tactics and questionable charges concerning the extent of communist subversion. In June 1950 five of her fellow Senate moderates joined Margaret Chase Smith in issuing a "Declaration of Conscience," decrying the pursuit of electoral success "through the selfish political exploitation of fear, bigotry, ignorance, and intolerance."[118] Taft worried that McCarthy was going too far. "The Republican situation has been going pretty well until McCarthy overstated a good case," he wrote that April.[119] But Taft also encouraged McCarthy to pursue the attack. Within the context of the Korean War, anticommunist concerns were especially intense.[120]

Democrats resorted to a variety of tactics to deflect the accusations of softness on communism, frequently with success. During the 1948 campaign, vice-presidential candidate Alben W. Barkley said that a Republican victory was "the quickest way to bring on communism in the country," because it was sure to lead to the economic distress on which such extremism fed.[121] Echoing Barkley's theme, Truman added that the Republicans' anticommunist rhetoric against his party was "absurd and ridiculous," an effort "to distract the people's attention with false issues." He also stressed his administration's steps against the international "Red menace."[122] Within weeks of the 1946 elections, Truman had established a President's Temporary Commission on Employee Loyalty, which in early 1947 recommended – and Truman then implemented – the creation of a loyalty program in the federal government. But such steps were far from successful in satisfying the anticommunist zeal.[123] Still, some Democrats had little need to fear accusations of softness on communism because they were at the forefront of the attack, notably including Senator Pat McCarran of Nevada, chief sponsor of the 1950 Internal Security Act that restricted the Communist Party and created a Subversive Activities Control Board to identify and regulate front organizations.[124] Moreover, some of the most intense bouts of anticommunism occurred within Democratic primaries.[125]

[116] Hugh D. Scott, Jr., "The Chairman's Letter," Aug. 15, 1948, box 6, Scott Papers.
[117] Philip Jenkins, *The Cold War at Home: The Red Scare in Pennsylvania, 1945–1960* (Chapel Hill: University of North Carolina Press, 1999), 53–54.
[118] Westerfield, *Foreign Policy and Party Politics*, 380.
[119] Robert A. Taft to B. L. Noojin, April 7, 1950, box 34, Taft Papers.
[120] Fried, *Nightmare in Red*, 125–131.
[121] *NYT*, Oct. 2, 1948, 8.
[122] *NYT*, Oct. 28, 1948, 26.
[123] Fried, *Nightmare in Red*, 67–70.
[124] Fried, *Nightmare in Red*, 116–117.
[125] Fried, "Voting Against the Hammer and Sickle," 110.

Anticommunism's anti-Democratic power was limited. Its peak of success was probably in 1950, helping Republicans to achieve gains in a number of contests. How many is open to question. Senator Herman Welker of Idaho claimed that McCarthy's campaign against communist influence in government accounted for the election of at least seven new Republican senators in those midterms.[126] But Welker exaggerated both the issue's salience and, at a time of extensive anticommunist rhetoric, McCarthy's own responsibility for its electoral exploitation. McCarthyism probably made little difference to the party's advance in McCarthy's own state, for example. His clearest impact occurred in Maryland, where he helped fan anti-Red flames of opposition to Senator Millard E. Tydings, who chaired a hostile investigation of McCarthy's initial allegations of communist subversion, but Tydings's reelection bid was vulnerable in other respects.[127]

Still, for a time anticommunism energized many Republicans' attacks on their Democratic rivals, and the issue overheated some contests. Moreover, it did experience some success in peeling some support away from the Democrats within constituencies that were generally hostile toward Republicans – Catholics and ethnic Americans of eastern European origins, overlapping groups with special cause for anticommunist anxieties.[128] But McCarthy's own appeal was strongest among existing Republican supporters; his campaign did not extend the party's reach among Democratic supporters.[129] The larger, longer-term power of anticommunism in tackling the party's minority problem was weak. By 1952, relatively few Americans saw domestic communism as a significant threat or as an important issue. In response to a poll that year asking for the "two or three biggest problems facing the country," only about one in eight mentioned domestic communism.[130] In that year, Republicans sloganeered "Corruption, Korea, and Communism" as their case against the Democrats; another survey found that the first two issues won support for the party, but the third had no salience for most.[131]

[126] *NYT*, July 1, 1951, 98.

[127] Richard M. Fried, "Electoral Politics and McCarthyism: The 1950 Campaign," in Robert Griffith and Athan Theoharis, eds., *The Specter: Original Essays on the Cold War and the Origins of McCarthyism* (New York: New Viewpoints, 1974), 190–222.

[128] Donald F. Crosby, "The Politics of Religion: American Catholics and the Anti-Communist Impulse," in Robert Griffith and Athan Theoharis, eds., *Specter: Original Essays on the Cold War and the Origins of McCarthyism* (New York: New Viewpoints, 1974), 36–37.

[129] Nelson W. Polsby, "Towards an Explanation of McCarthyism," *Political Studies* 8 (1960), 250–271.

[130] Samuel A. Stouffer, *Communism, Conformity, and Civil Liberties: A Cross-section of the Nation Speaks Its Mind* (Garden City, N.Y.: Doubleday, 1955), 58–88 (quotation, 86). Even in 1949, a poll reported that only 3 percent of respondents said that communism was the most serious issue facing the nation. John Earl Haynes, *Red Scare or Red Menace? American Communism and Anticommunism in the Cold War Era* (Chicago: Dee, 1996), 188.

[131] Angus Campbell, Philip E. Converse, Warren E. Miller, and Donald E. Stokes, *The American Voter* (New York: John Wiley, 1960), 50–51.

Rogers Dunn, who had aimed to quantify the "bought vote" during the 1930s, now modified his thesis about the Republicans' minority status. Then he had insisted that New Deal spending deprived the Republican Party of victory. In the post–World War II period he argued that the "payroll vote" had exerted a longer-term deleterious impact on the party by diverting Republicans from the realization that only a minority of Americans genuinely supported New Deal liberalism, which secured victory at the polls thanks to the support Democrats gained from the various beneficiaries of federal largesse. This misunderstanding led the party to embrace a me-too approach that consolidated the welfare state – according to Dunn, "only the sugar coating serving as bait for totalitarian government."[132] Dunn furthermore claimed that the party was now failing to recognize that the doctrine of federal spending – "subsidy politics" – was losing favor in labor and farm areas. The result was that Republican politicians did not press home their advantage by attacking Democratic shortcomings.[133]

Dunn was thus among others who emphasized low turnout as the party's key electoral problem, who were concerned about the forty-five million Americans who did not vote in 1948, compared with about thirty-four million in 1936 and 1940, and thirty-three million in 1944, suspecting that the mobilization of these nonvoters might unlock a Republican majority.[134] Tracing this gradual decline in turnout, Dunn concluded that the phenomenon revealed still another Republican failure – a failure to wage campaigns persuasive, and conservative, enough to mobilize the party's potential support. In support of the thesis, he argued that the more conservative among Republican congressional candidates were better at winning, even in areas where many were the direct financial beneficiaries of programmatic liberalism.[135] Most of the "stay-at-home" vote was potentially Republican, he claimed, provided that Republicans made clear their differences with New Deal liberalism.[136] Dunn stressed Taft's 1950 victory as an example of this strategy's promise.[137]

This answer to the minority problem was attractive, especially to the more conservative among Republicans. It suggested that their ideas enjoyed latent popular confidence, that the party simply needed to articulate this conservatism with clarity in order to translate its fundamental popularity into electoral success. In this view, any compromise with New Deal liberalism or any dilution of the conservative message was not only unnecessary but even hostile to the mobilization of Republican support. Senator William E. Jenner, an Indiana conservative, promoted a particularly bold version of this thesis. "Forty-five million voters in the United States refused to exercise their franchise because they were given no choice and there was no vehicle through

---

[132] Rogers C. Dunn, speech, April 28, 1950, box 4, Dunn Papers.
[133] Cleveland, Ohio, *Plain Dealer* clipping, Oct. 1, 1950, box 4, Dunn Papers.
[134] Hugh D. Scott, Jr., to F. M. Stapleton, June 30, 1949, box 6, Scott Papers.
[135] *Saturday Evening Post* clipping, May 30, 1954, box 4, Dunn Papers.
[136] *New York Sunday News* clipping, Nov. 7, 1954, box 4, Dunn Papers.
[137] Rogers C. Dunn, "The Political H Bomb," printed in *Congressional Record*, April 23, 1956, box 4, Dunn Papers.

which they could register their protest against the do-good patronage boost-ing, internationally-minded, Socialist government of the past 16 years," he said.[138] Low turnout in 1948, when Dewey secured slightly fewer votes than in 1944, fueled such claims.[139] During his quest for the 1952 presidential nomi-nation, in answer to the attack that his conservatism was incapable of winning the general election, Taft offered a sophisticated version of this argument. He claimed that a strong focus on party principles and a rejection of a me-too strategy were necessary to enthuse party workers so that they would cam-paign energetically, effectively mobilizing the Republican vote and thus secur-ing victory.[140]

Though attractive to many, the idea that nonvoters as a whole amounted to a nonmobilized majority for conservative politics was a myth. Instead, low turnout actually tended to favor their party, as the 1942 elections had dem-onstrated. In 1948, four out of five nonvoters preferred Truman to Dewey, though the party's official analysis evaded this conclusion in referring to thin evidence and a "mixed picture."[141] It was unquestionably advantageous for the party to maximize its own support at the polls through effective mobi-lization, which offered a reminder of the importance of good organization. "A strong, vigorous year-around organization, based on the precincts, is the only formula I know for political success," national chair Gabrielson told a meeting of state party chairs from the Midwest in October 1949, emphasizing the turnout problem.[142] But effective mobilization of the party's own vote was different from the generalized goal of turnout maximization.

Dunn's revision of the bought-vote thesis reflected its larger decline. It nev-ertheless remained a feature of how some Republicans viewed the New Deal coalition – noted in 1951 by Joe Martin, who criticized Republicans' "despair and defeatism" about their prospects, partly explained by the assumption that "the voters have been bought with their own money and that we will go up against a controlled vote."[143] Still, on the whole, Republicans recognized that it made little sense to think of a bought vote when many fewer Americans were direct beneficiaries of programmatic spending currently than during the New Deal. Instead, Truman's 1948 strategy in particular encouraged Republicans to modify the thesis to see the Democratic Party as pandering to interest groups in search of victory. They characterized their own party's mis-sion as the pursuit of a national interest, aloof from the selfishness of group interests.[144] This theme was not new. In his 1944 campaign against Roosevelt,

---

[138] *Times-Herald* clipping, Aug. 1, 1949, box 7, Scott Papers.

[139] Patterson, *Mr. Republican*, 425.

[140] John Robert Greene, *The Crusade: The Presidential Election of 1952* (Lanham, Md.: University Press of America, 1985), 75.

[141] Campbell et al., *The American Voter*, 110–111; Lubell, *The Future of American Politics*, 241–243; "The 1948 Elections: A Statistical Analysis," May 1949, reel 1, *Papers of the Republican Party*, part II.

[142] Guy George Gabrielson, speech, Oct. 15, 1949, box 787, Taft Papers.

[143] Joseph W. Martin, Jr., "The Three Great Issues for 1952," Oct. 1, 1951, box 7, Scott Papers.

[144] See, for example, Hugh Scott, speech, Nov. 18, 1948, box 10, addition 10200-ab, Scott Papers.

Dewey spoke of the need for a government that did not pit class against class, race against race.[145]

During this period a new response to the minority problem also emerged. This response was particularly iconoclastic and more promising than concern about the bought vote or turnout. It was the work of Richard Nixon and his campaign manager, Murray M. Chotiner; the response was controversial as well as iconoclastic. This was because an insight informing their strategic approach was the belief that opposition rather than support mobilized voters, an insight that dismissed as unproblematic any concern about Republican negativity. Chotiner later explained to an RNC-organized "campaign school" that "if we like it or not, the American people in many instances vote against a candidate, against a party, or against an issue, rather than for a candidate or an issue or a party."[146]

The particularly innovative contribution to the minority debate, however, was the conclusion that it was hopeless for Republicans to question New Deal liberalism's achievements, in an effort to explain the party's alternative, whether moderate or conservative. These achievements were the reason for the Democratic Party's majority status, and such discussion simply reinforced these issues' electoral salience, which was advantageous to the Democrats. According to Chotiner, "it is too difficult to sell the public the idea that welfare is to be shunned or that fair dealing is to be avoided." The Republican challenge was to identify more advantageous territory for campaign debate and then push debate toward this territory; this was the purpose that anticommunism served in Nixon's 1950 Senate campaign against Helen Gahagan Douglas. Reacting to revelations of corrupt practices in the federal government, Chotiner concluded that this was the next promising front of attack for the party. "If the Democratic party refuses to meet us on the issue WE declare, their silence will convict them," he wrote in May 1951. "If they do attempt to meet us, they are hopelessly lost because the facts are overwhelmingly against them."[147] But some were reluctant to accept the Chotiner strategy's wisdom. Kenneth Wherry challenged the key conclusion that New Deal liberalism was beyond attack, writing "that it is true everybody loves Santa Claus, yet I think there is another issue on which the Democrats are vulnerable, and that is the wasteful expenditure of money for these welfare ideas and the toll in taxes it has taken from the individual."[148]

The iconoclastic insight that informed Nixon's attacks on Democrats was not always easy to see. In conceding New Deal liberalism's electoral strength, Nixon nevertheless used communism as a means to share his party's antiliberal rhetoric. In 1946, like many Republicans, Nixon compared his Democratic

[145] Thomas E. Dewey, speech, Oct. 7, 1944, box 10, series 2, Hickenlooper Papers.
[146] Transcript, "RNC Campaign School," n.d., PPS 300.424, Nixon Vice Presidential Collection.
[147] Murray M. Chotiner to Richard Nixon, May 24, 1951, PPS 300.74A.2, Nixon Vice Presidential Collection.
[148] Kenneth S. Wherry to Richard Nixon, June 8, 1951, PPS 300.108, Nixon Vice Presidential Collection.

opponent, Jerry Voorhis, with Vito Marcantonio, demonizing Voorhis as being soft on communism. In 1950 he directly equated Douglas's views with communism.[149] Because Douglas placed the Fair Deal's strenuous promotion at the center of her campaign, Nixon's attacks on Douglas sometimes sounded like the rejection of New Deal liberalism. But Nixon concentrated on foreign policy and anticommunism in developing the case for his candidacy, rather than challenging New Deal liberalism systematically.[150] Even if difficult to detect, the approach was a fresh and apparently promising response to the party's minority problem. Its aggressive emphasis on anticommunism earned controversy for Nixon, however, as did its dependence on the creation of a demon to oppose.

Among the clearest examples of Truman's interest in pursuing New Deal liberalism's agenda beyond the Roosevelt administration's achievements involved race. In 1948 Truman advocated legislation on civil rights including measures against lynching and the poll tax and the permanent establishment of a Fair Employment Practices Commission (created by executive order in 1941). During the 81st Congress, Senate opposition killed the proposals, so Truman's achievements were limited to executive orders against segregation in the armed forces and in federal employment. Still, the national Democratic Party was obviously moving away from equivocation in its commitment to the cause of racial progress. This encouraged African Americans' movement away from the Republican Party, a trend that most leading Republicans did little to challenge, even though the party on Capitol Hill and elsewhere remained supportive of civil rights initiatives.[151] It also fostered dissatisfaction among segregationist southerners with the Democratic Party. In 1946 Taft privately observed that southern whites' refusal to consider Republican support made northern African Americans a more promising electoral target.[152] But developments within the Democratic Party might change the equation, he thought. "[I]f the Democratic Party nominated Henry Wallace, and the Southern Democratic organizations were willing to walk out of the convention to form a separate Democratic Party," wrote Taft, "we could perhaps work out an amalgamation with them."[153] Though developments in 1948 were different from the scenario that Taft outlined, the platform promises of Truman's Democratic Party alienated many southern politicians enough to precipitate a walkout, leading not to an "amalgamation" between Republicans and southern Democrats, but to the creation of the Dixiecrat party and the Thurmond presidential candidacy.

Although Taft at first suspected that African Americans' support was likelier than white southerners', he nevertheless doubted his party's ability to

---

[149] Bell, *Liberal State*, 202.
[150] Gellman, *The Contender*, 306–334 (quotation, 308).
[151] Sinclair, *Congressional Realignment*, 38–42.
[152] Robert A. Taft to Richard B. Scandrett, Jr., March 4, 1946, box 879, Taft Papers.
[153] Robert A. Taft to Stanley M. Rowe, Dec. 31, 1946, box 879, Taft Papers.

"outbid Mrs. Roosevelt." In his view, the importance to African Americans of permanence for the Fair Employment Practices Committee created an incompatibility between their community's political concerns and his party's anti-government tenets, though "[t]here are other measures like the bill to outlaw the poll tax and the anti-lynching bill which are hard to find good argument against."[154] In New York, Dewey had developed a promising record on civil rights to promote in his 1948 campaign against Truman, but within the general context of complacency he did not – even though Herbert Brownell had previously believed in African Americans' importance to the improvement of the party's fortunes. The possibility of southern gains might have influenced this silence; although Dewey and Brownell later disclaimed any such expectation, both Gallup and Crossley polls predicted, inaccurately, that Dewey would win Virginia.[155]

Such neglect was consequential. Julius J. Adams, the *Amsterdam News*'s managing editor and a Republican sympathizer, observed that "the Republican Party has completely departed from its traditional role as the champion of civil and human rights." He tempered this criticism, however, by emphasizing that the Dewey campaign's key shortcoming was a failure to communicate its message effectively and to cultivate African American leaders, not one of policy substance.[156] Not all interpretations of Dewey's record were so favorable; one NAACP staffer wrote that he "has not been forthright on many of these racial issues [involving antidiscrimination measures in New York] and has never moved until he was pushed into it."[157] Nevertheless, Dewey's northeastern awareness of civil rights decisively placed him among the party's more liberal. The party at large had little enthusiasm for racial liberalism, as the 1950 principles statement indicated. Despite efforts by some Capitol Hill northeasterners to ensure the inclusion of an unequivocal commitment to action on civil rights, the result was "weak and vacillating" in this area, according to one of them, Senator George Aiken of Vermont. Senator Hubert H. Humphrey, a Minnesota Democrat helping to lead his party toward action on civil rights, said that it amounted to an appeal to segregationists.[158]

Expectations of potential African American support were now modest. A. B. Hermann, the RNC official responsible for minority liaison, urged Republican concentration on the problem, telling an executive session of the national committee, "If we can get 20 per cent of them back into this Party,

[154] Robert A. Taft to Charles D. Hilles, May 21, 1945, box 786, Taft Papers; Taft to Stanley M. Rowe, Dec. 31, 1946, box 879, Taft Papers.
[155] Smith, *Thomas E. Dewey*, 523–524; Simon Topping, "'Never Argue with the Gallup Poll': Thomas Dewey, Civil Rights and the Election of 1948," *Journal of American Studies* 38 (2004), 179–198; Frederick Mosteller et al., *The Pre-Election Polls of 1948: Report to the Committee on Analysis of Pre-election Polls and Forecasts* (New York: Social Science Research Council, 1949).
[156] Julius J. Adams to Hugh Scott, Jan. 5, 1949, box 1, series 5, Dewey Papers.
[157] Madison Jones to Walter White, March 15, 1948, box A232, series II, NAACP Records.
[158] Bruce H. Kalk, "Yankee Party or Southern Strategy? George Aiken and the Republican Party, 1936–1972," *Vermont History* 64 (1996), 241.

and 5 or 10 per cent of the vast minorities, who today are the balance of power in America, we can't help but be victorious."[159] The "balance of power" reference echoed NAACP claims of African Americans' electoral importance; according to Walter White before the 1948 elections, there were at least seventeen states with 293 electoral votes "in which the Negro vote acting with reasonable unanimity as a bloc can determine the winner in any fairly close election."[160]

Leading Republicans were, by contrast, stepping up their interest in cultivating the South. In 1948 national chair Hugh Scott, a Virginia native though a Pennsylvania politician, paid a campaign visit to Dallas, where he stressed Republican support for states' rights and specifically for Texas's, rather than federal, ownership of the oil-rich tidelands.[161] Visiting Nashville, Robert Taft more starkly asserted the common ground of conservatism that united Republicans and most Tennessee Democrats against the Truman administration's "radical" agenda of ideas, which he said was the brainchild of CIO-PAC activists. Unlike Scott, he explicitly mentioned race as a reason for southern support of the GOP. "The President would center in Washington the entire field of control over questions involving civil rights," Taft said, "without even considering the proper functions of the Federal Government, the states and local communities in dealing with different features of the problem."[162] Guy George Gabrielson, Scott's successor as national chair, told RNC members that the need for electoral votes in the South "might not have been too serious at the time when we had solid Republican states north of the Mason-Dixon line, but some of those states that at one time were very solidly Republican are now becoming marginal areas, and if we are going to build towards a stronger Republican Party that can carry a national election we must do some effective and constructive work south of the Mason-Dixon line."[163]

Internal institutional obstacles to party growth in the South, with which Hoover ineffectually and even counterproductively grappled during his presidency, remained. John Wesley Kilgo, the party's 1944 gubernatorial candidate in Tennessee, observed that the party there was "busy with its intra-party strife and neglected its opportunity as well as its duty in State politics." In the party's eastern Tennessee stronghold, Republicans concentrated on congressional politics alone, according to Kilgo.[164] Similarly, though Georgia once had nine traditionally Republican counties, after World War II it had only

[159] Transcript, RNC executive session, Sept. 14, 1950, reel 10, *Papers of the Republican Party*, part I, series A.

[160] Walter White, "Will the Negro Elect Our Next President?" n.d., box A83, series II, NAACP Records.

[161] Hugh Scott, speech excerpts, Sept. 20, 1948, box 10, addition 10200-ab, Scott Papers; Scott to Edward L. Bacher, July 19, 1948, box 10, addition 10200-ab, Scott Papers.

[162] Robert A. Taft, news release, Oct. 11, 1948, box 10, addition 10200-ab, Scott Papers.

[163] Transcript, RNC executive session, Dec. 8, 1950, reel 10, *Papers of the Republican Party*, part I, series A.

[164] John Wesley Kilgo, *Campaigning in Dixie: With Some Reflections on Two-Party Government* (New York: Hobson Book Press, 1945), 87–88 (quotation, 88).

one, partly attributable to the party's patronage-focused leadership there.[165] The RNC created a committee to study the party's development in the South, declared to be "the great frontier of the Republican Party from this point out."[166] Its chair, Louisiana's John E. Jackson, reported that the committee identified as an enduring obstacle "the selfish greed and venality of the contending political forces which oppose the growth and competition of the Republican Party because of the ever lurking fear that the great power of public office and control of political patronage will be wrested from them." The committee advocated a long-term commitment to candidate recruitment and grassroots organization, foreseeing that two decades of such efforts were perhaps necessary to achieve a real breakthrough.[167] Jackson saw the absence of county-level candidates and the poor overall quality of state-level candidates as a compelling problem; he also saw a need for Republicans among "men of outstanding prominence, women of standing in their communities, men and women who have public confidence," in order to build the party.[168]

Senator Karl E. Mundt of South Dakota promoted a quicker fix to the problem, one designed to transform the party's ideological nature as well as its electoral fortunes. Mundt's explanation for conservatism's electoral decline involved the parties' internal dynamics; it posited that the Democrats' 1936 abandonment of the two-thirds convention rule effectively undermined southern influence within their party – exactly as this removal of southern delegates' veto power over candidate selection and platform creation intended. The rule change allowed the Democrats to embrace an urban liberal agenda. According to Mundt, the southern disinclination to support Republican candidates encouraged his own party to compete with the Democrats for urban and interest-group voters through the pursuit of an unsuccessful me-too strategy. This interparty competition for liberal support was driving the nation toward socialism, even though most Americans opposed such policies; Mundt pointed to 1948's low turnout as partial evidence for this claim. The way to halt "our trends toward total centralized political power and economic socialism" was an alliance between Republicans and southern Democrats, thus consolidating at an electoral level the conservative coalition visible in Congress since the late 1930s.[169] This stress on the importance of unity between northern and southern conservatives as a route to a majority challenged the view that a turnout boost in itself would ensure that enough conservative voters would go to the polls.[170]

---

[165] *New Republic*, July 21, 1947, 22.
[166] Transcript, RNC meeting, Jan. 26, 1951, reel 10, *Papers of the Republican Party*, part I, series A.
[167] RNC, press release, [c. Jan. 26, 1951], reel 10, *Papers of the Republican Party*, part I, series A.
[168] Transcript, RNC executive session, Dec. 8, 1950, reel 10, *Papers of the Republican Party*, part I, series A.
[169] Karl E. Mundt, "Should Need for a Southern Democrat-Northern Republican Alliance in 1952 Be Explored?" Sept. 15, 1951, box 42, Richberg Papers.
[170] Lichtman, *White Protestant Nation*, 169.

In September 1951 Mundt announced the creation of a short-term Committee to Explore Political Realignment to investigate the mechanics of such an alliance, chaired by Albert W. Hawkes, a former Republican senator from New Jersey and former United States Chamber of Commerce president, and Edward A. O'Neal, an Alabama Democrat and former American Farm Bureau Federation president.[171] Those who did not share Mundt's conservatism viewed with discomfort such a plan for party growth. Critics of this realignment project praised the parties' broadness as encouraging compromise, as promoting pragmatic engagement with the nation's problems, and as enhancing the polity's stability. "If anybody can think of a more tragic eventuality than that he must indeed have a good imagination," observed Willkie clubs founder Oren Root of an ideology-based realignment, viewing such a cleavage as likely to involve an unwelcome clash between society's poorer and wealthier people.[172] Republican opponents of the Mundt plan also worried about the implications for the party's relationship with African Americans of its embrace of states' rights and cultivation of southern conservatism.[173] On the committee's announcement, RNC officials made clear the official preference for the party's own development in the South, as opposed to a formalized alliance with Democrats. The project won no endorsement from any leading southern Democrat. Apart from Mundt, the only active politician openly interested in the committee's work was Senator Owen Brewster, a Maine Republican.[174]

The assumptions informing the committee's work included the confidence that a clear-cut choice between conservatism and liberalism promised electoral success for conservatives. In addition to a belief in the wisdom of an appeal to southern segregationists, they also included suspicions of the mass electorate, which were sometimes ethnophobic. Its staffers, John Underhill and J. Harvie Williams, wrote an analysis that searched for "creeping socialism's" electoral roots and found them in the "new immigration" from southern and eastern Europe in the late nineteenth and early twentieth centuries and its "feudal tradition" – "[t]he socialistic program of the New Deal and Fair Deal, wholly alien to the American heritage, violated none of their traditions" and even "conformed to them."[175] The committee's report did not draw on this analysis, however. The committee drew support for the Mundt thesis from a novel interpretation of the British Conservatives' 1951 victory, attributed to the absence of any sizeable vote for the Liberal Party; with a clearer-cut choice between Labour and Conservatives, a majority in the United Kingdom chose the latter, the report argued. On visits to the South in early 1952, Mundt urged

171 John Underhill, news release, Sept. 24, 1951, box 42, Richberg Papers.
172 *Commonweal*, April 15, 1949, 6–8.
173 Scripps-Howard clipping, n.d., box 42, Richberg Papers.
174 *Richmond Times Dispatch* clipping, Sept. 23, 1951, box 42, Richberg Papers.
175 [John Underhill and J. Harvie Williams,] "Chapter I: The Existing Political Situation in the United States," sent by Albert W. Hawkes to Donald R. Richberg, Nov. 27, 1951, box 3, Richberg Papers.

sectional support for Senator Richard Russell of Georgia as president in order to create an electoral college deadlock, throwing the presidential choice to the House, which "would undoubtedly bring about a permanent realignment of party forces in this country," he claimed.[176]

Mundt continued to promote a conservative realignment throughout the 1950s, advocating a series of institutional modifications friendly to conservatism in addition to a formalized coalition between southern Democrats and many Republicans. He called for electoral college reform, involving the replacement of the winner-takes-all system with the creation of single-elector districts, to undermine the influence of the big states. To dramatize his point, Mundt said that "one vote cast by Mr. Stumble Bum in New York City can put in action 45 electoral votes which mean more than all of the votes cast by intelligent people voting unanimously in 12 or 13 separate states of the United States." At the state level he advocated the modification of laws to facilitate cross-party voting in primaries, so that a registered Democrat in Georgia, for example, could participate in the Republican primary without imperiling that party attachment. He had recommendations for the other party, too. For the Democrats he favored the reintroduction of the two-thirds rule at the national convention, which Roosevelt terminated in 1936, to restore southern influence and to undermine liberalism; he hoped that the Republican Party might then create a similar rule. Similarly, to discourage liberal influence at the national conventions, he opposed the unit rule, according to which a state delegation cast its entire vote as a unit, reflecting the preference of a majority. The recommendation in which Mundt had least confidence was the GOP's revitalization in the deep South; in Mundt's view, though the potential implications of such a development were great, it remained difficult to achieve.[177]

Both Democrats and Republicans saw World War II hero Dwight D. Eisenhower as the answer to their party's problems. There was some early speculation that he was the ideal Republican opponent to Truman in 1948, but more serious pro-Eisenhower activity that year took place in the Democratic Party.[178] A diverse array of Democrats – including some conservatives but mostly liberals – sought in vain to persuade and later even to draft Eisenhower as a replacement for Truman, who seemed destined for defeat.[179] When Truman won the White House, it was the Republicans' turn, although, according to journalist Arthur Krock, in 1951 Truman himself offered to support Eisenhower if he decided to seek the Democratic nomination.[180] Looking for a leader to return

[176] *WP*, April 28, 1952, 6.
[177] James MacGregor Burns, *The Deadlock of Democracy: Four-Party Politics in America* (1963; London: John Calder, 1964), 295–299 (quotation, 296).
[178] John A. Wells, "General Conclusions," Sept. 30, 1947, box 41, series 2, Dewey Papers.
[179] Robert J. Donovan, *Conflict and Crisis: The Presidency of Harry S Truman, 1945–1948* (New York: Norton, 1977), 388–404.
[180] Stephen E. Ambrose, *Eisenhower*, vol. 1: *Soldier, General of the Army, President-elect, 1890–1952* (New York: Simon and Schuster, 1983), 515.

them to power, those who urged Eisenhower to enter electoral politics first tended to emphasize the need to halt New Deal liberalism.[181] Among them was Dewey. In July 1949, telling Eisenhower of his concerns about the nation's future, Dewey argued that no candidate who opposed liberalism's centralizing, paternalistic policies was able to win – as his own experience, as well as that of Hoover, Landon, and Willkie, indicated. The answer, according to Dewey, was the candidacy of a popular figure not associated with such unpopular ideas; Dewey told him, Eisenhower noted, "that only I (if I should carefully preserve my assets) can save this country from going to hades in the hand basket of paternalism – socialism – dictatorship."[182]

Eisenhower was receptive to Dewey's stress on freedom. As Columbia University president after World War II, Eisenhower spoke publicly about the dangers of big government, advocating instead a path "down the middle of the road between the unfettered power of concentrated wealth on one flank, and the unbridled power of statism, or partisan interest, on the other," as he put it in a 1949 speech.[183] Indeed, he echoed Republicans' antistatist anxieties so vividly that some placed his views on domestic policy to Taft's right. When efforts to recruit Eisenhower as a candidate stepped up in fall 1951, Eugene C. Pulliam, an Indiana newspaper publisher, noted to Harry Darby, part of these efforts, that "General Eisenhower is as completely fed up with socialism and bureaucracy as either you or I," believing "that only freedom and a strong economy can save America from going down the road to totalitarianism."[184] But it was not this concern about liberalism's trajectory that led Eisenhower to conclude that he should start a new career in politics.[185]

Instead, Eisenhower's views on foreign policy caused him to run. The arguments employed by those who tried to persuade him to enter party politics had shifted in this direction. Senator Henry Cabot Lodge, Jr., of Massachusetts, for example, told him that he was the only potential candidate who could challenge the statist drift at home while avoiding the "fatal errors of isolationism."[186] "I'm running because Taft is an isolationist," Eisenhower told journalists off the record in June 1952. "His election would be a disaster."[187] In particular, what precipitated his decision to run was his conclusion that a Taft presidency would pose a threat to international arrangements for European security, developed by the Truman administration and implemented in part by Eisenhower,

[181] Louis Galambos, ed., *The Papers of Dwight David Eisenhower*, vol. X: *Columbia University* (Baltimore: Johns Hopkins University Press, 1984), 755–756, 808–809, 839–841.

[182] Galambos, ed., *Papers of Dwight David Eisenhower*, X: 677–679 (quotations, 678).

[183] Galambos, ed., *Papers of Dwight David Eisenhower*, X: 745.

[184] Eugene C. Pulliam to Harry Darby, Oct. 11, 1951, box 41, series 10, Dewey Papers.

[185] Louis Galambos, ed., *The Papers of Dwight David Eisenhower*, vol. XI: *Columbia University* (Baltimore: Johns Hopkins University Press, 1984), 882–886.

[186] Louis Galambos, ed., *The Papers of Dwight David Eisenhower*, vol. XII: *NATO and the Campaign of 1952* (Baltimore: Johns Hopkins University Press, 1989), 608.

[187] Robert A. Divine, *Foreign Policy and U.S. Presidential Elections, 1952–1960* (New York: New Viewpoints, 1974), 31.

who in early 1951 assumed duties as NATO's first supreme commander.[188] Eisenhower believed, too, that the implementation of Cold War policy under Truman was flawed and demanded improvement.[189] The concern about internationalism's future was also especially significant to those Republicans who urged him to challenge Taft.[190]

Despite his enormous popularity, Eisenhower did not find it easy to defeat Taft, who had deep reservoirs of party support. Victory in many primary elections did not create enough Eisenhower delegates to outweigh decisively those selected in states where party leaders and activists, rather than Republican-supporting voters, were responsible for delegate selection. Taft, moreover, won enough primaries to demonstrate that he possessed at least some electoral appeal.

Arguments about the party's minority problem informed the battle between Eisenhower and Taft. Taft insisted that enthusing grassroots Republicans led to good organization, which in turn maximized the party's vote. The way to enthuse activists was via a stress on conservatism. In response, Eisenhower supporters believed that such a conservative stress was likely to alienate voters – independents and disaffected Democrats – whose support was necessary for victory. Furthermore, they did not agree that the maximization of turnout would involve the mobilization of a conservative "hidden vote."[191]

The evenness of the nomination battle meant that crucial to the overall outcome were decisions that the national convention made over a number of contested delegations from the South – Georgia, Louisiana, and Texas. In each case both Eisenhower Republicans and Taft Republicans claimed to be the rightful delegates. Taft's long-term wooing of state party leaders brought him a set of delegates, but Eisenhower enthusiasm led to activists' selection of a different set of delegates; state leaders dismissed the Eisenhower activists as often newcomers to the party who, as Democrats, had no right to participate in the selection process. A successful publicity drive about shenanigans such as the "Texas steal" helped the Eisenhower camp to build convention support for its "fair-play" proposals; superior cultivation of delegates also helped. Eisenhower's candidacy gained momentum when the convention seated the three states' friendly delegations, leading to victory over Taft.[192]

Wounded by his defeat, Taft wrote a remarkable – almost conspiracy-minded – analysis of its causes, in which he blamed first "the power of the New York financial interest and a large number of business men subject to New York influence, who had selected General Eisenhower as their candidate at least a year ago," and second the propaganda-like opposition he detected

---

[188] William B. Pickett, *Eisenhower Decides To Run: Presidential Politics and Cold War Strategy* (Chicago: Dee, 2000), 51, 119, 210–211.

[189] Robert R. Bowie and Richard H. Immerman, *Waging Peace: How Eisenhower Shaped an Enduring Cold War Strategy* (New York: Oxford University Press, 1998), 11.

[190] Brownell, *Advising Ike*, 91–92.

[191] *Business Week*, March 29, 1952, 94–96.

[192] Brownell, *Advising Ike*, 105–119; Mayer, *The Republican Party*, 487–491.

in four-fifths of the nation's press.[193] The analysis offered evidence of the geographic tensions underlying the party. Eisenhower was indeed the candidate of Dewey and his supporters. But it was finally the conclusion among enough Republicans that Eisenhower was likelier to win than Taft that was probably decisive; two decades outside the White House had sharpened the appetite for a return.[194] Seeking party unity, Eisenhower soothed Taft's disappointment by asking for his policy and strategy advice. The exercise helped to allay Taft's concerns about Eisenhower, but it did not change the Eisenhower project. On the one hand, Eisenhower's and Taft's beliefs about the Fair Deal's dangers had much in common anyway; on the other, Taft's preference for a rerun of 1950's "liberty-versus-socialism" theme did not dissuade the Eisenhower team from an emphasis on "Korea, Communism, and Corruption" – K_1C_2.[195] The first element was particularly important.

Gradually and successfully the Eisenhower campaign elevated Korea's salience to the choice between the candidates, a winning emphasis for the anti-incumbent war hero. Recognizing its threat, Truman suggested the removal of foreign policy from campaign debate, as in 1948, but Eisenhower refused. Democratic presidential nominee Adlai Stevenson's response to the threat involved a strategy, similar to Truman's in 1948, to remind farmers and workers of New Deal liberalism's benefits and to warn them of a Republican depression.[196] The worrying developments of the early Cold War – especially the outbreak of the Korean War – brought a tide of popular dissatisfaction with the Democratic record on peace. As World War II closed, one-half of respondents to a poll expected the Democrats to "do the best job of making the peace with other nations," compared with only one in five who named the Republicans.[197] In 1952 those most concerned about the Korean War by three to one thought Eisenhower the better candidate in achieving what he called "an early and honest end" to the war when he promised to visit Korea in search of peace.[198]

Eisenhower won, and the Republican Party secured control of both the House and the Senate. While Eisenhower's victory suggested that the Republican Party was at last posing a real challenge to the Democrats' majority status, its nature offered fresh evidence that the turnout argument was a myth. His candidacy did boost turnout, but the implications were different from those that party conservatives had projected. Eisenhower supporters who did not vote in

[193] Robert A. Taft, "How I Lost the Nomination," *Human Events*, Dec. 2, 1959, sec. III, no pagination.

[194] Mayer, *The Republican Party*, 491.

[195] Patterson, *Mr. Republican*, 572–580.

[196] Barton J. Bernstein, "Election of 1952," in Arthur M. Schlesinger, Jr., and Fred L. Israel, eds., *History of American Presidential Elections, 1789–1968*, vol. IV (New York: Chelsea House, 1971), 3249–3260.

[197] Claude Robinson, "Truman, the Republicans and 1948" (Opinion Research Corporation), July 5, 1945, box 40, Stassen Papers.

[198] Harris, *Is There a Republican Majority?* 24–26 (quotation, 24).

1948 lacked the attachment to Republican policies demonstrated by party loyalists (those who voted for both Dewey and Eisenhower), and they were thus similar to those who defected from a Truman vote in 1948 in order to support Eisenhower in 1952. In this way, Eisenhower crafted his Republican majority among those weakly supportive of what the party offered; there was no hidden majority of conservatives. Eisenhower won because one in five Democrats and three in four independents voted for him; Republicans numbered only one in three among the electorate.[199]

Eisenhower's majority drew on all major components of the Democratic coalition – union members, Catholics, city dwellers, and skilled and semiskilled workers. One survey suggested that Eisenhower turned Dewey's 15 percent share of people in skilled and semiskilled occupations into a total of 34 percent, for example. The key exception to this pattern of success was among African Americans, who showed no pro-Republican trend.[200] Eisenhower made a geographic breakthrough for the party, too, significantly undermining the Democrats' "solid South" at the presidential level. He carried Virginia, Florida, Tennessee, Oklahoma, and Texas, and lost Kentucky by only seven hundred votes. Early returns suggested that he might even win South Carolina under the "Independents for Eisenhower" ticket, and the same label spectacularly lifted his share in Mississippi to 39 percent from the usual Republican result of about five thousand votes.[201] Patterns varied from state to state; sometimes the strongly pro-Dixiecrat precincts of 1948 returned to support of the national Democrats, and sometimes they switched to Eisenhower. But the key pattern involved Eisenhower's strength among wealthier people in the urban areas, which often displayed similar socioeconomic voting cleavages to the North, although no inclination to vote for other Republicans below the presidency accompanied this strength.[202] Outside the South this newcomer to party politics also lifted the Republican vote at subpresidential levels. According to one estimate, Eisenhower's coattail effect was decisive enough to secure Republican victory in thirty-nine congressional districts, thirteen Senate seats, and seven governorships.[203]

Samuel Lubell's exploration of public opinion at the time of the election found a nation torn between two impulses that encouraged simultaneous yet contradictory sympathy for both parties – one seen as the party of peace but depression, the other seen as the party of prosperity but war.[204] Lubell

[199] Harris, *Is There a Republican Majority?* 5.

[200] Angus Campbell, Gerald Gurin, and Warren E. Miller, "Political Issues and the Vote: November, 1952," *APSR* 47 (1952), 359–385.

[201] Paul T. David, Malcolm Moos, and Ralph M. Goldman, eds., *Presidential Nominating Politics in 1952* (Baltimore: Johns Hopkins Press, 1954), III: 4–5.

[202] Donald S. Strong, "The Presidential Election in the South, 1952," *Journal of Politics* 17 (1955), 343–389.

[203] Alfred De Grazia, *The Western Public: 1952 and Beyond* (Stanford, Calif.: Stanford University Press, 1954), 14–15.

[204] Samuel Lubell, *Revolt of the Moderates* (New York: Harper, 1956), 37–43.

perhaps exaggerated the extent to which voters had confidence in the party, as opposed to Eisenhower personally, on foreign policy.[205] Still, the immediacy of the Korean War's problems encouraged Americans to turn to the national hero of World War II. The Republican Party nevertheless had much to prove in office in order to demonstrate itself no longer the party of Herbert Hoover and hard times. The Depression era still powerfully shaped Americans' views of the parties.[206]

[205] Angus Campbell, Gerald Gurin, and Warren E. Miller, *The Voter Decides* (Evanston, Ill.: Row, Peterson, 1954), 56–58.
[206] Donald E. Stokes, Angus Campbell, and Warren E. Miller, "Components of Electoral Decision," *APSR* 52 (1958), 372.

5

"Modern Republicanism": 1953–1961

Dwight Eisenhower's popularity and 1952's victories encouraged high hopes for the Republican future. "There is every reason to suppose," wrote journalist Richard Rovere in June 1953, "that with good management and just a small amount of luck [the Republicans] can build as formidable a series of political alliances as the Democrats built back in the thirties."[1] Eisenhower's remarkable political appeal was especially important in fostering such hopes; he enjoyed national popularity of a breadth and depth rarely paralleled in American history.[2] A crowd's enthusiasm for him at a 1956 appearance caused one foreign journalist to remark, "I haven't seen anything like this since Hitler."[3] At the White House he lost little of his popularity gained as a war hero; studies suggested that positive personal evaluations of him were even more extensive among Americans in 1956 than 1952 – enough to suggest to poll analysts that his reelection success relied more heavily on his strength as a political personality than on his presidential achievements.[4]

The Republican Party failed to realize the hopes that Rovere outlined, however. Instead, the 1950s proved to be a decade of declining fortunes. In 1954, the party lost its narrow majorities in Congress. In 1956, despite Eisenhower's landslide reelection to the presidency, Republicans failed to regain any ground on Capitol Hill. The results indicated, according to one reporter, "both the increasing grass-roots popularity of President Eisenhower and the increasing grass-roots unpopularity of the Republican party." The results of the 1958 midterms then provided unambiguous evidence of the party's weakness, as

[1] Richard H. Rovere, *Affairs of State: The Eisenhower Years* (New York: Farrar, Straus and Cudahy, 1956), 115.
[2] Herbert H. Hyman and Paul B. Sheatsley, "The Political Appeal of President Eisenhower," *POQ* 17 (1953–1954), 443–460.
[3] Katie Louchheim diary, July 17, 1956, box 77, Louchheim Papers.
[4] Campbell et al., *The American Voter*, 56.

GOP representation sank to 34 seats in the Senate and 154 seats in the House.[5] This was a midterm setback of unusually large proportions, which illustrated the enduring – growing, even – strength of the Democratic Party.[6] The Eisenhower years ended on a barely more encouraging note; in 1960 Richard M. Nixon lost to John F. Kennedy, if narrowly, in the race for the presidency, and congressional Republicans won back only some of the seats lost two years before. Polls suggested that in 1960 no more than three in ten Americans identified themselves as Republicans.[7] One reflection of Republican weakness then was the presidential candidates' use of their party attachment during the campaign; Nixon downplayed his party attachment while Kennedy stressed his – a clear indicator of the labels' contrasting value.[8] The Republican Party in the 1950s unquestionably remained America's minority.

Some Republicans of this era, together with other political observers, suspected that Eisenhower was significantly responsible for the party's disappointments and setbacks. An outsider to party politics, he supposedly showed little interest in GOP fortunes, investing barely any effort in the challenge to share his popularity with his fellow Republicans. At an RNC meeting in early 1959, Representative Richard M. Simpson of Pennsylvania ridiculed a message from the president extolling the virtues of "unremitting effort" in support of the party. "I call upon the White House to give us some of that 'unremitting effort' on behalf of the Republican party," said Simpson, whose anti-Eisenhower hostility won enthusiastic applause among an audience smarting from the 1958 defeats.[9] Liberal and moderate as well as conservative Republicans found fault with Eisenhower's party leadership. New York's Senator Jacob K. Javits saw his record in this regard as insubstantial because "he showed no real taste for leading a political movement or marshalling [sic] the personalities to support him in its leadership."[10]

But the 1950s Republican decline does not mean that Eisenhower neglected the party. He had a partisan edge that many contemporaries did not notice, and although he burnished his image as a war hero above party politics – an image that helps to account for the enormity of his political success – he had a vision for the GOP's future and worked with some commitment toward its achievement. Despite his lack of background in Republican politics, he saw

---

5 *Congress and the Nation, 1945–1964: A Review of Government and Politics in the Postwar Years* (Washington, D.C.: Congressional Quarterly Service, 1965), 13, 20, 23, 29, 32; *New York Herald Tribune* clipping, Nov. 13, 1956, BBC Press Cuttings Collection.

6 Sundquist, *Dynamics of the Party System*, 240–297.

7 Warren E. Miller and Santa A. Traugott, *American National Election Studies Data Sourcebook, 1952–1986* (Cambridge, Mass.: Harvard University Press, 1989), 81.

8 Stanley Kelley, Jr., "The Presidential Campaign," in Paul T. David, ed., *The Presidential Election and Transition 1960–1961* (Washington, D.C.: Brookings Institution, 1961), 65.

9 *Newsweek*, Feb. 2, 1959, 21–22.

10 Jacob K. Javits, "The GOP – and Modern Republicanism," sent Jan. 7, 1959, box 3, subseries 2, series 5, Javits Papers.

the party's revitalization as a key goal of his presidency. The adverse implications for the two-party system of the GOP's long consignment to minority status worried him, and this worry was among the more important factors that encouraged him both to enter electoral politics in 1952 and to run for a second term in 1956.[11]

Eisenhower's effort to revitalize the Republican Party involved two key elements, one designed to broaden the appeal of its principles and policies and the other to improve the capacity of its organization. "Modern Republicanism" sought to moderate the party's antigovernment emphasis, while Citizens for Eisenhower was the key institution aiming to recruit new activists to work for the party's cause. This twofold project was a compelling response to the minority problem.

As Simpson's attack on Eisenhower suggests, by no means all Republicans agreed that the revitalization effort was a promising path for the party to take. Disillusionment with conservative opposition to this project sometimes clouded Eisenhower's desire to work for the party. It even led him to well-publicized contemplation that the creation of a new party was a more promising route to his "middle-way" politics than the apparently impossible task of modernizing the GOP.[12] In private he often complained about congressional Republicans, and, after the 1954 loss of Congress, he sometimes mused that Democratic control was preferable.[13] In turn, many Democratic politicians told voters that they supported Eisenhower more effectively than conservative Republicans did, particularly on foreign policy. Upon announcing his party's program during the 1954 campaign, Senator Lyndon B. Johnson of Texas began with a pledge of full cooperation with the administration's foreign policy.[14] "The sober fact, of course, is that when the President denounces the Democrats as enemies of his program," said Adlai Stevenson that October, in remarks that acknowledged the significance of Eisenhower's work on behalf of his party, against the Democratic opposition, "he must know that on many key measures – foreign trade, housing, health, the conduct of foreign relations – the Democrats were far better supporters than the Republicans."[15]

When Javits questioned the energy that Eisenhower brought to his work as party leader, he also praised him – for his challenge to conservative Republicans and for his success in confirming the party's capacity to win elections.[16] Eisenhower would enjoy limited success at best in pursuing the positive goal of fashioning and consolidating a moderate brand of Republicanism that won

[11] Charles Murphy, notes, n.d., box 719, Luce Papers; Arthur Larson, *Eisenhower: The President Nobody Knew* (1968; London: Leslie Frewin, 1969), 45; Galvin, *Presidential Party Building*, 41–69.
[12] Robert Donovan, *Eisenhower: The Inside Story* (New York: Harper, 1956), 142–153.
[13] Ann Whitman diary, Feb. 13, 1956, box 8, Ann Whitman Diary Series, Eisenhower Papers [hereafter AWDS].
[14] *Manchester Guardian* clipping, Oct. 25, 1954, BBC Press Cuttings Collection.
[15] *NYT*, Oct. 10, 1954, 1, 44.
[16] Javits, "The GOP – and Modern Republicanism."

a majority's electoral support, beyond his personal victories, but he enjoyed more success in challenging anti-internationalist sentiment within the party. This victory was partly pyrrhic in nature, however, because the resentful reaction of conservatives to the Eisenhower project helped to ignite a powerful mobilization of new conservatism within the party. Still, the new conservatism that emerged was different from the old, because it generally lacked any isolationist impulse (except for a skeptical view of foreign aid).

The second rationale for Javits's praise involves less tangible, though equally important, developments. Since the New Deal, Republican engagement with the minority problem had frequently edged toward desperation – a sense of hopelessness in viewing the party's prospects of any significant electoral success, despair about New Deal liberalism's implications for the country. In the 1930s many Republicans saw the United States as no more than a few steps from dictatorship; in the 1940s they feared socialism's approach. Under Eisenhower, this desperation largely disappeared. In the 1960s some Republicans would return to pessimism, but the tenor of debate remained calmer and more hopeful after Eisenhower's presidency than it was before. Electoral success under Eisenhower fostered this new sobriety.

Eisenhower's challenge to the isolationist legacy among Republicans – the tenets of which were offensive to his internationalist commitment – was a particularly important component of his mission to transform the party. When he decided to seek the Republican candidacy, the desire to protect bipartisanship against the skeptics was a leading consideration.[17] His concerns about the significance of Republican opposition to his views on foreign policy were well founded. The congressional party contained many Republicans who opposed his internationalism, especially in the House.[18] In response, Eisenhower devoted considerable energy to the defense of his foreign policy.

One early challenge involved opposition to his nominee as ambassador to the Soviet Union, Charles Bohlen, a confirmation struggle that Eisenhower almost lost in the Senate; controversy surrounded Bohlen's advisory role with the U.S. delegation at Yalta in 1945. A more wide-ranging challenge was the Bricker amendment – first introduced in September 1951 and Senate Resolution 1 in 1953 – which proposed to restrict the president's treaty-making powers. On its introduction by Senator John Bricker of Ohio, the 1944 vice-presidential nominee, the proposed amendment was co-sponsored by all but four of the forty-eight Senate Republicans, also receiving support from eighteen Democrats, mostly southern conservatives.[19] The proposed amendment enshrined GOP concerns about the presidency's expanding powers and the Roosevelt and Truman administrations' unchecked diplomacy. But Eisenhower sought to

[17] Pickett, *Eisenhower Decides To Run*, 96–97.
[18] Gary W. Reichard, *The Reaffirmation of Republicanism: Eisenhower and the Eighty-Third Congress* (Knoxville: University of Tennessee Press, 1975), 14–50.
[19] Duane Tananbaum, *The Bricker Amendment Controversy: A Test of Eisenhower's Political Leadership* (Ithaca, N.Y.: Cornell University Press, 1988), 68–69.

protect the Cold War presidency's freedom of action and did not line up with these fellow Republicans. Thanks to Democratic assistance, his opposition was successful. Success was nevertheless incomplete; he failed to persuade some Republicans to change their mind about the amendment, which Bricker again offered in new versions for the next three years.[20]

Party loyalty and the success of Eisenhower's leadership helped ensure that congressional Republicans shifted away from anti-internationalism.[21] A similar change was visible among Republican voters, who were much more likely than before to approve of Cold War bipartisanship.[22] A skeptical element remained, however. This skepticism dependably emerged not just in the reappearances of the Bricker amendment but in Republican responses to foreign aid; opposition to administration proposals also occurred, for different reasons, among both fiscal conservatives and liberal internationalists in the Democratic Party. Throughout his White House years, Eisenhower needed to work hard to maintain party support for what he considered an essential component of American foreign policy, and appropriations were always less generous than the requested amounts. In 1957, for example, Congress appropriated $2.8 billion for the Mutual Security Program, more than a billion dollars lower than the sum Eisenhower described as "a minimum figure considering the issues at stake."[23] There were thus limits to the success of Eisenhower's promotion of Republican internationalism, especially when money was involved; still, he managed to contain the policy threat of anti-internationalism.

Achieving a more fundamental transformation of the party proved difficult. The failure of Franklin Roosevelt's "purge" effort against conservative Democrats demonstrated the limits of presidential authority as party leader. The tools available to Eisenhower extended little beyond private encouragement of the friendly, measured persuasion of the hostile. Within the constraints that existed, he acted. In 1954, persuasion was the tool in the case of Representative Joseph T. Meek – no enthusiast for modern Republicanism – who was the Republican challenger to Senator Paul Douglas of Illinois. In exchange for presidential help during the campaign, Eisenhower urged Meek to downplay his criticism of the administration's foreign policy and his support for Joseph McCarthy.[24] In the same year, Eisenhower wished to support a moderate Republican seeking election to the Senate from New Jersey – Clifford Case, who met opposition from McCarthy and state conservatives.[25] Sherman Adams, Eisenhower's chief of staff, assigned an aide to monitor Case's campaign and lend help where possible, while Eisenhower encouraged

[20] Chester J. Pach, Jr., and Elmo Richardson, *The Presidency of Dwight D. Eisenhower*, rev. ed. (Lawrence: University Press of Kansas, 1991), 58–62.
[21] Reichard, *Reaffirmation of Republicanism*, 69–96.
[22] Campbell et al., *The American Voter*, 199.
[23] Pach and Richardson, *Presidency of Dwight D. Eisenhower*, 166.
[24] Meeting notes, Dwight D. Eisenhower, Joseph T. Meek, and Everett Dirksen, April 28, 1954, and meeting notes, Eisenhower and William Stratton, April 27, 1954, box 2, AWDS.
[25] Bernard Shanley diary, Aug. 9, 1954, box 2, Shanley Diaries.

Secretary of the Treasury George Humphrey to speak for Case, thus offering conservative credibility.[26] These contests' results were not unfavorable to Eisenhower's cause, even if the outcome was mixed for the party. Meek lost decisively to Douglas, who talked of his support for the administration in many areas, notably foreign affairs.[27] Case won in New Jersey, partly because a McCarthyite independent drew votes away from the Democrat.[28]

Eisenhower tried again in 1956, this time encountering a different obstacle – the electorate's reluctance to support his preferred candidates. To promote the party's transformation, he encouraged a number of sympathetic Republicans to run for the Senate. But Douglas McKay in Oregon, Arthur Langlie in Washington, and Dan Thornton in Colorado all met defeat.[29] Eisenhower's search for promising candidates, such as these three, reflected his belief that the overall quality of Republican candidates was problematic, hostile to party growth. "If you look at the whole gamut of Republicans nominated," he confided to a journalist after the 1954 elections, "you know you have people there that [although] they have character and principle, they are certainly stupid."[30] Nixon agreed, attributing the congressional decline of the 1950s to candidate quality.[31] Together, these examples illustrate the limitations Eisenhower faced in seeking to influence the party's direction. They also demonstrate his desire to take action, within these constraints.

The larger congressional picture was not entirely disappointing from the Eisenhower project's perspective. Republicans newly elected to the House in 1954, 1956, and 1958 were collectively more moderate than existing members – an overall shift away from the Republican Right.[32] In the Senate, the 1958 Republican downturn was, by contrast, a setback for moderates; one result was that the Republican contingent in the Senate, formerly more liberal on race than Senate Democrats as a whole, turned more conservative.[33] The limitations of Eisenhower's powers as party leader mean that the responsibility for these developments was not his, though the trend toward moderation suggests that potential candidates responded positively to his efforts to promote a modern Republicanism. It also perhaps suggests a popular appetite for Eisenhower Republicanism.

[26] Shanley diary, July 27, 1954, box 2, Shanley Diaries; Dwight D. Eisenhower to George [Humphrey?], Sept. 8, 1954, box 8, DDE Diary Series, Eisenhower Papers [hereafter DDEDS].

[27] Dwight D. Eisenhower, *The White House Years*, vol. I: *Mandate for Change, 1953–1956* (Garden City, N.Y.: Doubleday, 1963), 433.

[28] Survey analysis, unsigned, n.d., box 2, Campaign Series, Eisenhower Papers.

[29] *NYT* clipping, Nov. 8, 1956, BBC Press Cuttings Collection.

[30] Wagner, *Eisenhower Republicanism*, 116.

[31] Nixon Volunteers, "Vice President Richard Nixon Answers Questions About Politics," n.d., box 8, subseries 2, series 5, Javits Papers.

[32] Kevin S. Price, "The Partisan Legacies of Preemptive Leadership: Assessing the Eisenhower Cohorts in the U.S. House," *Political Research Quarterly* 55 (2002), 609–631.

[33] Edward G. Carmines and James A. Stimson, *Issue Evolution: Race and the Transformation of American Politics* (Princeton, N.J.: Princeton University Press, 1989), 69–72.

Eisenhower's interest in developing a new rationale for electoral support of the Republican Party – framed as modern Republicanism – was all the more important because the anti-incumbent issues that secured the 1952 breakthrough lost salience. Once out of office, Democrats shed the taint of corruption.[34] Republican politicians were often slow to notice the change, however, perhaps due to experiences similar to those of Nixon, who during 1956 campaign appearances still found that references to government's improved "moral tone" gained an enthusiastic reception while those to economic policy did not.[35] Like the corruption theme, domestic anticommunism ebbed away as a political issue.[36] It made little sense for the in-party to assail internal subversion. By the late 1950s, Republican campaigners attacked Democrats for "extremism" or "radicalism," rather than softness on communism.[37] This disappearance accompanied the political decline of Joseph McCarthy, the issue's most avid exponent. Eisenhower played a role in McCarthy's decline, thus contributing to the party's move away from McCarthyism as an electoral issue. Caution characterized this work, however, with the result that it made little difference to the outcome, which McCarthy's own excesses were primarily responsible for precipitating.[38] The other element of the 1952 K_1C_2 formula – the Korean War – also lost electoral relevance for the party, because of the war's end. A demonstration of Eisenhower's foreign-policy prowess, this was often a personal rather than party advantage – especially because many Democrats emphasized their agreement with the administration's aims in foreign policy, and also because some Republicans remained skeptics about internationalism. Nevertheless, success of this kind encouraged positive associations among the electorate between the Republican Party and peace.[39]

The administration's path to establish the GOP as sympathetic to the post–New Deal electorate's concerns was one of moderate conservatism. Modern Republicanism sought to redefine the party's antigovernment principles by accepting a larger federal role in dealing with socioeconomic problems. "We should keep in mind at all times," Eisenhower told aides during a 1954 meeting, "the principle upon which our program is based, that is that we are conservative in our economics and liberal in dealing with our people."[40] Although intraparty critics labeled modern Republicanism a me-too echo of Democratic policies, the first part of this formula was just as important as the second.

[34] Campbell et al., *The American Voter*, 50.

[35] Charles A. H. Thomson and Frances M. Shattuck, *The 1956 Presidential Campaign* (Washington, D.C.: Brookings Institution, 1960), 223, 248.

[36] The issue sometimes retained local significance. M. J. Heale, *McCarthy's Americans: Red Scare Politics in State and Nation, 1935–1965* (Basingstoke, U.K.: Macmillan, 1998).

[37] Fried, "Voting Against the Hammer and Sickle," 114–115.

[38] Fred I. Greenstein, *The Hidden-Hand Presidency: Eisenhower as Leader* (New York: Basic, 1982), 155–227.

[39] Donald E. Stokes, Angus Campbell, and Warren E. Miller, "Components of Electoral Decision," *APSR* 52 (1958), 375.

[40] Shanley diary, May 10, 1954, box 2, Shanley Diaries.

Eisenhower's commitment to fiscal conservatism was significant – all the more so because of Cold War imperatives, given that Eisenhower saw long-term economic health as key to withstanding the Soviet threat. Moreover, Eisenhower's support for liberalism "in dealing with our people" was no endorsement of New Deal liberalism in the Democrats' mold. He accepted the need for activist government in tackling socioeconomic ills, but his solutions were usually less generous than the Democrats' version and more conscious of a need for balanced budgets. They also looked for state- and local-level alternatives to federally run programs.

Eisenhower's own instincts were yet more antistatist. The paradox of the Eisenhower project to revitalize the party in a purportedly me-too shape is that Eisenhower privately harbored beliefs that often aligned him more closely with conservative Republicans. While president of Columbia University in the years after World War II, he sometimes expressed these beliefs publicly. On one occasion, he warned of a "constant drift toward centralized government" that would lead to "a swarming of bureaucrats over the land," increasingly to government ownership of private property, "and finally you have to have dictatorship as the only means of operating such a huge organization."[41] Still, modern Republicanism's electoral imperative seemed clear to him. Eisenhower believed that conservative Republicanism lost elections. Shortly after California's William Knowland became Senate majority leader following Robert Taft's untimely death in 1953, he told the conservative Knowland, "There is nothing wrong with [the Republican Party] that a hell of a good enactment of legislation won't cure." The legislation he favored was of a "progressive" nature.[42] "If we could get every Republican committed as a Moderate Progressive," he told a friend in 1954, "the Party would grow so rapidly that within a few years it would dominate American politics."[43] Antistatism still informed these "progressive" innovations. "The preceding Administration claimed a monopoly of the goals of a good society and their formula was always the same: a federal program financed by new federal taxes or new federal debt," he wrote in July 1953, thinking already about his 1954 State of the Union. "Our task is to demonstrate that the goals our people want – in every field – can be achieved by other means than those that result in making Big Government bigger."[44] According to such views, modern Republicanism was a better way to oppose New Deal liberalism because electoral support was a likelier means to achieving that end.

[41] Mark Sullivan, "Eisenhower's Views on Domestic Policy," Aug. 12, 1951, box 7, Scott Papers.

[42] Memo of telephone calls, Dwight D. Eisenhower and William Knowland, March 10, 1954, box 5, DDEDS.

[43] Dwight D. Eisenhower to Cliff Roberts, Dec. 7, 1954, box 27, Name Series, Eisenhower Papers.

[44] Dwight D. Eisenhower to Oveta Culp Hobby, July 30, 1954, vol. 41, series O.6, Record Group 4, Rockefeller Family Archives.

Modern Republicanism's proponents believed that this approach to public policy addressed a national mood for an alternative to New Deal liberalism, stressing harmony rather than conflict between the goals of different groups.[45] In *A Republican Looks at His Party*, a 1956 exposition of "New Republicanism" that Eisenhower endorsed, Arthur Larson, who served as under secretary of labor and then as a presidential speechwriter, celebrated the administration's success in embracing and promoting a new climate of consensus. Eisenhower and the administration "discovered and established the Authentic American Center in politics," returning more power to the states and more responsibility to individuals and achieving balance between business and labor interests. Seeking to distinguish this New Republicanism from the "1896 ideology's" excessive conservatism as well as the "1932 ideology's" excessive liberalism, Larson called in essence for a cautiously conservative modification of New Deal liberalism.[46] It is a sign of Larson's disagreement with right-wing Republicans that he studied the United Kingdom's welfare state not to identify how it endangered liberty but to seek ideas for the improvement of American social insurance. Larson's exploration of the British system encouraged him to underscore a reliance, wherever possible, on state-level rather than federal-level solutions, on private rather than government provision – different from that model. But it also informed his support for a variety of welfare extensions. Such concerns distinguished the modern Republican agenda from that of Democrats as well as the Republican Right.[47]

Modern Republicanism was imaginative, and it engaged with the minority problem's policy dimension not by mimicking New Deal liberalism (as some critics insisted) but by crafting an alternative approach that answered a desire or need for welfare protections while remaining wary of statist expansions.[48] However, the Eisenhower agenda's quiet modesty and the constraints to enactment it faced conspired to make modern Republicanism an unproductive route to the genuine revitalization of the party. It was not modest enough, nevertheless, to escape stinging criticisms from party conservatives and even to encourage the reassertion of their alternative agenda, which was less interested in accommodation with New Deal liberalism.

Implementation of modern Republicanism was not straightforward. Under their unified control of government during the 83rd Congress, Republican politicians certainly demonstrated that they did not pose a threat to the New Deal era's liberal achievements, but they did not manage to offer a coherent program of "progressivism" as a plausible alternative to the Democrats' agenda. Congress revealed this commitment to the protection of the New Deal's legacy through Social Security changes: payment increases; coverage

---

[45] Robert Griffith, "Dwight D. Eisenhower and the Corporate Commonwealth," *AHR* 87 (1982), 87–122.

[46] Arthur Larson, *A Republican Looks at His Party* (New York: Harper, 1956); Stebenne, *Modern Republican*, 157–169 (quotation, 159).

[47] Stebenne, *Modern Republican*, 99–114.

[48] Stebenne, *Modern Republican*, 114, 125–126.

extensions to encompass new occupational groups; and the creation of a new class of entitlement – that of disabled people. Moreover, the Department of Health, Education, and Welfare was inaugurated under the leadership of Oveta Culp Hobby, a Texas Democrat and the first woman in the Cabinet since Frances Perkins, Franklin Roosevelt's secretary of labor. Other achievements of this kind included the St. Lawrence Seaway Act, an omnibus housing bill, extended coverage of unemployment insurance, and – an example of a more traditional Republican concern – a significant tax cut.[49]

But there were disappointments as well as achievements. The administration's health reinsurance bill suffered defeat due to opposition not only from Democrats, for whom it was insufficiently liberal, but also from conservative Republicans, for whom it represented an unacceptable expansion of the federal government's role. The agenda's disappointments partly reflect the lack of commitment that Eisenhower demonstrated in this area, when contrasted with the energies he expended to shift the party wholeheartedly toward internationalism.

The record during Eisenhower's first two years underscored fiscal conservatism's importance in qualifying the "progressive" goals of modern Republicanism. The administration and the 83rd Congress took an approach to fiscal and economic matters that did little to challenge existing expectations of Republican policy – emphasizing a balanced budget, low taxation, and private enterprise.[50]

Without control of Congress, in 1955 and afterward, Republicans were less able to build a modern reputation. Still, Eisenhower included reform proposals along these lines in State of the Union messages; responding to the 1955 message, Senator Stuart Symington, Democrat of Missouri, in private labeled him jokingly as Franklin Harry Eisenhower.[51] Nevertheless, because they were the product of a Democratic Congress as well as a Republican administration, any reform achievements were not likely to change substantially public perceptions of the party.

Modern Republicanism's message, moreover, often did not reach its audience within the electorate. Republican rhetoric's noisier element often remained attack. For example, in Duluth, Minnesota, during the 1954 campaign, Nixon defended "the moderate Eisenhower way." But his focus was an assault on Democrats as a socialist force and a warning of dire prospects should they regain Congress that year: "The United States will swing back down the leftward road toward Socialism, toward more Big Government that robs States of their historic rights and our people of their historic freedoms, toward ever-mounting taxes, toward more of the crisis-to-crisis maneuvering that once kept our farm and industrial economy on a perpetual hot seat."[52]

49 Stephen H. Hess to Oliver Gale, Aug. 18, 1960, box 2, Hess Records.
50 Reichard, *Reaffirmation of Republicanism*, 97–147.
51 Louchheim diary, Feb. 5, 1955, box 77, Louchheim Papers.
52 Richard Nixon, speech, Sept. 23, 1954, PPS 208(1954).29.4 (1), Nixon Pre-Presidential Speech File.

Throughout the Eisenhower administration, Nixon, in leading the party's campaign efforts, spoke of the Republicans' modern goals but tended to place greater stress on the Democrats' failings.[53] This reflected Nixon's central insight about the nature of electoral politics during the era of Democratic dominance – that Republicans were sure to lose when bread-and-butter New Deal liberalism was at the heart of political debate. "Remember, they can always *out*-promise us on economic issues," he told a Republican audience in 1954. It was therefore wise to move the focus of debate to the party's strong issues, "peace, Communism, corruption, taxes," he advised – even though the salience of many of these issues was in decline.[54] As the administration's chief campaigner, Nixon not only relied on his own strategic ideas and flair for aggressive rhetoric in programming such a course but also received encouragement from Eisenhower and key White House aides to go on the attack.[55]

Nixon was by no means alone in publicly downplaying modern Republicanism. On the campaign trail in Indiana in 1958, Representative Charles Halleck, a leading Republican in the House, sounded similar themes to Nixon's, in yet stronger terms. Emphasizing his party's commitment to liberty, Halleck denounced the Democrats' dominant northern wing as "radical and socialistic" – "the champion of heavy spending, high taxes, and centralized power in Washington at the expense of authority at the state and local levels." He discussed the anti-Democratic imperative to prevent "more years of wild-eyed spending, of mounting deficits, heavier taxes or ruinous inflation," to end "radical schemes that promote federal bureaucracy at the expense of individual freedom." Halleck did not, by contrast, discuss the modern Republican agenda much.[56] Eisenhower himself sometimes displayed his partisan edge, attacking Democrats as "easy-spending, paternalistic, business-baiting inflationists" in a 1957 speech about modern Republicanism, for example.[57]

Democrats stressed their opponents' conservatism more strenuously than Republicans promoted modern Republicanism. As Henry Cabot Lodge, Jr., ambassador to the United Nations, noted to Eisenhower in 1954, it was the Democratic strategy to campaign against the Republican Party as a reactionary force. "They never attack anything that comes from the modern Republican side," he wrote.[58] Along these lines, Tennessee's Senator Albert Gore remarked in 1958, "If the Republican Party were ever reincarnated into a homing pigeon, no matter where it was released in the universe, whether from a jet plane or in outer space, it would go directly home to Wall Street

---

[53] William Costello, *The Facts About Nixon: An Unauthorized Biography* (New York: Viking, 1960), 93–176.

[54] Richard Nixon, speech, n.d. (filed Dec. 7, 1954), LBM 116, Small Deeded Collections, Nixon Library.

[55] Richard Nixon, notes, Sept. 12, 1956, PPS 324.92, Nixon Vice Presidential Collection.

[56] Charles Halleck, speech, n.d., box 101, Halleck Papers.

[57] *Newsweek*, June 17, 1957, 38.

[58] Henry Cabot Lodge, *As It Was* (New York: Norton, 1976), 149.

without a flutter of the wing."[59] In a 1956 speech Katie Louchheim of the Democratic National Committee borrowed from a journalist in referring to Eisenhower's health problems when asking a Democratic audience, "which will you vote for; the party with the heart or the party with the heart attack?"[60] Modern Republicanism did little to confound such attacks, which had assisted Democrats to victory since the time of Herbert Hoover.

If modern Republicanism's first-term implementation was imperfect, the second-term pursuit of this vision was still less substantial. Eisenhower signaled his commitment to its pursuit by announcing that his 1956 reelection landslide was an endorsement of and mandate for modern Republicanism.[61] The claim was a dubious one, given his party's inability to make many congressional gains and the presidential campaign's domination by issues of foreign, not domestic, policy. It counterproductively infuriated those Republicans who distrusted this goal. Still, Eisenhower's State of the Union messages continued to show vestiges of modern Republican ambition – but with little consequence. The second term was defined not by party reinvention or repackaging; a climate of economic difficulties encouraged a stress on fiscal conservatism instead of policy innovation.

First, a "Battle of the Budget" broke out in response to Eisenhower's tax-and-spend proposals for fiscal 1958, projecting a small surplus but calling for record peacetime expenditures. Secretary of the Treasury George M. Humphrey made incautious remarks about the adverse implications of high spending, and just as incautiously Eisenhower challenged Congress to cut the budget if possible. Congressional conservatives then provided evidence of their skepticism toward modern Republicanism, with Knowland and others assaulting spending proposals; partisanship encouraged Democrats to attack the budget, too. Successful in slicing $4 billion from Eisenhower's $73.3 billion budget, Congress dramatized the weak foundations within the party on which modern Republicanism stood.

Second, the economy experienced a recession in 1957–1958, the seriousness of which the administration was slow to recognize. The administration then took steps designed to stimulate the economy, but Democrats found it easy to brand these steps as inadequate, to remind voters of connections between the GOP and hard times, and to draw electoral advantage from them in the 1958 midterms.[62] The downturn also deprived the administration of the money considered necessary for modern Republican proposals.

Even in a "modern" guise, Republicans remained confident in the wisdom of fiscal conservatism, however qualified – an approach that, regardless of its policy merits or demerits, reinforced the Democrats' electoral advantage, rather than challenging it. This confidence in fiscal conservatism and

[59] *Time*, Nov. 3, 1958, 17.
[60] Katie Louchheim to "Pu," March 4, 1956, box 77, Louchheim Papers.
[61] *NYT*, Nov. 15, 1956, 1.
[62] Pach and Richardson, *Presidency of Dwight D. Eisenhower*, 167–169, 175–185.

Eisenhower's preference for solutions that did not promote bigger government show that those their intraparty critics called me-too Republicans did not imperil the antistatist agenda; indeed, they shared it, if in different measure. A priority to ward off inflation united most Republicans. In early 1959, administration economist Don Paarlberg wrote of his hope that this concern possessed electoral promise because it should "have us be *for* an honest dollar rather than *against* public services," thus confounding the Democratic message that "[casts] us as the party which wishes to veto the Twentieth Century."[63] Polls suggested instead that there was widespread support for spending limits in general, but such support coexisted with opposition to specific program cuts; public opinion continued to favor the Democrats' activism.[64]

Modern Republicanism was a twofold failure as a majority-seeking strategy. First, it failed to challenge the party's image as the friend of big business and the enemy of the ordinary American. Although the experience of the Eisenhower years led fewer Americans to see Republicans as a threat to New Deal achievements, the administration "was not equally successful ... in dispelling the popular belief that the Republicans were the party of the great and the Democrats the party of the small," according to a University of Michigan research team.[65] The social scientists who reached this conclusion were conducting groundbreaking work on the politician–voter relationship, finding ample evidence that it was extraordinarily difficult for a party to win the lasting affiliation of a voter who supported the rival party. Their work underscored what Republicans had discovered over the previous decades – that the minority party's best efforts seemed powerless to challenge the majority party's supremacy in any enduring manner.

Confidence in modern Republicanism reflected the belief that the nation's growing prosperity would foster new GOP strength and that "consensus" was the country's defining characteristic during this period. But such observations overlooked the persistent political significance of socioeconomic difference, whether perceived or real, and Democratic loyalties were thus far from vulnerable to attack. Stewart Alsop, a leading political journalist, took a trip away from Washington in 1956 to assess public opinion; the pervasive incidence of class consciousness – to the Democrats' benefit – astonished him. "It seems strange that so many Americans, in this prosperous egalitarian country, should think of themselves as 'little guys,'" wrote Alsop. "But they do. Many of the people who think of themselves as 'little guys,' moreover, live in neat houses with well-kept lawns, with a good car parked outside, and like as not a freezer and a washer-dryer in the kitchen."[66] "Little-guy" identity aided the Democrats and hurt the Republicans. Indeed, in some respects the New Deal coalition

[63] Iwan W. Morgan, *Eisenhower versus "the Spenders": The Eisenhower Administration, the Democrats and the Budget, 1953–60* (London: Pinter, 1990), 80–135 (quotation, 135).

[64] James L. Sundquist, *Politics and Policy: The Eisenhower, Kennedy, and Johnson Years* (Washington, D.C.: Brookings Institution, 1968), 430–466.

[65] Campbell et al., *The American Voter*, 47.

[66] *Saturday Evening Post*, Jan. 12, 1957, 25.

achieved a pinnacle of strength during Eisenhower's tenure in the White House. Not only did the recession boost the Democratic Party to renewed levels of success in the 1958 midterms, but the party also gained strength in formerly Republican-dominated states of the North and West, including California, the Dakotas, Oregon, Pennsylvania, and Wisconsin. It was a trend that extended to the two Republican states of 1936, Maine and Vermont.[67]

Modern Republicanism's second failure was yet more significant for the party's longer-term development. Not only did Eisenhower fail to mobilize the more conservative members of his party in support of this modernization, but his initiatives encouraged the development of a new conservatism, which would, in time, prove more successful than his moderately conservative agenda in securing intraparty support. Midway through the first term, buoyant reports suggested that the job of party transformation was almost done, that the grassroots GOP was now a force of modern Republicanism.[68] But those reports were misleading. Eisenhower himself recognized that "he was forced down the throats of a lot of people in '52," as he privately noted in 1957. "Some will never forget it.... There is so much resentment, and those people will never give up."[69]

An RNC survey in 1957 of Midwest party leaders exemplified modern Republicanism's failure to transform the party. It found pessimism about GOP prospects, together with conservative prescriptions for these problems. Although they identified the president personally as a key party strength, many criticized his ideas. One wrote, "Bring Bob Taft back to life – I mean this sincerely, not facetiously." Another wrote, "Register all 'Modern Republicans' as Democrats." It did not necessarily seem inconsistent to support Eisenhower but criticize his initiatives, as still another revealed. "Ike is strong on foreign relations," he argued, "but weak on some domestic issues: (1) Compromising with socialistic matters; (2) Taking bad advice on domestic matters; (3) Could cut some spending." Principle mattered to Republicans for whom opposition to New Deal liberalism inspired their involvement in politics, and Eisenhower was wrong to conclude that factional resentments alone accounted for resistance to modern Republicanism. "We have no Republican Party as we knew it in the past," one concluded. "We have changed the label, yes, but the bottle is the same New Fair Deal contents."[70] A broader survey of convention delegates and alternates found that these leading activists identified closely with business and its political needs – concerns that separated them from many Americans within the electorate. Indeed, the survey found that on issues of social welfare, the ideas of Republican supporters were closer to those of leading Democrats than Republicans.[71] A 1957 Gallup poll of Republican voters provided similar

[67] Sundquist, *Dynamics of the Party System*, 240–268.
[68] *Newsweek*, April 4, 1955, 27–30.
[69] Notes of prepress conference briefing, May 15, 1957, box 24, DDEDS.
[70] Public Opinion Polls, survey report, May 28, 1957, box 42, Pyle Papers.
[71] Herbert McCloskey, Paul J. Hoffman, and Rosemary O'Hara, "Issue Conflict and Consensus Among Party Leaders and Followers," *APSR* 54 (1960), 406–427.

findings. Offered a choice between Eisenhower Republicanism and conservative Republicanism, nearly three-quarters preferred the former and less than one-fifth indicated a preference for the latter.[72] Eisenhower was thus right to believe in modern Republicanism's appeal, but many Republicans did not similarly recognize its potential strength.

Frustration with the Eisenhower record fueled the revitalization of intellectual conservatism, which over time would bolster the strength of a conservative response to the minority problem.[73] In 1955, William F. Buckley, Jr., launched *National Review*, a magazine animated by disillusionment with modern Republican thinking and driven by the goal to refashion American conservatism in a more attractive form and, in a "fusionist" project, to achieve unity of purpose between traditionalist and libertarian conservatism – between those who believed that government should encourage morality and those who believed that government should take a strictly laissez-faire approach, remaining aloof from moral as well as economic concerns. For the moment, it was a distinction much more relevant to the world of ideas than party politics.

William Rusher, who became *National Review*'s publisher in 1957, later underscored the significance of disillusionment during the 1950s with modern Republicanism in explaining conservatism's growth. "As a matter of fact, modern American conservatism largely organized itself during, and in explicit opposition to, the Eisenhower Administration," he wrote to Buckley in 1972: "Under your leadership."[74] How to pursue this conservatism in the world of practical politics was not at first clear, and the 1956 election divided the magazine's editors – some of whom concluded that abstention, designed to promote conservatism, was preferable to support for Eisenhower and modern Republicanism. Buckley himself did not vote, in a campaign-period editorial attacking the administration for its "easy and whole-hearted acceptance of all that came before, of the great and statist legacy of the New Deal."[75] Rusher's disenchantment with party politics was more fundamental. Arguing in 1960 that it was "pointless" to criticize a political party for caring more about votes than principles, he preferred work in pursuit of conservatism through an opinion-influencing vehicle such as *National Review*, rather than the Republican Party "where [advocates of conservatism] will forever be forced into enervating compromises," he observed to Buckley.[76]

Dissatisfaction with modern Republicanism was consequential within the party, too. The lack of electoral advance under Eisenhower encouraged his critics to advocate an alternative solution to the minority problem, in line with their policy concerns. Appearing on CBS's *Face the Nation* in April 1959, Senator Barry Goldwater of Arizona argued that an emphasis on "individual

[72] Note of Gallup poll, March 24, 1957, box 7, subseries 2, series 5, Javits Papers.

[73] Critchlow, *Conservative Ascendancy*.

[74] William A. Rusher to William F. Buckley, Jr., March 9, 1972, box 121, Rusher Papers.

[75] John B. Judis, *William F. Buckley, Jr.: Patron Saint of the Conservatives* (1988; New York: Touchstone, 1990), 144–146 (quotation, 145).

[76] William A. Rusher to William F. Buckley, Jr., Oct. 10, 1960, box 121, Rusher Papers.

freedom" and "fiscal responsibility" would uncover new support. He said that "my judgment is there is something like 20 and 25 million people in this country, disenfranchised Democrats and Republicans, who would rush to the Republican Party if that's done."[77] Goldwater had won election to the Senate in 1952 as an Eisenhower Republican, but modern Republicanism disappointed him, encouraging a move further rightwards. His belief in conservatism's electoral promise partly involved the insight, supported by his Arizona experience of campaigning, that staunch opposition to New Deal liberalism energized activists, whose grassroots work then helped to bring victory.[78] He used his own 1958 reelection victory against labor opposition – one of the few Republican highlights amid the midterm woes of that year – as a key example. In short, Goldwater was pressing into service the turnout thesis of the minority problem.

Goldwater's rhetoric of personal freedom provided common ground with many less conservative Republicans. But the content of his domestic proposals took a much more avowedly antigovernment emphasis than those of modern Republicans. His approach to foreign policy was strongly anticommunist and, skeptical of international cooperation, often nationalist rather than internationalist. Chair of the Republicans' campaign committee in the Senate, Goldwater traveled extensively during the late 1950s to promote his brand of conservatism. Within the party's activist ranks, there were many ready to listen.

Unhappy about minority status, leading Republicans looked across the Atlantic with admiration at the success of the Conservative Party in the United Kingdom. Conservatives had suffered a crushing defeat in 1945, when voters overwhelmingly supported the Labour Party and its promise to build a comprehensive welfare system. They soon staged an impressive comeback, however, and in 1951 their party was back in government, where it would remain for more than a decade. During the Truman administration, the U.K. postwar experience had provided Republicans with a cautionary tale about "socialism's" dangerous appeal. In time, however, British politics instead offered a lesson about the importance of organization, as it had during the New Deal years. Most Republicans did not dwell on the accommodationism developed by the Conservatives on welfare questions – a key aspect of their strategy to engineer a return to power – but instead examined their organizational revitalization under Lord Woolton (Fred Marquis before ennoblement) as chair.[79]

---

[77] Transcript, "Face the Nation," April 19, 1959, box 293, series 320, Nixon Pre-Presidential Papers.

[78] Barry Goldwater to Jacob K. Javits, May 25, 1960, box 9, subseries 2, series 5, Javits Papers; Elizabeth Tandy Shermer, "Origins of the Conservative Ascendancy: Barry Goldwater's Early Senate Career and the De-legitimization of Organized Labor," *Journal of American History* 95 (2008), 678–709.

[79] See, for example, Richard Nixon to Raymond Moley, Aug. 19, 1958, box 524, series 320, Nixon Pre-Presidential Papers, and Fred A. Seaton, speech, Jan. 23, 1959, box 682, series 320, Nixon Pre-Presidential Papers.

After meeting with Woolton, pollster Claude Robinson noted, "They operate like the Jehovah's witnesses do in this country." An extensive network of trained party workers identified and mobilized the Conservative vote through door-to-door campaigning and canvassing.[80] The interest in organization, to the exclusion of policy, was the same approach to transatlantic lesson learning that John Hamilton took during the 1930s. By contrast, when Woolton visited Washington in 1950, he noticed differences – rather than similarities – between British and American politics, telling a journalist that "one of the things that struck him most was the hostility of Republicans here toward their adversaries which, he thought, was quite alien."[81]

These lessons seemed especially relevant because many Republicans remained convinced that a key obstacle to electoral success was their party's lack of organizational capacity compared with that of the Democrats. Thomas Dewey argued in 1950, for example, that Republicans were less attuned to the necessary chores of politics than Democrats. According to Dewey, Republicans were interested simply in deciding policy, and there were few activists available to canvass voters, people the polls, or learn the hard business of campaign management.[82] Eisenhower commented similarly that the party "wanted to have too many generals and too few fighting men."[83]

The problem seemed to become more significant during the 1950s as a result of the vitality of labor support for the Democratic Party. Republicans connected labor with the further losses they suffered in historic areas of party strength in the Northeast and upper Midwest. When Senator Homer Ferguson of labor-strong Michigan lost his bid for reelection in 1954, he blamed the organizational might of unions, predicting that his state "would be controlled from now on by labor, and will probably be lost to the Republican Party."[84] Labor leaders took a different view of their influence, seeing themselves as far from dominant, but engaged in a difficult struggle to promote liberalism within the Democratic Party. The 1954 races were among labor's most promising, but in general Republican evaluations were an exaggeration of the organizations' significance, though in financial terms their contribution to the Democrats was important.[85] Moreover, a 1952 study suggested that the canvassing efforts fielded by the Republican Party – despite its smaller size – were probably a little more extensive than those of their rivals, though poorly targeted and thus

[80] Notes, n.d., box 646, series 320, Nixon Pre-Presidential Papers.
[81] Henry Brandon diary, June 3, 1950, box 2, Brandon Papers.
[82] John A. Wells, ed., *Thomas E. Dewey on the Two-Party System* (Garden City, N.Y.: Doubleday, 1966), 30.
[83] Dwight D. Eisenhower to William S. Paley, Nov. 14, 1956, box 25, Name Series, Eisenhower Papers.
[84] Earle D. Chesney to Stan Rumbough, Nov. 16, 1954, box 689, Official File, Eisenhower Records.
[85] Robert H. Zieger, *The CIO, 1935–1955* (Chapel Hill: University of North Carolina Press, 1995).

too often mobilizing Democratic supporters rather than Republican ones.[86] Nevertheless, many Republicans believed in labor power and in an organizational disparity. The RNC's Robert Humphreys, for example, concluded the party "was out-maneuvered, out-manned and out-financed" in 1954, but mostly by organized labor rather than the Democratic Party itself; this was "only an indication of what is to come."[87]

Such analysis tended to overlook a turnout disparity that favored the Republican Party. Republican supporters were more likely to vote than Democratic supporters, a disparity suggesting that the party was already achieving at least some success in maximizing its support at the polls, if also suggesting that the connection between voting or nonvoting and socioeconomic status or racial group favored the Republicans.[88] Indeed, together with a greater disinclination among Republicans to vote for an opposition candidate, this meant that the GOP minority at the polls was not as pronounced as it seemed in data about Americans' party preferences. A study of the survey data about the 1960 election, for example, found that, while only one in three Americans self-identified as Republican, the party's normal share of the presidential vote was 46 or 47 percent.[89] The problem of organization nevertheless seemed compelling; a party report on the 1956 election emphasized organization in explaining electoral disappointments, indicating that the party's direct campaigning reached about 10 percent of the electorate, and concluding that this figure was inadequate.[90] Pollster George Gallup argued, "Roughly, there should be a volunteer worker for every five Republican votes," claiming that this ostensibly unrealistic target was actually realistic because yet more respondents to his surveys indicated a willingness to undertake such participation in politics.[91] An important attraction of the organizational thesis for Republican difficulties remained its superficial avoidance of divisive discussion about the appropriate ideological direction for the party to take. Still, organization mattered to contemporary Republicans.

Central to the desire to revitalize the party during the 1950s was Citizens for Eisenhower. Citizens's key goal was the mobilization of activism in support of Eisenhower, whose extraordinary power as a politician fostered political excitement, energy, and commitment among many who were outside existing

---

[86] Morris Janowitz and Dwaine Marvick, *Competitive Pressure and Democratic Consent: An Interpretation of the 1952 Presidential Election*, 2nd ed. (Chicago: Quadrangle, 1964), 22–23, 76–83, 107–108.

[87] Harold Lavine, *Smoke-Filled Rooms* (Englewood Cliffs, N.J.: Prentice-Hall, 1970), 135.

[88] William F. Connelly, Jr., and John J. Pitney, Jr., *Congress' Permanent Minority? Republicans in the U.S. House* (Lanham, Md.: Rowman & Littlefield, 1994), 131. Although this discussion primarily relates to a later period, it also has relevance to this one.

[89] Jones, *Republican Party*, 66–67.

[90] "Preliminary Report on a Study of Congressional Districts in the Following States," unsigned, n.d., box 1, Administration Series, Eisenhower Papers.

[91] George Gallup to Ogden Reid, Sept. 5, 1956, PPS 324.93.2, Nixon Vice Presidential Collection.

ranks of activists, first in 1952 and later in 1956. But Eisenhower and other Republicans were anxious that these activists would not rest with the war hero's election and reelection to the presidency but would instead boost the ranks of the GOP itself. Peter Clayton, a leader of Citizens, observed in 1955 that the mission for Citizens was "to translate the enthusiasm which the Eisenhower name has created into a bigger, richer, Republican Party with a Republican President and a Republican Congress in office *long after Eisenhower leaves office.*"[92] Citizens's leaders thus encouraged members to join the GOP – to protect their organization's "spirit," as one put it after the 1952 election.[93]

To some moderates, a key attraction of the project was the prospect that Citizens activists would infuse the party with modern Republicanism; Eisenhower enthusiasts outside conventional party circles were assumed to share that vision. As Jacob Javits put it to Eisenhower, their permanent recruitment to party ranks had promise because "the indefatigable worker is rarely to be denied."[94] Charles P. Taft, who had played little part in national politics since the Landon campaign, saw the very expansion of participation in politics as likely to have a moderating effect on the party, positing that weak grassroots organization was the obstacle to the creation of "a strong middle-of-the-road party."[95]

Citizens had emerged in 1951 as a grassroots expression of enthusiasm for the Eisenhower candidacy. At a time when this candidacy remained speculative rather than real, Charles F. Willis and Stanley Rumbough, two young business-people, established an organization to foster the creation of Eisenhower clubs nationally. Willis and Rumbough later said that they used the General Foods sales manual for guidance on publicity, emblematic of their newness to politics and their business orientation. The organization quickly enjoyed success, claiming eight hundred clubs and thirty-eight state chairmen when Henry Cabot Lodge, Jr., invited Willis and Rumbough to make it part of the now-official campaign as Citizens for Eisenhower.[96] It became not just a grassroots movement. At the national level it also involved an elite group of Eisenhower associates, often outsiders to party politics, whose financial support was important; those with closer links to political activity retained a distance from the organization to emphasize its volunteer identity.[97] When the nomination was won, some suspected that Citizens – which claimed an active membership of 250,000 in some 29,000 clubs by the convention – was essential in securing victory.[98]

[92] Peter Clayton to "Frank," June 2, 1955, box 32, Stephens Records. Italics capitalized in original.

[93] Walter Williams, form letter, box 822, series 320, Nixon Pre-Presidential Papers.

[94] Jacob K. Javits to Dwight D. Eisenhower, Dec. 27, 1954, box 3, subseries 2, series 5, Javits Papers.

[95] *Fortune*, Feb. 1955, 214.

[96] Jane Dick, *Volunteers and the Making of Presidents* (New York: Dodd, Mead, 1980), 67.

[97] Brownell, *Advising Ike*, 107; Robert F. Burk, *Dwight D. Eisenhower: Hero and Politician* (Boston: Twayne, 1986), 117.

[98] *Saturday Evening Post*, Sept. 27, 1952, 53; Leonard W. Hall, foreword, in Stephen A. Mitchell, *Elm Street Politics* (New York: Oceana, 1959), i; Dick, *Volunteers and the Making of Presidents*, 110; *NYT*, Aug. 1, 1952, 6.

The success of the nomination season and their political differences with the "regulars" who supported Taft discouraged Citizens leaders from merging with the RNC after Eisenhower won the nomination. In turn, hostile memories of the Willkie "amateurs" as well as a desire to maintain their decision-making powers encouraged RNC officials to resist any separation. The disagreement was intense. Under a compromise that the groups reached between the convention's end and the fall campaign's start, Citizens maintained a separate if coordinated existence, in this role achieving further success in Eisenhower's campaign against Stevenson. At the campaign's height, Citizens claimed an active membership close to two million.[99] Despite the compromise, the Citizens–RNC relationship was always tense.[100]

The organization served a variety of useful purposes in different states. In Illinois, Republican disaffection with the Eisenhower candidacy meant that the Citizens organization was at first entirely responsible for the anti-Stevenson effort, though regulars eventually joined in.[101] In the South, the Citizens movement – often known as Democrats for Eisenhower or Independents for Eisenhower – facilitated activism outside the Republican label. On launching the Charlottesville, Virginia, branch, Mills F. Neal, the head of the state's Democrats for Eisenhower, emphasized to his audience a recent interpretation of state law affirming that registered Democrats who supported a Republican presidential candidate did not lose their party standing provided that they supported state-level Democratic candidates.[102] In this respect, the organization's southern manifestation enlarged the activist ranks, as it did elsewhere, and rationalized southern Democratic support for a Republican. But it did not create a formula for party growth. And it did not necessarily promote a moderate brand of Republicanism. Campaigning as a Democrat for Eisenhower at a Virginia rally, former New Deal agency head Donald R. Richberg devoted special attention to attacks on the Truman administration's liberalism on race and its disregard for states' rights.[103] Citizens's leaflets in Greensboro, North Carolina, even adopted a quite assertively segregationist tone; state Republicans apologized for this racist appeal.[104]

A great success in mobilizing support for Eisenhower himself, the Citizens movement failed as an organizational effort to revitalize the GOP. A clear indication of this failure was the apparent need for its continuing existence as a separate organization, well beyond the 1952 election. Citizens first established a congressional committee in 1954 to secure the election of Eisenhower's

[99] "Eisenhower-Nixon Club News," Oct. 29, 1952, box 1, Political File, Thayer Papers.

[100] Craig Allen, *Eisenhower and the Mass Media: Peace, Prosperity, and Prime-time TV* (Chapel Hill: University of North Carolina Press, 1993), 77–82.

[101] David et al., *Presidential Nominating Politics*, IV: 111.

[102] "E. J. Oglesby Elected Chairman Of Local Democrats For Ike," clipping (no publication), n.d., box 42, Richberg Papers.

[103] Donald R. Richberg, speech summary, Oct. 8, 1952, box 24, Richberg Papers.

[104] Julian M. Pleasants, "'Call Your Next Case': H. F. 'Chub' Seawell, Jr., the Gubernatorial Election of 1952, and the Rise of the Republican Party in North Carolina," *North Carolina Historical Review* 76 (1999), 88.

supporters in the midterms. Arguing that the loss of congressional control would lead to the loss of the presidency two years later, the committee
sought to secure marginal seats for Republicans by appealing to Eisenhower-
supporting Democrats and independents.[105] It reappeared not only in 1956
but in 1958, too. After the 1960 election, when a Nixon–Lodge Volunteers
operation replicated Citizens, Walter N. Thayer, one of its leaders, concluded
that "the Republican Party, for whatever reason, during the past eight years
has not found the way to avail itself of the energy and enthusiasm these people
have to offer."[106]

This failure was not the result of absent effort. Charles Willis joined the
White House as an assistant to chief of staff Sherman Adams, looking after
patronage matters and promoting the integration of Citizens with the national
committee as a way to diffuse Eisenhower Republicanism through the
party. At the RNC, national chair Leonard Hall appointed Clancy Adamy,
another 1952 Citizens leader, as the chair's consultant on enrollment of new
Republicans and convened an advisory board of other leading members.[107]
The failure of such efforts revealed the distinction between personal politics
and party politics; Eisenhower activists often had little interest in GOP activism. It also revealed a difference between the ways amateurs, on the one hand,
and regulars or professionals, on the other, engaged in politics. For the former,
the purity of the cause – the "crusade" of 1952 – was important.[108] Regular
party politics usually involved compromise rather than such crusading purity.
Professionals were wary of amateurism and jealous of any perceived threat to
their intraparty power, but amateurs were at least as wary of professionalism
and anxious of any challenge to their purity of purpose.

An alternative way to challenge labor's contribution to the Democratic Party
involved the mobilization of business to support the Republicans actively.
Leading Republicans noted the absence of party work among businesspeople, by contrast with labor unionists; Tom Stephens, a White House political
aide, regretted "[the] woeful lack of political activity on the part of successful
businessmen in their local political organizations."[109] A young AT&T executive who joined his local suburban Republican club similarly concluded, "Our
party strength is poor because our good young people who are smart and ambitious gravitate naturally toward business and not toward politics."[110] Ignoring
the prospect that such corporate involvement was likely to reinforce their party's elitist image, Republicans developed recruitment efforts. An inspiration

[105] "Statement of Policy and Objectives," Sept. 27, 1954, box 5, Political File, Thayer Papers.
[106] Walter N. Thayer to Richard Nixon, Dec. 5, 1960, box 7, Political File, Thayer Papers.
[107] Cornelius P. Cotter, "Eisenhower as Party Leader," *Political Science Quarterly* 98 (1983),
268–269; Leonard W. Hall to Dwight D. Eisenhower, June 20, 1955, box 9, Office of the
Chairman of the Republican National Committee (Leonard W. Hall) Records.
[108] James Q. Wilson, *The Amateur Democrat: Club Politics in Three Cities* (Chicago: University
of Chicago Press, 1962).
[109] Notes, "from TES [Thomas E. Stephens]," March 1955, box 4, AWDS.
[110] Anonymous letter to Walter N. Thayer, Dec. 19, 1960, box 7, Political File, Thayer Papers.

was the "Ohio Plan," part of Robert Taft's 1950 Senate campaign, under which companies ran schemes of political education, encouraging registration and precinct-level participation.[111] Along these lines, Republicans established the "1956 Plan" to create "a well-informed segment of voters who will have had the benefit of receiving the studied business viewpoint as reflected by top executives of business and industry."[112] Ostensibly nonpartisan, the effort had obviously partisan intent, securing Eisenhower's appreciation and Hall's blessing.[113] Some corporations already spoke to employees about politics, a contemporary version of some business owners' older practice of instructing workers how they should vote. At the start of the decade, for example, General Motors management circulated among employees a cartoon pamphlet called *Crossroads to Tomorrow*, which depicted a historic threat to individual liberties by liberal policies, representing a "drift to Socialism," and which urged political activity in their defense: "We're all Americans, and every person in America must be alert for freedom's protection."[114]

The business-in-politics initiatives achieved some success. By decade's end, many companies, including General Motors as well as Ford, Johnson & Johnson, Gulf Oil, and Monsanto Chemical, ran schemes of this kind.[115] A pioneer in this area, General Electric launched a "citizen education" initiative as well as its "Syracuse plan" to encourage managers and supervisors to engage in politics.[116] But from a Republican perspective their practical achievements were limited. Few among the many businesspeople who took a course on politics then became a party worker, encouraging leading Republicans in the early 1960s to conclude that they still faced the same problem of enjoying business sympathy but no meaningful support from these quarters.[117] Indeed, the initiatives were likely to have a counterproductive effect, partly at least; such business association with the party could only reinforce the fat-cat image at the heart of its minority status.[118] George Meany of the American Federation of Labor and Congress of Industrial Organizations (AFL–CIO) – the 1955 merger of which only served to boost Republican anxiety about labor power – wrote that he supported such business activity because it would encourage greater political interest among workers and then "we will do all right, because there happen to be a few more of us than there are of them."[119]

[111] Leonard Hall to Ann Whitman, March 1, 1955, box 4, AWDS.

[112] "The 1956 Plan," unsigned, n.d., box 31, Stephens Records.

[113] Dwight D. Eisenhower to Edward Durrell, April 23, 1956, box 689, Official File, Eisenhower Records.

[114] *Crossroads for Tomorrow* (Detroit: Ross Roy, 1950), box 1157, Taft Papers.

[115] *The Times* clipping, April 19, 1960, BBC Press Cuttings Collection.

[116] Lichtman, *White Protestant Nation*, 219; Phillips-Fein, *Invisible Hands*, 87–114.

[117] "Oklahoma City Presentation of Big City Politics Report," Jan. 12, 1962, box 36, subseries 2, series 5, Javits Papers.

[118] Francis A. Jamieson to Nelson A. Rockefeller, March 26, 1956, box 17, Record Group 13, Rockefeller Family Archives.

[119] *Congressional Record – Senate*, Sept. 10, 1959, 17443; Lodge, *As It Was*, 152.

Any success in pursuing the desire to strengthen the party's organizational capacity depended on the contribution of women. By the 1950s, the gender dimension of political activity still differed little from that of the Hoover years. Women carried out essential grassroots work while generally excluded from the party hierarchy and elected office.[120] According to Representative Jessica McCullough Weis, Republican of New York, there were perhaps four times as many women as men among campaign activists of this period, though other estimates were generally rather lower.[121] Leonard Hall attributed the extent of Eisenhower's electoral success to the increasing involvement of women in politics. "I would trade two ordinary men workers for a woman worker any day," he said. "Women have a capacity for ringing doorbells and talking to housewives that men will never have."[122] The RNC's Robert Humphreys also emphasized women's importance, observing to an audience that they "gain a sense of achievement in attacking tasks that most men supposedly find too boring or time-consuming."[123] Not all men in politics shared this patronizing view, and in his 1949 report to the RNC, outgoing chair Hugh Scott had advocated "more recognition" for women and expressed his hope that "they will grow less and less modest – in their political demands, that is"; Scott blamed women for failing to secure influence that reflected their work for their party, as well as men for denying the women a meaningful voice in party affairs.[124]

In the aftermath of the 1948 Dewey defeat, Senator Margaret Chase Smith connected electoral failure with "male dominance of the party."[125] Such male dominance discouraged any significant engagement with the reality of Republican electoral success among women. The Republican Party's emphasis on liberty encouraged it to associate itself with gender egalitarianism more closely than did the Democrats – who were more supportive of special protections for women – but these philosophical proclivities did not lead to meaningful embrace of reform proposals in either party.[126] Still, according to RNC figures, women were much more likely than men to vote for Eisenhower in both 1952 and 1956 – a difference that garnered relatively little attention as a facet of electoral politics.[127]

---

[120] Paula Baker, "'She Is the Best Man on the Ward Committee': Women in Grassroots Party Organizations, 1930s–1950s," in Melanie Gustafson, Kristie Miller, and Elisabeth I. Perry, eds., *We Have Come To Stay: American Women and Political Parties, 1880–1960* (Albuquerque: University of New Mexico Press, 1999), 151–160.

[121] Jessica McC. Weis, "Organizing the Women," in James M. Cannon, ed., *Politics U.S.A.: A Practical Guide to the Winning of Public Office* (Garden City, N.Y.: Doubleday, 1960), 172; Baker, "'She Is the Best Man on the Ward Committee,'" 158.

[122] *Life* clipping, April 25, 1960, box 313, series 320, Nixon Pre-Presidential Papers.

[123] Robert Humphreys, speech, n.d., box 361, series 320, Nixon Pre-Presidential Papers.

[124] Hugh Scott, report, Aug. 4, 1949, box 5, Scott Papers; Hugh D. Scott, Jr., *How to Go into Politics* (New York: John Day, 1949), 143–152.

[125] *NYT*, Feb. 5, 1949, 12.

[126] Christina Wolbrecht, *The Politics of Women's Rights: Parties, Positions, and Change* (Princeton, N.J.: Princeton University Press, 2000), 127.

[127] Thomson and Shattuck, *1956 Presidential Campaign*, 354.

Despite their exclusion from decision-making responsibilities and the generally patronizing attitude of party men, women seized opportunities for political participation. In many areas, they provided much of the vitality within the Citizens organization; the newness of Citizens perhaps helped to maximize such opportunities. Speaking of the 1952 victory, India Edwards, DNC vice chair, dismissively observed that "a lot of silly, unthinking women ... who hadn't voted or worked in politics before ... did get out and work for [Eisenhower]."[128] In 1956 Clifford Roberts, a Citizens leader, noted that "in some states, the woman Co-Chairman is doing work that in part makes up for the weak [male] Chairman."[129] Women were welcome as party activists; indeed, the male design for party revitalization depended on their activism. But women remained unwelcome in positions of power. In 1950 a journalist wrote that leading House Republicans "privately believe that few women possess the political savvy, shrewdness, and, above all, the level-headed qualities needed to function properly as a party legislator."[130] Although there were more women among Republican than Democratic officeholders – among state legislators in 1953, for example, there were 197 Republicans and 86 Democrats – the smallness of these numbers nevertheless emphasized women's underrepresentation in elected positions, even while their contribution to practical politics was crucial.[131] Many men were unwilling, or unable, to explore the electoral power that attentiveness to women's party contributions – both as activists and as voters – might unlock. This was an opportunity to tackle the minority problem that men missed.

The interest in organizational regeneration persisted in spite of Republican mastery of technical innovations. During the late 1940s and 1950s, television quickly became the dominant communication medium in the country; already in 1952 television's audience for political information was larger than that for either radio or newspapers.[132] Television offered a new, more direct way for politicians to reach the electorate, to some extent reducing the need for precinct-level organization – the opinion-sounding importance of which was also less important due to polling developments.[133] Under Eisenhower, the Republicans made pioneering, innovative use of television, overshadowing the Democrats' efforts in this regard.[134] But politicians did not consider television an adequate replacement for older – more intensive and personal – forms of political communication. Leonard Hall argued there was "no substitute" for "the local organization, ... for doorbell ringing and shoe leather."[135] An

[128] *WP*, March 17, 1953, 30.
[129] Clifford Roberts to Richard Nixon, Oct. 22, 1956, box 645, series 320, Nixon Pre-Presidential Papers.
[130] *Collier's*, Aug. 19, 1950, 27.
[131] RNC, "Women in 1953 State Legislatures," March 1953, box 722, Luce Papers.
[132] Janowitz and Marvick, *Competitive Pressure and Democratic Consent*, 22.
[133] Kelley, "The Presidential Campaign," 85–86.
[134] Allen, *Eisenhower and the Mass Media*.
[135] *Life* clipping, April 25, 1960, box 313, series 320, Nixon Pre-Presidential Papers.

enthusiast nonetheless about the political exploitation of television, he saw the medium as especially important for outreach to areas where the party was weak organizationally, such as the South.[136]

Demographic developments amended understandings of the minority problem. Because of the party's relative suburban strength, and because of rapid postwar suburbanization, its urban weakness – a concern since the New Deal years – seemed less problematic during the 1950s.[137] In 1952, Eisenhower's suburban success in six states decisively wiped out Stevenson's urban pluralities, and seventeen of twenty-four congressional districts in the suburbs of the twenty largest metropolitan areas elected a Republican. "The Democratic Party will never win another national election until it solves the problem of the suburbs," Robert Taft commented.[138]

The suburbs' growth seemed to hold great promise for the party; contemporaries associated suburbanites with Republican support. One theory posited that a move to the suburbs often encouraged a change of party allegiance because of the suburban context of upward mobility, property ownership, and social conformity, because of an environment where people were likelier to encounter Republican ideas than in the cities, and because of a community that more closely resembled small-town America of conservative strength than big-city America's Democratic strongholds. According to such observations, a moderate form of Republicanism was especially likely to encourage movement away from the Democrats. But another theory – of transplantation rather than conversion – offered less encouragement to Eisenhower Republicanism because it saw no special connection between the suburbs and Republican support. When people moved to the suburbs, they took their existing party allegiance with them, and any partisan change was the cause of other factors, such as new affluence. Indeed, between 1948 and 1952, Republican presidential support increased by a greater proportion in central cities than the surrounding suburbs.[139] According to this perspective and research, the trend was less promising than it first appeared.

Research suggested that the popular conversion thesis lacked credibility, but socioeconomic factors apparently did not alone explain Republican success in the suburbs.[140] In small measure, at least, there seemed to be a distinctively suburban outlook on politics, and some evidence to support author William H. Whyte's conclusion in studying what he called "Organization Man" that "it is true that something does seem to happen to Democrats when they get

[136] Allen, *Eisenhower and the Mass Media*, 69.
[137] In 1940, one in ten Americans lived in "satellite" communities; by 1955, the proportion was almost three in ten. Fred I. Greenstein and Raymond E. Wolfinger, "The Suburbs and Shifting Party Loyalties," *POQ* 22 (1958–1959), 473.
[138] Robert C. Wood, *Suburbia: Its People and Their Politics* (Boston: Houghton Mifflin, 1958), 139.
[139] Wood, *Suburbia*, 135–153; Greenstein and Wolfinger, "Suburbs," 479–480.
[140] Greenstein and Wolfinger, "Suburbs."

to suburbia."[141] The suburban effect was not nearly great enough, however, to make much difference to Republican fortunes more broadly.

When Eisenhower decided to run for reelection, he contemplated Nixon's removal from the ticket. Despite the vice president's assiduous work in support of the administration's political goals, there were other politicians who might now offer a stronger contribution to the majority-seeking cause. A favored candidate, promoted by national chair Hall as a means to win conservative Democrats over to the Republican Party, was Frank Lausche, Ohio's Democratic governor, who possessed "middle-way" credentials.[142] Eisenhower's preference was different; he told Hall that "if you did not have to answer the segregation problem, [the] answer would be to get a really good Southern Democrat."[143]

Nixon survived, but these discussions demonstrated Eisenhower's interest in the white South as a source of new GOP support. In May 1956, for example, Eisenhower privately noted that "he had many times in conversation remarked on [the] fact that like-minded people in north and south cannot get together in the same political tent and vote."[144] In 1952, Eisenhower had campaigned in the South, in defiance of RNC officials, who thought it wiser to concentrate his efforts elsewhere. Still, this defiance was no act of political apostasy, and Taft had similar plans to develop southern support had he won the nomination instead.[145] Eisenhower became the first Republican candidate to break the solid South since Herbert Hoover in 1928, enjoying further success there in 1956.

The party as a whole did not achieve a similar southern breakthrough, however.[146] In 1954 Republicans picked up two urban districts, in Dallas and in Tampa–St. Petersburg, though there was also a loss of one Virginia district. There were then no further House gains in the South during the decade, and the party still lacked a U.S. senator representing a southern state.[147] Nevertheless, belief in the South's promise persisted, and the RNC increased its southern efforts, creating "Operation Dixie" in 1957 under I. Lee Potter, the Virginia chair.[148]

But Eisenhower supporters in the South often showed little interest in becoming Republican supporters. According to a study of a Florida precinct in 1956, Eisenhower voters explained this support in overwhelmingly personalized terms; for them, the Eisenhower vote was for an individual and

---

[141] William H. Whyte, *The Organization Man* (New York: Simon and Schuster, 1956), 332.
[142] Memo of calls, Dwight D. Eisenhower with Sherman Adams, Sept. 11, 1953, box 5, DDEDS; *Life* clipping, Nov. 15, 1954, box 29, Name Series, Eisenhower Papers.
[143] Whitman diary, Feb. 9, 1956, box 8, AWDS.
[144] Notes of prepress conference briefing, May 23, 1956, box 8, AWDS.
[145] *Collier's*, April 12, 1952, 74.
[146] *Newsweek*, Nov. 29, 1956, 50–51.
[147] Black and Black, *Rise of Southern Republicans*, 65–66.
[148] *NYT*, June 11, 1957, 10.

not a party, even though their socioeconomic characteristics were similar to Republican voters elsewhere – they were more numerous among wealthier and better educated people. They were also more likely to have lived outside the South than Stevenson supporters.[149]

There was much less interest within the party in revitalizing African American support for the party of Lincoln – despite a record of moderate activism on civil rights. The administration completed the armed forces' desegregation, implemented integration in Washington, D.C., and in 1957 initiated the first post-Reconstruction piece of civil rights legislation. This was, indeed, the one area where impetus for change lay clearly with the Republicans; the southern congressional contingent prevented Democratic innovation in this regard. Progress on civil rights during the 1960s would overshadow these achievements, but they were substantial, reflecting Eisenhower's concern to eradicate discrimination in areas of federal authority. However, his attentiveness to the separation of powers constrained the prospects for bolder initiative.[150]

Eisenhower, distrustful of bully pulpit tactics and concerned about separated powers, showed little enthusiasm in public for the goal of racial equality. He announced no more than the most lukewarm endorsement of the Supreme Court's 1954 *Brown v. Board of Education* decision, which ended the constitutional doctrine of "separate but equal." Only a direct challenge to executive authority in Little Rock, Arkansas, in 1957 brought real support for *Brown's* enforcement – real enough to take the edge off the mild signs of Republican growth in the South. In 1958, there were fewer Republican candidates in southern districts than in the previous few elections. One Virginian who had predicted real progress for the party in the state in 1960 now thought that this would take about another decade.[151] Given his unwillingness to trumpet the administration's interest in civil rights, Eisenhower's unspectacular success overall in restoring Republican fortunes among African Americans was not surprising. This was nevertheless a surprise to Eisenhower and key aides. They thought that this disappointment revealed the ingratitude of African Americans who, Eisenhower complained following Nixon's 1960 defeat, "just do not give a damn."[152]

A similar attitude was evident when in summer 1958 Eisenhower met with a group of African American leaders, including Martin Luther King, Jr., and A. Philip Randolph. Eisenhower offered few words of any support for or sympathy with their freedom struggle. Instead, he was unhappy to hear that the progress achieved during his presidency did not satisfy their call for legal equality. Eisenhower told them that "he was extremely dismayed to hear that after 5½ years of effort and action in this field these gentlemen were saying that bitterness on the part of the Negro people was at its height. He

[149] James W. Prothro, Ernest Q. Campbell, and Charles M. Grigg, "Two-Party Voting in the South: Class vs. Party Identification," *APSR* 52 (1958), 131–139.

[150] David A. Nichols, *A Matter of Justice: Eisenhower and the Beginning of the Civil Rights Revolution* (New York: Simon & Schuster, 2007).

[151] *Wall Street Journal* [hereafter *WSJ*], Oct. 1, 1958, 1; Black and Black, *Rise of Southern Republicans*, 66.

[152] Bryce Harlow for record, Dec. 28, 1960, box 55, DDEDS.

wondered if further constructive action in this field would not only result in more bitterness."[153] African Americans made decisions about voting according to economic self-interest, Eisenhower thought, and the welfare liberalism of the Democratic Party had more appeal than modern Republicanism's more restrained policies. During an April 1955 meeting he argued, "As of now, the Negroes have one interest only: Who is going to promise him the greatest in social security."[154] In this way Eisenhower articulated a cynicism that betrayed an attitude unlikely to foster a party climate friendly to the cultivation of African Americans.

This lack of interest persisted in spite of some signs suggesting a willingness among some African Americans to reconsider their support for the Democrats. Eisenhower's share of African American voters was modestly higher in 1956 than 1952, with some strikingly good improvements in southern cities.[155] The strength of southern segregationists among Democratic ranks provided a particularly compelling argument for Republicans to develop.[156] But many Republicans did not. "Basically and sociologically," wrote journalist Theodore H. White, "Republican state organizations are unlikely to go out for the predominantly working-class Negro unless flogged into it by the White House."[157]

No such leadership existed. E. Frederic Morrow, who broke new ground as the first African American member of the White House executive staff, also found that the party as a whole was failing to break similarly new ground in cultivating nonwhite support.[158] According to Robert Humphreys of the RNC, the party's grassroots identity – as a largely white and middle-class organization – undermined such initiatives. "How many Republicans would sit down in their own home and break bread with a Negro?" he asked Hall. "I've done it, but even I don't say much about it for fear other Republicans would look down their noses at me."[159] Val Washington, the highest-ranking African American at the RNC, noted in 1956 that "the attitude of the Republican Party as a whole from the county level, is just about as bad as it was in 1924 when I first became a worker."[160] In few cases did constituency pressures encourage congressional Republicans to develop a more affirmative approach to civil rights. No more than a handful of House Republicans represented a district with a sizeable African American minority.[161] Not only

[153] Rocco C. Siciliano for files, June 24, 1958, box 33, DDEDS.

[154] Meeting memo, Dwight D. Eisenhower and Robert Merriam, April 28, 1955, box 30, Administration Series, Eisenhower Papers.

[155] Thomson and Shattuck, *1956 Presidential Campaign*, 352–353.

[156] *New York Herald Tribune* clipping, April 9, 1956, BBC Press Cuttings Collection.

[157] *Collier's*, Aug. 17, 1956, 47.

[158] E. Frederic Morrow, *Black Man in the White House: A Diary of the Eisenhower Years by the Administrative Officer for Special Projects, The White House, 1955–1961* (New York: Coward-McCann, 1963).

[159] Robert Humphreys to Leonard Hall, Dec. 31, 1958, box 10, Humphreys Papers.

[160] Val Washington to Sherman Adams, Jan. 4, 1956, box 28, Pyle Papers.

[161] Julius Turner, *Party and Constituency: Pressures on Congress*, rev. ed. by Edward V. Schneier, Jr. (Baltimore: Johns Hopkins Press, 1970), 134.

did the Republican Party's antistatism impede the construction of a positive agenda on civil rights, then, but many Republicans also lacked the inclusive attitude necessary to foster real interest in the African American cause.

The Cold War fed deep concern among Americans.[162] For much of the 1950s, this concern helped the Republicans electorally. Their party developed an advantageous reputation as the one better able to preserve peace, especially due to the Korean War. The advantage was, however, of limited use in securing a party majority because – despite anxieties about national security – congressional campaigns tended to focus on domestic rather than international issues. It was, nevertheless, much more significant in battles for the presidency, thanks to the national nature of this contest and, more importantly, because of the president's responsibilities as commander-in-chief and de facto leader of American foreign policy.[163] Eisenhower's personal reputation as a special expert on foreign policy reinforced the party's advantage in this area on his way to victory in two elections in which international issues were particularly important. His 1952 promise to end the Korean War was crucial for many voters; in fall 1956 the Suez crisis and the Soviet Union's invasion of Hungary both underscored foreign policy's significance to the contest for the White House; more Americans considered Eisenhower abler than Adlai Stevenson to meet such challenges.[164]

Foreign policy was equally central to the presidential campaign of 1960. But Republicans lost their advantage as the party of peace, and in search of the White House Senator John F. Kennedy of Massachusetts persuasively developed an argument that the military strength of the United States was dangerously slipping behind its Soviet adversary's. The "missile gap" would help to thwart Nixon's ambition to succeed Eisenhower as president. An August 1958 Gallup poll signaled the arrival of this fresh dimension of Republican decline. "GOP Loses Important '56 Edge as 'Party of Peace' to Voters," read its headline.[165] Confidence in U.S. strength against the Soviet Union faced a number of challenges. First, the Soviet Union asserted its lead in space with *Sputnik*'s 1957 launch. The event generated considerable alarm; Lyndon Johnson spoke of "the atmosphere of another Pearl Harbor." Second, and more significant still, the report of the Gaither committee, convened by the administration to investigate national defenses, suggested that these were inadequate against the USSR's ever-strengthening forces, calling for a military buildup. Breaking the news of the secret report in December 1957, the *Washington Post* characterized its findings as "[portraying] a United States in the gravest danger in its

---

[162] W. J. Rorabaugh, *Kennedy and the Promise of the Sixties* (Cambridge: Cambridge University Press, 2002).

[163] Byron E. Shafer, "The Notion of an Electoral Order: The Structure of Electoral Politics at the Accession of George Bush," in Shafer, ed., *The End of Realignment? Interpreting American Electoral Eras* (Madison: University of Wisconsin Press, 1991), 49.

[164] Campbell et al., *The American Voter*, 524–528.

[165] George Gallup, "GOP Loses Important '56 Edge as 'Party of Peace' to Voters," Aug. 22, 1958, box 646, series 320, Nixon Pre-Presidential Papers.

history," stating: "It shows an America exposed to an almost immediate threat from the missile-bristling Soviet Union."[166] There was, in fact, no missile gap. But the political debate diverged from the substance. Democrats seized the opportunity to coalesce behind accusations that the administration's guardianship of national security was inadequate.[167] Republicans swiftly tried to advance the argument that the Truman administration had neglected missile development.[168] But it was the current White House party that was the likelier target of such concerns.

Eisenhower's Republican Party was vulnerable to criticism of this kind due to the administration's economy-minded approach to defense. Profoundly concerned about the emergence of a garrison state in response to the demands of the Cold War, Eisenhower initiated a modification of foreign policy on arrival at the White House, seeking to realize the goal of containment while controlling the level of military spending and the size of the armed forces. The "new look" emphasized nuclear rather than conventional defenses, as well as the development of covert operations. Guiding its design was the understanding that U.S. success against the Soviet Union depended on the nation's long-term economic vitality, and that an extravagant approach to foreign policy would prove to be counterproductive. Regardless of its merits, when the administration faced setbacks in foreign policy, the new look was open to the criticism that security had fallen victim to economy.

The challenge to foreign policy did not emerge from Democrats alone. Governor Nelson Rockefeller joined the critics. From a northeastern family of immense wealth and privilege, Rockefeller won the New York governorship in 1958. He found support for his criticisms in the findings of a panel on national security convened by his family's Rockefeller Brothers Fund; reporting in early 1958, the panel fed missile-gap anxiety. Part of a Special Studies Project established explicitly to nourish Rockefeller's political ambitions, the panel called for greatly increased spending on defense, claiming that the Soviet Union's military strength would soon outstrip that of the United States otherwise.[169] Rockefeller's gubernatorial victory that defied the 1958 pro-Democratic trend catapulted him to the party's leading ranks, confirming the promise of his political glamour. Setting his sights on the presidency, he combined welfare liberalism with hawkish internationalism. In June 1960, to Eisenhower's annoyance, he attacked the White House for spending too little on defense.[170] Republican disunity in foreign policy had thus returned, though

[166] David L. Snead, *The Gaither Committee, Eisenhower, and the Cold War* (Columbus: Ohio State University Press, 1999), 80, 139.

[167] Gary W. Reichard, "Divisions and Dissent: Democrats and Foreign Policy, 1952–1956," *Political Science Quarterly* 93 (1978), 51–72.

[168] *Newsweek*, Feb. 3, 1958, 18.

[169] Cary Reich, *The Life of Nelson A. Rockefeller: Worlds to Conquer, 1908–1958* (New York: Doubleday, 1996), 649–667.

[170] Ann Whitman to Dwight D. Eisenhower, June 9, 1960, box 11, AWDS; Whitman, memo of telephone call, June 11, 1960, box 50, DDEDS.

the overt dissent was grounded this time not in a form of isolationism that advocated a reduced U.S. role in global affairs, but in active internationalism that advocated a more ambitious pursuit of the nation's Cold War mission to hold the line against communism. Rockefeller defended his actions against critics who accused him of fomenting party disunity by insisting "that unless the Vice President and the Party take strong and affirmative positions on the great issues involving the security and survival of the nation, the chances for a Republican victory in November will have been substantially diminished."[171]

This argument led Rockefeller to criticize the draft of the platform for the 1960 election as inadequately forceful on national defense, also finding its domestic planks too conservative. Although Nixon easily overwhelmed Rockefeller's challenge for the party nomination, he reached an agreement with Rockefeller about the platform in the "Compact of Fifth Avenue" – infuriating conservatives including Goldwater, who dubbed the compromise the "Munich of the Republican Party," as it lacked principle and was sure to bring defeat. The implication that the nation's defenses were inadequate infuriated Eisenhower, too. A modified compromise scaled back the "Compact's" impact, leaving the platform with a more assertive plank on civil rights and a reworked plank on national defense, which called for an "intensified" program and accepting "any necessary increased expenditures to meet new initiatives."[172]

Rockefeller represented the "eastern establishment." His embrace of moderation in domestic policy – outflanking modern Republicanism – and interventionist internationalism in foreign policy placed him within a Republican tradition that had exercised much influence at least since Wendell Willkie's candidacy. In 1952 Eisenhower had enjoyed establishment support, and his agenda of modern Republicanism promoted a moderate vision of party policy. Rockefeller's criticism of the administration's record signaled his personal ambition but also suggested that modern Republicanism had fallen short of establishment ambitions for the party. The impact of Rockefeller's influence-seeking intervention would soon prove to be counterproductive, however. What Goldwater called the "Munich" of the Republican Party encouraged conservative mobilization against such influence, and the rise of Goldwater conservatism during the 1960s would spell the eastern establishment's decline in the party.[173]

In the shorter term, such problems were barely evident. Despite the intraparty disagreements that facilitated extraparty attacks, Nixon remained confident in the electoral power of the GOP reputation as the party of peace. In

[171] Nelson A. Rockefeller to Benjamin A. Javits, July 6, 1960, box 97, series L, Record Group 4, Rockefeller Family Archives.
[172] Theodore H. White, *Making of the President 1960* (New York: Atheneum, 1961), 191–205 (quotations, 199, 205).
[173] Leonard Silk and Mark Silk, *The American Establishment* (New York: Basic, 1976), 280–285.

June he wrote to pollster Claude Robinson that "if foreign policy is uppermost in the people's minds we will do well. If not, the Democrats will tend to bene-fit, particularly if the economic situation should fall off to any extent" – once more reflecting his belief that a focus on New Deal liberalism was always to the Democrats' benefit.[174] Robinson agreed, reporting in September that Nixon's experience was crucial to voter evaluations of his candidacy: "The factor that is likely to tip the balance your way is public concern over the chal-lenge of the Russians and the belief that you are better qualified than Kennedy to deal with this situation." The votes of women, somewhat more concerned than men about the preservation of peace, were important, he thought.[175]

Despite his stress on foreign policy's electoral power, Nixon did not neglect domestic policy in pursuing the presidency. He fretted about the electoral impact of the economy's continuing sluggishness, later observing that the administration's failure to tackle unemployment more strenuously in 1959 and 1960 may have cost him the election.[176] He was also anxious to pro-mote an image of sympathy toward welfare liberalism. When, in the after-math of the 1958 setbacks, Eisenhower convened the Republican Committee on Program and Progress under businessperson Charles H. Percy to define the party's ideological direction, Nixon emphasized to Percy the significance of the Democratic position on social welfare to the Republicans' minority status. He hoped that Percy's committee would identify initiatives that Republicans could advocate to tackle what were seen as emerging social problems of the day, such as welfare dependency and juvenile delinquency. Rather paradox-ically, given his own campaign-trail condemnations of Democratic radical-ism, Nixon bemoaned the Republican tendency to respond to the opposition's programs "with cries of 'Socialism', 'too much', or make dire references to ruining the moral fibre [sic] of the people."[177] In 1960 Nixon sought to bur-nish his modern Republican credentials with proposals such as federal aid to education and a healthcare program for the elderly – outflanked by Kennedy's more generous and wide-ranging alternatives, which Nixon condemned as too expensive.[178] According to Nixon's conceptualization of interparty conflict, such positions sought to immunize the party against Democratic attack and did not involve the expectation that a Republican advantage in this area might be possible.

Cold War developments again underlined foreign policy's salience to the presidential contest. Superpower relations turned more tense in 1960 – the result of such events as the collapse of a summit conference, the Soviet Union's

[174] Richard Nixon to Jackie Robinson, June 15, 1960, box 647, series 320, Nixon Pre-Presidential Papers.
[175] Jackie Robinson to Richard Nixon, Sept. 1, 1960, box 647, series 320, Nixon Pre-Presidential Papers.
[176] Richard M. Nixon, *Six Crises* (Garden City, N.Y.: Doubleday, 1962), 293–426.
[177] Richard Nixon to Charles Percy, March 21, 1959, box 588, series 320, Nixon Pre-Presidential Papers.
[178] Kelley, "The Presidential Campaign," 69.

support for the Fidel Castro regime in Cuba and for the Patrice Lumumba faction in the newly independent Congo, and Soviet premier Nikita Khrushchev's assertive rhetoric at fall meetings of the UN General Assembly. In response to Nixon's stress on his leadership experience, Kennedy emphasized the need for fresh momentum at home and overseas.[179] Kennedy thus neutralized the Cold War advantage from which Eisenhower had benefited, even managing to construct a compelling argument that he was better able than Nixon to lead the nation against the communist threat. This argument, combined with the enduring Democratic advantage of New Deal liberalism's popular appeal, helped Kennedy to secure a narrow victory over Nixon. Kennedy's Catholicism provided his victory with some distinctive characteristics. His candidacy encouraged the return to the Democratic Party of Catholic voters who had voted for Eisenhower; it also fostered the return of the anti-Catholicism that Al Smith experienced in 1928 – not nearly to the same degree, but enough that his Catholicism was an obstacle rather than a help to his victory.[180]

The demographic dimension of the 1960 results involved continuity as well as change. African American support for the GOP declined still further – seven in ten voted for Kennedy – a reflection of the Democrats' more convincing commitment to civil rights, symbolized during the campaign by Kennedy's intervention to secure Martin Luther King's release from jail, but involving a broader preference for the Democrats' policies.[181] The white South demonstrated that its support for the presidential Republican Party was not for Eisenhower alone; visiting three southern states in late August, Nixon found a warm, enthusiastic welcome, most notably in Atlanta. Nixon increased the Republican vote there, outrunning Eisenhower in Alabama, Georgia, Mississippi, and South Carolina (though losing all four), and he almost matched Eisenhower's victory margins in winning Florida and Virginia. Altogether, in the eleven states of the former Confederacy, Nixon won 47.7 percent of the vote, compared with Eisenhower's 48.1 percent in 1952 and 50.5 percent in 1956. Goldwater saw the Compact of Fifth Avenue as crucial in depriving Nixon of the additional votes needed for victory, later claiming that the original, weaker, version of the platform plank on civil rights would have ensured such success; in his eyes, the modified version that Nixon and Rockefeller agreed was responsible for defeat.[182]

In explaining his failure, Nixon identified enduring features of the New Deal coalition as damaging; in addition to the recession's reinforcement of the

[179] Kelley, "The Presidential Campaign," 59–60, 67–68, 75–77.

[180] Philip E. Converse, Angus Campbell, Warren E. Miller, and Donald E. Stokes, "Stability and Change in 1960: A Reinstating Election," *APSR* 55 (1961), 269–280; V. O. Key, Jr., "Interpreting the Election Results," in Paul T. David, ed., *The Presidential Election and Transition 1960–1961* (Washington, D.C.: Brookings Institution, 1961), 150–175.

[181] James H. Meriwether, "'Worth a Lot of Negro Votes': Black Voters, Africa, and the 1960 Presidential Campaign," *Journal of American History* 95 (2008), 737–773.

[182] White, *Making of the President 1960*, 321–323, 354, 268–272, 203.

connection between Republicans and bad times, he attached some responsibility for his defeat to labor's organizational efforts against him.[183] However, the narrowness of Nixon's defeat indicated Republican presidential strength that extended beyond Eisenhower's personal popularity. Still, the Eisenhower years thus ended with disappointment for the Republicans. Not only had the two-stranded project of party revitalization – modern Republicanism and Citizens for Eisenhower – failed to share Eisenhower's popularity with the party at large, but Eisenhower's vice president had also failed to translate this legacy into sustained presidential success at the polls. This disappointment encouraged new engagement with the minority problem, which took the party in a very different direction from that of modern Republicanism.

[183] Kelley, "The Presidential Campaign," 64.

6

"A Choice, Not an Echo": 1960–1968

According to Senator Barry Goldwater of Arizona, Richard Nixon's defeat to John F. Kennedy – the very narrowness of which fostered intraparty conflict – offered the party a lesson in electoral strategy.[1] "This election outcome does suggest the Republican Party should reexamine its position and should be prepared to reject all those who advocate a 'me-too' position for future election contests," Goldwater argued within days of the defeat.[2] A little over three years later, Goldwater spoke of his alternative to me-too politics when in January 1964 he announced his candidacy for the party's presidential nomination. "I will offer a choice," he said, "not an echo."[3] The strategic argument that an electoral majority existed in support of conservative principles – in support of "a choice, not an echo" – was at the heart of his presidential quest, and it enthused pro-Goldwater activists. The idea alarmed Goldwater's opponents within the party, who considered the belief in a "hidden" conservative majority not only wrong-headed but dangerous, too; advocacy of such conservatism threatened to reduce the Republican Party to political irrelevance, they thought.

Race informed the strategic disagreement. For Goldwater, it was a matter of electoral reality that his party's best opportunity for growth was among the South's white conservatives who still tended to support Democratic candidates. His opponents believed that their cultivation involved a rejection of the party's fragile Lincolnian inheritance as the proponent of racial progress. Against the background of the tumultuous struggle for civil rights, the Republican Party moved in Goldwater's direction. The disastrous showing by Goldwater against Lyndon Johnson in fall 1964 confirmed his strategy's electoral fallacy, and the contest helped to complete the disaffiliation of African Americans from the Republican Party. However, while losing the battle, party conservatives won the war. Although in the shorter-term aftermath of Goldwater's

---

[1] *New Republic*, March 27, 1961, 10.
[2] Press release, statement by Barry Goldwater, Nov. 9, 1960, box 222, Strauss Papers.
[3] Robert D. Novak, *The Agony of the G.O.P. 1964* (New York: Macmillan, 1965), 269.

defeat, conservatism's future in the Republican Party was unclear, its dominance became clear in time.

In contemplating the mobilization of a Republican majority, Goldwater commandeered Franklin D. Roosevelt's 1932 rhetorical cultivation of ordinary Americans by issuing an appeal to "forgotten Americans." A January 1961 statement characterized these "silent Americans" as neglected by New Deal liberalism, which instead responded to the demands of noisy pressure groups. Goldwater concluded "that there are literally scores of millions of Americans who are either outside the organized pressure groups or find themselves represented by organizations with whose policies they disagree in whole or in part." His statement called for government action to reverse the pattern of neglect.[4] The policy detail of Goldwater's search for forgotten Americans was subject to change. Goldwater quickly stepped away again from positive references to government activism. But its spirit remained unchanged. During his campaign against Johnson, Goldwater again said that his appeal was to "the forgotten American" – a 95 percent slice of the electorate, he claimed – who was "the man who pays taxes, the man who works, the man who stays out of trouble."[5] Confidence in a majority's fundamental conservatism informed his candidacy. So, too, then, did a rejection of interest-group politics; Goldwater insisted that his focus was a national interest and did not seek to engage in the selfish and base politics of brokerage among a variety of special interests, a belief that during the 1964 campaign led him to condemn the administration's "War on Poverty" in economically deprived Appalachia and its Medicare proposals for healthcare for the elderly in Florida's retirement communities.[6]

The Nixon defeat encouraged another argument about the party's electoral future, one very different from Goldwater's. This emphasized the problem of light support for the party in the big cities, especially in the East. Election returns showed that in many cases big-city deficits wiped out vote surpluses elsewhere in a state. Republicans noted with concern that 1960 also saw a decline for the party in the eastern cities' suburbs, areas often associated in the 1950s with upward mobility and party growth.[7] The urban problem was by no means new; since the New Deal large majorities in the cities had helped to account for Democratic victories. But the detail of the Nixon defeat encouraged fresh attention to the problem and a shift away from the emphasis of the 1950s on the suburbs as a strength able to neutralize or even overwhelm the cities' hostility.

According to an RNC report, the party carried only fourteen of forty-one big cities, mostly in the South and West. It suggested that success in minimizing urban losses would have secured another eight states, 173 votes in

---

[4] Novak, *Agony of the G.O.P.*, 28–35 (quotation, 30).

[5] *NYT*, Oct. 7, 1964, 27.

[6] Richard Hofstadter, "Goldwater and Pseudo-Conservative Politics," in *The Paranoid Style in American Politics and Other Essays* (1965; London: Jonathan Cape, 1966), 120–122.

[7] RNC Research Division, "Preliminary Analysis of the 1960 Presidential Vote," Nov. 23, 1960, box 36, subseries 2, series 5, Javits Papers.

the electoral college, and certain victory for Nixon.[8] In its rawest form, the urban concern involved the belief that the Nixon defeat was a stolen election, that the lack of Republican personnel to watch polling places permitted Democratic irregularities to maximize the Kennedy vote. But the concern also had further-reaching implications, involving the sense that the party had lost touch with urban Americans, widely perceived during the 1960s as an increasingly important strand of society; if the 1950s was the decade of suburban optimism, then the 1960s was the decade of the city – first associated with cosmopolitan modernity, but later associated with decay and unrest. One reflection of the larger worry about the party's fortunes in the cities was a postelection idea of a Nixon campaign aide. Charles McWhorter suggested the creation of community programs to display the merits of grassroots, volunteer-based solutions to local problems, thus building in a practical way electoral support for Republican antistatism.[9] The way McWhorter wrestled with the policy implications of the party's urban problem revealed an assumption, shared by many, that Republicans needed to display problem-solving imagination, if not the me-too position that Goldwater condemned, in order to boost its city support. Not all those who promoted a new urban focus for the party were moderates, but many were. It was usually a focus that led in a different direction from Goldwater's conservatism.

Still, the urban lessons of 1960 seemed too clear for the party at large to ignore. Observing that it was an "obvious fact that this election was lost for the Republican candidates in big cities," national chair Thruston B. Morton, senator from Kentucky and a moderate, successfully recommended the RNC's creation of a Committee on Big City Politics under Ray C. Bliss, the Ohio party chair.[10] Bliss was an exponent of organizational improvements as a way to boost the party's chances, leaving debates about ideology and policy to officeholding and -seeking politicians; his own views were on the more conservative rather than more moderate side. The committee's remit was to embrace this technocratic approach, and it found much that was at fault with the party's capacity to wage an effective campaign in the cities; the Republican engagement during the Eisenhower years with its organizational deficiencies had apparently failed to secure significant improvements in this regard. Reporting in January 1962, the committee found that the party had neither the funds nor the personnel in the cities to pose a vigorous opposition to the Democratic Party, the beneficiaries of labor support and local political patronage. "In most big cities, the Republican Party generally is out-manned, out-organized, out-spent and out-worked," concluded Bliss. The committee's report advocated permanent organization to mobilize the Republican vote. Better organization would improve

---

[8] "Oklahoma City Presentation of Big City Politics Report," Jan. 12, 1962, box 36, subseries 2, series 5, Javits Papers.

[9] Charles McWhorter, memo draft, Nov. 22, 1960, box 6, Safire Papers.

[10] Philip A. Klinkner, *The Losing Parties: Out-Party National Committees, 1956–1993* (New Haven, Conn.: Yale University Press, 1994), 45.

the quality of candidates interested in running for office as Republicans, and through publicized attention to their special concerns it would allow the party to win more support among union members, ethnic Americans, and African Americans. While advocating new efforts to challenge the work of the AFL–CIO's Committee on Political Education (COPE) that aimed to consolidate labor backing for Democratic candidates, the committee also recommended further pursuit of business-in-politics initiatives.[11]

The emphasis on organization had met with staunch objections internally from L. Judson Morhouse, chair of the New York State party, who led a subcommittee dealing with polling, television, and public relations. Believing that an inadequately progressive approach to welfare questions – especially on medical care for the elderly – accounted for Nixon's 1960 defeat, Morhouse insisted that the consideration of issues was central to success in understanding the party's urban problem. He was also concerned about a structural problem; the national committee then consisted of two members for each state, together with a third member for states where Republicans had enjoyed recent presidential, gubernatorial, or congressional success, thus overrepresenting smaller and more conservative states. Effective engagement with big-city concerns required a different kind of national committee, Morhouse thought, and he told fellow New York Republicans that the division of RNC membership among the states should be decided according to population. Morhouse was unable to persuade the committee to look at issues as well as organization, however, instead using his subcommittee's report to suggest the need for a more liberal set of policies. "Until the Republican Party listens to the people, it will remain a minority party," he wrote.[12]

Despite the avoidance of policy controversies, Bliss's emphasis on organization failed to gain momentum as a response to the minority problem. Under the leadership of William E. Miller, a New York congressperson and Morton's replacement, the national committee showed no interest in the implementation of the big-city report. The RNC instead invested more attention and money in the party's southern development, a focus usually compatible with Goldwater conservatism.[13]

Beyond the national committee, an urban-oriented modernity persisted as some leading Republicans' hallmark. The most liberal among them was New York's Senator Jacob K. Javits, whose 1964 book, *Order of Battle*, set out his belief that the poor quality of Democratic city governments created a Republican opportunity to win "metropolitan man's" support. He advocated innovation in housing, transportation, intergovernmental relations, and the arts to do so, warning that by 1970 four in five Americans would live in major urban areas. "Metropolitan man" lived in the South, too, according to Javits,

---

[11] "Oklahoma City Presentation of Big City Politics Report," Jan. 12, 1962, box 36, subseries 2, series 5, Javits Papers.
[12] Klinkner, *Losing Parties*, 47–48 (quotation, 47).
[13] Klinkner, *Losing Parties*, 53–60.

who forecast party growth among urban professionals there, thus challenging the assumed connection between white southerners and conservatism.[14] Joining Javits and his fellow New Yorker, Nelson Rockefeller, within these moderate ranks were Charles H. Percy, an Illinois businessperson who headed the Republican Committee on Program and Progress before chairing the 1960 platform committee; John V. Lindsay, a New York City congressperson; and Michigan's George W. Romney.

Within these ranks, Romney first joined Rockefeller in generating most interest as a presidential prospect and, less liberal than Javits or Rockefeller, drew on his experience in his labor-stronghold state to offer a thoughtful response to the minority problem. When Romney gained national party prominence in early 1962, his business success and maverick-like politics encouraged comparisons with Wendell Willkie. As the president of American Motors, he had led a successful challenge to the auto industry's gas-guzzling obsession by promoting a "compact" car that significantly increased his company's market share against its much bigger Detroit rivals. Opposition to bigness defined his agenda, both in business and in politics. As an auto executive, he attacked the excessive size of big corporations (such as Ford and General Motors) and – despite qualified achievement in securing management–union relations that were harmonious by Detroit's standards – he made a similar attack on organized labor, advocating a maximum size for a union of ten thousand members. He also spoke of consumerism – which "places economic control in the hands of all citizens as consumers," he said in 1958 – as having replaced a capitalistic system that concentrated such control.[15] One journalist commented that his David-against-Goliath background made him "probably the only big businessman in the country with whom the average voter can easily identify."[16] This consumer-oriented skepticism of bigness was, Romney thought, a formula for Republican growth among the urban Americans whose support the party needed.[17]

The party's position in the cities was also among the key concerns of a resuscitated Citizens movement. More than a decade after the organization's first emergence in support of Dwight Eisenhower as the Republicans' presidential nominee, a group of leading Eisenhower supporters reassembled it in spring 1962 as the National Republican Citizens Committee (later renamed the Republican Citizens Committee of the United States), once more with the intention to achieve the permanent mobilization of activists who had worked for the presidential candidacies of Eisenhower and then Nixon outside regular party organizations.[18] In addition to the creation of "a permanent reservoir of citizen talent which can be called upon by Republican nominees

[14] Jacob K. Javits, *Order of Battle: A Republican's Call to Reason* (New York: Atheneum, 1964), 313–314.
[15] *The Nation*, Feb. 3, 1962, 95–97.
[16] *Harper's*, March 1962, 18–24.
[17] *New Republic*, March 5, 1962, 17–27.
[18] Austin J. Tobin, Jr., to Walter N. Thayer, June 4, 1962, box 18, Safire Papers.

in national elections," the committee set out to support the work of other Republican citizens groups that had developed here and there and to "[tap] the vast, un-utilized potential for creative political effort in the business, managerial and professional community particularly in the large urban centers."[19] The new Citizens operation argued that experience revealed that organizational revitalization was not enough to boost fortunes and indicated a need as well for policy development.[20] Milton S. Eisenhower, the former president's brother and a university president, therefore launched a research offshoot, the Critical Issues Council, "to articulate a Republican-citizens' position on the great problems that face our people and our government."[21]

Conservatives' response to the return of Citizens revealed the bitterness of intraparty factional conflict and the low regard they had for Eisenhower as party leader. Goldwater attacked Citizens leaders as "the same people who caused most of our present Party troubles," because he believed they sidelined Republican regulars during campaigns and downplayed Republican principles during the Eisenhower administration, arguing that such "splinter groups" undermined rather than assisted efforts to grow the party.[22] According to Ohio RNC member Katharine Kennedy Brown, the initiative was a left-wing takeover attempt; Eisenhower "did nothing to help build the Republican Party organization in the eight years of his presidency," she wrote, and his "modern Republicanism" was "a natural course for people who have never worked in the Party in their lives and hardly know to which Party they belong."[23]

Goldwater's cause had nothing to fear, however. By sharp contrast with its origins as a mass grassroots movement, the new Citizens organization was primarily an elite group of former Eisenhower supporters and administration officials whose hopes to foster volunteer-based politics were rather forlorn. The contrast with pro-Goldwater activism that was developing at the party's grass roots was equally sharp. A lack of funds – the result of a lack of members – fatally undermined the pursuit of its ambitious goals. Despite a mailing list of 300,000 names inherited from the Nixon campaign, by summer 1963 the organization had fewer than 300 members.[24] Despite issuing twelve papers by August 1964, the Critical Issues Council had little success, too, in leading or informing Republican policy debate.[25] The results of Citizens activism disappointed Dwight Eisenhower. "Every individual with whom one talks

[19] National Republican Citizens Committee, progress report, n.d., box 5, Political File, Thayer Papers.
[20] Republican Citizens Committee of the United States, progress report, June 1963, box 5, Political File, Thayer Papers.
[21] Republican Citizens Committee of the United States, progress report, Oct. 1963, box 5, Political File, Thayer Papers.
[22] Barry Goldwater to William E. Miller (released), July 5, 1962, box 4, series I, Goldwater Papers.
[23] Katharine Kennedy Brown to William E. Miller, July 12, 1962, box 155, Rusher Papers.
[24] John von Stade to Joseph E. Sheffield and Walter N. Thayer, Aug. 22, 1963, box 5, Political File, Thayer Papers.
[25] Walter N. Thayer to Barry Goldwater, Aug. 4, 1964, box 5, Political File, Thayer Papers.

is quite ready to sound off on the importance of free enterprise and sound fiscal policy, preservation of the value of our currency and so on," he confided to
his brother. "When it comes to getting them to do any work themselves – or
even to contribute out of personal, unneeded funds to support such work –
one usually runs into blank walls."[26] In short, Eisenhower had discovered that
his faith in an elite to revitalize the party now met with an even more lackluster response than it did when he was in the White House.

"The Republican Party, like it or not, has a rendezvous with a brand new
idea," wrote *National Review* publisher William Rusher in early 1963. He
argued that the previous fall's elections conclusively demonstrated that no
Republican presidential candidate was capable of defeating John F. Kennedy
in New York and California; the margin of Nelson Rockefeller's reelection
victory was disappointing, while Richard Nixon lost his challenge to Edmund
G. "Pat" Brown for California's governorship. Instead of seeking a presidential candidate considered likely to win the big states, the party should develop
a different strategy, for which the obvious candidate was not Rockefeller but
Barry Goldwater. What struck Rusher as significant was the party's southern growth; in the 1962 midterms, GOP candidates for the House garnered
31 percent of the southern vote – almost twice the proportion achieved in
1958 – despite the party's failure to field a challenger in many districts. At
the presidential level, the South was available for cultivation by a Republican,
who could then piece together a majority in the electoral college, despite the
inescapable loss of New York and California to Kennedy. The only prominent Republican with the necessary appeal to the South – with the necessarily conservative views – was Goldwater, Rusher concluded.[27] Such analysis
supported the case made by Goldwater himself. "We ought to forget the big
cities," he said at a conference of southern Republicans in late 1961, because
"[w]e can't out-promise the Democrats," arguing that any victory relied on
"strong support from the hinterland" instead.[28]

According to its opponents, this "southern strategy" required the party to
take a racist turn, not just a repudiation of its pro–civil rights tradition but also
a way to alienate permanently millions of its supporters outside the South.[29]
Emblematic of the moderate Republican position, a *New York Herald Tribune*
editorial warned that the party was in danger of committing "as immoral a
political act as any by a major party in American history."[30] Rusher dismissed
such objections as simply a factional effort to maintain intraparty power,
insisting that racism did not characterize southern Republicans, pointing out

---

[26] Dwight D. Eisenhower to Milton S. Eisenhower, Feb. 17, 1964, box 5, Political File, Thayer
Papers.
[27] *National Review*, Feb. 12, 1963, 109–112 (quotation, 110).
[28] WP, Nov. 26, 1961, E1.
[29] NYT magazine, Oct. 27, 1963, 15, 105–107.
[30] *New York Herald Tribune*, July 2, 1962, 18.

that the Democratic Party there remained the more conservative on race. The party's growth was founded on a new middle class that benefited from the South's economic development, part of a socioeconomic transformation that was reducing the region's distinctiveness, he argued.[31]

Others supportive of the thesis were less willing to downplay race's significance. The pro-Goldwater argument made sense to Peter Clayton, a Citizens leader during the 1950s, after a visit to the South, for example. In Clayton's eyes it was a growing resentment toward what he saw as African Americans' militancy that made Goldwater a potential winner at the height of the movement for civil rights. Clayton wrote that "it is widely suspected that his views on segregation differ from those of, say, Governor [Ross] Barnett [of Mississippi]; yet there is a kind of wishful thinking evident throughout the South that Senator Goldwater will not articulate these differences too much." Discussion of racial problems in a manner sympathetic to the white South, together with an emphasis on states' rights, presented the possibility of Goldwater victory, according to Clayton, who suspected that states in the industrial Northeast and Midwest might support such a candidacy if the administration maintained its pro–civil rights momentum.[32]

Goldwater was no foe of racial progress. He voted for the 1957 and 1960 Civil Rights Acts, designed to protect voting rights, and he both denounced discrimination and worked to eradicate it. At home in Arizona he had joined the NAACP and promoted the Air National Guard's integration, as well as owning some of the first Phoenix stores to employ African Americans.[33] But his conservatism placed him in opposition to federal action to achieve such progress, an approach that seemed to offer little promise of much change in the South at least in the near future. "I would like to see our party back up on school integration," he told southern Republicans in 1961, speaking more bluntly than usual on civil rights. "The Supreme Court decision is not the supreme law of the land."[34] Goldwater's position was very different from moderate Republicans', which usually endorsed much of the administration's pro–civil rights program. But especially when the Kennedy administration started to work more unequivocally in pursuit of civil rights legislation in 1963, there was accumulating evidence that African Americans were unwilling to support any Republican, however moderate, against the president. A *Newsweek* poll that summer found that moderates Rockefeller and Romney were likely to fare barely any better against Kennedy than Goldwater among African Americans; the percentage of respondents planning to vote for Kennedy in a contest against any of these Republicans was overwhelming.[35]

---

31 *National Review*, Feb. 12, 1963, 111–112.
32 Peter H. Clayton, "November, 1964 – As Seen in June, 1963," June 25, 1963, box 1, Political File, Thayer Papers.
33 Robert Alan Goldberg, *Barry Goldwater* (New Haven, Conn.: Yale University Press, 1995), 89–91, 121, 140, 154–155.
34 *WP*, Nov. 26, 1961, E1.
35 *Newsweek*, July 29, 1963, 29.

In seeing clear signs of a pro-Republican trend in the South, party conservatives identified it as friendly to their ideological agenda as well as electoral aspirations. A newcomer who fostered confidence in a southern opportunity for the party was John G. Tower. Surprise winner of the 1961 Texas special election to replace Lyndon Johnson in the Senate and the first twentieth-century Republican senator from a state of the former Confederacy, Tower benefited from Democratic divisions, as he would, too, in 1966 – Texas liberals were unwilling to support the conservatives their party fielded.[36] Tower spoke of "a conservative resurgence," and insisted on Americans' fundamental conservatism. "They have a basic trust in that which is of proven value," he wrote. "They are by nature patriotic, and they enjoy the comfort the present economic system affords them, along with its attendant individual liberties." But he spoke, too, of an influential "Liberal Establishment," successful in misleadingly characterizing liberalism as fostering prosperity and socioeconomic progress, while demonizing conservatives as backward-looking and self-interested.

For Tower, then, the conservative mission was to find a way to communicate effectively a message with which many Americans sympathized. It was also important to provide tangible evidence that conservatives were not liberalism's negative opponents, by promoting conservative solutions to contemporary problems. To do so, Tower presented eight bills and resolutions to the Senate in March 1962. The issues and concerns he raised included "a policy of victory" against the Soviet Union, tax cuts and a bill to balance the budget, antitrust legislation to deal with unions, and the protection of states' rights.[37] Although there was ideological diversity among southern Republicans (as among Republicans elsewhere), Tower was much closer to the ideas of more of them than the urban-oriented moderates were. At a Republican meeting in Atlanta, Leonard Nadasby, Young Republican National Federation chair, remarked that it was "full of young zealots," who were "full of pep and ambition" and "mostly young Jaycees who want to get into politics but can't find any place in the one-party system."[38]

John Kennedy's death and the ascendance to the presidency by Texan Lyndon Johnson in November 1963 challenged the southern strategy's logic. The RNC's A. B. Hermann projected that Kennedy's 85 to 90 percent share of African Americans might decline to 60 or 70 percent for Johnson, provided that the party publicized the new president's congressional record of neglect on civil rights and achieved organizational revitalization in the cities. He forecast similar Republican gains among predominantly urban and Catholic "Nationality groups," such as Irish Americans and Italian Americans.[39] But

---

[36] Black and Black, *Rise of Southern Republicans*, 90–91.
[37] John G. Tower, *A Program for Conservatives* (New York: Macfadden, 1962), 16–18 (quotation, 16).
[38] WP, Nov. 26, 1961, E1.
[39] A. B. Hermann to Republican leaders, Dec. 20, 1963, box 25, Scott Papers.

Johnson pursued his predecessor's egalitarian agenda with yet more energy and determination, mobilizing nonsouthern Democratic and sufficient Republican support in Congress to secure the 1964 Civil Rights Act, a legislative landmark. This Republican support, guided in the Senate by minority leader Everett Dirksen of Illinois, was crucial in overwhelming southern Democrats' opposition. Unlike many of his fellow Republicans in the Senate, Goldwater voted against the bill because he viewed it as an unconstitutional expansion of federal powers. Despite significant Republican support for the Civil Rights Act, then, the line between Goldwater and Johnson on race was thus clear.

During his campaign for the 1964 nomination, Goldwater discussed his view of the party's electoral problem. "This Republican Party of ours is no longer a minority party that has to apologize for its principles or double-talk to squeeze out votes," he told an April rally. Acknowledging that registration figures remained decisively in the Democrats' favor, he nevertheless emphasized the existence of "a spirit, a warm and rising spirit that you can't miss in this election," which indicated that "Republican chances are on the rise everywhere – and everyone knows it whether they want to admit it or not."[40] The most powerful argument in support of the conservative response to the minority problem was the work of Republican activist Phyllis Schlafly in her 1964 self-published book, *A Choice Not an Echo*. Schlafly criticized eastern-establishment "kingmakers" who, she argued, had since 1936 dictated the selection of presidential candidates to conform to their me-too policy concerns, concerns that reflected their financial interests. The me-too path to which the kingmakers committed the party repeatedly led to defeat. Between April, its month of publication, and November 1964 the book achieved sales of three and a half million copies.[41]

It was not the power of his strategic argument that won the nomination for Goldwater. Instead, it was the success of the pro-Goldwater movement within the party. This movement benefited from the shortcomings of the efforts during the Eisenhower years to improve the party's organization because its continuing grassroots weakness allowed Goldwater enthusiasts to take control of local Republican committees.[42] Among conservatives the Goldwater candidacy developed a crusade-like meaning, as the Eisenhower candidacy had in 1952 among its supporters, and the mobilization it inspired drew new activists to the party, seeking to promote conservatism. Some Republicans viewed this mobilization with alarm. A New Mexico Republican, for example, worried that "a minority of far-right extremists" were taking control of the party in his state.[43]

---

[40] Barry Goldwater, speech, April 28, 1964, box W12, Goldwater Papers.
[41] Critchlow, *Phyllis Schlafly and Grassroots Conservatism*, 124–125.
[42] Jack L. Walker, "The Republican Party and the Birth Rate," *Antioch Review* 25 (1965), 299.
[43] James R. Gay to Hugh Scott, June 20, 1964, box 25, Scott Papers.

First working without any commitment from Goldwater to become a candidate, a draft-Goldwater operation at the national level provided support to local activities. "The best guarantee that each state will get the maximum number of Goldwater delegates is to perfect the organization down to the precinct level," wrote Peter O'Donnell, Jr., to leading activists. "Precinct organization means political power."[44] As the committee's national director, F. Clifton White applied organizational expertise partly gained through his work in the business-in-politics phenomenon of the 1950s to the challenge of building support for a conservative Republican.[45] As White noted to the group's other founders, their goal was to transform the party into the vehicle for conservatism in American politics.[46] One of the effort's supporters was William Rusher, who not long before had preferred to pursue his conservatism outside the framework of political parties, disliking the compromise of principles they demanded. The draft-Goldwater goal conceptualized a different kind of party, dedicated to principle. Some saw the Goldwater movement as a centralized effort to take over the party, but White insisted that "all we did was give direction and focus to a great grassroots movement."[47] The activists' energy supported the construction of an argument that their organizational revitalization of the party was likely to aid its quest for electoral victory. A draft-Goldwater leaflet predicted Republican gains with Goldwater but twenty years more of defeat without.[48]

Among the developments that fostered this movement, White later stressed the significance of the Supreme Court's 1962 *Engel v. Vitale* decision banning prayer in public schools.[49] School prayer's importance signaled the emergence of a new kind of political issue, stemming from anxieties about the nature of American society – in this case the role of religion – rather than involving New Deal liberalism's bread-and-butter concerns or Cold War internationalism's security and defense concerns. Related concerns, such as the content of school textbooks, frequently drew Goldwater activists to involvement in politics. Goldwater himself was only starting to tackle such concerns, which he previously viewed as outside government's proper interests.[50] But Goldwater's wider agenda of strong antistatism and a nationalist critique of Cold War policy won him support, too. To critics, this agenda was a backward-looking embrace of the conservatism that consigned the party to minority status. In Jacob Javits's view, Goldwater "kind of satisfies a hankering for the 5-cent

---

[44] Peter O'Donnell, Jr., "Progress Report #4," n.d., box 155, Rusher Papers.
[45] F. Clifton White with Jerome Tuccille, *Politics as a Noble Calling: The Memoirs of F. Clifton White* (Ottawa, Ill.: Jameson, 1994).
[46] F. Clifton White to "our original group," Dec. 4, 1963, box 155, Rusher Papers.
[47] F. Clifton White with William J. Gill, *Suite 3505: The Story of the Draft Goldwater Movement* (1967; Ashland, Ohio: Ashbrook Press, 1992), 28.
[48] National Draft Goldwater Committee, "Key to Republican Victories in 1964," n.d., box 214, series I, C. P. Taft Papers.
[49] White with Gill, *Suite 3505*, 54.
[50] Goldberg, *Goldwater*, 155.

beer and the 5-cent cigar"; his brand of conservatism was "nice and comfortable and convenient" but outdated.[51] Goldwater, by contrast, insisted that, instead, New Deal liberalism was outdated, referring to its exponents as "men who live in the political past – who would apply the out-moded and discredited programs of the 1930's to the problems of the 1960's."[52]

Weak intraparty opposition was also important in explaining Goldwater's success. Belief in Kennedy's political strength – as opposed to the conservative conviction in his vulnerability – first discouraged the development of an active field of contenders.[53] But those ranks were in any case thin. Among the advocates of urban-oriented modernity, only Rockefeller was ready to embark on a serious fight for the candidacy. Chance played its part, too. During the nomination season, Rockefeller and Goldwater, articulating very different visions for the party's future, remained so evenly matched that the many convention delegates from California, a state holding an early June primary, were crucial to the overall outcome. Rockefeller and Goldwater were evenly matched in California, too. What helped to account for Goldwater's victory there, narrowly achieved, was news of a baby for Rockefeller and his second wife three days before election day, reminding voters of his divorce. The effectiveness of the Goldwater campaign at the grass roots was also significant.[54]

As the convention approached, a stop-Goldwater movement coalesced in support of Governor William W. Scranton of Pennsylvania. It was too late to stop Goldwater, but time enough to stir up further party conflict. Electoral arguments were an important element of the pro-Scranton ammunition. Reminding fellow Republicans of the 1960 big-city problem, his supporters insisted that Goldwater was sure to lose but that Scranton was capable of adding needed Democratic and independent voters, especially in urban and suburban areas, to the party's minority base.[55] The argument had force. Polls suggested that a minority of Republican identifiers among voters – who in any case amounted to a minority of the national electorate – preferred Goldwater. But among the constituency that counted – delegates at the national convention – the argument carried much less force. The idea of a hidden, nonmobilized pro-Republican vote influenced their thinking. So did an interpretation of Republican history, as promoted by Schlafly, viewing the Scranton candidacy as yet another eastern-establishment effort to divert the party not only from its true beliefs but also from a better chance of electoral success.

Many delegates also displayed a preference for principle to victory. "I would rather be one against 20,000 and believe I was right," said one. "That's what

---

[51] *Albany Times Union* clipping, Sept. 30, 1963, box 9, subseries 2, series 5, Javits Papers.

[52] Barry Goldwater, speech, March 3, 1961, box 38, subseries 2, series 5, Javits Papers.

[53] *New Republic*, June 13, 1964, 10–11.

[54] Harold Faber, ed., *The Road to the White House: The Story of the 1964 Election by the Staff of The New York Times* (New York: McGraw-Hill, 1965), 41–43; Rick Perlstein, *Before the Storm: Barry Goldwater and the Unmaking of the American Consensus* (New York: Hill and Wang, 2001), 333–353.

[55] Clifford P. Case et al., news release, July 5, 1964, box 26, Scott Papers.

I admire about Goldwater. He's like that."[56] Karl Hess, a Goldwater speech-writer, later observed that any electorally informed centrism was not only a strategic miscalculation because, "just as importantly for anyone who feels that politics *is* more important than mere job-holding, it isn't right."[57] This zest for conservatism, reinforced by a dislike for compromise that sullied the pursuit of principle, distinguished the Goldwater phenomenon. It exposed the folly of the Citizens belief that an influx of Republican "amateurs" was sure to moderate the party's appeal. The influx instead pushed the party toward no-compromise conservatism.

Although there were many differences between Goldwater supporters and opponents, race and concern about "extremism," often relating to foreign policy, were especially important to the case against Goldwater. In a publicly released letter to Goldwater, Scranton told him he had "too often casually prescribed nuclear war as a solution to a troubled war," "too often allowed the radical extremists to use you," and "too often stood for irresponsibility in the serious question of racial holocaust."[58] Like other moderate Republicans, Scranton thus associated Goldwater with right-wing extremism, a phenomenon attracting widespread concern during the early 1960s. The John Birch Society particularly kindled this concern, and many society members became conservative activists. Its founder, Robert Welch, peddled conspiracy-influenced ideas about liberalism's success, which members did not necessarily share, but which heightened the antiextremist anxiety.[59]

The idea of a silent or hidden vote in favor of conservatism was a myth. Voting studies still suggested instead that Republican supporters were more likely to go to the polls than their Democratic counterparts and that any increase in turnout tended to benefit Democratic candidates.[60] It was, however, a potent myth, one that helped conservatives to explain the long-term decline in Republican support during the 1940s and 1950s, which coincided with a decline in voter turnout. The myth informed the conservative view that any pursuit of a modern Republicanism, as promoted by the Eisenhower administration, was electoral folly as well as the abandonment of principle, and it reflected a conservative observation that America was not the politically liberal nation that Democratic majorities intimated. A study of public opinion conducted during 1964 provided a persuasive explanation for the illusion. Its authors, Lloyd A. Free and Hadley Cantril, argued that Americans were "ideological conservatives" but "operational liberals" – that they often favored conservative ideals

[56] Aaron Wildavsky, "The Goldwater Phenomenon: Purists, Politicians, and the Two-Party System," *Review of Politics* 27 (1965), 394.

[57] Karl Hess, *In a Cause That Will Triumph: The Goldwater Campaign and the Future of Conservatism* (Garden City, N.Y.: Doubleday, 1967), 39–41 (quotation, 40).

[58] William W. Scranton to Barry Goldwater (released), July 12, 1964, box 26, Scott Papers.

[59] Critchlow, *Conservative Ascendancy*, 56–72.

[60] Philip E. Converse, Aage R. Clausen, and Warren E. Miller, "Myth and Reality: The 1964 Election," *APSR* 59 (1965), 321–336.

of individualistic self-reliance but just as often supported specific examples of government activism at odds with the conservative agenda.[61]

Even those who believed in the hidden vote suspected that 1964 was not a good time to mobilize a conservative majority, however. Goldwater was sure that Americans did not want to have three presidents in little more than a year. Throughout 1964, Johnson's popularity was evident. The unpromising prospects for a conservative majority in the short term encouraged its proponents to look forward to its longer-term mobilization, to establish their strength within the party. "The American voter has been subjected to 30 years of unremitting Liberal propaganda, most of it from the heights of power," wrote William Rusher in July, "and it is asking too much to expect that this will wash off in a single scrubbing."[62]

The myth was nevertheless compelling enough to retain some believers, especially because of the unknown strength of the "backlash" – hostility to racial progress that caused Democratic supporters to turn away from their liberal convictions. Some Democrats, fearful of electoral trends, joined conservatives in the belief.[63] Within traditionally Democratic communities, support for Goldwater was a guilty secret that people were reluctant to voice, some thought. "[O]ur guys are so indoctrinated they'll never admit they're going to vote for Goldwater, but they'll just go in there and vote for him anyway," said one union leader. "The silent vote is what scares me."[64] In analyzing the phenomenon of the silent vote, journalist Robert Spivack found race important. But he argued that other factors also encouraged such support, including Goldwater's "common touch" and what critics labeled his simplistic answers to the Cold War's complexities. Goldwater offered "freedom from frustration," Spivack concluded.[65]

The idea of the hidden vote gained popular currency in 1964. In a poll conducted for the Goldwater campaign in early October, one that revealed that its candidate's prospects were bleak, nearly four in ten respondents said that the idea of a hidden vote was probably true – almost as many as those who did not.[66] Among Goldwater supporters, one-half thought there were many people who would vote for their candidate but were not prepared to admit it.[67] There were efforts to boost the belief; in mid-October Dean Burch, the national chair, claimed that a private poll suggested that the election was too close to call.[68] Members of the Ripon Society, a group of moderate and

[61] Lloyd A. Free and Hadley Cantril, *The Political Beliefs of Americans: A Study of Public Opinion* (New Brunswick, N.J.: Rutgers University Press, 1967).

[62] *National Review*, July 28, 1964, 641.

[63] *WP*, Aug. 30, 1964, E1, E3.

[64] *WSJ*, Aug. 26, 1964, 1, 18.

[65] Press summary, June 27–29, 1964, box 25, Scott Papers.

[66] "October 5 campaign survey," unsigned, box 8, Goldwater Papers.

[67] Thomas W. Benham, "Polling for a Presidential Candidate: Some Observations on the 1964 Campaign," *POQ* 29 (1965), 196.

[68] *NYT*, Oct. 10, 1964, E1.

liberal Republicans, later asserted that "the private and unreal vision of the Goldwater leaders," involving belief in the hidden vote, encouraged "foolish statements and foolish decisions" that led to defeat.[69]

Confusion between "operational liberalism" and "ideological conservatism" does not alone explain the myth of the hidden vote. The grassroots mobilization of conservatives demonstrated that conservatism had energy and vitality of a kind that others simply failed to recognize. Goldwater campaign contributors were a broader-based group than the party normally depended on, and the campaign boasted of their socioeconomic diversity. An appeal for more funds as election day approached, for example, brought a flood of small contributions, usually no more than a few dollars – from ordinary Americans "who truly make up grassroots America," said Republican National Finance Committee treasurer J. William Middendorf. A Pittsburgh steelworker endorsed his weekly paycheck of $96 to the Republican Party, explaining that he was "sick and tired of being pushed around by union bosses."[70] The volume of small contributions helped the party to finish the campaign with a surplus, by sharp contrast with the deficits that generally plagued political candidacies, especially losing ones.[71]

The potential of backlash at the polls intrigued and horrified Republicans. When Goldwater considered his vote on the civil rights bill, his view of its constitutionality and his dislike for the expansion of federal power were decisive factors. But the electoral implications of his decision were clear. A negative vote increased the likelihood that backlash would benefit his candidacy, and some believed that this offered his only chance of victory against Johnson.[72] The foray into Democratic presidential primaries of segregationist George C. Wallace, Alabama's governor, demonstrated the potential electoral power of backlash in Indiana, Wisconsin, and Maryland.[73] After a summer visit to Polish neighborhoods in Buffalo, Cleveland, and Pittsburgh, Goldwater campaign aide Theodore L. Humes reported that "substantial blocs of these normally Democratic voters are very likely to break for Goldwater on this issue."[74]

Labor leaders took steps to discourage backlash within their ranks, both initiating an education program about civil rights and reminding union members of the reasons for their Democratic loyalties.[75] In a ten-minute film created by the steelworkers union, president David McDonald told his members, "If you want to destroy your union, all you need to do is support Goldwater

---

[69] Thomas P. Petri, ed., *Election '64: A Ripon Society Report* (Cambridge, Mass.: Ripon Society, 1965), 7.

[70] RNC press release, Oct. 26, 1964, box W5, Goldwater Papers.

[71] Herbert E. Alexander, "Money and Votes: Party Finance, 1964," in Bernard Cosman and Robert J. Huckshorn, eds., *Republican Politics: The 1964 Campaign and Its Aftermath for the Party* (New York: Praeger, 1968), 113–151.

[72] *WP*, June 8, 1964, A19.

[73] *WP*, June 9, 1964, A2.

[74] Theodore L. Humes, memo, Aug. 8, 1964, box 1, Humes Papers.

[75] *WSJ*, Sept. 3, 1964, 4.

for President; and if you want to be unemployed and live in filth and degrada-
tion, go out and support Goldwater."[76]

An August Harris poll suggested that the summer's race-related unrest
was indeed fostering backlash; in a series of disturbances in cities outside the
South, nine were killed and nearly six hundred were wounded. According to
its analysis, about a third of Americans were concerned about race in ways
that made them susceptible to a backlash appeal. Most were already Goldwater
supporters, but Louis Harris argued that one in five Johnson supporters fitted
this category, numerous enough to decide the election.[77] White House aides
were more sanguine about the threat. Although their polls projected losses
due to backlash, they also projected much heavier Republican losses due to
"frontlash" – involving anxieties about Goldwater's candidacy – and designed
a campaign to maximize these anxieties.[78] Less sanguine were moderate
Republicans. At a mid-August meeting in Hershey, Pennsylvania, designed to
promote party unity, George Romney and Charles Percy raised their concerns
about backlash with Goldwater. Goldwater told leading Republicans there of
his fear of civil rights as a political issue, vowing that he would not talk about
race during the campaign. He afterwards released a statement emphasizing
that as president he would fully implement the Civil Rights Act.[79] Following
race-connected unrest in Harlem, he met with Johnson to suggest that the two
candidates avoid discussion that might add to tensions.[80]

Goldwater's assurances were well intended but unrealistic. The news of a
single day, September 8, revealed the implausibility of a campaign without
race in 1964. In New York City, a boycott of city schools took place in protest of an affirmative program to achieve their integration through methods
including busing. In California, Episcopal bishops spoke out against a proposition designed to overturn the state's 1963 Rumford Act, which banned housing discrimination. In Prince Edward County, Virginia, the public schools
reopened after a five-year closure designed to avoid implementation of the
Brown desegregation order, but most white children were expected to remain
in private, segregated institutions. In the African American section of Summit,
Mississippi, there were bomb explosions, though without injuries. Finally, an
AFL–CIO spokesperson announced that in the absence of backlash organized
labor hoped to secure a large enough increase of congressional support to
permit the overturn of the Taft-Hartley Act.[81] Against this backdrop, it was
impossible to avoid the subject of race.

The Republican campaign was not one that eschewed anxieties about race
as an electoral advantage. William E. Miller, the vice-presidential candidate,
spoke extensively about concerns usually interpreted as a way to foment

[76] *WSJ*, Aug. 26, 1964, 1, 18.
[77] *WP*, Aug. 17, 1964, A1; Goldberg, *Goldwater*, 213.
[78] Joseph W. Alsop, release, Aug. 14, 1964, box 83, series II, Alsop and Alsop Papers.
[79] *WP*, Dec. 3, 1966, A1, A6.
[80] Goldberg, *Goldwater*, 215–216.
[81] "Civil Rights," n.d., box W3, Goldwater Papers.

backlash without explicit racism – promising to make "our Nation's streets and parks safe, once again for your wife and mine to use without fear," and implying that the Johnson administration softly treated civil rights demonstrators who committed illegal acts, for example.[82] Goldwater himself discussed his conservative view of racial progress, implicitly referring to the civil rights movement as "the mobs in the streets," who were postponing a return to violence until after the elections. Toward the campaign's end he criticized busing as a method to seek racial balance in schools as "morally wrong" because "forced integration is just as wrong as forced segregation."[83] He spoke against "quotas" in Chicago and for "freedom of association" in South Carolina.[84]

The clarity of the difference between the parties on civil rights had stark consequences for the level of Republican support among African Americans. Already low, it dwindled to almost-complete insignificance. Four years earlier, Nixon's most prominent African American supporter in his campaign against Kennedy was former baseball player Jackie Robinson, who had urged the candidate to take action as African Americans turned away from the party.[85] In Goldwater's case, Robinson did not make similar efforts, believing him to be hopelessly tied to an anti–civil rights and pro–states' rights position, and he would not support him.[86] Robinson's opposition symbolized the party's problem of disappearing African American support.

Goldwater attributed Democratic success among African Americans to economic benefits rather than egalitarian protections. He later insisted that no Republican nominee would have won significantly more African American support than he did "because the professional Negro organizations like the NAACP, etc., are dead set politically against the election of a Republican to the office of President and this can be traced with any degree of study to the fact that the Democratic Party, the AFL–CIO, the UAW (United Auto Workers), the ADA (Americans for Democratic Action), and other left-wing extremist groups have been practically the sole source of financial support for the activities of this group." He believed "that the average Republican has a much kindlier, more natural, more brotherly feeling toward the members of the minority groups in this country than has his Democratic counterpart who looks upon him only as a ballot box and not with the warm eye of friendship and sincere effort to do something for them." Better communication of this concern might boost Republican support among African Americans, Goldwater thought. Moreover, he identified Latino Americans, numbering

[82] *WP*, Sept. 9, 1964, A22.

[83] Timothy N. Thurber, *The Politics of Equality: Hubert H. Humphrey and the African American Freedom Struggle* (New York: Columbia University Press, 1999), 164, 166.

[84] Timothy N. Thurber, "Goldwaterism Triumphant? Race and the Republican Party, 1965–1968," *Journal of the Historical Society* 7 (2007), 351.

[85] Jackie Robinson to Richard Nixon, May 25, 1961, box 649, series 320, Nixon Pre-Presidential Papers.

[86] Jackie Robinson to Barry Goldwater, July 25, 1964, box 5, Robinson Papers.

more than six million, as an unexplored source of potential support, possibly significant in California, New Mexico, Texas, and New York City, as well as his home state of Arizona.[87]

Goldwater used the campaign to promote his conservatism. He questioned the effectiveness of defense policy and he attacked big government.[88] As election day neared, Miller tried to assert confidence about conservatism's appeal in remarks that nevertheless seemed to sound a note of defeatist disbelief in the hidden-majority thesis: "[W]e know that if 51 per cent of the American people wanted to be Federally born and Federally housed and Federally educated and Federally subsidized in business and on the farm and finally buried in a Federal box, Barry and I will lose."[89] Hubert Humphrey, Miller's rival for the vice presidency, branded the Republican ticket as radical – consolidating the intraparty attacks of nomination season. This was a charge that Lyndon Johnson echoed, while often downplaying partisanship in search of defecting Republican supporters, even in one speech praising Herbert Hoover's "humane leadership."[90]

The Goldwater campaign introduced a new set of concerns into presidential politics, involving public morality. The agenda began with the resuscitation of anticorruption themes that Republicans had used against the Truman administration. It raised ethics questions about presidential aides and – because of the family fortune amassed at an Austin, Texas, broadcasting company apparently shielded from local competition – about Johnson himself. More broadly, Johnson was branded a politician without principle, in Miller's words "a man who has no set of convictions except a dedication to his own political victory."[91] Concerns about morality extended to rising crime rates, though the perception of a law-and-order crisis outstripped the reality of little change in the incidence of crime.[92] The agenda also involved a vaguer sense of unease about the nation's direction. "[Goldwater] talks about the unrest and uncertainty that is beginning to plague all Americans, even though their standard of living continues to rise and their material needs and wants are pretty much attainable by most of our citizens," national chair Dean Burch said in September.[93]

[87] Barry Goldwater, "Minority Groups," n.d. [1966?], box 5, Personal and Political series II, Goldwater Papers.
[88] Theodore H. White, *The Making of the President 1964* (New York: Atheneum, 1965), 311–319; Brennan, *Turning Right in the Sixties*, 82–103.
[89] Faber, *Road to the White House*, 189–190.
[90] Faber, *Road to the White House*, 193, 252, 257; Robert David Johnson, *All the Way with LBJ: The 1964 Presidential Election* (New York: Cambridge University Press, 2009), 190–193, 204–214.
[91] RNC news release, Sept. 22, 1964, box W5, Goldwater Papers.
[92] Fred P. Graham, "A Contemporary History of American Crime," in Hugh Davis Graham and Ted Robert Gurr, eds., *Violence in America: Historical and Comparative Perspectives – A Report Submitted to the National Commission on the Causes and Prevention of Violence* (New York: Bantam, 1969), 487–502.
[93] RNC news release, Sept. 26, 1964, box W6, Goldwater Papers.

As an ideology, conservatism faced a dilemma in raising the morality agenda when it moved beyond accepted government functions to combat crime and corruption (though the former was for the most part a matter for the states and localities, not the federal level). The traditionalist desire to promote morality was at odds with the libertarian desire to roll back government. Goldwater tackled the dilemma by asserting that the moral crisis he identified was a facet of liberalism's reliance on government rather than the individual. Calling for a return to "the traditional virtues of honesty, courage, self-control, truth, and justice," he linked the problem with a disregard for individualism and the family. "Government seeks to be parent, teacher, leader, doctor, and even minister," he said in March. "And its failures are strewn about us in the rubble of rising crime rates, juvenile delinquency, scandal, self-seeking and greedy grabs for power, even in evasion and distortion of issues in order to create false public relations images."[94]

The electoral benefits of the new agenda seemed obvious. In analyzing campaign coverage, Goldwater aides discovered that, among the barrage of negative observations about their candidate's irresponsibility and radicalism, concerns about Johnson's qualities as a leader were a rare positive in their favor.[95] As polls that fall made clear the scale of Goldwater's failure against Johnson, one aide concluded that "a *theme of moral crisis*" was "the one direction which may be able to rescue the campaign by providing us with a common denominator whose theme will appeal to all major groups whose vote we must obtain – AND, at the same time, will strike at Johnson's only point of real vulnerability." The conclusion was a desperate one. An emphasis on "moral crisis" was attractive because the popularity of the administration's record and anxieties about Goldwater left few options. In fact, Johnson's personal vulnerability was not great. According to a campaign poll, only about one in five respondents agreed that Johnson was "too much of a politician"; despite his reputation for frank straight-talk, the figure for Goldwater was closer to one in four.[96]

Another benefit of the morality agenda was the opportunity it provided to talk about race without mentioning race, as Miller's remarks about crime indicated. This was rhetoric that Goldwater echoed, speaking of the "growing menace to personal safety ... in homes, churches, playgrounds and places of business" when discussing civil rights activism.[97] In the South, by contrast, Goldwater emphasized the revitalization of states' rights and the shortcomings of the Supreme Court, rather than the problem of crime.[98]

[94] Goldwater for President Committee, news release, March 19, 1964, box W3, Goldwater Papers.

[95] Pam Rymer to Denison Kitchel, Dean Burch, John Grenier, and Wayne Hood, Sept. 22, 1964, box 8, Goldwater Papers.

[96] "Strategy analysis of campaign survey," unsigned, n.d., box 4, Goldwater Papers.

[97] Goldberg, *Goldwater*, 218.

[98] Gene Shalit and Lawrence K. Grossman, eds., *Somehow It Works: A Candid Portrait of the 1964 Presidential Election by NBC News* (Garden City, N.Y.: Doubleday, 1965), 170.

The development of a morality-based appeal reflected the existence of such concerns among the grassroots conservatives who were the activist base of the Goldwater movement. For Americans at large, the imminence of a moral crisis did not necessarily make sense in 1964, but many right-wing activists were involved in community-based struggles that informed the development of such themes. Although anticommunism had until the early 1960s often provided the glue that bound together grassroots conservatism, morality was now sometimes taking its place.[99] The theme of a moral crusade had frequently informed Republican women's involvement in politics for much longer, and women played an important role in the grassroots pro-Goldwater mobilization.[100] But Goldwater and his aides saw the issue as powerful beyond the activist base. As election day approached, Goldwater placed increasing stress on "moral rot."[101] David Brinkley of NBC News noted, "Morality, or immorality, now has become the dominant and most discussed issue in the Republican campaign."[102] Among the campaign's initiatives to make the emphasis was the recruitment of five hundred clerics as signatories to a statement "that immorality without corrective influence from the White House is permeating our country, resulting in crime, pornography, rioting and degeneracy."[103]

Many in the party were uncomfortable with Goldwater's innovative approach to the pursuit of a majority. His candidacy sparked Republican defections among the party's leading figures as well as among voters. The *New York Herald Tribune*, the voice of eastern Republican moderation, refused to endorse Goldwater – regarding him as unfit for the presidency and dangerous to the party. Critical of "his simplistic views on world affairs," the newspaper reserved special disapproval for "his appeal – whether calculated or not – to ugly racial passions in this climactic year of the struggle for equal rights." Goldwater threatened to "reduce a great political organization to a permanent, ineffectual opposition," it warned.[104] The choices made by leading Republicans in responding to Goldwater, choices that activists remembered, would have important consequences for their subsequent careers. Rockefeller pledged support but failed to campaign actively for Goldwater – an absence that helped to consolidate him further as the conservatives' *bête noire*. By contrast, Nixon's speeches in support of the ticket would smooth his return to party prominence.[105]

Rockefeller's response was by no means unusual. The Goldwater campaign discovered that outside the South, where association with Goldwater

[99] McGirr, *Suburban Warriors*; Jeff Roche, "Cowboy Conservatism," in David Farber and Roche, eds., *The Conservative Sixties* (New York: Peter Lang, 2003), 79.

[100] Rymph, *Republican Women*, 160–172.

[101] *NYT*, Oct. 25, 1964, E1.

[102] Shalit and Grossman, *Somehow It Works*, 195.

[103] RNC release, Nov. 2, 1964, box W5, Goldwater Papers.

[104] *New York Sunday Herald Tribune* clipping, Oct. 4, 1964, box 1, Political File, Thayer Papers.

[105] Faber, *Road to the White House*, 142–143.

offered a Republican the best chance of success, many candidates were to various degrees seeking to avoid linkage with the national ticket. A pocket of notable loyalty was the rural Midwest, but in eastern states such as Massachusetts and New York, wrote an aide in September, there was "panic" among local Republican leaders who believed that Goldwater had no electoral interest in their region.[106] Democratic opponents made the most of the Goldwater connection. Supporting Robert F. Kennedy's Senate campaign in New York, New York City Mayor Robert F. Wagner associated moderate Republican incumbent Kenneth Keating with Goldwater, "the erratic, irrational, self-contradictory candidate who, like a Western bandit, kidnapped the Republican nomination" and whose election "would be a catastrophe: a nightmare come true" – even though Keating refused to endorse Goldwater.[107] In Pennsylvania, Senator Hugh Scott, another moderate, found his reelection effort "tough": "Our opponent has no issues except Goldwater and is using that issue all over the State," he wrote.[108] Unease about Goldwater permeated the party's base as well as his factional opponents. A journalist's informal soundings in September among Republican-supporting easterners vacationing in Catskill and Adirondack resorts found a large majority uncomfortable with Goldwater as radical, erratic, and "trigger happy." Only 37 out of 212 were avowed Goldwater supporters. One complained that his area's activists were "about as conservative as Adolf Hitler."[109] By contrast, his national party's support for civil rights led Senator Strom Thurmond of South Carolina, the 1948 Dixiecrat candidate for the presidency, to join the Republicans in September, condemning the Democrats as radical.[110] On joining the party, he spoke of his desire to see a realignment making it "the true, great conservative party," mentioning his hope that other conservative Democrats would follow him and saying that liberal Republicans "might move over."[111]

The 1964 elections were a disaster for Goldwater and the Republican Party. Their most notable feature involved the impact of civil rights. Thanks to the clarity that existed between Goldwater and Johnson on race, five states of the Deep South – Mississippi, Alabama, South Carolina, Louisiana, and Georgia – supported a Republican presidential candidate for the first time since Reconstruction, decisively or even overwhelmingly. They were Goldwater's only states beyond Arizona.[112] Goldwater did not replicate Eisenhower's and Nixon's success in other southern and border states. Fewer than one in ten

---

[106] Pam Rymer to Denison Kitchel et al., Sept. 22, 1964, box 8, Goldwater Papers.
[107] Robert F. Wagner, transcript, Oct. 9, 1964, box 13, subseries 2, series 5, Javits Papers; Faber, *Road to the White House*, 143.
[108] Hugh Scott to Albert Leman, Oct. 14, 1964, box 27, Scott Papers.
[109] Binghamton, N.Y., *Press* clipping, Sept. 15, 1964, box 8, Goldwater Papers.
[110] Nadine Cohodas, *Strom Thurmond and the Politics of Southern Change* (New York: Simon & Schuster, 1993), 355–362.
[111] *NYT*, Sept. 23, 1964, 24.
[112] Carmines and Stimson, *Issue Evolution*, 45.

African Americans voted for him, compared with about one in three for Nixon in 1960.[113] Voters in 1960 perceived relatively little difference between Kennedy and Nixon on civil rights and less still between the parties; in 1964, however, many perceived a clear-cut distinction between Goldwater as hostile to civil rights and Johnson as friendly, a distinction that influenced evaluations of the parties as well as the candidates.[114] In some northern cities, the backlash seemed to find some new Republican support in eastern European, Catholic communities of strong Democratic traditions, if not nearly enough to take the edge off the Goldwater defeat.[115] The House losses associated with the Johnson landslide were concentrated among northern moderates, with the effect that congressional sentiment on race among Republicans moved in a conservative direction, compounding the effect of the 1958 midterms, which involved the loss of Senate moderates.[116] Although Goldwater's opposition to federal action to achieve progress in civil rights did not characterize the outlook of most party officeholders, his candidacy helped to define the party in these terms.

Predictions of the Republican Party's demise – or, at least, its decisively long-term relegation to minority status – were not uncommon. Political scientist Walter Dean Burnham observed that "the GOP is becoming less and less relevant to the central issues and concerns of American politics in the last half of the century."[117] One especially gloomy interpretation of the Goldwater candidacy involved the logic of a minority party. Work by another scholar of politics, V. O. Key, Jr., on state parties suggested that over time the minority's diminished chances of victory encouraged moderates to join the majority party, thus further reducing its prospects and concentrating power in the hands of more extreme activists, who were unlikely to make their party more attractive to more voters. Application of this theory to the Republican Party in 1964 helped to explain its declining levels of party identification among the electorate and the rise to prominence of conservatism.[118]

Many party conservatives did not view the resounding extent of Goldwater's defeat as indicating the bankruptcy of their strategic argument, however. They believed instead that the 1964 campaign offered an inadequate test of conservatism's electoral strength. Goldwater received a share of the blame. Willis Johnson, for example, who helped to run the campaign in the South, concluded "that Goldwater in his heart did not want the nomination and thus passively allowed his own defeat," failing to make a real and active issue of conservatism against liberalism.[119] Another campaign aide, Theodore Humes, similarly regretted "Barry's desultory approach to campaigning," which squandered

[113] Carmines and Stimson, *Issue Evolution*, 46.
[114] Converse et al., "Myth and Reality," 329.
[115] Faber, *Road to the White House*, 274–275.
[116] Carmines and Stimson, *Issue Evolution*, 65–77.
[117] *Commonweal*, March 19, 1965, 781.
[118] Wildavsky, "The Goldwater Phenomenon," 412.
[119] Willis Johnson, report, Nov. 9, 1964, box W8, Goldwater Papers.

conservatives' investment of energy and money in his cause; Goldwater was, he thought, "charismatic but not anywhere near profound enough to carry a campaign."[120] Poll data provided some evidence in support of such criticisms. Across a range of issues involving government activism, a substantial majority of Americans with liberal beliefs voted for Johnson, but Goldwater failed to maximize his potential share of the conservatives. Almost four in five Americans in favor of Medicare were Johnson supporters, for example, whereas Goldwater's share of those against Medicare was three in five. Unlike the issues involving federal activism, there was no correlation between opinion on school prayer and voting choice – despite the Goldwater campaign's morality agenda.[121] The same data, however, revealed New Deal liberalism's strength. Even the full mobilization of antigovernment sentiment could not have saved the Goldwater cause; polling found this sentiment among only a minority of Americans.

Willis Johnson and Theodore Humes sounded a theme common among conservative critics of the campaign when they attacked the chaotic nature of its organization. Goldwater fulfilled a promise to place the national committee again at the center of the presidential campaign's management but brought neither unity nor order to the process by doing so. The arrival of Goldwater loyalists at the RNC created conflict and encouraged the departure of some long-standing staffers.[122] Goldwater himself acknowledged organizational problems that suggested a need for the RNC to adopt a permanent operation of campaign planning. His other explanations for the campaign's problems included press misrepresentations, party disunity, and the bitterness of the presidential primaries that encouraged the view that Goldwater was a radical. He estimated that the primary campaigns cost him between six million and eight million votes in the general election.[123] An exaggeration, the argument nevertheless possessed some merit in observing the dangers of division to a party's fortunes. After 1964 many in the party developed a new appetite for unity, but many also remained eager to promote their own approach to Republican politics as the focus for this unity.

Among the Republicans alarmed about Goldwater was Charles P. Taft, an early advocate of a me-too strategy in his 1936 book, *You and I – and Roosevelt*. After his work for the Landon campaign, Taft, unlike his brother, did little at the national level, instead concentrating his efforts in Cincinnati. Then, expanding previous fundraising efforts on behalf of party moderates, during the 1964 campaign he launched the Committee to Support Moderate

[120] Theodore L. Humes to William J. Gill, Aug. 1, 1965, box 1, Humes Papers.
[121] C. Anthony Broh, *Toward a Theory of Issue Voting* (Beverly Hills, Calif.: Sage, 1973), 13–32.
[122] Karl A. Lamb, "Under One Roof: Barry Goldwater's Campaign Staff," in Bernard Cosman and Robert J. Huckshorn, eds., *Republican Politics: The 1964 Campaign and Its Aftermath for the Party* (New York: Praeger, 1968), 20–45.
[123] Barry Goldwater, "Suggestions to the National Committee relative to a Presidential Campaign," n.d. [1966?], box 5, Personal and Political series II, Goldwater Papers.

Republicans, intended to provide assistance to Republican candidates who did not share Goldwater's views but whose prospects for reelection faced danger in the anti-Goldwater tide.[124] The committee raised $55,000 and endorsed seventy-one candidates, mostly for Congress.[125]

After the elections, Taft relaunched the committee as Republicans for Progress, which sought "to assist creative and constructive Republicans strengthen not just the Party's 'image' with the American people, but its record of achievement." In addition to campaign assistance, Republicans for Progress aimed to offer research support to members of Congress who were "interested in making the Republican Party a more effective instrument for progress."[126] The weakness of the congressional minority's staff was a continuing concern for Taft and other Republicans, who believed that a lack of capacity in legislative research helped to account for the party's reputation for negativity in response to Democratic initiatives. In association with Yale University–based Republican Advance, it issued a report arguing that the party's development in the South depended not on segregationists or conservatives but on moderate whites and African Americans, many of whom the 1965 Voting Rights Act newly enfranchised.[127] Most ambitiously, A. E. Abrahams, its executive director, sought to create an operation to foster activity among rank-and-file moderates designed to influence the selection of delegates to the 1968 convention – a recognition of the importance of grassroots activism to Goldwater's control of the 1964 convention. Abrahams launched a pilot project in a handful of cities, including St. Louis, Missouri, where he estimated that the recruitment of three hundred activists would form the foundation of a successful organization for the selection of moderate delegates. The budget Abrahams projected was modest (though not much more modest than the early costs of the draft-Goldwater activities), but still beyond the organization's means.[128] By 1967, when Abrahams was working on the delegate project, Republicans for Progress depended heavily on Taft himself for its financial survival, and Taft concluded that a political organization of this kind did not deserve survival.[129] A scaled-back organization made some disappointing efforts in that year to raise funds once more for moderate candidates, and in 1968 it issued endorsements to favored candidates.[130] But Republicans for Progress was by then little more than a letterhead for Taft's hopes for the party.

[124] Charles P. Taft to Robert W. Johnson, Sept. 2, 1959, box 199, series I, C. P. Taft Papers; Taft, form letter, Oct. 14, 1960, box 200, series I, C. P. Taft Papers; Taft to Joe M. Baker, Jr., Jan. 11, 1965, box 199, series I, C. P. Taft Papers.

[125] Charles P. Taft to Elmer F. Bennett, Jan. 22, 1965, box 215, series I, C. P. Taft Papers.

[126] Republicans for Progress, news release, Feb. 3, 1965, box 219, series I, C. P. Taft Papers.

[127] Republicans for Progress and Republican Advance, "Southern Project Report," released on April 13, 1966, box 2, Political File, Thayer Papers.

[128] A. E. Abrahams to Charles P. Taft, May 11, 1967, box 218, series I, C. P. Taft Papers; F. Clifton White to Roger Milliken, Jan. 9, 1963, box 155, Rusher Papers.

[129] Charles P. Taft to A. E. Abrahams, July 1, 1967, box 218, series I, C. P. Taft Papers.

[130] Charles P. Taft to Margot Lindsay, Nov. 7, 1966, box 218, series I, C. P. Taft Papers; Republicans for Progress, news release, Oct. 31, 1968, box 219, series I, C. P. Taft Papers.

Republicans for Progress was one of a number of moderate groups that cooperated as the Congress of Republican Organizations.[131] The most influential among these groups was the Ripon Society. In late 1962 a small group of Cambridge, Massachusetts, students and professionals took inspiration from the U.K. Conservative Party's Bow Group in founding the organization as a forum for the development of Republican ideas among like-minded young people. At the start of 1964, the society issued "A Call to Excellence in Leadership," which argued that the Democratic coalition was in decay but that conservative Republicans' "platform of negativism" offered "rancor, violence, and extremism," presenting no hope of party growth or effective leadership for the nation. Instead, to win a majority for the Republican Party, it called for moderation that would appeal to the "new Americans" within the middle classes outside the South, young graduates and professionals, and the racial moderates of the "new South."[132] The policy proposals developed by Ripon members included a plan to share federal tax revenues with the states and localities, allowing those jurisdictions to make decisions about their use; a scheme to develop an all-volunteer military, thus ending the draft; an idea to help the poor through the introduction of a negative income tax; proposed protections for the rights of the mentally ill; and suggestions for the improvement of U.S.-Sino relations.[133] The society's imaginative, energetic endeavors earned it attention on a scale that far outmatched the small size of its membership. John M. Ashbrook, an Ohio congressperson active in conservative circles, grumbled that the attention was so extensive that media reports sometimes seemed to treat Ripon as the party's official mouthpiece.[134] Ashbrook was wrong to worry about Ripon and other liberal Republican organizations, however. In the longer term, the cultivation of an elite constituency was a strategy unlikely to overwhelm the conservatives' grassroots organization.[135]

Still, Ashbrook's irritation with media interest in Ripon reflected the shorter-term travails of the American Conservative Union (ACU), of which he was president. Conservative organizations enjoyed little more success than their moderate counterparts. Such activity by conservatives involved a recognition of their movement's institutional and intellectual immaturity and of the dominance of liberal ideas and organizations. "Where is our ADA on a national level?" Donald C. Bruce, the ACU's chair, asked. "Where is our COPE going into the precincts on an organized basis? Where is our coordinated support in the academic community? Where are our new programs and new ideas?"[136]

---

[131] Walter N. Thayer, memo, Jan. 28, 1965, box 2, Political File, Thayer Papers.
[132] Lee W. Huebner and Thomas E. Petri, eds., *The Ripon Papers 1963–1968* (Washington, D.C.: National Press, 1968), 3–9 (quotations, 5).
[133] Huebner and Petri, *Ripon Papers*, 225–230.
[134] John M. Ashbrook to ACU board of directors and advisory assembly, Sept. 22, 1966, box 132, Rusher Papers.
[135] Rae, *Decline and Fall of the Liberal Republicans*, 84–86.
[136] *D.C. Young Republican Rally*, June 1965, box 132, Rusher Papers.

The ACU aimed to meet this challenge, as did some other organizations. The Free Society Association (FSA) was a short-lived organization that sought to channel the political engagement of Goldwater supporters reluctant to join the party. In its absence, Denison Kitchel claimed, an eight- or nine-million-strong group "might just disappear," and the FSA aimed "to hold them away from a third party, to pull them toward the Republican party and to pull the Republican party toward the conservative viewpoint they share."[137] Even though the FSA did not last long, *National Review* and Young Americans for Freedom, an organization that William F. Buckley, Jr., helped to create in 1960, were extraparty institutions already building the infrastructure that Bruce identified as important.

A desire to heal divisions characterized party activities after the 1964 defeat.[138] Ray Bliss, who replaced Burch as national chair in early 1965, was especially responsible for this emphasis. Bliss pursued nonideological initiatives designed to improve the party's organization, as his unimplemented big-city report had earlier advised. He oversaw, for example, a series of workshops in 1966 on techniques of campaign management, and then disseminated a published collection of workshop presentations.[139] Although he was ready to offer support to the Citizens movement's final, abortive plans to look for new voters, he condemned "splinter groups," especially – though needlessly, as it turned out – concerned about the FSA's threat to the RNC's capacity to raise funds and its apparent focus on the presidential nomination rather than the larger party cause.[140] The RNC meeting that chose Bliss as Burch's replacement also created the Republican Coordinating Committee (RCC) as a broad-based forum for policy discussion.[141] Invited to join the committee, Alf Landon reminded Burch of the 1940 convention's neglect of the Frank report and his own conviction that congressional Republicans created party policy. "I do not believe the Republican party is going to furnish the leadership our country needs by new committees and new conventions," he warned.[142] Landon was right to downplay the RCC's creative potential. Nevertheless, it had a valuable role in pulling the party together and in cautiously but decisively moderating its position in the sensitive areas of civil rights, right-wing extremism, and U.S. military involvement in Vietnam.[143]

[137] *NYT* clipping, July 17, 1965, box 30, Scott Papers.
[138] Critchlow, *Conservative Ascendancy*, 78–81.
[139] "Campaign Management: Remarks of Some of America's Foremost Political Experts" (Washington, D.C.: RNC in association with RSCC and RCCC, 1966).
[140] Elmer L. Andersen to Walter N. Thayer, Feb. 16, 1965, box 5, Political File, Thayer Papers; *NYT*, July 1, 1965, 30.
[141] John F. Bibby and Robert J. Huckshorn. "Out-Party Strategy: Republican National Committee Rebuilding Politics, 1964–66," in Bernard Cosman and Robert J. Huckshorn, eds., *Republican Politics: The 1964 Campaign and Its Aftermath for the Party* (New York: Praeger, 1968), 218–223.
[142] Alf M. Landon to Dean Burch, Jan. 27, 1965, box A30, Ford Congressional Papers.
[143] Hess and Broder, *Republican Establishment*, 51–52.

A thirst for a new direction was evident on Capitol Hill. Senate Republican Policy Committee staffers produced a report, "Where the Votes Are," which provided the gloomy confirmation that only one in four Americans was a Republican. Not only did the report emphasize the need to cultivate independents and disaffected Democrats, but it also argued that the post–World War II baby-boom generation "offers Republicans their first opportunity in nearly forty years" to achieve majority status. According to the report, the concerns of these new voters, often located in the cities, involved the array of urban problems, including pollution, crime, race relations, housing, and education; Republican success in addressing these problems was likely to lead to success in picking up a group of metropolitan voters to offset labor members' electoral power. Such conclusions supported a desire to create constructive alternatives to Great Society programs.[144] House Republicans similarly emphasized the need for the party to develop a more constructive reputation in opposing the Democrats. Michigan's Gerald R. Ford represented a new congressional generation, barely less conservative than the old leadership against which Ford and others rebelled, but pragmatically engaged in a quest for constructiveness. The challenge began in early 1963 with Ford's successful opposition to Iowa's Charles Hoeven as House Republican Conference chair. "The goal was to become the majority party in the House," Donald Rumsfeld, one of Ford's chief supporters, who represented an Illinois district, later explained, "and the question was: Is it possible to use the Republican Conference in a more constructive way?" After the 1964 elections, Ford then defeated Charles Halleck to become minority leader, in this role not only leading attacks on the administration's shortcomings, but also attempting to offer imaginative alternatives to its policies.[145]

Impatience with the party's minority status led Ford to an iconoclastic rejection of the conservative coalition. He spoke of "my Southern strategy" – avoiding agreements with southern Democrats, but instead seeking to encourage them to join with the administration in favor of a unified Democratic position, against a coherently Republican position. Such partisanship accepted the likelihood of more legislative defeats for the Republican agenda but hoped to advance an association between these Democrats and liberalism, which would assist Republican efforts to take their seats.[146] Rhetoric outstripped reality; Great Society liberalism was reinforcing rather than undermining the conservative coalition. In 1967, a majority of southern Democrats and Republicans opposed a majority of northern Democrats in more than a third of House roll calls.[147] Although his efforts faced obstacles, Ford's rhetoric demonstrated

---

[144] Scott, *Come to the Party*, 232–234 (quotation, 233).

[145] James M. Cannon, *Time and Chance: Gerald Ford's Appointment with History* (1994; Ann Arbor: University of Michigan Press, 1998), 73–75, 81–96 (quotation, 73).

[146] *Albany* [Georgia] *Herald* clipping, May 17, 1967, box A70, Ford Congressional Papers.

[147] W. Wayne Shannon, "Revolt in Washington: The South in Congress," in William C. Havard, ed., *The Changing Politics of the South* (Baton Rouge: Louisiana State University Press, 1972), 647.

his desire not to rely on the politics of opposition in pursuit of a Republican agenda but to achieve a congressional majority.

Exemplifying the congressional quest for an alternative, Wisconsin's Melvin R. Laird, Ford's replacement as House Republican Conference chair, edited *Republican Papers*, a 1968 book of essays on policy issues by House colleagues and others. Laird stressed the enterprise's pragmatism in response to the perception that the Democrats' programmatic efforts from the New Deal to the Great Society had achieved disappointing results.[148] Among the proposals the book contained was Laird's own bill for revenue sharing, which intended to send federal money to the states and localities in order to address their needs in a more effective, decentralized manner.[149] Economist Milton Friedman advocated a negative income tax as a more efficient, less bureaucratic way to help the poor, a policy also designed to foster self-help and self-reliance by assisting the working poor.[150] In sum, the project represented the Republican desire to find more efficient solutions to society's problems in ways that challenged the federal government's growth. Opposition was not a fertile location to achieve their implementation, however. House Republicans in 1967 endeavored to amend legislation on elementary and secondary education to transfer responsibilities from the federal to state level, for example, but achieved just a limited increase in the states' decision-making role.[151]

The initial vitality and momentum of Johnson's Great Society agenda left moderates little space to craft a rationale for their Republicanism.[152] Still, Goldwater's failure merely boosted the belief that a racially progressive, urban-oriented approach was electorally essential as well as ideologically congenial.[153] The obstacle to its success was the party's conservatism, unlikely to accept a moderate Republican with any enthusiasm.[154] George Romney's interest in reaching a balance between antistatism and government activism led him later in the 1960s to emphasize the voluntary sector as the appropriate location for welfare innovations. He picked up the ideas of writer Richard C. Cornuelle, who argued that the independent sector's development answered the Republican problem.[155] "Though the average American opposes big government, he also believes that he has more and more problems which only the government wants to tackle," he wrote. "So he applauds the conservative

[148] Melvin R. Laird, ed., *Republican Papers* (Garden City, N.Y.: Anchor, 1968), ix–xiii.
[149] Melvin R. Laird, "The Case for Revenue Sharing," in Laird, ed., *Republican Papers* (Garden City, N.Y.: Anchor, 1968), 60–84.
[150] Milton Friedman, "The Case for the Negative Income Tax," in Melvin R. Laird, ed., *Republican Papers* (Garden City, N.Y.: Anchor, 1968), 202–220.
[151] Hess and Broder, *Republican Establishment*, 28.
[152] Walter De Vries to George Romney, Jan. 19, 1965, box 6, De Vries Papers.
[153] Walter De Vries and Joseph Bachelder, "Times, Issues, Strategy, & Organization," Sept. 8, 1966, box 6, De Vries Papers.
[154] Walter De Vries to George Romney, Nov. 24, 1965, box 6, De Vries Papers.
[155] T. George Harris, *Romney's Way: A Man and an Idea* (Englewood Cliffs, N.J.: Prentice-Hall, 1967), ix–xi.

rhetoric and supports the liberal program."[156] Engagement with city problems
thus unlocked a fertile strand of Republican thinking but failed to recast the
party within the model of urban-oriented modernity that its promoters sought.
In Romney's case, it was not only intraparty conservatism that frustrated moderation's pursuit; ill-judged remarks that military officials "brainwashed" him
on a visit to Vietnam supported the suspicion that Romney lacked the foreign
policy ability to be president, undermining his presidential opportunity.[157]

In 1961 a *New Republic* editorial suggested that the Republican Party was
likely to remain the nation's minority for the foreseeable future. "Short of
a national catastrophe, the GOP can only hope to capture an occasional
Presidential election either through the choice of a spectacular candidate not
too closely associated with the party, or through the accumulation of some
truly major grievances against the Democrats," the magazine argued.[158] Many
such grievances arrived during the post-1964 period, significant enough that
by 1968 some suspected they were even catastrophic. They certainly shook
confidence in New Deal liberalism.

Divisions of agonizing dimensions developed over civil rights. After the 1965
Voting Rights Act, white support for the pursuit of racial justice fractured.
Claims of socioeconomic equality were less successful politically than guarantees of legal equality. By 1968, more than one-half of Americans believed that
the federal government's pursuit of integration was "too fast."[159] Divisions
also emerged over the nation's military support of the South Vietnamese government against the National Front for the Liberation of Viet Nam rebels,
popularly known as the Viet Cong, and against the North Vietnamese, who
supported the rebels. By 1968, this support involved a peak of 535,000 troops,
and the administration's policies had sparked a large-scale antiwar movement
and were starting to meet opposition among congressional Democrats.[160]
Public opposition to the war was growing, too. Before the end of the Johnson
years, a majority reached the conclusion that American involvement in the
war was a mistake, though most did not advocate withdrawal, and many
viewed antiwar protesters negatively.[161]

The shortcomings of the Johnson administration's Great Society programs
were more visible than their achievements. Because of a focus on War on

[156] Richard C. Cornuelle, *Reclaiming the American Dream: The Role of Private Individuals and Voluntary Associations* (1965; New Brunswick, N.J.: Transaction, 1993), 10.
[157] Tom Wicker, *One of Us: Richard Nixon and the American Dream* (New York: Random House, 1991), 297–299.
[158] *New Republic*, June 5, 1961, 5–6.
[159] Dan T. Carter, *From George Wallace to Newt Gingrich: Race in the Conservative Counterrevolution, 1963–1994* (Baton Rouge: Louisiana State University Press, 1996), 9.
[160] Robert D. Schulzinger, *A Time for War: The United States and Vietnam, 1941–1975* (New York: Oxford University Press, 1997), 182, 215–245.
[161] William L. Lunch and Peter W. Sperlich, "American Public Opinion and the War in Vietnam," *Western Political Quarterly* 32 (1979), 25–32; Philip E. Converse and Howard Schuman, "'Silent Majorities' and the Vietnam War," *Scientific American* 222 (June 1970), 17–25.

Poverty initiatives, the misleading perception developed that the Great Society tackled the problems of the few rather than the many – a perception that notably overlooked Medicare's introduction, as well as other actions such as consumer protections and assistance for students in higher education. The broad-based foundation of support for the liberal agenda was starting to crack.[162] So, too, was agreement among liberals about their goals. The programs' inability to achieve their lofty ambitions caused some liberals to contemplate more radical ideas, which accepted the need for the government to guarantee equal outcomes rather than simply to guarantee opportunity for socioeconomic advancement. The shift toward "entitlement," as opposed to "opportunity," liberalism created divisions among Democrats, and over time it would encourage the party to adopt policy proposals that struggled to win over a majority of Americans.[163]

Moreover, the dark warnings of the 1964 morality agenda seemed to win some vindication. Crime was on the increase.[164] So was the use of illegal drugs, first concentrated within a "counterculture" small in size but large in its critique of mainstream society. "Permissiveness" became a catchword to describe acceptance of unconventional ways of life and of previously unacceptable content in film, art, television, and literature.[165] The Supreme Court extended constitutional protection to sexually explicit content in works that had some "redeeming social value," one of many controversial decisions during an era in which the Court was redefining national conceptions of individual rights.[166] On the one hand, then, the liberal agenda was broadening and advancing; on the other, the incumbent Democratic Party was earning unpopularity for its policies at home and overseas. These developments offered Republicans the opportunity for electoral gain.

The 1966 midterms provided the first signs of a Republican resurgence. The party made net gains of three Senate seats, forty-seven House seats, and eight governorships.[167] An RNC postelection study found that the number of Republican-identifying Americans was at last on the increase, from 25 percent before the election to 29 percent afterward. "The important thing is not the four percentage points, but the fact that a downtrend in the sales [curve] of the Republican Party that has been going on for some twenty years has been reversed for the first time," pollster Thomas W. Benham told an RNC executive session, noting that Democratic numbers had fallen from

[162] David Burner, *Making Peace with the 60s* (Princeton, N.J.: Princeton University Press, 1996), 178–179.

[163] Gareth Davies, *From Opportunity to Entitlement: The Transformation and Decline of Great Society Liberalism* (Lawrence: University Press of Kansas, 1996), 235–243.

[164] Graham, "Contemporary History."

[165] Allen J. Matusow, *The Unraveling of America: A History of Liberalism in the 1960s* (New York: Harper & Row, 1984), 275–307.

[166] John Morton Blum, "The Politics of the Warren Court," in *Liberty, Justice, Order: Writings on Past Politics* (New York: Norton, 1993), 342, 357–358.

[167] Hess and Broder, *Republican Establishment*, 1–11.

53 percent in 1964 to 43 percent in his latest study.[168] Republican politicians of all stripes benefited. Among the new Republicans in the Senate, for
example, were Massachusetts's Edward W. Brooke and Oregon's Mark O.
Hatfield, both forward-looking moderates.[169] In California, Ronald Reagan
beat gubernatorial incumbent Pat Brown by mounting an avowedly conservative challenge to his liberalism, harnessing public concerns about crime
and campus radicalism. He mobilized enthusiastic activism at the grass roots,
but disassociated his candidacy from the "extremist" tag that had plagued
Goldwater.[170] In Arkansas, the gubernatorial victory of Winthrop Rockefeller,
Nelson's older brother, supported the moderate argument that a "new South"
was an area of Republican opportunity. A critic of aspects of federal legislation while a supporter of civil rights, Rockefeller achieved victory mostly
thanks to a good-government emphasis. But more typical of the party in the
South was the successful U.S. Senate candidacy of Claude R. Kirk, Jr., in
Florida, whose stress on conservatism extended to race.[171]

Another victor in 1966 was Richard Nixon, though not a candidate for
office in that year. His indefatigable work for the Republican cause helped to
rescue him from an apparently irreversible decline, the result of his 1960 presidential and 1962 California gubernatorial defeats.[172] Similarly, when Nixon
became a candidate for the party's 1968 presidential nomination, his 1964
efforts for Goldwater ensured conservative support. His quest for the candidacy demonstrated an understanding that a more conservative approach was
now necessary to win convention delegates.[173] The significance of this insight
was clear when the 1968 national convention met; there was a groundswell
of pro-Reagan sentiment, even though Reagan had waged no active nomination campaign. In 1960 Nixon sought to appease Rockefeller; he now endeavored to placate conservatives, however, enlisting Strom Thurmond to convince
southern delegates that he would be sympathetic to their concerns and no liberal on civil rights.[174] The Reagan momentum was not strong enough to topple
Nixon, but it offered evidence for William Rusher "that the troops are in good
shape for the future."[175]

The belief that the Democratic Party's problems created a great opportunity
for the Republican Party informed the Nixon campaign.[176] During nomination

[168] Transcript, RNC executive session, Jan. 23, 1967, 96, reel 5, *Papers of the Republican Party*,
part I: *Meetings of the Republican National Committee, 1911–1980*, series B: *1960–1980*
(Bethesda, Md.: University Publications of America, 1986).
[169] Hess and Broder, *Republican Establishment*, 1–11.
[170] Matthew Dallek, *The Right Moment: Ronald Reagan's First Victory and the Decisive
Turning Point in American Politics* (New York: Free Press, 2000).
[171] Hess and Broder, *Republican Establishment*, 349–353.
[172] Jules Witcover, *The Resurrection of Richard Nixon* (New York: Putnam's, 1970), 175.
[173] *New Republic*, Sept. 17, 1966, 12–18.
[174] Harry S. Dent, *The Prodigal South Returns to Power* (New York: Wiley, 1978), 81–104;
Critchlow, *Conservative Ascendancy*, 42–52, 87–88.
[175] William Rusher to John Ashbrook, Aug. 23, 1968, box 7, Rusher Papers.
[176] Garry Wills, *Nixon Agonistes: The Crisis of the Self Made Man* (1970; New York: Mentor,
1971), 246–247.

season Nixon spoke once of "a new alignment for American unity" as his vision for the party coalition. According to this vision, common ideas, rather than selfish economic interest, brought a variety of groups together – all skeptical of big government and preferring instead individualism's reassertion. Nixon listed "new liberals," promoting participatory democracy; the "new South," wanting to "[interpret] the old doctrine of states' rights in new ways"; African American militants, emphasizing self-help in place of government assistance; and the "silent center," the most numerically significant of these groups, consisting of "the millions of people in the middle of the American political spectrum who do not demonstrate, who do not picket or protest loudly."[177] The speech "was in part realistic and in part unrealistic," as Nixon later noted.[178] Certainly New Leftists and black nationalists were unlikely GOP recruits. The "silent center" was another matter. This group included those Democratic voters anxious about the party's response to late-1960s upheavals; Nixon maintained a campaign focus on seeking their support. As a presidential candidate, he spoke to "the great majority of Americans, the forgotten Americans, the non-shouters, the non-demonstrators," described as "those who did not indulge in violence, those who did not break the law, people who pay their taxes and go to work, people who send their children to school, who go to their churches, people who are not haters, people who love this country, and because they love this country are angry about what has happened to America."[179]

This Nixon strategy cast aside the party's flirtation of the 1960s with an urban focus. Instead, it developed an appeal to suburbanites – whose number among voters exceeded city dwellers for the first time – including attacks on Great Society efforts to tackle the problems of the city. Nixon employed "law and order" as an issue to exploit anxieties about urban disintegration.[180] It was widely understood that this focus was a covert way to signal anxieties about the implications of African American gains for whites because a common misconception connected black people with the decade's rise in crime.[181] By no means all Americans understood the issue in such a way. The crime problem was real, and the Democrats' answers to the problem were securing little success. To many, anticrime policy offered an example of liberalism's shortcomings, allowing Republicans to argue in favor of a conservative alternative.[182] Still, in Nixon's hands, this alternative did not celebrate

177 New Republic, July 13, 1968, 19.
178 Richard Nixon to H. R. Haldeman, Nov. 30, 1970, box 2, White House Special Files – Staff Member and Office Files: President's Personal Files [hereafter PPF].
179 Jules Witcover, The Year The Dream Died: Revisiting 1968 in America (New York: Warner, 1997), 306; Lewis Chester, Godfrey Hodgson, and Bruce Page, An American Melodrama: The Presidential Campaign of 1968 (London: André Deutsch, 1969), 609–610; Theodore H. White, The Making of the President 1968 (New York: Atheneum, 1969), 403–404.
180 Lassiter, The Silent Majority, 232–237.
181 Carter, From George Wallace to Newt Gingrich.
182 Michael W. Flamm, Law and Order: Street Crime, Civil Unrest, and the Crisis of Liberalism in the 1960s (New York: Columbia University Press, 2005).

conservatism's promise but demonized the city in search of suburban support. By contrast, Hubert H. Humphrey, the vice president and his Democratic opponent, promised a "Marshall Plan for the Cities."[183]

In developing the message, vice-presidential candidate Spiro T. Agnew was especially important. A suburban politician, Agnew made a leap in 1966 from his low-profile office as Baltimore County Executive to become Maryland's governor thanks to a moderate campaign against George P. Mahoney, a Democrat who stressed opposition to integration. In addition to representing the suburbs, Agnew, of Greek heritage, was an example of the ethnic Americans, traditionally part of the Roosevelt coalition, whom Nixon sought for the Republican Party. Agnew had caught Nixon's attention for his angry criticisms of civil rights protesters after the assassination of Martin Luther King, Jr. He thus fused an acceptance of limited African American progress with a tetchy irritation toward egalitarian and integrationist claims.[184] This was a formula for suburban success both within and outside the South.

Despite Nixon's reference in his "new alignment" speech to the party's common ground with some African Americans, he was not a candidate well placed to challenge its low level of black support. In late 1967 a campaign adviser urged him to improve his relationship with the African American community – not in the hope that his share of its vote might grow but simply to discourage an active mobilization of African Americans against him.[185] Matters were even difficult for much more strongly pro–civil rights GOP candidates. The experience of the successful 1968 House campaign fought by Robert Taft, son of Robert A. Taft, encouraged Carl B. Rubin, his campaign manager, to conclude that it was exceptionally difficult for Republicans to overcome the calamitous weakness of their support among African Americans, though he rejected as inadequate the neutralization strategy suggested to Nixon. Considered a candidate with a good record of engagement with the community's problems, Taft avoided connection with Nixon and other Republicans in search of African American support. The result was apparently the strongest performance of any House candidate, but still "only a small fraction of the vote," in Rubin's words. "An overall return of 35–40% of the negro [sic] vote is the maximum realistic objective and as a matter of fact may not, against a strong opponent, be obtainable," he wrote.[186]

The boldness of Nixon's speech about a "new alignment" was a rare commodity in his campaign against Hubert Humphrey and, as a third-party candidate, George Wallace. While aides contemplated a realignment to the Republicans' benefit, caution usually characterized Nixon's strategy, which relied on anti-incumbent sentiment instead of pro-Republican enthusiasm. A year that was full of upheaval, especially involving the Vietnam War and

---

[183] *Life*, Oct. 20, 1968, 42.
[184] Jules Witcover, *White Knight: The Rise of Spiro Agnew* (New York: Random House, 1972).
[185] Rita E. Hauser to Leonard Garment, Nov. 13, 1967, box 10, Safire Papers.
[186] Carl B. Rubin, report, n.d., box 302, Robert Taft Papers.

civil rights, 1968 confounded the incumbent party's efforts to retain power. Wallace's dissident, segregationist candidacy demonstrated the Democrats' inability to hold together its incoherent coalition of liberalism and racism, while chaotic scenes at their Chicago convention suggested that differences between mainstream liberalism and more leftist liberalism were also disrupting the party's effectiveness. But Humphrey fought back to remind voters of New Deal liberalism's benefits and edged toward criticism of Johnson's Vietnam policy. Anxious about Wallace's appeal, leaders of organized labor reinforced Humphrey's message. Against all odds, these efforts came close to achieving another triumph for the New Deal coalition. Nixon won only a half-million votes more than Humphrey, achieving 43.4 percent of the popular vote against Humphrey's 42.7 percent and Wallace's 13.5 percent. In the eleven states of the former Confederacy, Nixon won 34.7 percent of the vote, only slightly more than the 34.3 percent share secured by Wallace, who won Alabama, Arkansas, Georgia, Louisiana, and Mississippi. Although Republicans made some House and Senate gains, Democratic majorities were still large in both. Fifty-five percent of Americans still saw themselves as supporters of the Democratic Party, while barely more than one in three had a similar attachment to the Republican Party.[187] Despite the Democrats' disarray in 1968, New Deal liberalism retained strength; Republicans still faced electoral problems.

---

[187] This calculation counts "independent" party identifiers together with weak or strong identifiers. Philip E. Converse, Warren E. Miller, Jerrold G. Rusk, and Arthur C. Wolfe, "Continuity and Change in American Politics: Parties and Issues in the 1968 Election," *APSR* 63 (1969), 1083–1105.

7

"There's a Realignment Going On": 1968–1976

"Now for the first time since Teddy Roosevelt, it is we who have the initiative, we who stand for sweeping change, we who stand for restoring power to the people – and the other side on Capitol Hill who suddenly become the party of the Status Quo." Meeting with congressional Republicans in early 1971, Richard Nixon argued that it was an important moment for the party. According to Nixon, the party's few post–World War II victories had depended on opposition – opposition to postwar frustrations in 1946, to "the mess in Washington" in 1952, and to "crime and Vietnam and campus anarchy and riots" in 1968. An opposition psychology pervaded the party, he told them, characterizing its congressional politicians' actions even when Republicans won power. It was this reliance on opposition – together with the Republican refusal to outspend Democrats – that accounted for the party's minority status, Nixon said.[1] A few days earlier the president had outlined his proposals for "sweeping change" in his State of the Union address, in which he indulged his taste for political hyperbole by speaking of a "new American revolution." This intended revolution involved welfare reform, environmental protections, healthcare, revenue sharing (which sought to shift control over spending in certain areas from the federal government to the states and localities), reform of the federal government, as well as the assurance of prosperity, fed by an expansionary budget. Together, the initiatives amounted to a Republican version of activist government: an expansion of the welfare state but a reassertion of state and local responsibility for its oversight, therefore compromising the party's antistatism while maintaining a stress on its skepticism of federal action.

Nixon's message to congressional Republicans repudiated the approach to electoral politics that had characterized his own career. His understanding of the party's minority status had discouraged him from any defense

---

[1] The quotations feature Buchanan's paraphrasing of Nixon's remarks. Patrick J. Buchanan to Ronald Ziegler, Jan. 29, 1971, box 1, White House Special Files – Staff Member and Office Files: Buchanan.

of a conservative alternative to New Deal liberalism, still less any promotion of such an alternative. Nixon believed that voter support for activist government accounted for the Democratic Party's electoral advantage, and that any campaign engagement with related questions was unlikely to win converts but sure to elevate the salience of those issues – thus reminding a majority of Democratic strengths. This is why, according to Nixon's perspective, Republican success depended on Democratic failure, rather than any affirmative mobilization in support of a nonliberal agenda. A related strategy looked for other issues, beyond the key concerns of New Deal liberalism around which U.S. politics had usually centered now for a generation. Nixon had encouraged Republicans to cultivate different foci of campaign debate, to the Democrats' disadvantage. His advocacy of anticommunism as such an issue during the 1940s and 1950s was the preeminent example of this strategy, a tactic that helped to earn him his controversial reputation as "Tricky Dick." The nature of his advice to fellow Republicans in early 1971 was thus a departure from his previous insights about the implications of the party's minority status. It did not represent a surrender of his earlier argument, however. Nixon still believed that any emphasis on a conventionally conservative response to New Deal liberalism was a sure route to defeat. But he now thought that a Republican version of activist government was worthy of policy development and political defense.

Nixon was ready to rethink his career-long understanding of interparty competition because he believed that the crisis of the Democratic coalition, visible in 1968, created an opportunity for an electoral realignment to the Republicans' benefit. He was hardly alone in this belief. The prospect of such change was the talk of political Washington and even, in journalist David S. Broder's words, "almost a national sport."[2] Nixon saw himself as especially well qualified to lead the Republican Party at such a time of opportunity, believing he had a good understanding of ordinary Americans' concerns.[3] His qualifications included a long engagement with his party's minority problem and a career of party service that equipped him with deep reservoirs of Republican knowledge. "Dick knows almost everything there is to know about the party's inner workings and geography," an aide remarked in 1968.[4] Obsessed with campaign politics, Nixon ran an administration unusually attentive to the political implications of policy.[5] This attentiveness was so acute, indeed, that

---

[2] David S. Broder, *The Party's Over: The Failure of Politics in America* (New York: Harper & Row, 1972), 192.

[3] Robert Mason, "'I Was Going To Build a New Republican Party and a New Majority': Richard Nixon as Party Leader, 1969–1973," *Journal of American Studies* 39 (2005), 463–483.

[4] Wills, *Nixon Agonistes*, 17.

[5] John Ehrlichman, *Witness to Power: The Nixon Years* (New York: Pocket Books, 1982), 183–184; Herbert G. Klein, *Making It Perfectly Clear* (Garden City, N.Y.: Doubleday, 1980), 107; *Atlantic*, Oct. 1970, 51; Karen M. Hult and Charles E. Wolcott, *Empowering the White House: Governance under Nixon, Ford, and Carter* (Lawrence: University Press of Kansas, 2004).

the administration sometimes seemed to care more about public relations than substantive achievement.[6]

A victory-at-all-costs mentality harbored even greater dangers, as the administration's demise in the Watergate scandal vividly revealed. But there were other aspects of Nixon's campaign obsession that undermined his ability to reap the maximum benefit from this opportunity. According to reporter Tom Wicker, clouding his sense of connection with "middle America" was a "condescending and contemptuous attitude toward the commonality of the American people."[7] Moreover, his skill as a campaign politician was open to question. The divisive nature of Nixon's political personality limited the extent of his appeal, most acutely demonstrated by the loser reputation Nixon developed as a result of his 1960 and 1962 defeats. He was not the most compelling salesperson for a new direction for the Republican Party.

Among the arenas for Broder's "national sport" were two books agreeing with Nixon's belief that the party needed to take some steps toward activism to achieve majority status. *The Real Majority*, a 1970 work about electoral change, presented such a thesis. Its authors, Richard M. Scammon and Ben J. Wattenberg, had both served in the Johnson administration, Scammon as census director and Wattenberg as a presidential speechwriter, and in writing the book their key goal was to alert their fellow Democrats to the danger of declining support. The book discussed the emergence during the 1960s of the "Social Issue," first associated with concerns about crime before broadening in scope as disorder became increasingly connected with racial tensions, antiwar activism, and college radicalism. This Social Issue also involved issues of the "counterculture" and "permissiveness," subjects like drug use and sexual behavior. Scammon and Wattenberg emphasized that the electorate remained "unyoung, unpoor, unblack" – their median voter was a forty-seven-year-old machinist's wife in Dayton, Ohio – and did not share the Social Issue liberalism that was making gains among Democratic politicians.[8] Race was perhaps a more important element of the Social Issue than the book suggested. At a meeting in early 1972, Scammon told Nixon, curious about the Social Issue, that key contemporary manifestations of these concerns were busing and scatter-site housing, both affirmative measures toward racial integration.[9] The "real majority," according to Scammon and Wattenberg, was conservative on the Social Issue, but it remained liberal – in favor of activist goverment – on the "Economic Issue." As an auxiliary to their book's key mission to tell Democratic politicians about the strength of Social Issue conservatism, their message to the Republican Party recognized "that a good deal

---

[6] Patrick J. Buchanan to Charles W. Colson, Jan. 12, 1972, box 9, White House Special Files – Staff Member and Office Files: Buchanan.

[7] Tom Wicker, "Richard M. Nixon 1969–1974," *Presidential Studies Quarterly* 26 (1996), 254.

[8] Richard M. Scammon and Ben J. Wattenberg, *The Real Majority* (New York: Coward-McCann, 1970).

[9] Charles W. Colson to Richard Nixon's file, Jan. 28, 1972, box 24, White House Special Files – Staff Member and Office Files: Colson.

of Republican gardening will be done on the Social Issue," but pointed out that "Republicans must move on the Economic Issue to capture the center." Scammon and Wattenberg explained, "A Republican Party perceived of as go-slow on the problems of unemployment or the cities or transportation or pollution or against Medicare or Social Security will be vulnerable."[10]

Another book about the Republican opportunity stressed more explicitly race's electoral salience. *The Emerging Republican Majority*, a 1969 book, was the work of Kevin P. Phillips, a Department of Justice aide. A manuscript of the book had won Phillips a job with the Nixon campaign the previous year.[11] *The Emerging Republican Majority* revealed an encyclopedic knowledge of historical demography, knowledge that Phillips marshaled in support of his central insight that intergroup animosities informed political conflict over time. In an interview, he made the point bluntly: The key to understanding electoral politics was to know "who hates who," he said.[12] It was an approach that critics thought characterized Nixon's career in electoral politics, which they often saw as dependent on the exploitation of resentments, especially surrounding anticommunism during the 1940s and 1950s. The current nature of this "ethnic polarization" made Phillips's book controversial. According to Phillips, it involved white opposition to civil rights advances; the mobilization of this emerging Republican majority required the Democratic Party's association with the concerns of African Americans. Phillips shared the interpretation of the 1968 election that the Wallace vote was a way station for disaffected supporters of the Democrats, now ready to support the GOP. In its simplest form, this projection of a Republican majority involved the unification of those who did not support Humphrey in 1968, whether they voted for Nixon or for Wallace.

Perhaps because of his administration role, Phillips did not elaborate his electoral theory's policy-making implications in the book. But he agreed with Scammon and Wattenberg that the Republican Party needed to revise its opposition to activist government to consolidate this emerging majority's support. Great Society liberalism, not New Deal liberalism, was responsible for its alienation from the Democratic Party. "The emerging Republican majority spoke clearly in 1968," he wrote, "for a shift away from the sociological jurisprudence, moral permissiveness, experimental residential, welfare and educational programming and massive federal spending by which the Liberal (mostly Democratic) Establishment sought to propagate liberal institutions and ideology – and all the while reap growing economic benefits."[13] Phillips thus viewed this majority's concerns as antielitist, a characteristic that supported his conceptualization of the Republican opportunity as reflecting the

---

[10] Scammon and Wattenberg, *The Real Majority*, 292.
[11] Leonard Garment, *Crazy Rhythm: My Journey from Brooklyn, Jazz, and Wall Street, to Nixon's White House, Watergate, and Beyond* ... (New York: Times Books, 1997), 134.
[12] *NYT* magazine, May 17, 1970, 106.
[13] Kevin P. Phillips, *The Emerging Republican Majority* (New Rochelle, N.Y.: Arlington House, 1969), 471.

cyclical nature of electoral politics – a conceptualization informed by the realignment paradigm. Across American history he saw periods of a party's dominance as enduring for a generation, between twenty-eight and thirty-six years in length – a view implying that the New Deal coalition's decline was now due. Challenges to the dominant party generally emerged in the South and West as frustrations with the unresponsive agenda of an eastern elite, Phillips emphasized. To harness this populist tide against a liberal agenda now tackling the concerns of the few rather than the many, the Republican Party needed to shed its own elitist reputation for privileging the economic concerns of big business and the wealthy.[14] "I wish we could drop into the Potomac all those obsolescent conservatives who are still preoccupied with Alger Hiss and General MacArthur, and who keep trotting out *laissez faire* economics and other dead horses," he said. "They make the Republican party look musty to millions of ignored working-class people who are looking for a party that relates to their needs."[15]

Both books were part of a current interest in "middle Americans," whom *Time* editors named as 1969's "man and woman of the year."[16] "Middle America" was a vague construct, often referring to blue-collar workers who were not poor and white-collar workers who were not affluent.[17] Its political significance was much clearer. Middle Americans were the heart of the Democrats' New Deal coalition – New Deal liberalism's key supporters – now harboring concerns that encouraged a reassessment of this traditional loyalty. As the differences between Phillips's "emerging Republican majority" and Scammon and Wattenberg's "real majority" suggest, there was disagreement about the nature of these concerns. One interpretation emphasized economic factors. Middle Americans were not poor, but they were not affluent, either – often not affluent enough, arguably, to achieve contemporary expectations of a good standard of living – and in real terms the average income of factory hands and clerks fell slightly during the second half of the 1960s. Mundane work and limited opportunity compounded this problem of nonaffluence.[18] Another perspective suggested that race influenced this sense of nonaffluence. African Americans' median income rose at twice the rate of whites' during the 1960s (though the latter remained much wealthier), a disparity of increase that perhaps fed insecurity.[19] A similar argument suggested that government efforts during the 1960s to help minorities and the poor – part of Great Society

---

[14] Kevin P. Phillips, "Middle America and the Emerging Republican Majority," n.d., box 8, White House Special Files – Staff Member and Office Files: Dent.

[15] *NYT* magazine, May 17, 1970, 106.

[16] *Time*, Jan. 5, 1970, 10–17.

[17] William B. Hixson, *Search for the American Right Wing: An Analysis of the Social Science Record, 1955–1987* (Princeton, N.J.: Princeton University Press, 1992), 146.

[18] *Time*, Aug. 8, 1969, 42; *Time*, Nov. 9, 1970, 68–78.

[19] Hixson, *Search for the American Right Wing*, 147; Richard Parker, "The Myth of Middle America," in Stanley N. Katz and Stanley I. Kutler, eds., *New Perspectives on the American Past*, vol. II: *1877 to the Present*, 2nd ed. (Boston: Little, Brown, 1972), 408–422.

liberalism – encouraged disaffection that middle America's problems had lost similar attention.[20]

Other understandings of middle Americans' woes emphasized race much more, an emphasis that George Wallace's 1968 political appeal outside as well as within the South supported – that objections to the Democratic Party largely involved its commitment to civil rights.[21] Still another observation perceived a broad-based anxiety toward the tumultuous change that the nation was experiencing. According to former Johnson aide Bill Moyers, Americans "don't know what to make of it all: of long hair and endless war, of their children deserting their country, of congestion on their highways and overflowing crowds in their national parks, of art that does not uplift and movies that do not reach conclusions; of intransigence in government and violence; of politicians who come and go while problems plague and persist; of being lonely surrounded by people and of being bored with so many possessions; of being poor; of the failure of organizations to keep the air breathable, the water drinkable, and man peaceable."[22]

When Nixon sought administration aides' views about middle American troubles, most posited some formula of racial tensions and economic problems to explain them.[23] But the detail divided them, as did the prescription to tackle the troubles. Daniel Patrick Moynihan, a Democrat working on domestic policy for Nixon, commended the administration's nascent reform agenda on the grounds that it promised to help "the people-in-between," as well as "the people at the bottom," thus possessing "the making of a social revolution which preserves the fabric of American society, rather than tearing it to sheds."[24] Department of Labor officials similarly advocated reform as a way to meet middle America's ills. Jerome Rosow, an assistant secretary, noted that racial tensions obscured much common ground that existed between black and white "troubled Americans," who shared not only similar socioeconomic concerns but also anxieties about rising crime and about traditional values apparently under attack.[25] Rosow wrote a report, which won support among leading administration figures, that not only endorsed the reform agenda but also advocated a host of other measures designed to ease employment-related frustrations, such as the improvement of access to education, the funding of

[20] *Time*, Aug. 8, 1969, 42.

[21] Thomas F. Pettigrew with Robert T. Riley, "The Social Psychology of the Wallace Phenemenon," in Pettigrew, *Racially Separate or Together?* (New York: McGraw-Hill, 1971), 231–256.

[22] Bill Moyers, *Listening to America: A Traveler Rediscovers His Country* (1971; New York: Dell, 1972), 377.

[23] Robert Mason, *Richard Nixon and the Quest for a New Majority* (Chapel Hill: University of North Carolina Press, 2004), 43–47.

[24] Daniel Patrick Moynihan to Richard Nixon, May 17, 1969, box 46, White House Central Files – Subject Files: BE.

[25] Jerome Rosow to George Shultz, April 16, 1969, box 154, General Records of the Department of Labor: Shultz Records.

childcare facilities, and better regulation of workplace conditions.[26] Others in the administration developed a very different interpretation of middle America's needs. Some conservatives met as the Middle America Committee, and their deliberations acknowledged the significance of the perception that government ignored this group, but concluded that "the large and politically powerful white, middle class is deeply troubled primarily over the erosion of what they consider to be their values." They therefore encouraged Nixon "to visit blue collar areas and follow through with a tough pitch for law and order and emphasis on the good old values."[27] One of the committee's members dismissed the Rosow report as "a blue-print for an expanded welfare state."[28]

The clearest manifestation of middle America's support for Nixon did not involve race or economics, but foreign policy. By fall 1969 disaffection with the Vietnam War was becoming acute. Antiwar protest reached the mainstream both among the growing contingent of congressional politicians calling for swift withdrawal and within the wider public; October's "moratorium" demonstrations mobilized many who had previously eschewed such activism. This protest threatened to force Nixon to revise his Vietnam policy, which took a gradualist approach to disengagement, through "Vietnamization" of the war, as the way to achieve "peace with honor." That promise retained popular power, however. While most Americans now believed that involvement in Vietnam was a mistake, there was also a majority against immediate withdrawal without the achievement of war aims.[29] To buy time for his policy, in a televised address of early November Nixon appealed for the support of "the great silent majority." The speech achieved a spectacular impact. Nixon later agreed with aide Patrick J. Buchanan that the day of the speech "was probably the critical turning point in the election of 1972 – and Nixon Presidency."[30] White House polls suggested that three in four Americans identified with the "silent majority," and an easy majority of those were Nixon supporters.[31] Nixon aimed not only to maintain this show of public confidence in his Vietnam policy but also to develop other reasons for this silent majority to support the administration.[32]

As the analyses of middle America's political concerns emphasized, racial progress remained very controversial. The civil rights agenda was changing

[26] *U.S. News & World Report*, July 20, 1970, 18–20; Jerome M. Rosow, "The Problems of Lower-Middle-Income Workers," in Sar A. Levitan, ed., *Blue-Collar Workers: A Symposium on Middle America* (New York: McGraw-Hill, 1971), 76–94.

[27] Harry S. Dent to Richard Nixon, Oct. 16, 1969, White House Special Files – Staff Member and Office Files: President's Office Files [hereafter POF].

[28] Tom Charles Huston to Harry Dent, Aug. 11, 1970, box 293, White House Special Files – Staff Member and Office Files: Haldeman.

[29] Lunch and Sperlich, "American Public Opinion and the War in Vietnam," 27–28.

[30] Patrick J. Buchanan to Richard Nixon's files, Nov. 30, 1972, box 2, White House Special Files – Staff Member and Office Files: Buchanan.

[31] Opinion Research Corporation, poll report, June 1970, box 376, White House Special Files – Staff Member and Office Files: Haldeman.

[32] Klein, *Making It Perfectly Clear*, 200.

in nature. The eradication of de jure segregation of southern schools was at last almost complete, but the inequalities among the races and their geographic separation that endured suggested a need for bolder remedies, in order to tackle de facto segregation, present both within and outside the South. Remedies that moved beyond desegregation in search of integration in the North as well as the South – busing and scatter-site housing – were often unpopular. Nixon viewed such remedies as coercive actions of social engineering and as wrong, even though he realized that their rejection repudiated an integrationist dream of a society in which blacks and whites lived equally together.[33] He also realized that their rejection – as Scammon reminded him during their early 1972 meeting – possessed electoral promise.[34] Nixon therefore accepted that racial tensions helped to explain middle Americans' anxieties and that a halt in the tide of racial progress would contribute to their mobilization at the polls.

Busing programs to achieve school desegregation despite patterns of de facto residential segregation generated much opposition. The Supreme Court's 1971 *Swann v. Charlotte-Mecklenburg Board of Education* decision endorsed such a program to correct past de jure school segregation, and lower courts soon heard cases with wider-ranging implications, involving interdistrict and nonsouthern busing. Outspoken opposition to these plans played an important role in the success of George C. Wallace in the 1972 Democratic presidential nomination primaries until a May assassination attempt cut short his campaign. Wallace's success encouraged Nixon to take action against busing. Aide Harry Dent, a former Strom Thurmond staffer, counseled that an initiative of this kind would deprive Wallace of "the only leverage issue that remains to him."[35] Although Nixon's impulse was to propose an antibusing constitutional amendment, a degree of restraint induced him instead to call for a "moratorium" on court-ordered busing and for increased funding for needy schools. Neither achieved enactment, but the moratorium proposal was the politics of symbolism – intended to make a point.[36] Despite Wallace's exploitation of busing and despite Nixon's impulse to emulate him, the difference between the parties was by no means clear-cut. Although some liberal Democrats argued vigorously for busing as a means to achieve a meaningful form of desegregation, others, mindful of its unpopularity, took a more equivocal position or even opposed busing measures on Capitol Hill.[37]

---

[33] Richard Nixon to John Ehrlichman, Jan. 28, 1972, box 20, White House Special Files – Staff Member and Office Files: Ehrlichman.

[34] Richard Nixon to John D. Ehrlichman, May 17, 1972, box 24, White House Special Files – Staff Member and Office Files: Ehrlichman.

[35] Jeb Stuart Magruder to John Mitchell, Jan. 28, 1972, box 401, White House Special Files – Staff Member and Office Files: Haldeman.

[36] Edward Morgan to John Ehrlichman, May 30, 1972, box 17, White House Special Files – Staff Member and Office Files: Ehrlichman.

[37] Steven M. Gillon, *The Democrats' Dilemma: Walter F. Mondale and the Liberal Legacy* (New York: Columbia University Press, 1992), 131–135; Thurber, *Politics of Equality*, 227–232.

Unlike the moratorium proposal, the appointment of conservatives to the Supreme Court substantially changed the fortunes of busing (among a broader array of important public issues). Nixon hoped that his successful nominees – Harry Blackmun, William Rehnquist, and Lewis Powell as justices, together with Warren Burger as chief – would shift the Supreme Court away from the rights-expanding trajectory of Earl Warren's chief justiceship. Though Blackmun would often prove to be that tradition's defender, Burger, Powell, and Rehnquist more reliably helped to check its development. They soon contributed to the 1974 majority in *Milliken v. Bradley* against interdistrict busing, in essence ending the prospect of desegregation plans across suburbs and central cities in the North.[38]

Opposition to racially egalitarian projects was geographically wider-ranging than talk of a "southern strategy" suggested, but party growth in the South remained an important ambition, as Phillips's *The Emerging Republican Majority* indicated. An appeal to white conservatism was Nixon's focus. At the start of the Nixon administration, it was almost fifteen years since the Supreme Court had handed down the *Brown v. Board of Education* decisions (1954 and 1955), ordering the desegregation of dual-school systems; because of action by the judiciary and initiatives by the Johnson administration, *Brown*'s promise of desegregated schools was at last close to realization across the South, a transition that the administration took steps to encourage in a peaceable fashion. The administration also took steps to disassociate itself from desegregation's implementation, however, by transferring responsibility for desegregation from the executive to the judiciary. Notably in *Alexander v. Holmes County Board of Education* (1969), the administration supported Mississippi's efforts to delay implementation of *Brown*, the first time the federal government had taken a stance in such a case contrary to that of the NAACP Legal Defense and Educational Fund.[39]

Nixon's judicial appointments, moreover, aimed to make a sectional point as well as ideological impact. Before selecting Blackmun for the Supreme Court, Nixon unsuccessfully nominated conservative southerners Clement Haynsworth and G. Harrold Carswell, seeking political benefit in the Senate's failure to confirm either by speaking of an "act of regional discrimination."[40] But Nixon saw his agenda as a whole – not only his approach to school desegregation and judicial nominations – as compatible with southern conservatism, noting to aides in October 1972 that what he described as his "New American Majority" consisted of "Americans to the core," sharing the same values and exhibiting the same characteristics of patriotism, antipermissiveness, and antielitism. "The Southerners are more so than the rest of the United

[38] J. Harvie Wilkinson, III, *From Brown to Bakke: The Supreme Court and School Integration, 1954–1978* (New York: Oxford University Press, 1979), 147–149.
[39] Dean J. Kotlowski, *Nixon's Civil Rights: Politics, Principle, and Policy* (Cambridge, Mass.: Harvard University Press, 2001).
[40] Reg Murphy and Hal Gulliver, *The Southern Strategy* (New York: Scribner's, 1971), 139.

States, because they are not poisoned by the elite universities and the media," Nixon said.[41]

Nixon did not believe that a meaningful challenge to anti-Republican sentiment among African Americans was possible, expecting any increase in support to be "minimal" at best.[42] Such an increase would probably be among the growing, but still small, black middle class, he anticipated. The Office of Minority Business Enterprise, created in 1969 within the Department of Commerce, promoted African American ownership; Nixon was mindful of the political promise of this emphasis on "black capitalism."[43] The prospect of increased Latino support, by contrast, intrigued Nixon. "While our gains will not be spectacular," he wrote, "I believe that we can win a considerable number of Mexicans to our side simply by paying more attention to them."[44] The existing record was unimpressive. In 1968 just 10 percent of Mexican Americans and 15 percent of Puerto Ricans in the United States voted for Nixon. The results in New Mexico, where Nixon won almost four in ten votes in Latino precincts, suggested that better was possible; the state party there paid attention to Latino concerns and incumbent Republican Governor David F. Cargo had developed popularity within the Latino community.[45] In addition to a boost in the number of Spanish-surnamed presidential appointees, Nixon offered Latinos "more attention" through the creation of the Cabinet Committee on Opportunities for Spanish-Speaking People and the inclusion of Hispanics in affirmative action programs.[46] Interest in the cultivation of Latino support was, moreover, one of the factors that encouraged the administration to promote bilingual education.[47] A Mexican American group resuscitated the balance-of-power argument to claim that its community was able to decide elections in three southwestern states and Illinois, a claim similar to one that the League of United Latin American Citizens offered as early as 1960. Probably an overstatement, the claim nevertheless underscored the growth of Latino groups, whose needs Nixon acknowledged that government had historically neglected; according to the census, 4.5 percent of Americans were of Spanish origin. Nixon accepted a different version of the Latino balance-of-power argument, thinking that the votes of Cuban Americans,

---

[41] H. R. Haldeman, *The Haldeman Diaries: Inside the Nixon White House*, complete multimedia ed. (Santa Monica, Calif.: Sony Electronic Publishing, 1994), Oct. 14, 1972. The quotations feature Haldeman's summary of Nixon's remarks.

[42] Richard Nixon to John Ehrlichman, Nov. 30, 1970, box 2, White House Special Files – Staff Member and Office Files: PPF.

[43] Kotlowski, *Nixon's Civil Rights*, 134–136.

[44] Richard Nixon to John Ehrlichman, Nov. 30, 1970, box 2, White House Special Files – Staff Member and Office Files: PPF.

[45] Mark R. Levy and Michael S. Kramer, *The Ethnic Factor: How America's Minorities Decide Elections*, with new epilogue (1972; New York: Touchstone, 1973), 79–80, 94.

[46] Kotlowski, *Nixon's Civil Rights*, 264.

[47] Gareth Davies, "The Great Society after Johnson: The Case of Bilingual Education," *Journal of American History* 88 (2002), 1405–1429.

whose opposition to the Castro regime helped to account for their high degree of Republican support, were potentially decisive in Florida.[48]

"There's a realignment going on," Nixon told aides in early September 1970 who were working on that fall's midterm campaign. To harness the benefits of this realigning moment, he charged them with the implementation of an ambitious plan. Democratic candidates, he said, were seeking to use economic issues as ammunition against the party; Republican candidates must avoid the defensive posture that such an attack invited. Instead, permissiveness and the Vietnam War were issues of potential strength for them. But Scammon and Wattenberg had published *The Real Majority* not long beforehand, and Nixon thought that they were succeeding in their goal to warn fellow Democrats that Social Issue liberalism was dangerous. "All the Democrats are reading it," he said. "All Democrats are trying to blur their image; they are petrified about permissiveness being hung on them – toward crime, toward students." An all-out attack, grounded in Social Issue concerns, aimed to thwart the effort.[49] The campaign he designed chose as its target "radical liberals," defined as politicians with permissive and antiwar views, out of step with most Americans.

The strategy was classically Nixonian. It accepted the Democrats' Economic Issue advantage, looking elsewhere for a winning appeal. Finding one in the Social Issue, it relied on aggressive attack. Economic conditions encouraged Nixon to develop this strategy; unemployment approached 6 percent, and inflation was at 6 percent, too, while strikes were at a level nearly unmatched since World War II. Most likely to suffer economic woes were the middle Americans whose support Nixon coveted.[50] Moreover, the administration had failed to make much progress toward the enactment of a reform agenda or its public promotion. The Post Office Department's replacement by the Postal Service, a public corporation, was a rare exception that Nixon was able to identify soon after the midterm elections: "We haven't gotten across the whole area of reform," he wrote.[51] Nixon was therefore unable to develop the claim, as recommended by Scammon and Wattenberg, that the party was moving toward the Economic Issue center. He needed to retreat to his old attack tactics.

The strategy also acknowledged that the Republican tag remained unappealing to many. The campaign aimed to mobilize voters against "radical liberalism" and to elect a Congress supportive of the president, rather than secure pro-Republican conversions – downplaying the Republican tag. The avoidance of party labels was in line with Nixon's desire to offer some help

[48] Levy and Kramer, *The Ethnic Factor*, 77; John A. García, *Latino Politics in America: Community, Culture, and Interests* (Lanham, Md.: Rowman & Littlefield, 2003), 111–112; Richard Nixon to John Ehrlichman, Nov. 30, 1970, box 2, White House Special File – Staff Member and Office Files: PPF.

[49] William Safire, *Before the Fall: An Inside View of the Pre-Watergate White House* (Garden City, N.Y.: Doubleday, 1975), 318–319.

[50] *Time*, Nov. 9, 1970, 68–78.

[51] Richard Nixon to H. R. Haldeman, Dec. 1, 1970, box 2, White House Special Files – Staff Member and Office Files: PPF.

not only to Republican candidates. The administration withheld support from two Republicans, Senator Charles Goodell of New York and Ray L. Garland, the party's Senate candidate in Virginia. The liberalism of Goodell's record and especially his opposition to the war led to his categorization as a radical liberal. One of Goodell's challengers was James L. Buckley, representing the state's Conservative Party, who was much more supportive of the administration and whose antipermissiveness, law-and-order campaign made him a model exponent of Social Issue conservatism.[52] Considered by state Republicans an excellent representative of the "New South's" moderation, Garland, unlike Goodell, did not lose administration support on the grounds of his political views, but because Nixon hoped to persuade Harry Byrd, the Democratic incumbent, to switch to the Republican Party. Byrd was seeking reelection as an independent, a decision he made when his faction's decline within the state Democratic Party made his renomination unlikely.[53]

Nixon's cultivation of Byrd was one example of his immersion in party and campaign politics. His belief in a historic opportunity for GOP growth encouraged him to take an assertive approach to his presidential duties of party leadership. The most important strand of this activity in 1970 was a national campaign against what Nixon labeled radical liberalism, reinforced by thoroughgoing White House promotion of the theme, most extensively by Vice President Spiro T. Agnew, but by Nixon himself, too. It also encompassed Nixon's recruitment of Senate candidates he considered promising. To help them, Nixon directed major contributors to donate money to a White House–based fund and to send only token amounts to the Capitol Hill campaign committees; he thus maintained control over fund distribution. This fundraising drive secured several million dollars, topping up candidate funds according to a White House–devised formula.[54]

Agnew faithfully developed the theme of opposition to radical liberalism. "Today's radical-liberal posturing in the Senate is about as closely related to a Harry Truman, as is a chihuahua to a timber wolf," he said in his first speech of the campaign. He attacked radical liberals for big spending, but mostly for their antiwar views – encouraging voters to "sweep out the salons of sellout in foreign affairs" – and their approach to the Social Issue. "The radical liberal will not get exercised over the presence of hard-core pornography at the corner drugstore – but don't let him watch your son praying in the public schools," he said in Albuquerque. "The radical liberal will not hesitate to demand immediate use of the 82nd Airborne to integrate the schools of a Southern state – but he will buy his house so far out in the suburbs that you have to take the Metroliner to get there."[55] When Nixon made campaign appearances, he instructed

[52] George J. Marlin, *Fighting the Good Fight: A History of the New York Conservative Party* (South Bend, Ind.: St. Augustine's Press, 2002), 162–183.

[53] James R. Sweeney, "Southern Strategies: The 1970 Election for the United States Senate in Virginia," *Virginia Magazine of History and Biography* 106 (1998), 165–168.

[54] Mason, "'I Was Going To Build.'"

[55] John R. Coyne, Jr., *The Impudent Snobs: Agnew vs. the Intellectual Establishment* (New Rochelle, N.Y.: Arlington House, 1972), 361, 374, 376.

advance people to admit some protesters to dramatize his antiradical rhetoric. "The President's whole pitch is built around having a few demonstrators in the hall heckling him so that he can refer to them and their 'obscenities,'" aide Dwight L. Chapin explained.[56] In San Jose, California, Nixon mentioned the demonstrators both inside the auditorium and outside, "shouting their hatred for the United States and shouting also the usual obscenities that you expect from this kind of crowd."[57] The campaign reran Nixon's old solution to the minority problem. He tried to sideline New Deal liberalism that encouraged majority status for the Democrats by promoting other concerns, and he did so by fostering a political demon – on this occasion radicalism prepared to use violence – and by connecting his opponents with this demon.

The Nixon strategy faced obstacles, however, which the Minnesota campaign illustrated. Hubert H. Humphrey was seeking a return to the Senate, challenged by Clark MacGregor, one of Nixon's campaign recruits. Humphrey's presence in the race increased its importance to Nixon, who hoped that the assaults on radical liberalism would damage some of the Democratic Party's leading presidential contenders; he intended the campaign to brand Edmund Muskie in Maine and Edward M. Kennedy in Massachusetts, as well as Humphrey, as leftists rather than moderates, thus aiding his own 1972 reelection prospects.[58] Like other Democrats, Humphrey declined to act as the radical-liberal campaign's fall guy, and with Ben Wattenberg as an adviser, he insulated himself from the Social Issue attack before launching his own Economic Issue attack on Republicans.[59] As the campaign season unfolded, most congressional Democrats went on the record in ways that confounded the Nixon strategy; there was barely a dissenting voice among them in joining Republicans to vote for crime and drugs bills.[60] A further obstacle to the strategy's implementation in Minnesota was MacGregor's reluctance to emphasize the Social Issue and to attack Humphrey in the dramatic way White House aides exhorted, although many other Republican candidates were much more willing to take up the theme.[61]

Judged by the expectation of midterm losses for the White House party, the results were encouraging. Republicans made a net gain of two Senate seats,

[56] Dwight L. Chapin to Ron Walker, Oct. 21, 1970, box 12, White House Special Files – Staff Member and Office Files: Chapin.

[57] Richard Nixon, remarks, Oct. 29, 1970, doc. 411 in "Public Papers of Richard Nixon, 1970," at<www.nixonlibrary.org/clientuploads/directory/archive/1970_pdf_files/1970_0411. pdf>, accessed June 29, 2007.

[58] Haldeman, *Diaries*, Sept. 26, 1970; H. R. Haldeman to Bryce Harlow, Sept. 26, 1970, box 64, White House Special Files – Staff Member and Office Files: Haldeman; Richard Nixon to Haldeman, Sept. 21, 1970, box 2, White House Special Files – Staff Member and Office Files: PPF.

[59] Carl Solberg, *Hubert Humphrey: A Biography* (New York: Norton, 1984), 418–419.

[60] *Congress and the Nation: A Review of Government and Politics*, vol. 3: 1969–1972 (Washington, D.C.: Congressional Quarterly Service, 1973), 256–277.

[61] H. R. Haldeman to Murray Chotiner, Sept. 24, 1970, box 64, White House Special Files – Staff Member and Office Files: Haldeman; Chotiner to Clark MacGregor, Sept. 29, 1970, box 65, White House Special Files – Staff Member and Office Files: Haldeman.

and three targets of the radical-liberal campaign – Goodell, Albert Gore in Tennessee, and Joseph Tydings in Maryland – met defeat at the hands of Buckley, William E. Brock, III, and Glenn Beall, respectively. In House races, the party suffered a net total of nine losses; in a setback that the administration attributed to statewide rather than national issues, Republicans lost eleven governorships. On the crucial question of Vietnam, however, the new Congress was modestly more dovish than the old.[62] Besides, judged in terms of Nixon's own expectations of greater gains, the results were a disappointment and certainly did not resemble the realigning moment that he glorified to aides before the campaign.[63] They demonstrated that the hope that the Social Issue might outweigh the Economic Issue was unrealistic, at least at an economically troubled time.[64] Moreover, administration polling suggested that the campaign failed to disseminate adequately the radical-liberal message, despite its shrillness. An October poll reported that only about a half of respondents were aware of the radical-liberal tag, and that reactions to the campaign reflected general evaluations of Nixon and the Republican Party; it reinforced existing partisan sentiment instead of challenging current allegiances and winning converts.[65] Still, Nixon did not allocate much blame to his strategy's shortcomings, privately complaining about the quality of Republican candidates.[66]

According to Kevin Phillips, the 1970 elections showed that Republicans were making gains only against excessively leftist Democrats. Victory elsewhere demanded not only social conservatism but also a "positive" domestic agenda; Phillips mentioned national health insurance, welfare reform, and aid to needy areas as possible examples.[67] Nixon's "new American revolution" acknowledged such an imperative.[68] But over the next two years this revolution's pursuit failed to transform the Republican Party into what Nixon called "the party of change ... of imagination, of innovation," however.[69] A number of counterrevolutionary impulses were problematic. First, Democrats in control of Congress were often unsupportive. They sometimes favored more liberal

---

[62] Charles DeBenedetti with Charles Chatfield, *An American Ordeal: The Antiwar Movement of the Vietnam Era* (Syracuse, N.Y.: Syracuse University Press, 1990), 293.

[63] Haldeman, *Diaries*, Nov. 4, 1970.

[64] H. R. Haldeman, notes, July 10, 1970, in *Papers of the Nixon White House, part 5: H. R. Haldeman: Notes of White House Meetings, 1969–1973* (Frederick, Md.: University Publications of America, 1989); *Newsweek*, Nov. 16, 24–30; *Time*, Nov. 16, 1970, 14–24.

[65] David R. Derge to H. R. Haldeman, Oct. 13, 1970, box 403, White House Special Files – Staff Member and Office Files: Haldeman.

[66] H. R. Haldeman, notes, Nov. 2, 1970, in *Papers of the Nixon White House*, part 5.

[67] Transcript, Republican Governors Conference, Dec. 14, 1970, box 91, Hartmann Papers.

[68] *NYT*, Jan. 7, 1971, 1; *NYT*, Jan. 24, 1971, sec. 4, 1.

[69] Bill Safire to Alex Butterfield, Jan. 27, 1971, and Lee Huebner, "Color Report on Breakfast for Republican Congressmen – Thursday, January 28, 1971, 8:00 A.M.," box 8, White House Special Files – Staff Member and Office File: POF; Patrick J. Buchanan to Ron Ziegler, Jan. 29, 1971, box 1, White House Special Files – Staff Member and Office Files: Buchanan.

versions of Nixon's initiatives, a response that impeded achievement of those initiatives, and they were reluctant to help improve the Republican Party's poor reputation for reform. Second, congressional Republicans did not in all cases join the reform drive with enthusiasm. Some preferred more ambitious reform than Nixon did, but many were skeptical of the proposals' wisdom. For example, Georgia's Representative Ben Blackburn wrote that the Family Assistance Plan (FAP) to reform welfare "is not only contrary to the best interests of the [people] it purports to help, but is destructive of the philosophy and hence of the success of the Republican party ... and, more importantly, destructive of the very foundations and cornerstones of the American federal system." Blackburn blamed aides for providing Nixon with misleading advice in order to explain the administration's promotion of FAP.[70] Discomfort with the new American revolution was probably yet more acute among many grass-roots Republicans. Buchanan, against the reform agenda, asked, "Can one seriously imagine in 1972 those little old ladies in tennis shoes ringing doorbells in Muncie for 'FAP,' 'FHIP' [National Health Insurance Partnership, an element of the healthcare proposals] and the 'full employment budget'[?]"[71]

Third, Nixon himself – always more interested in foreign policy – did not devote adequate energy to his own agenda's pursuit. The administration failed to create a relationship with Congress of an effectiveness that would maximize its legislative success.[72] Observing the plight of administration proposals for executive reorganization, novelist Allen Drury perceived a weakness, common in his view to much of the administration's domestic policy, that "there is a curious lack of follow-through, a curious inertia that could almost be called disinterest, a curious reluctance, almost, to come to grips with it – to get down to the guts of it – to get into the arena, tear off those nice neat ties, unbutton those nice neat shirts, muss up that nice neat hair and *fight*."[73] A partial explanation for this disengagement is Nixon's uncertainty about the initiatives' electoral promise and even their desirability.[74] Indeed, Nixon chose hyperbolic packaging for his State of the Union "great goals" because he doubted their intrinsic appeal.[75] A fourth obstacle stemmed from institutional conflict. Government reform and revenue sharing met resistance from interest groups and congressional politicians, preferring the existing frameworks that benefited them.[76]

[70] *Human Events*, July 17, 1971, 12.
[71] Patrick J. Buchanan to H. R. Haldeman, January 14, 1971, box 9, White House Special Files – Staff Member and Office Files: POF.
[72] Nigel Bowles, *The White House and Capitol Hill: The Politics of Presidential Persuasion* (Oxford: Clarendon, 1987).
[73] Allen Drury, *Courage and Hesitation: Inside the Nixon Administration* (1971; London: Michael Joseph, 1972), 312.
[74] Haldeman, *Diaries*, May 13 and June 2, 1971.
[75] Safire, *Before the Fall*, 501–504.
[76] Otis L. Graham, Jr., *Toward a Planned Society: From Roosevelt to Nixon* (1976; New York: Oxford University Press, 1977), 209–213; Timothy Conlan, *New Federalism: Intergovernmental Reform from Nixon to Reagan* (Washington, D.C.: Brookings Institution, 1988), 31–64.

Nixon's domestic agenda nevertheless scored some notable successes. The administration won enactment of revenue sharing in a reduced form, together with a series of green initiatives to follow the 1970 creation of the Environmental Protection Agency.[77] Although FAP failed, Congress passed omnibus legislation expanding benefits for the needy elderly, blind, and disabled, and instituted an automatic cost-of-living adjustment to raise Social Security payments in line with inflation, following the implementation of a 20 percent increase. Much of the impetus for this reform emerged within Congress, rather than from the administration, however.[78] Other agenda elements secured less success. Little progress was made toward government reorganization, and the healthcare proposal fell by the wayside. Despite the legislative achievements, in the electoral arena this reform drive did not transform the party's image. In June 1972 aides Patrick Buchanan and Kenneth Khachigian observed that the "countless hours and unrecorded effort selling the bold dynamic 'New American Revolution'" had delivered results that were "not encouraging"; it was thus pointless to emphasize the theme in the campaign.[79]

The determination to achieve economic prosperity, one of the 1971 State of the Union's "six great goals" and probably the most important to the president, led Nixon away from Republican tradition. In early 1971 he remarked to a journalist that he was "now a Keynesian in economics." His budget for fiscal 1972 called for large spending increases, designed to stimulate the economy and described as a "full-employment budget."[80] The embrace of government activism and the emphasis on unemployment instead of inflation were marks of a different approach, even though the change in economic policy at this time involved presentation more than substance, and this policy actually showed evidence of the increasing influence of Milton Friedman's focus on the control of money supply, a focus that sought to repudiate John Maynard Keynes's fiscal paradigm. Phillips's speech analyzing the 1970 elections made clear the electoral dimension of such policy. To win the "emerging Republican majority," Phillips advocated "the type of expansive economics which would put the interests of middle America ahead perhaps of the needs of the board room" – the prioritization of unemployment's reduction rather than inflation's.[81]

Nixon took a bigger step away from a conservative approach to economics in August 1971. Impatient with his policy's lackluster impact on unemployment and inflation, and anxious about an overvalued dollar that imbalanced foreign trade, Nixon introduced wage and price controls, among other measures

[77] J. Brooks Flippen, *Nixon and the Environment* (Albuquerque: University of New Mexico Press, 2000), 1–89.

[78] Julian E. Zelizer, *Taxing America: Wilbur D. Mills, Congress, and the State, 1945–1975* (Cambridge: Cambridge University Press, 1998), 317–346.

[79] Patrick Buchanan and Kenneth Khachigian to H. R. Haldeman, June 18, 1972, box 299, White House Special Files – Staff Member and Office Files: Haldeman.

[80] Allen J. Matusow, *Nixon's Economy: Booms, Busts, Dollars, and Votes* (Lawrence: University Press of Kansas, 1998), 87–104.

[81] Transcript, Republican Governors Conference, Dec. 14, 1970, box 91, Hartmann Papers.

that included the end of the dollar's gold convertibility. In the shorter term, the
economy made improvements so that in 1972 it was not the electoral liability
that had impeded the 1970 campaign. In time, however, it became clear that
controls had failed to undercut inflationary pressures and that the measures
intended to grow the economy had misread its capacity, further fostering inflation instead.[82] Nixon nevertheless viewed the short-term success not as the
creation of a party advantage ripe for electoral exploitation, but as the neutralization of a potential disadvantage. He remained wedded to his conviction
that the economy was a Democratic issue, best avoided by Republicans.[83]

In Nixon's eyes, foreign policy, unlike the economy, was a winning issue.
His pursuit of détente in the Cold War secured a Moscow summit where superpower leaders signed the first treaty limiting strategic arms. More dramatically, Nixon visited China, seeking rapprochement with the People's Republic.
Opposition to Red China was a key conservative concern, and during his early
career Nixon had sought electoral advantage in the so-called loss of China
under Truman. Détente was an effort to stabilize the Cold War and protect national interests, but Nixon thought it presented him with an electoral
advantage, too. After the Moscow visit's announcement, H. R. Haldeman,
the White House chief of staff, noted Nixon's view that "we should really
go to work playing the 'Man of Peace' issue all the time, move all the other
issues to a lower level and really build that one up, because it's our issue and
we have to use it."[84] Similarly, when in the Soviet Union Nixon and Haldeman
talked about "the general political approach that it's not domestic issues that
we should spend our time on, that's their issue, not ours," and the desirability
instead of "[concentrating] on the international, which is where we make the
gains."[85] Polls supported the view.[86]

Nixon's conduct of the Vietnam War developed popular appeal, too, even
though his quest for "peace with honor" incurred a large death toll and
unleashed further havoc on southeast Asia. At first, signs were not good. By
early 1971 public patience that the appeal to the silent majority had created
was running out; there were rumors that Nixon might not seek a second term
because of his lack of progress in Vietnam.[87] During 1971 and 1972, peace
talks were often disappointing, and sometimes so too was the military situation. But the Vietnamization policy reduced the size of the nation's forces there
and the number of U.S. battle deaths. By the middle of 1972 Nixon's promise to
end the nation's involvement in Vietnam was a source of electoral strength.[88]

[82] Matusow, *Nixon's Economy*, 126–255.

[83] Haldeman, *Diaries*, July 6, 1972.

[84] Haldeman, *Diaries*, Oct. 12, 1971.

[85] Haldeman, *Diaries*, May 27, 1972.

[86] William Bundy, *Tangled Web: The Making of Nixon's Foreign Policy, 1968–1974* (New
York: Hill & Wang, 1998), 240–241, 331–332.

[87] Dwight Chapin to Charles W. Colson, March 8, 1971, box 46, White House Subject Files –
Central Files (Confidential Files).

[88] Lou Harris, "Nixon Ahead of Rival on 15 of 16 Key Issues," July 17, 1972, box 399, White
House Special Files – Staff Member and Office Files: Haldeman.

Foreign policy was especially significant in accounting for Nixon's success within middle America. One of middle America's most important elements was organized labor, the party's traditional foe. A signal of foreign policy's power in challenging this hostility was a May 1970 demonstration, dominated by construction workers, in New York City to show opposition to antiwar activists, soon following a Washington rally against the administration's Cambodia "incursion" and the National Guard's shooting of protesters at Kent State University. Aide Stephen Bull wrote that "this display of emotional activity from the 'hard hats' provides an opportunity, if under the proper leadership, to forge a new alliance and perhaps result in the emergence of a 'new right.'"[89] The administration was already winning support from George Meany, the AFL–CIO president. Meany spoke in favor of the administration's policies on Vietnam and defense, and the organization's executive issued statements similarly supportive of its foreign policy. Underpinning this support was Meany's disaffection with what he saw as the Democrats' leftward drift, which he interpreted as hostile to labor's interests.[90] His friendliness to the administration thus involved at least partly a strategy to reassert his organization's influence within the Democratic Party.[91] Nixon believed that the Vietnam War and domestic turbulence deepened links between workers and Republican politics. He told aides, as one noted, "that the country is going through a moral crisis, 'a crisis of character' and that the strength of the nation will not be found in its leader class now, but with its working men and that the character of the country was changing."[92] Some union leaders resisted the strategy by stressing New Deal liberalism's enduring importance. "If they all get swept up in something emotional like a lot of student bombings, workers are going to work against their economic interest," Bill Dodds of the liberal United Auto Workers commented. "But there is no reason why we cannot articulate that interest."[93] Meany himself remained critical of the GOP in this regard.

The administration's labor strategy was not its only special appeal to middle Americans, and foreign policy was not the only front of attack. The creation of an office of public liaison at the White House institutionalized outreach to many groups, especially segments of middle America.[94] In addition to labor, Catholic Americans were notable among these groups. Nixon cultivated members of the Catholic hierarchy and sought Catholic votes through aid to parochial schools and opposition to abortion.[95] A number of white

[89] Stephen Bull to Charles W. Colson, May 22, 1970, box 26, White House Special Files – Staff Member and Office Files: Colson.

[90] Charles W. Colson to H. R. Haldeman, box 61, White House Special Files – Staff Member and Office Files: Haldeman.

[91] *WP* clipping, Aug. 31, 1970, box 77, White House Special Files – Staff Member and Office Files: Colson.

[92] Charles W. Colson for file, July 26, 1971, box 14, White House Special Files – Staff Member and Office Files: Colson.

[93] *NYT*, Sept. 7, 1970, 1, 12.

[94] Hult and Wolcott, *Empowering the White House*, 78–90.

[95] Mason, *Richard Nixon*, 151–155.

ethnic groups, too, won special attention, part of a contemporary rediscovery of ethnicity's enduring salience in American society. Nixon saw Americans of Italian and eastern European descent as key targets.[96] This outreach tended to involve symbolism rather than substance, including appointments and attention to group identity.[97] These often overlapping groups of middle America – labor members, Catholics, and ethnic Americans – were all key parts of the coalition assembled by Franklin Roosevelt in the 1930s, usually hostile rather than friendly to the Republican Party. Nixon's search for a realignment was trying to unravel that coalition.

Women were not the similar beneficiaries of electorally inspired outreach. They remained significant within the ranks of grassroots activism, but their lack of formal party influence persisted. Few had positions of power. At a National Republican Congressional Committee conference for candidates in 1972, spouses discovered that their preferred role did not challenge traditionalist expectations. "A wife who seems overly ambitious is detrimental to her candidate-husband," was one piece of advice.[98] Some Republicans recognized that change was overdue, however. At a 1969 National Federation of Republican Women meeting, Senator Robert W. Packwood of Oregon challenged his audience to seize power; a dominant concern of the meeting was the need for women to move on from a concentration on party activism toward an increase in their numbers in elected office.[99] Second-wave feminism, which emerged during the 1960s, denounced the secondary status of women in society and politics. The Nixon administration's response to the mainstream feminist agenda was lukewarm at best. The climate of increased support for women's rights created some anxiety at the White House that there might be punishment at the polls for neglect, but this anxiety did little more than to secure Nixon's unenthusiastic endorsement of the Equal Rights Amendment (ERA), passed by Congress in 1972.[100]

Republican feminists won more influence in the wider party. Those who joined the multipartisan National Women's Political Caucus, founded in 1971, successfully promoted the 1972 platform's inclusion of some key concerns, such as support for ERA's immediate ratification and a proposal for daycare provision opposed by Nixon. The national convention also adopted a new rule that state parties should actively seek equal representation of men and women in their convention delegation and amended the party's antidiscrimination statement to include age and sex. The changes stemmed from the work of a commitment established by the 1968 convention to tackle the delegate body's unrepresentative nature – a less ambitious version of the McGovern-Fraser

[96] Richard Nixon to John Ehrlichman, Nov. 30, 1970, box 2, White House Special Files – Staff Member and Office Files: PPF.

[97] Mason, *Richard Nixon*, 98–99, 168–169, 188.

[98] "Wives' Manual" (Washington, D.C.: National Republican Congressional Committee, n.d. [1972]).

[99] *Republican Congressional Committee Newsletter*, Sept. 29, 1969, box 55, Robert Taft Papers.

[100] Kotlowski, *Nixon's Civil Rights*, 222–258.

commission that brought major change to the Democratic Party's system of presidential nomination. Just as worries about the loss of women's support pushed the administration toward a limited acceptance of gender equality, Republican feminists comparably claimed that a more inclusive party was an electoral necessity.[101] In advocating "Emergent Responsible Feminism," Rita Hauser – a former campaign aide and U.S. representative to the United Nations Commission on Human Rights – warned Nixon, "Not to reach out for [the New Woman] would, truly, be 'missing the boat' in 1972."[102]

But the search for votes also led away from women's rights, which social conservatism did not easily accommodate, as Nixon's opposition to daycare signaled. Important, too, to many feminists were abortion rights, growing in political salience and the subject of contentious battles in state legislatures and the courts. The desire to win Catholic support led Nixon to voice guarded opposition to abortion reform. He emphasized that abortion was a state, not federal, concern. When in 1973 the Supreme Court handed down its landmark decision of *Roe v. Wade*, which announced constitutional protection for abortion rights, Nixon withheld any comment.[103] But his opposition was already clear by 1972, and it reflected electoral priorities. In response to criticism from Hauser about the administration's position on abortion, Buchanan retorted that if Nixon modified it, "he will cost himself Catholic support and gain what, [leading feminist] Betty Friedan?"[104] Moreover, the masculine, rather than feminine, dimension of Nixon's electoral enterprise was significant. Notably, the rationale of his search for labor and blue-collar support celebrated traditional notions of masculinity – workers "are men, not softies," Nixon told aides – and conceptualized workers as male, in common with much of the contemporary debate about middle America's problems.[105] The Nixon strategy thus went beyond an ostensible neutrality to display a lack of sympathy for contemporary feminism, and its social conservatism loomed with probable hostility to its claims.

The Democrats' nomination of George McGovern for the presidency encouraged Nixon to adopt an electoral strategy of opposition, rather than any effort to achieve an affirmative mobilization in support of his new Republican agenda of reform-minded initiatives. The Nixon campaign argued that the nature of McGovern's liberalism placed him outside his own party's mainstream, that this Democrat therefore did not deserve the votes of Democratic supporters.

---

[101] Rymph, *Republican Women*, 188–211.

[102] Rita Hauser to Richard Nixon, April 12, 1971, box 10, White House Special Files – Staff Member and Office Files: Colson.

[103] Tanya Melich, *The Republican War Against Women: An Insider's Report From Behind the Lines*, updated ed. (New York: Bantam, 1998), 16–37; Kotlowski, *Nixon's Civil Rights*, 250–252.

[104] Patrick J. Buchanan to Rita Hauser, Jan. 10, 1972, box 2, White House Special Files – Staff Member and Office Files: Buchanan.

[105] Jefferson Cowie, "Nixon's Class Struggle: Romancing the New Right Worker, 1969–1973," *Labor History* 43 (2002), 257–264.

McGovern was the choice of a changing, divided Democratic Party. The disappointing progress of Great Society programs, the persistence of racially connected socioeconomic inequalities, the foreign-policy questions raised by American involvement in Vietnam, and the counterculture's challenge to social norms all encouraged some Democrats to interpret their liberal commitments in ways that worried others, such as Scammon and Wattenberg, who saw their leftward drift as electorally dangerous. Opposition to the Vietnam War inspired McGovern's candidacy; speedy withdrawal was a key position. McGovern spoke sympathetically about, if not directly supportive of, the liberalization of marijuana and abortion laws, and he supported a guaranteed income more generous than FAP's formula.[106] His candidacy was thus decisively more liberal than Hubert Humphrey's in 1968; although his ideas owed more to New Deal liberalism than to leftward-leaning "New Politics" liberalism, the influence of the latter was significant enough to assist the Nixon campaign in characterizing him as a radical.[107]

McGovern's victory was assisted by an institutional transformation that the Democratic Party was undergoing. Sparked by concerns that the 1968 convention had failed to represent party sentiment effectively, a commission, chaired first by McGovern and later by Donald Fraser, revised its nomination process. The new rules moved the power of selection away from party leaders and toward primary voters and called for affirmative steps to achieve better representation of minority members, young people, and women. By boosting activists' influence at the leaders' expense, this democratizing effort seemed to help candidates who took a less compromising approach to party ideals.

Liberalization's advocates denied any surrender of their party's electoral advantage. In *Changing Sources of Power* Fred Dutton, who acted as an adviser to McGovern, argued that a liberal middle class, members of minority groups, and the poor represented a winning coalition. During the 1970s, according to Dutton, young Americans' votes would move the political agenda in a more radical direction.[108] As things stood in 1972, about a third of Democratic primary voters supported McGovern, about a third preferred the more traditional formulation of New Deal liberalism advocated by his rivals Humphrey and Senator Henry "Scoop" Jackson of Washington, and the final third chose Wallace.[109] The confidence in youth's influence was not the only belief that informed the McGovern candidacy in ways that at first made such a challenge to Nixon seem plausible and even promising. McGovern

---

[106] Herbert S. Parmet, *The Democrats: The Years after FDR* (1976; New York: Oxford University Press, 1977), 300–304.

[107] Bruce Miroff, *The Liberals' Moment: The McGovern Insurgency and the Identity Crisis of the Democratic Party* (Lawrence: University Press of Kansas, 2007), 119–141.

[108] Frederick G. Dutton, *Changing Sources of Power: American Politics in the 1970s* (New York: McGraw-Hill, 1971), 15–56.

[109] Walter Dean Burnham, "American Politics in the 1970's: Beyond Party?" in William Nisbet Chambers and Burnham, eds., *The American Party Systems: Stages of Political Development*, 2nd ed. (New York: Oxford University Press, 1975), 343.

supporters noted that through 1971 and early 1972 Nixon was an unpopular incumbent, likely again to face a third-party challenge from Wallace. The public mood of alienation was one that McGovern could answer successfully, and despite party divisions, they expected unity in the presidential campaign against Nixon. Most of all, they believed that the Democrats remained the nation's majority party.[110]

McGovern's potential weaknesses as a candidate had encouraged the White House to take surreptitious steps to damage Edward Kennedy and Edmund Muskie, whose candidacies Nixon feared. While the 1970 campaign included attempts to brand their views as extreme, "dirty tricks" later sought to undermine them. The fondness for dirty tricks and political intelligence led to the break-in in June 1972 at the Democratic National Committee headquarters, housed in Washington's Watergate complex, which in time led to the scandal that ended the Nixon presidency. In the shorter term, the break-in did very little damage to the reelection campaign. A central strand of that campaign was the promotion of McGovern's weaknesses. Buchanan, worried about his potential appeal as the defender of ordinary Americans' interests, advised Nixon that the campaign should "portray McGovern as a candidate of the Elite, 'Professor McGovern,' the leader of the party of the PHds. [sic] and limousine liberals, whose elitist shock troops took over the party of the people, the 'noise-makers' and the 'exotic,' the tiny minority who are imposing an asinine social policy of bussing on a country, eighty-five percent of whose people do not want bussing."[111]

A central element of the Nixon campaign was Democrats for Nixon, under John Connally, the former Texas governor who joined the administration in late 1970 as treasury secretary. The organization secured endorsements from leading Democrats to legitimize Democratic voters' support for Nixon, and its speakers attacked McGovern as outside the party's traditions. Facilitating these efforts was the unwillingness of many Democratic congressional candidates to associate themselves with McGovern's cause. In turn, Nixon did not want to oppose Democratic incumbents friendly to him, especially over foreign policy.[112] He was even willing to lend them some support, inviting a number of southern Democrats to the White House for photographs with the president.[113] Not only did Nixon withhold support from the Republican challengers to Senators James Eastland of Mississippi and John McClellan of Arkansas, but he also asked his daughter, Tricia Nixon Cox, to mention her support for the Democratic incumbents on a visit to the South.[114] Nixon did not seek to

[110] Miroff, *Liberals' Moment*, 49–52.

[111] Patrick J. Buchanan to Richard Nixon, July 12, 1972, box 117, White House Special Files – Staff Member and Office Files: Haldeman.

[112] *WP*, March 21, 1973, A6; Dent, *Prodigal South*, 223; Raymond Price to file, Nov. 5, 1971, box 119, White House Special Files – Staff Member and Office Files: PPF.

[113] John E. Niedecker to file, Sept. 12, 14, 18, 19, and 21, 1972, box 89, White House Special Files – Staff Member and Office Files: POF.

[114] Richard Nixon, *RN: The Memoirs of Richard Nixon* (New York: Grosset & Dunlap, 1978), 669; Haldeman, *Diaries*, Sept. 26, 1972.

convert disaffected Democrats into Republicans, however; a Democrat's support was a more powerful symbol than that of a new Republican, even if this was unhelpful to the cause of the party at large.

"The real issues of the election are the ones like patriotism, morality, religion – not the material issues," Nixon told aides. "If the issues were prices and taxes, they'd be for McGovern."[115] This conceptualization of the contest suggested that Nixon had not traveled at all far from his early insight that debate about economic issues inescapably worked to the Democrats' advantage. It revealed the shortcomings of Nixon's engagement with the minority problem and his lack of a larger ambition beyond a landslide reelection. Critical of the strategy, Douglas Hallett, a young aide, wrote that "our present approach – because it is based on the idea that McGovern is some kind of radical freak and not representative of the Democratic Party – does not allow us to set ourselves apart from the past Democratic failures and claim that we are offering new kinds of solutions to national problems – and thus it bodes for us to win this election on negative grounds with no necessary, or even likely, permanent cross-over into a new Republican majority."[116] Nixon understood the larger demands of a majority-building project, but he prioritized the maximization of his own vote, which demanded a personally concentrated rather than party-oriented campaign. The fragility of the new American revolution's achievements made a focus on Nixon's reinvention of the Republican Party implausible in any case.

The positive issue that won support for Nixon was foreign policy. Robert Teeter, his pollster, called Vietnam "truely [sic] the gut issue in the campaign"; according to his analysis, détente was second to Vietnam in importance.[117] McGovern's denunciation of the war and his call for swift withdrawal failed to match the popularity of Nixon's insistence on the nobility of the nation's mission and his Vietnamization of the fighting. The campaign attacked the McGovern position in sharp terms. Calling McGovern a "spokesman for the enemy," Secretary of Defense Melvin Laird said that his proposals amounted to "unconditional surrender."[118] Nixon told voters on election eve that they faced a choice between "peace with honor" and "peace with surrender," between "a strong America" and "a weak America."[119]

Nixon won his landslide. He secured 60.7 percent of the vote, including 42 percent of self-identified Democratic supporters and 66 percent of independent voters.[120] The South and middle America were important elements

---

[115] Raymond Price, *With Nixon* (New York: Viking, 1977), 122.

[116] Douglas Hallett to Charles Colson, Aug. 10, 1972, box 99, White House Special Files – Staff Member and Office Files: Colson.

[117] Robert Teeter to H. R. Haldeman, Aug. 15, 1972, box 1, Teeter Papers; Frederick T. Steeper and Robert M. Teeter, "Comment on 'A Majority Party in Disarray,'" *APSR* 70 (1976), 806–813.

[118] DeBenedetti with Chatfield, *American Ordeal*, 341.

[119] Richard Nixon, *Public Papers of the Presidents of the United States: Richard Nixon*, vol. 4: *1972* (Washington, D.C.: U.S. Government Printing Office, 1974), 1138–1139.

[120] Arthur H. Miller, Warren E. Miller, Alden S. Raine, and Thad A. Brown, "A Majority Party in Disarray: Policy Polarization in the 1972 Election," *APSR* 70 (1976), 768.

of this landslide. Nixon won 57 percent of voters in union households, 60 percent of Catholic voters, 61 percent of blue-collar voters, and 66 percent of the two-party presidential vote in the South.[121] The Nixon majority's size was not reflected in congressional results. Of 377 Nixon-supporting districts, 188 elected a Republican to the House and 189, a Democrat.[122] Republicans made a net gain of just twelve in the House and suffered a net loss of two in the Senate. There were also state-level losses, which Nixon interpreted as a demonstration of the party's weakness.[123]

Nevertheless, the prospect of a Republican House did not seem entirely lost. Rumors suggested that enough House Democrats were ready to change party in order to throw organization to the Republicans; Nixon mulled such conversions as the route to a congressional majority.[124] Minority leader Gerald Ford had been looking for such potential converts in what he called "operation switch over."[125] This interest among conservative Democrats in changing party allegiance stemmed from their concern that liberals' reform plans might undercut their seniority-based influence.[126] But optimism outstripped reality in fueling the rumors. The number of likely converts was not great enough to change House organization to the Republican Party, thus greatly reducing legislators' motivation to switch.[127]

"Operation Switch Over" was also the name of a Tallahassee, Florida, event that Agnew attended in December 1972, designed to welcome former Democratic activists who were joining the Republican Party. The GOP was the party of "individual rights," Agnew told them, a commitment that leading Democrats increasingly abandoned, and a party offering such activists a voice when their old party excluded them.[128] Among leading Democrats, the number of converts was small. Without any prospect of advancement within the Democratic Party, John Connally joined the Republicans in May 1973.[129] A former speaker of the Texas House was a rare politician who followed suit.[130]

[121] Miller and Traugott, *American National Election Studies Data Sourcebook*, 316; Harold W. Stanley and Richard G. Niemi, *Vital Statistics on American Politics* (Washington, D.C.: CQ Press, 1988), 77.

[122] Burnham, "American Politics," 320–321.

[123] Haldeman, *Diaries*, Nov. 13, 1972.

[124] Hodgson, *World Turned Right Side Up*, 123–127; William A. Rusher, *The Rise of the Right* (New York: William Morrow, 1984), 251; Haldeman, *Diaries*, Dec. 2, 1972.

[125] H. R. Haldeman to file, May 5, 1971, box 85, White House Special Files – Staff Member and Office Files: POF; Haldeman, *Diaries*, July 21, 1972.

[126] Julian E. Zelizer, *On Capitol Hill: The Struggle to Reform Congress and Its Consequences, 1948–2000* (Cambridge: Cambridge University Press, 2004), 137.

[127] James Reichley, interview with Bud Shuster, Oct. 6, 1977, box 2, Reichley Interviews; Reichley, interview with William Timmons, Nov. 29, 1977, box 1, Reichley Interviews; Reichley, interview with Joe Waggoner, Feb. 8, 1978, box 2, Reichley Interviews; Richard K. Cook to Timmons, box 17, White House Special Files – Staff Member and Office Files: POF.

[128] Spiro T. Agnew, speech, Dec. 12, 1972, box 10, subseries 7, series III, Agnew Papers.

[129] James Reston, Jr., *The Lone Star: The Life of John Connally* (New York: Harper & Row, 1989), 453–454.

[130] *WP*, May 15, 1973, A4.

The state where conversion was most promising was perhaps Virginia, where Mills Godwin, its governor between 1966 and 1970, agreed to seek the Republican nomination for a return to that office.[131] Successful in doing so, Godwin won the 1973 gubernatorial election. In developing a successful appeal to dissident Democrats, the party repelled some of its leading liberals. John Lindsay, the New York mayor, became a Democrat in August 1971 and the following year launched a brief effort to win his new party's presidential nomination. Representative Ogden R. Reid, whose House district was in New York City's affluent Westchester County suburbs, a former *New York Herald Tribune* editor-publisher, also switched. Though personal ambition precipitated Reid's move as well as Lindsay's, that judgment reflected a recognition that liberal Republicans of the "eastern establishment" were increasingly no longer at home in their party, which was developing a southern, western, and anti-establishment orientation instead.[132]

After his landslide, Nixon took steps to consolidate the new majority. New-majority credentials were an important factor in second-term appointments – one part of much larger, if hazily formed, plans to make this coalition permanent.[133] Their focus was more party-oriented than before; Nixon wanted to revitalize the party as a vehicle for the new majority.[134] There was no time, however, to develop and implement these plans. It was not long before the Watergate scandal overwhelmed his administration. Nixon resigned in August 1974, and former House minority leader Gerald R. Ford replaced him as president; in December 1973 Ford had been sworn in as vice president after Agnew's resignation, the result of a Maryland kickbacks scandal. Scandal drove the party toward decline, rather than the new majority's consolidation. The 1974 midterms saw the party incur further losses in a year when fewer than two in five Americans took part in House elections, a similar proportion to 1942's wartime contest and an indicator of a national frustration with politics.[135] In late 1974, pollster Robert Teeter told the national committee that Republican identification stood at just 19 percent, commenting that if present trends continued, the party would be "extinct" within two or three decades.[136]

[131] Ed DeBolt and Jim Galbraith to George H. W. Bush, Feb. 22, 1973, box 20, White House Special Files – Staff Member and Office Files: POF; Peter Flanigan to Richard Nixon, Feb. 26, 1973, box 47, White House Special Files – Central Files (Confidential Files).

[132] Theodore H. White, *The Making of the President 1972* (New York: Bantam, 1973), 93–113; *NYT*, March 22, 1972, 1, 34.

[133] H. R. Haldeman, memo, Nov. 12, 1972, box 112, White House Special Files – Staff Member and Office Files: Haldeman; Gerald S. Strober and Deborah H. Strober, *Nixon: An Oral History of His Presidency* (New York: HarperCollins, 1994), 271; Patrick J. Buchanan, *The New Majority: President Nixon at Mid-passage* (no place of publication [Philadelphia?]: Girard Bank, 1973), 77.

[134] Nixon, *RN*, 769.

[135] Burnham, "American Politics," 357.

[136] Gwen Anderson to Robert T. Hartmann, Dec. 9, 1974, box 3, Calkins Files.

Through his search for a new majority, Nixon infuriated many on the Right. In August 1971, a group of leading conservatives announced their dissatisfaction with the administration's record in a *National Review* article, and by year's end this dissatisfaction involved a challenge to Nixon's renomination. The group, known as the "Manhattan Twelve," included the magazine's William F. Buckley, Jr., and William A. Rusher; J. Daniel Mahoney, chair of the New York Conservative Party; Jeffrey Bell and John L. Jones of the American Conservative Union (ACU); and Randal C. Teague of Young Americans for Freedom. Representing an extensive cross section of the conservative movement, the Twelve wanted change across a broad range of administration policies.[137] Patrick Buchanan determined that Nixon's foreign policy of détente with the Soviet Union and of negotiations with China was especially responsible for this conservative elite's alienation, and that a commitment to high defense spending might cause the group to withdraw its interest in a nomination challenge.[138] There was no compromise, however, and the Twelve found a candidate in ACU chair John Ashbrook, a House member from Ohio. On the announcement of his candidacy, Ashbrook made conservative concerns clear when he said he would drop his candidacy in return for a confirmation of Agnew's renomination as vice president, an indication that welfare reform was no longer an administration priority, an increase in defense spending, and an announcement that Nixon would visit Taiwan after Beijing.[139] Nixon needed to make no concessions to shrug off Ashbrook's challenge easily; Ashbrook won just 7.9 percent of the vote in the primaries he actively contested.[140]

Gerald Ford faced much more significant opposition from conservatives. Less skilled in presidential politics than his predecessor, Ford was also unfortunate in that conservatism experienced fresh growth during his administration. Richard A. Viguerie, a leading organizer of and fundraiser for what became known as the New Right, attributed this movement's emergence to Ford's vice-presidential nomination of Nelson A. Rockefeller, whose earlier resistance to the Goldwater movement still left him as anathema to conservatives, even though he was no longer a model of liberal Republicanism.[141] Conservative opponents to Ford believed that, even as the Republican Party plummeted to new depths of popular disapproval, conservatism was gaining strength. For example, a poll taken on the eve of the 1974 midterm elections, which were

[137] Lee Edwards, *The Conservative Revolution: The Movement That Remade America* (New York: Free Press, 1999), 168–172.

[138] Patrick J. Buchanan to John Mitchell and H. R. Haldeman, Dec. 15, 1971, box 3, White House Special Files – Staff Member and Office Files: Buchanan.

[139] *NYT*, Dec. 30, 1971, 1, 9.

[140] Ernest R. May and Janet Fraser, eds., *Campaign '72: The Managers Speak* (Cambridge, Mass.: Harvard University Press, 1973), 296–297.

[141] Paul Gottfried, *The Conservative Movement*, rev. ed. (New York: Twayne, 1993), 98–99; Michael Barone, *Our Country: The Shaping of America from Roosevelt to Reagan* (New York: Free Press, 1990), 531–532.

disastrous for the party, suggested that more than half of Americans either called themselves a conservative or held mostly conservative views. This conservatism was not cohesive, however. The poll classified about three in five as classic liberals and the remainder as populist conservatives, an indication of their significantly different ideas about the economy.[142] Still, to conservatives, the lesson seemed simple. Nixon's quest for a new majority was a failure because it was a wrongheaded underestimation of conservatism's new strength.

William A. Rusher was among those confident in conservatism's electoral promise. Ford's nomination of Rockefeller encouraged Rusher to commandeer the rhetoric of the new majority for different purposes. Seeing it as a sign of the administration's return to a pre-Goldwater strategy that "[tried] to prize from the Democrats a handful of their moderate liberals, to add to the GOP's economic conservatives," Rusher wrote *The Making of the New Majority Party*, published in June 1975. The route to a majority that Rusher advocated involved a union of economic conservatives (already Republican supporters) and social conservatives (often still Democratic supporters). Conflicts between the two groups' concerns did not seem problematic to Rusher, who noted that the New Deal coalition had successfully brought together people with interests more disparate yet. In Rusher's eyes, however, the GOP seemed an unpromising vehicle for this goal's realization because its leaders "seemed gripped by paralysis at the prospect of reaching out to the formerly Democratic social conservatives," as he later put it, as a result of party liberals' influence. The exception was Ronald Reagan, whose gubernatorial tenure in California had ended in early 1975. Rusher therefore preferred the creation of a new party, which would replace the Grand Old Party.[143]

Rusher's book reflected as well as fostered some interest among conservatives in a new party; thirty-three House Republicans in March declined to sign a party pledge of loyalty, devised to undercut the separatist momentum.[144] Most did not agree with the wisdom of separatism, however, and Rusher saw Reagan's refusal to lead any such initiative as a crucial development.[145] At a February meeting of conservatives, where the idea of a new party was under discussion, Reagan asked, "Is it a third party we need, or is it a new and revitalized second party, raising a banner of no pale pastels, but bold colors which make it unmistakably clear where we stand on all of the issues troubling the people?"[146] His preference for the latter was a mature, pragmatic acceptance of the enormous obstacles to the creation of a new party. As the American Independent Party, Rusher's group managed to secure a ballot presence in many states in 1976, but, to his regret, the presidential candidate was Lester Maddox, the former Georgia governor, a southern Democrat notorious for his

---

[142] *Time*, Nov. 11, 1974, 17, 19.
[143] Rusher, *Rise of the Right*, 263–274 (quotations, 264, 268); William A. Rusher, *The Making of the New Majority Party* (New York: Sheed and Ward, 1975).
[144] *WP*, March 14, 1975, A9.
[145] Rusher, *Rise of the Right*, 269–288.
[146] *New Guard*, April 1975, box 21, Waldron Files.

segregationism and entirely unacceptable to some of its state organizations, which would not list him as their candidate.[147]

Despite the failure of the Rusher effort, Ford did encounter a serious conservative assault when Reagan challenged him for the party's 1976 nomination. Reagan's stress on an antigovernment agenda did not strengthen his candidacy, however, because Ford managed to exploit concerns among primary voters about the programmatic implications of such an emphasis. A proposal to transfer funding responsibility for a variety of programs to the states and localities met with alarm in New Hampshire, for example, as a threat to its regime of no income tax. In Florida, concerns about Reagan's plans for Social Security assisted Ford's victory there. Reagan enjoyed more success in developing a critique of deténte. "All I can see is what other nations the world over see: collapse of the American will and the retreat of American power," he said.[148] Opposition to the administration's rumored willingness to give up sovereignty of the Panama Canal Zone in negotiations about its future proved to be a crowd-pleasing example of such purported weakness. Reagan also spoke of his social conservatism, offering denunciations of permissiveness, abortion rights, and gun control, an emphasis that helped him to energize activists. Watching this activist energy, a White House aide noted that the Ford campaign was "in real danger of being out-organized by a small number of highly motivated *right wing nuts*."[149] The Reagan challenge was powerful enough that Ford's nomination remained in some doubt when delegates arrived in Kansas City for the national convention. Another sign of its power was the platform's inclusion of a plank on "morality in foreign policy," essentially a statement of Reagan's views and a rebuke to deténte.[150]

The Reagan challenge sapped the Ford administration's energies and publicized dissatisfactions with the president's record, thus impeding Ford's effort to win election in his own right. As a southern moderate and therefore no George McGovern, his Democratic opponent, Jimmy Carter, a former governor of Georgia, made it difficult for Ford to replicate Nixon's new majority. But Ford made a good campaign against Carter, who emphasized his outsider status, an appealing feature after Watergate. At the start of the campaign, Robert Teeter's analysis of opinion on Carter found that a majority of voters considered his ideas closer to theirs than Ford's were; voters saw Carter as mildly liberal on economic issues while mildly conservative on foreign policy, whereas they saw Ford as somewhat conservative on economic issues while somewhat liberal on matters of national security and what Teeter called "Traditional American Values." The campaign shifted these perceptions. According to Teeter's studies, by the end of the campaign voters viewed

[147] Rusher, *Rise of the Right*, 275–289.
[148] Jules Witcover, *Marathon: The Pursuit of the Presidency, 1972–1976* (New York: Signet, 1978), 398.
[149] Memo, unsigned, n.d., box 25, Jones Files.
[150] Witcover, *Marathon*, 485–486.

Ford edging toward the center of opinion and Carter moving away.[151] Ford lost to Carter, but only narrowly.

Although the Ford defeat, compounded by other disappointing results and woeful figures of party identification, encouraged another bout of Republican gloom about the party's future, attentive Democrats realized their party's traditional coalition was on shaky ground. Although Ford only won Virginia in the South, even native-son Carter was unable to secure a majority among white southerners, relying on African Americans for his margin of victory. Blue-collar urban Catholics – some of the middle Americans – did not turn out to vote for Ford in as great a number as they did for Nixon, but neither did they return overwhelmingly to the Democratic Party. Patrick H. Caddell, Carter's pollster, soon predicted a tough reelection fight for the victor. Traditional Democratic voters were economic liberals but social conservatives; however, there were new, younger Democratic voters who were not only socially liberal but also economically conservative. It was not at all easy to hold together this changing coalition.[152]

The Watergate scandal helped to check the Republican tide of the 1970s.[153] It fatally injured Nixon's efforts to consolidate his new majority during the second term, as did the fact that his replacement Gerald Ford did not share the same set of political concerns or a similar obsession with the detail of electoral politics. The scandal encouraged a decline, rather than any increase, in Republican identification among voters. It also fostered suspicions of government and the political process, which doubts about the Johnson and Nixon administrations' management of the Vietnam War had already encouraged. Jimmy Carter was the obvious beneficiary of a public desire for a different kind of politician, one more honest and open, as well as one untainted by Watergate. But as president Carter would become a victim of cynicism about politics, too, and the growth in antigovernment sentiment was a natural development for Republican exploitation during the late 1970s.

The travails of the Republican Party encouraged some to conclude that there was not a realignment going on during the 1970s, but a "dealignment." Fewer Americans felt a sense of attachment to either of the parties (though among those who did, more still preferred the Democratic Party), and more identified as a political independent instead.[154] Seen in earlier analyses as a

---

[151] Martin Schram, *Running for President 1976: The Carter Campaign* (New York: Stein & Day, 1977), 269–270, 367.

[152] Everett Carll Ladd, "The Shifting Party Coalitions – from the 1930s to the 1970s," in Seymour Martin Lipset, ed., *Party Coalitions in the 1980s* (San Francisco: Institute for Contemporary Studies, 1981), 135–146; Gillon, *Democrats' Dilemma*, 178–179.

[153] Kevin P. Phillips, *Post-Conservative America: People, Politics and Ideology in a Time of Crisis* (1982; New York: Vintage, 1983).

[154] In 1964 three in four Americans identified with a political party; in 1976 the proportion was 63 percent. Helmut Norpoth and Jerrold G. Rusk, "Partisan Dealignment in the American Electorate: Itemizing the Deductions since 1964," *APSR* 76 (1982), 522–537.

sign of limited interest in and knowledge of politics, independence was often now a sign of political sophistication, the choice of many people who knew a great deal about and paid close attention to politics, preferring to remain aloof from the parties in considering issues and evaluating candidates. A related trend was the shift from party- to candidate-centered campaigns. Nixon's 1972 reelection effort was the most uncompromising incarnation of candidate-centered politics, but it was by no means alone; over time congressional as well as presidential candidates increasingly downplayed party in campaigns. The party-oriented nature of the Republican quest for majority status therefore seemed increasingly obsolete, even as it moved to the very center of Republican thinking during the Nixon years. Indeed, a persuasive interpretation of political history viewed the twentieth century as the long decay of party, interrupted only by the surge of Democratic enthusiasm that accompanied the New Deal.[155] These trends nevertheless did not seem to absolve Republican leaders from responsibility for the party's decline. Political scientist Everett Carll Ladd called the GOP "half a party" and attributed the problem largely to the tendency toward increasing conservatism within the party, an ideological journey that left it decreasingly well equipped to communicate with ordinary voters who were generally more centrist.[156]

Republicans faulted Nixon for his emphasis on presidential fortunes to the exclusion of those of the party. The 1972 campaign saw a zenith of institutional and thematic separation between the presidential candidate and the party at large, because of Nixon's concern about Republican minority status and because of his desire to depict McGovern as a candidate outside the Democratic mainstream. But other elements of Nixon's party leadership show deep interest in its future. The belief in the possibility of a realignment encouraged Nixon to undertake a midterm campaign designed to boost the party's strength and later, once the goal was not in conflict with his personal desire to secure a reelection landslide, to look for party converts among conservative Democrats.[157] While many Republicans blamed Nixon for his lack of electoral coattails, Nixon declared many candidates' defeat the product of the party's own shortcomings.[158] John Connally told Nixon that the electorate favored the division of power between the parties, a view supported by some polling that reported many in favor of separated control for Congress and the White House.[159] Determined to avoid similar president–party separation, Gerald Ford instead emulated it.[160] Reform of campaign finance, which Congress

[155] Walter Dean Burnham, *Critical Elections and the Mainsprings of American Politics* (New York: Norton, 1970); Silbey, *American Political Nation*.
[156] Everett Carll Ladd, *Where Have All the Voters Gone? The Fracturing of America's Political Parties*, 2nd ed. (New York: Norton, 1982), 18–25 (quotation, xxvi).
[157] Mason, "'I Was Going To Build'"; Galvin, *Presidential Party Building*, 70–98.
[158] Haldeman, *Diaries*, Nov. 13, 1972.
[159] Haldeman, *Diaries*, Nov. 17, 1972; Harris press release, Jan. 25, 1972, box 17, White House Subject Files – Staff Meeting and Office Files: Colson.
[160] *First Monday*, April 1975, box 24, Hartmann Files.

enacted in response to Nixon's excesses, in some respects encouraged the revitalization of parties, but Ford aides concluded that the law's stringent reporting requirements made a separate committee advisable.[161] Ford's need to win the votes of independents and Democratic supporters meant that his campaign plan instructed him not to work for Republican candidates.[162] His experience as president therefore suggested that a candidate-centered approach to campaigning was difficult to escape. Far from the achievement of a Republican realignment, the Nixon and Ford years instead ended with the suspicion that such a goal was now entirely beyond reach.

[161] Jack Calkins and Gwen Anderson to Gerald R. Ford, April 28, 1975, box 18, Cheney Files; Fred Slight to Jerry Jones, April 2, 1975, box 18, Cheney Files.
[162] Campaign plan, unsigned, n.d., box 1, Downton Files.

8

"You Are Witnessing the Great Realignment": 1977–1989

The Republican Party's comeback from its slump of the mid-1970s, a time yet again of predictions about its demise, was swift and resounding. In fall 1977 the Gallup poll organization reported its lowest-ever figure for voter identification with the party: only one in five, against almost one in two for the Democrats.[1] But the results of the 1980 elections encouraged the belief that the GOP was finding an enduring majority at last, that Americans were decisively turning away from New Deal liberalism. Ronald Reagan won 51 percent of the popular vote against President Jimmy Carter's 41 percent share; independent John Anderson, a moderate Republican disillusioned with the party's conservatism, picked up most of the rest. The party won the Senate for the first time since 1952, defeating nine Democrats to achieve a margin of fifty-three to forty-six (with Virginia's Harry F. Byrd sitting as a conservative independent). In the House, the party made a net gain of 33 to reach 192, compared with the Democrats' 243.[2]

Frustrations with the Carter record created for the Republicans what political scientist Austin Ranney called "a great opportunity to become again the nation's majority party." According to Ranney, success depended on how Republicans responded to this opportunity under Reagan as president.[3] That leadership fostered confidence; optimism about the GOP future reached a zenith in 1984, buoyed by Reagan's reelection prospects as a popular incumbent and by disarray within the Democratic Party. Capturing the mood, a spectator at one campaign event held a sign that read, "You are witnessing the great realignment."[4] Once more, the hopes of realignment were to end in

[1] *NYT*, Aug. 21, 1977, 27.
[2] Ellis Sandoz, "Revolution or Flash in the Pan?" in Sandoz and Cecil V. Crabb, Jr., eds., *A Tide of Discontent: The 1980 Elections and Their Meaning* (Washington, D.C.: Congressional Quarterly Press, 1981), 2–3, 9.
[3] Austin Ranney, "The Carter Administration," in Ranney, ed., *The American Elections of 1980* (Washington, D.C.: American Enterprise Institute, 1981), 2.
[4] Richard Brookhiser, *The Outside Story: How Democrats and Republicans Reelected Reagan* (Garden City, N.Y.: Doubleday, 1986), 286.

disappointment. Once more, the party failed to share fully the electorate's confidence in a popular president.

Although it did not win a majority, the Republican Party made real, lasting gains. Richard Wirthlin, a pollster for the Reagan administration and the Republican National Committee, spoke of the Republicans as a "parity party," rather than the majority.[5] To achieve parity was a significant improvement for the party that had long languished as the nation's minority.

The surge of support that took the party to this parity status had distinctive demographic characteristics. In the late 1970s and 1980s, it was more frequently men and not women who turned away from the Democrats and boosted GOP fortunes. Senator Robert W. Packwood of Oregon, Senate Republican Campaign Committee chair, claimed in early 1982 that his party "[had] just about written off those women who work for wages," faulting Reagan's "idealized concept of America" that did not recognize the nation's diversity. "We are losing them in droves. You cannot write them off and the blacks off and the Hispanics off and the Jews off and assume you're going to build a party on white Anglo-Saxon males over 40. There aren't enough of us left."[6] In fact, the party won increasing support among younger Americans during the 1980s – age was no longer such an acute problem for the party – but Packwood was right to note its coalition's other characteristics, including its whiteness and its new problem of the "gender gap."

As a former Democrat, Ronald Reagan himself symbolized the transition within the electorate that the party sought. Less than a month after Gerald Ford's departure from the White House at the start of 1977, Reagan had spoken to a conservative audience about his vision for the party. He called for a "New Republican Party," jettisoning the current "country club–big business image," providing "room for the man and woman in the factories, for the farmer, for the cop on the beat and the millions of Americans who may never have thought of joining the party before but whose interests coincide with those represented by principled Republicans." Reagan thus echoed William Rusher's *The Making of the New Majority Party* in believing that the party's route to a majority involved a coalition between social conservatives and economic conservatives.[7] This argument underscored the differences that existed between Reagan's understanding of the Republican future and Richard Nixon's, even while there were similarities between their rhetoric about party support in middle America. Nixon believed that the common ground shared by these new recruits and existing Republican supporters was limited, and crucially it did not extend to economic conservatism. Reagan, by contrast, believed in his antistatism's popular strength. A further distinction involved the two leaders' political style and outlook.

---

[5] Hedrick Smith, "Congress: Will There Be Realignment?" in Paul Duke, ed., *Beyond Reagan: The Politics of Upheaval* (New York: Warner, 1986), 162.

[6] *NYT*, March 2, 1982, D22.

[7] Associated Press, Feb. 5, 1977.

Sunny optimism characterized Reagan's, quite unlike the dark, divisive appeals to which Nixon resorted.[8]

As the 1980 elections approached, Americans were increasingly receptive not only to this optimism but also to Reagan's message. Public opinion became more conservative during the 1970s, benefiting the GOP. Skepticism of government activism grew. According to Harris polls, in 1973 about a third of respondents agreed that "the best government is the government that governs least"; by 1981 this proportion had risen to three in five. Views on spending partly reflected this growth of antigovernment sentiment, though opposition to domestic programs increased more modestly; one survey reported that the number of Americans believing that "too much" was spent on welfare grew from 42 percent in 1974 to 56 percent in 1980.[9] Welfare, moreover, was among the less-popular examples of government spending, and Social Security, by contrast, retained much of its support. Still, Americans were now closer, at last, to the Republican view of the federal government. Speaking in 1981, Senate majority leader Howard H. Baker, Jr., of Tennessee even compared the political power of opposition to big government with that of nineteenth-century abolitionism and the New Deal. "You'd be amazed how I find people real excited about cutting the size of government," he said.[10]

There was change, too, to the Republicans' benefit in public opinion about other concerns. A conservative trend emerged at the end of the 1970s on social issues, including attitudes toward drug use, abortion, and the Equal Rights Amendment. This shift was rather glacial, however, by comparison with the pronounced transformation of ideas about foreign policy. In 1973 only about one in five Americans viewed the Soviet Union in a highly negative way, but the proportion had increased to more than three in five by the start of 1980. Support for détente declined. The perception that the military capacity of the United States was slipping behind that of the Soviet Union increased, and there was correspondingly a desire for higher defense spending. In 1979 the Soviet invasion of Afghanistan and the taking of hostages at the Tehran embassy allowed Republican critics to develop scathing attacks on the Carter administration's foreign policy; a new skepticism toward the Soviet Union had already developed, however.[11]

The results were positive for Republicans at large. A National Republican Congressional Committee poll in June 1980 found that voters had more confidence in Republicans than Democrats in tackling a host of foreign and domestic issues – with the lonely exception of unemployment, where the Democratic advantage endured. "For the first time in recent history," according to the

---

[8] Gil Troy, *Morning in America: How Ronald Reagan Invented the 1980s* (Princeton, N.J.: Princeton University Press, 2005).

[9] William G. Mayer, *The Changing American Mind: How and Why American Public Opinion Changed between 1960 and 1988* (Ann Arbor: University of Michigan Press, 1992), 79, 85.

[10] *NYT* magazine, June 14, 1981, 110.

[11] Mayer, *The Changing American Mind*, 19–73.

poll, "there are more positive mentions offered about the GOP than negative mentions; and more negative mentions offered about the Democratic Party than positive ones." Although more Americans still planned to vote for their Democratic House candidate, Representative Guy Vander Jagt of Michigan, the committee's chair, nevertheless remarked, "For the first time since the 1930s, the Republican label is not baggage."[12] The party's better image encouraged Republicans seeking office to emphasize rather than downplay their Republican identity and to call for a change of party, a notable development after many years when candidates had tended to conclude that their chances at the polls were better as an individual rather than as a representative of the Republican Party.[13]

The Democrats' problems helped Republicans to achieve and then maintain success during this period. Frustrations with Carter's record first fueled disenchantment with liberalism and encouraged public receptivity to conservative ideas. The electorate's turn away from the Democrats in 1980 then fostered divisive self-scrutiny within the party, undermining its ability to respond effectively to conservative revitalization. By challenging key liberal assumptions, the Reagan administration's initiatives demanded an imaginative response. The Democratic Party did not offer enough that was imaginative. In 1980, Senator Daniel Patrick Moynihan, Democrat of New York – who a decade before as an adviser to Nixon had diagnosed conservatism's intellectual shortcomings as a leading problem for the administration – remarked that "all of a sudden, the GOP has become a party of ideas."[14] Walter F. Mondale, Carter's vice president and the 1984 presidential nominee, later said, "I sensed late in my public career that we were running out of new ideas."[15] The Democrats' shortcomings helped shield the Republicans' vulnerabilities.

The 1980 breakthrough was, in fact, less formidable than at first it appeared. Victories in the less populated states west of the Mississippi help to account for the party's capture of the U.S. Senate, as do Republican wins in marginal races, where a relatively small switch between the parties would have secured a Democratic win instead.[16] More fundamentally, there was little evidence yet

---

[12] Market Opinion Research, "U.S. National Study: Statistical Summary," June 1980, and National Republican Congressional Committee news release, July 7, 1980, box 28, ERAmerica Records; *Fortune*, Aug. 25, 1980, 85.

[13] James W. Caeser, "American Parties in the Eighties: Declining or Resurging?" in Paul T. David and David H. Everson, eds., *The Presidential Election and Transition, 1980–1981* (Carbondale: Southern Illinois University Press, 1983), 220.

[14] Daniel Patrick Moynihan to Richard Nixon, Nov. 13, 1970, box 8, White House Special Files – Staff Member and Office Files: POF; Everett Carll Ladd, "The Reagan Phenomenon and Public Attitudes Toward Government," in Lester M. Salamon and Michael S. Lund, eds., *The Reagan Presidency and the Governing of America* (Washington, D.C.: Urban Institute Press, 1984), 221–249.

[15] Gillon, *Democrats' Dilemma*, 304.

[16] Roger H. Davidson and Walter J. Oleszek, "Changing the Guard in the U.S. Senate," *Legislative Studies Quarterly* 9 (1984), 638; Thomas E. Mann and Norman J. Ornstein, "Sending a Message: Voters and Congress in 1982," in Mann and Ornstein, eds., *The American Elections of 1982* (Washington, D.C.: American Enterprise Institute for Public Policy Research, 1983), 136–137.

that the party's new support was durable. Volatility characterized public opinion during the 1980 campaign, and perhaps more than one in three voters settled on a choice of presidential candidate only in the week before election day.

Moreover, apart from the growing opposition to welfare, support for spending on other government programs did not change significantly – despite increasing antistatism. The economic problems of the 1970s did not spell the end of the divided opinion that Lloyd Free and Hadley Cantril had analyzed in the 1960s as ideological conservatism but operational liberalism. Instead, those problems sharpened the former sentiment while continuing to demonstrate the latter's social benefits.[17] Although many in the party saw the 1980 results as full of promise – perhaps the start of a new Republican era – the rightward shift was not unqualified. As Ranney emphasized, how governing Republicans responded to victory was critical to the party's longer-term prospects.

Although the party's 1980 surge depended on disillusionment with Democrats and liberalism, the late 1970s was a time of extensive activity among conservatives to mobilize new support, improving the Republican infrastructure in a variety of ways. These efforts included the extraparty organizations of the "New Right" and the Religious Right. They also encompassed a growing conviction among Republicans that their economic conservatism possessed untapped popular appeal – that it was possible to recruit new support through the more effective communication of the conservative message.

A signal event of this mission took place in Youngstown, Ohio, in February 1978. Representative Marvin "Mickey" Edwards of Oklahoma and Representative Philip Crane of Illinois organized a meeting with union members there, seeking labor support for antigovernment ideas, trying to associate conservatives with the priority of job creation, not with a "country club image."[18] Edwards and Crane thought they found a receptive audience. Of their concerns about government workplace regulation, foreign countries' industrial subsidies, and high interest rates, Edwards said, "Few free-market conservatives have stated their arguments as well as did those union leaders in Youngstown." The meeting led to the introduction in the House of related legislation.[19] *National Review*'s William F. Buckley overlooked Nixon's strategy to woo middle America when he described the initiatives as "perhaps the first recognition in our time, by a prominent Republican, of the existence of labor unions."[20] But by seeking common cause in economic conservatism, rather than social conservatism or patriotic internationalism, they were certainly different from Nixon's efforts to cultivate labor. Indeed, Crane downplayed the electoral power of social issues, which he believed garnered only short-term support.[21]

[17] Ladd, "The Reagan Phenomenon."
[18] Philip M. Crane to William A. Rusher, Dec. 20, 1977, box 39, Rusher Papers.
[19] *National Review*, June 9, 1978, 717.
[20] *National Review*, May 26, 1978, 672–673.
[21] *Chicago Tribune* clipping, March 28, 1978, box 39, Rusher Papers.

Regardless of its wisdom as a strategy to undermine New Deal liberalism, such a message seemed of limited value in helping Crane to boost his party standing or Edwards to explain his House victory. Crane's relative lack of interest in social issues was an obstacle to New Right support for his 1980 presidential nomination quest.[22] Edwards did not emphasize his economic conservatism in accounting for his own majority in a traditionally Democratic, predominantly working-class district of Oklahoma City; he stressed an incumbent's ability to cultivate personal support, rather than the power of conservative ideas. "I don't go back to my district with placards proclaiming von Mises and Hayek," he said. "The voter votes for a candidate if he likes him."[23] He did, however, echo the long-time criticism of the party that it offered nothing positive in response to Democratic ideas, positing that "the national failure to more frequently embrace Conservative or Republican candidates may be found in the predominant negativism of conservative and Republican candidates."[24]

Another Republican representing a largely working-class community in the House – Buffalo, New York, in this case – was Jack Kemp. Believing that he understood how the party could unlock a majority's support, Kemp influentially promoted the recrafting of the party's economic message. He decried the negative electoral impact of the Republican concern with balanced budgets as allowing the Democrats to win support for their spending programs.[25] Similarly to Edwards, Kemp advocated the development of a more positive agenda, finding it in "supply-side economics," which drew on the work of economist Arthur Laffer. Supply-side economics called for tax cuts that would expand the economy through increases in productivity and investment.[26] The faith in supply-side economics was electorally attractive; it "gave Republicans a way of appealing to the blue-collar Democrats as well as to country-club Republicans," journalist John B. Judis noted.[27] During the 1978 campaign congressional Republicans supported a tax bill, based on supply-side principles, promoted by Kemp with Senator William Roth of Delaware; Congress later rejected the bill.

Convinced of the idea's political appeal, Ronald Reagan supported a form of supply-side economics during the 1980 campaign, even though his economic advisers had little enthusiasm for the decision.[28] Reagan's support marked a significant departure from the concerns of his earlier career. Always opposed

[22] *WP*, May 4, 1979, A3.
[23] *In These Times*, Feb. 21–27, 1979, 4–5.
[24] Mickey Edwards, "The State of the Conservative Movement and an Agenda for Further Development," n.d., box 29, Rusher Papers.
[25] *Los Angeles Times*, May 16, 1985, 1; *Esquire*, Oct. 24, 1978, 69.
[26] Iwan W. Morgan, *Deficit Government: Taxing and Spending in Modern America* (Chicago: Dee, 1995), 146.
[27] *The Progressive*, Jan. 1983, 22–27.
[28] Paul J. Quirk, "The Economy: Economists, Electoral Politics, and Reagan Economics," in Michael Nelson, ed., *The Elections of 1984* (Washington, D.C.: CQ Press, 1985), 164.

to high levels of taxation and always anxious about their impact on individual incentives to create wealth, he had nevertheless emphasized the importance of fiscal responsibility as a prerequisite to any tax cuts. In other words, Reagan had previously reflected the orthodox Republican view about economics, and his embrace of supply-side ideas helped to dramatize the significance of the shift taking place within the party, seeking to refashion its conservatism in a more appealing form.

Taxation grew as a public concern because of its increasing burden. In 1970 an average American paid 14.4 percent of income in direct individual tax, but in 1980 the proportion was 15.7 percent. Substantial increases in Social Security contributions and the multiplication of loopholes made the system less progressive, and the inflation-induced phenomenon of "bracket creep" subjected many people to a higher rate of taxation, even when their real income was not correspondingly higher. Discontent surfaced in the tax revolt that began in California with Proposition 13; this initiative, designed to limit the state's property taxes, passed by a two-to-one margin in June 1978.[29] Although the midterm elections later that year did not see major advances for the Republicans (who secured net gains of twelve seats in the House and three in the Senate), many viewed the contests as signaling a growth of antigovernment, antispending sentiment. Tax or spending limitations were on the ballot in an additional sixteen states, in thirteen cases successfully.[30]

The meaning of the California tax revolt was open to misinterpretation, however. There were limits to the antistatism it involved. Many of those who voted for the antitax initiative wanted to see most government spending stay at the same level, if not increase – with the significant exception of welfare programs that benefited relatively few.[31] This did not, then, amount to a rejection of New Deal liberalism's programmatic dimension, but merely a challenge to its cost. There was a reluctance to accept the logic that tax cuts were dependent on program cuts. Still, the tax revolt signaled a growing receptivity to a historically central objection of the Republican Party to New Deal liberalism. Moreover, the work of Kemp, Edwards, Crane, and others showed a new desire to recast economic conservatism in freshly appealing ways. The supply-side formula advanced the attractive claim that the old logic was wrong, that tax cuts – of the right nature – might increase revenues.

As policy concerns turned to the Republicans' advantage, the party improved its organizational capacity under William E. Brock, III, RNC chair between 1977 and 1981. Brock fashioned a new, more active role for the national committee, and his initiatives provided the party with electoral advantage. They included programs to train candidates and equip them with the financial and professional resources they needed to win office. Through

---

[29] Morgan, *Deficit Government*, 142–147.
[30] *Nation's Business*, Dec. 1978, 81.
[31] David O. Sears and Jack Citrin, *Tax Revolt: Something for Nothing in California* (Cambridge, Mass.: Harvard University Press, 1982).

its Local Elections Campaign Division, established in 1977, the RNC paid special attention to campaigns for state legislatures in order to develop candidates for higher office and to increase Republican prospects for influence over congressional redistricting. Alarmed that many local bodies were in a state of disarray or even demise, Brock placed importance on the party's grassroots revitalization. In order to maximize the overall effectiveness of party efforts, his reforms centralized power within the RNC, enabling Washington officials to make decisions about the support offered to individual campaigns. Although the more important element of Brock's work involved the party's organizational transformation, it also sought to foster policy discussion, reflecting the belief that the party was perceived to lack ideas. The national committee launched an opinion journal, *Commonsense*, and ran advisory councils, whose debates contributed to the formulation of the 1980 platform and notably encouraged intraparty support for supply-side economics. The RNC developed television commercials first to improve the party's image and then, during 1980, to attack the Democrats. The U.K. Conservatives' anti-Labour rhetoric helped to inspire the election-year ads, which encouraged voters to support Republicans "For a Change." In one, a jobless blue-collar worker asked, "If the Democrats are so good for working people, then how come so many people aren't working?"[32]

Brock's achievements were important. His perfection of a national infrastructure for the party facilitated effective engagement with its minority problem.[33] Pursuing the legacy of John Hamilton from the 1930s and Ray Bliss from the 1960s, Brock addressed this problem by maximizing the party's potential support through organizational initiatives that avoided ideological controversies. One observer posited that the effect of the RNC's revitalization was to offset the Democrats' advantage of labor support.[34] The effect was perhaps yet more dramatic in 1980. Opinion polls failed to predict the size of Reagan's victory over Carter, and what accounted for this failure was the Republicans' greater success in mobilizing their support. It is possible, then, that the improvement in the party's organizational capacity turned what might have been a marginal defeat of Carter into the convincing triumph that Reagan achieved.[35]

Crucially, an ample supply of money supported these activities. The number of RNC contributors increased from 250,000 in 1976 to 1.2 million in 1980.[36] Between 1976 and 1980 the National Republican Congressional Committee had ten times more money than the Democratic Congressional

---

[32] Klinkner, *Losing Parties*, 136–154.

[33] Milkis, *President and the Parties*, 266.

[34] *Fortune*, Aug. 25, 1980, 85.

[35] John R. Petrocik, "Voter Turnout and Electoral Performance: The Anomalous Reagan Elections," in Kay Lehman Schlozman, ed., *Elections in America* (Boston: Allen & Unwin, 1987), 251–258.

[36] Klinkner, *Losing Parties*, 139.

Campaign Committee, money that richly funded Republican campaigns in districts where a gain seemed possible.[37]

Partly the result of organizational innovation to harness grassroots support, the new wealth also showed the increased willingness of business to provide financial support for the Right. In the past, Republicans had often complained that business was a disappointing ally; the electoral victim of an unhelpful image as business's protector, the party frequently did not reap the associated benefits of business support. Now business leaders offered more active assistance. It was not only concerns about the sluggish economy that encouraged them to do so. So did the beliefs that the economic cost of a cooperative relationship with labor was now greater than its benefits for workplace harmony, and that an upsurge in government regulation excessively burdened productivity. Corporations launched advertising programs in support of their economic ideas and supported conservative think tanks – boosting old ones, such as the American Enterprise Institute and the Hoover Institution, and creating new ones, notably the Heritage Foundation. They increased their investment in politicians through Political Action Committees (PACs), and an ideological commitment to conservatism more frequently governed the choice of these funds' beneficiaries, rather than the pragmatic desire to support incumbents of most political stripes – the more usual impulse behind business contributions. The transformation was great. In the early 1970s, there were many more labor than business PACs, and the funds of the two groups were roughly similar. Within a decade, business PACs easily outnumbered and vastly outspent labor PACs.[38]

It was not only business PACs that fostered conservatism's revitalization. Many other extraparty groups, known collectively as the New Right, also organized support and raised money. New Right groups promoted supply-side economics and social conservatism, often with a populist edge criticizing a distant, out-of-touch liberal elite. In many cases, its leaders were not new to conservative politics, and its key concerns were not far from long-standing elements of conservatism; in these senses, the New Right was not so new. Its newness rested on updated applications of economic and social conservatism and the use of modern techniques of political mobilization – especially mass mailings.

New Right leaders believed in their capacity to activate a conservative majority, especially within blue-collar and religious constituencies, often beyond the reach of the Republicans' party organization. "Conservatives cannot become the dominant political force in America until we stress the issues of concern to ethnic and blue-collar Americans, born-again Christians,

[37] Thomas Byrne Edsall, "The Reagan Legacy," in Sidney Blumenthal and Edsall, eds., *The Reagan Legacy* (New York: Pantheon, 1988), 13–14.

[38] Jerome L. Himmelstein, *To the Right: The Transformation of American Conservatism* (Berkeley: University of California Press, 1990), 129–151; Phillips-Fein, *Invisible Hands*, 166–212.

pro-life Catholics and Jews," remarked Richard Viguerie, the leading New Right fundraiser. "Some of these are busing, abortion, pornography, education, traditional Biblical moral values and quotas."[39] The New Right therefore shared the argument that a coalition of economic and social conservatives represented an electoral majority, adding the claim that its organizational impetus was crucial in realizing this coalition. Women played an important role in the New Right, especially thanks to Phyllis Schafly and her anti–Equal Rights Amendment organization, STOP ERA; the abortion controversy as well as the question of constitutionally enshrined gender equality fostered antifeminism during the 1970s.[40]

The Religious Right shared some of the concerns and organizational infrastructure of New Right groups.[41] What were perceived as secularist assaults on tradition and religion's place in society encouraged evangelical leaders to enter politics – a decision made more influential thanks to a growth in the numbers of their churches' adherents. The 1973 *Roe v. Wade* abortion decision was an important precipitant of this activism, as was the Equal Rights Amendment campaign. Then in 1978 the Internal Revenue Service sought to ensure tax-exempt Christian private schools' compliance with integration policy, which led to complaints of federal interference, another spur to activism. By decade's end, Moral Majority, Christian Voice, and the Religious Roundtable were at the forefront of direct-mail campaigns and political lobbying, claiming to be powerbrokers at the vanguard of a national shift to the Right, able to mobilize many millions against secular liberalism.[42] There were clearly tensions between a culturally traditionalist agenda and a laissez-faire economic agenda – the classic obstacle to the creation of a socially and economically conservative coalition. But Christian Right leaders often insisted that their traditionalism was essentially antistatist, that their quest for power wanted to end government's secularist interference with religion. Jerry Falwell, a Southern Baptist minister who launched Moral Majority in 1979, more explicitly asserted this common interest by campaigning against big government and high taxes, as well as about social issues.[43]

Surveying the growth of extraparty conservatism, Brock did not interpret the trend as helpful to his goal of party revitalization. He doubted the coalition-building qualities of "those emotional social issues," believing that the New Right took money away from the party and distracted congressional attention from more important issues, such as "tax reduction, job creation, health care, housing – the American Dream issues," on which a majority could be mobilized.[44] Brock's skepticism was well founded. The Religious Right was

---

[39] Himmelstein, *To the Right*, 80–94 (quotation, 83).
[40] Rymph, *Republican Women*, 212–231.
[41] Himmelstein, *To the Right*, 83–84.
[42] Himmelstein, *To the Right*, 97–126; Gillian Peele, *Revival and Reaction: The Right in Contemporary America* (Oxford: Clarendon Press, 1984), 80–119.
[43] Phillips-Fein, *Invisible Hands*, 228–235.
[44] *The Atlantic*, Nov. 1978, 61.

less electorally influential than many suspected and than its leaders claimed, and social issues were much less important than bread-and-butter concerns to most voters. Nevertheless, in 1980 there was a connection between religiosity on the one hand and both conservatism and Reagan support on the other, and the most intensely religious Americans constituted about one out of ten Reagan voters.[45]

Some elements of the new conservatism echoed the themes of Nixon's new majority – the interest in ethnic and blue-collar Americans, the belief in the power of social issues. But the New Right did not usually share Nixon's conviction that a reform-minded approach to other domestic issues – operating within the tradition of New Deal liberalism – was also important in building support. Moreover, Nixon's search for Republican recruits had not involved much consideration of the electoral promise of "born-again" Protestants (as opposed to traditionally Democratic Catholics) or antifeminist women; the arrival of these targets signified the newness of the advance that conservatism achieved.

On the campaign trail in 1980, Ronald Reagan invoked positive recollections of Franklin D. Roosevelt. One of his intentions in doing so was to promote the theme that his goal was to overturn finally the Democratic Party's New Deal coalition and replace it with a similarly durable Republican alternative. Democrats responded with skepticism; Walter Mondale told the 1980 Democratic National Convention, "I've been in politics for many years, and I've noticed that the closer Republican oratory moves to Franklin Roosevelt, the closer their policies move to Herbert Hoover." Reagan insisted, however, that he did not seek to dismantle the New Deal's policy legacy, but instead to challenge what he saw as the liberal agenda's later excesses. "Like FDR, may I say I'm not trying to destroy what is best in our system of humane, free government – I'm doing everything I can to save it: to slow down the destructive rate of growth in taxes and spending; to prune non-essential programs so that enough resources will be left to meet the requirements of the truly needy," he said in 1982.[46]

In 1981 Reagan asserted his claim to be a transformative president when he stewarded to passage a major package of tax and budget cuts. The tax cuts amounted to 23 percent over three years, including the reduction of the top marginal rate for individuals from 70 to 50 percent, as well as cuts in lower rates for individuals and in corporate taxation. Spending cuts targeted various means-tested programs for the poor and reduced the numbers of beneficiaries covered by the Social Security disability program. Supply-side thinking, as well as a more straightforward Republican interest in tax reduction, shaped the package. The supply-side moment was short-lived, however. Because budget cuts did not match tax cuts, the federal deficit increased, a development

[45] Jeffrey L. Brudney and Gary W. Copeland. "Evangelicals as a Political Force: Reagan and the 1980 Religious Vote," *Social Science Quarterly* 65 (1984), 1072–1079.

[46] William E. Leuchtenburg, *In the Shadow of FDR: From Harry Truman to Ronald Reagan* (Ithaca, N.Y.: Cornell University Press, 1983), 209–235 (quotations, 220, 230).

that encouraged the reassertion of fiscal conservatism first among congressional Republicans and then at the White House. Although the deficit persisted, the economy experienced steady growth following a recession in late 1981 and 1982. But not all benefited from this growth, which instead increased economic inequality.

Democrats attacked Republicans for unfairness.[47] "The brilliance of this theme is that it turns the administration's greatest accomplishment, economic growth and opportunity, into a negative legacy of greed and selfishness," a White House political aide wrote in 1988.[48] But the net result of economic change for electoral fortunes was positive. There were clearly connections between Reagan's popularity and the economy, as fluctuations in the former reflected the state of the latter.[49] And more Americans now viewed the Republican Party as the better custodians of the nation's economy – a transformation of traditional party perceptions. Democrats nevertheless maintained an advantage as the protectors of social-welfare programs and as the party of ordinary people, rather than the privileged.[50]

Foreign policy also helped Reagan's popularity as president.[51] In waging the Cold War, he reasserted anticommunism in superpower relations and built up the nation's defenses. Especially after Mikhail Gorbachev became the Soviet Union's leader in early 1985, the strategy also involved negotiations on nuclear-arms reduction, which led to a December 1987 treaty to eliminate intermediate- and short-range missiles in Europe, a step toward the Cold War's end. But even in 1984 the belief that Reagan had successfully restored a strong defense contributed to his reelection, his easy defeat of Walter Mondale, as did the improving economy and confidence in his leadership skills.[52]

It was not long after the start of Reagan's second term that Kevin Phillips, author of *The Emerging Republican Majority* in 1969, wrote of his suspicion that conservatism's future was insecure. He sensed a growing appetite for activist government, detecting a particular danger if Republicans interpreted the 1984 victory as a mandate for "a new era of Social Darwinism," involving laissez-faire economics and welfare-state reform.[53] The Reagan

[47] James T. Patterson, *Restless Giant: The United States from Watergate to Bush v. Gore* (New York: Oxford University Press, 2005), 154–170.
[48] Frank J. Donatelli to Howard H. Baker, Jr., Kenneth M. Duberstein, and Tom Griscom, Jan. 6, 1988, box 3, series I, Duberstein Files.
[49] Sheldon D. Pollack, *Refinancing America: The Republican Antitax Agenda* (Albany: State University of New York Press, 2003), 60–68.
[50] John G. Geer, "The Electorate's Partisan Evaluations: Evidence of a Continuing Democratic Edge," *POQ* 55 (1991), 218–231.
[51] Clyde Wilcox and Dee Allsop, "Economic and Foreign Policy as Sources of Reagan Support," *Western Political Quarterly* 44 (1991), 941–958.
[52] Paul C. Light and Celinda Lake, "The Election: Candidates, Strategies, and Decisions," in Michael Nelson, ed., *The Elections of 1984* (Washington, D.C.: CQ Press, 1985), 83–110; Beth A. Fischer, *The Reagan Reversal: Foreign Policy and the End of the Cold War* (Columbia: University of Missouri Press, 1997).
[53] *Orlando Sentinel*, May 12, 1985, G1.

administration did not pursue the radical agenda that Phillips feared, but he was correct to believe that the public's rightward shift was easing. During the 1980s antitax and antigovernment sentiment subsided, while support for domestic spending increased – perhaps demonstrations of Reagan's success in reducing taxation, restoring confidence in government, and controlling programs.[54] This is not to say that the Republicans' tax-cutting agenda lost its electoral power; such ideas created a clear, attractive message that continued to work in the party's benefit. By contrast, the emphasis that Democrats developed on deficit reduction – beginning with Mondale's 1984 campaign – lacked similar appeal.[55] But the merits of spending, as well as tax cutting, were popular, blunting the conservative trend. There was a shift away, too, from the harder-line views of foreign policy that emerged during the 1970s – which again can be interpreted as the result of the administration's success. Fewer believed that the Soviet Union enjoyed military superiority over the United States, and more supported defense cuts and a return to détente.[56]

But many conservatives did not recognize the limits of public support for their agenda. They suspected that the Reagan administration offered too much compromise, not enough principle.[57] For example, some leading neoconservatives – an elite group of intellectuals disenchanted with liberalism, often characterized by strong Cold War anticommunism – were critical of Reagan's emphasis on negotiation with the Soviet Union during his second term.[58] Some other conservatives faulted Reagan for not achieving bigger cuts in domestic spending.[59] And there was early and particularly vocal disappointment among advocates of social conservatism, who insisted that Reagan's success relied on his identification with their cause and that action on such issues promised increased success for the Republican Party. At the White House, Morton C. Blackwell, responsible for liaison with conservative groups at the start of the Reagan administration, promoted this view. Blackwell claimed, first, that Reagan's success depended on "a call to faith in traditional American values."[60] Second, he added that the party's electoral fortunes depended on the extent and enthusiasm of activism in its support, a further reason for the administration to take action that energized conservatives. Thinking in particular of New Deal protection of organized labor, he argued that "this Administration is doing nothing analagous [sic] to the Roosevelt Administration efforts to

[54] Mayer, *The Changing American Mind*, 76–110.

[55] Mark A. Smith, *The Right Talk: How Conservatives Transformed the Great Society into the Economic Society* (Princeton, N.J.: Princeton University Press, 2007).

[56] Mayer, *The Changing American Mind*, 45–46, 62, 411–420.

[57] *National Review*, March 18, 1988, 24.

[58] Gregory L. Schneider, "Conservatives and the Reagan Presidency," in Richard S. Conley, ed., *Reassessing the Reagan Presidency* (Lanham, Md.: University Press of America, 2003), 71–72, 78–80.

[59] *Policy Review*, Winter 1984, 12–19.

[60] Morton C. Blackwell to Elizabeth H. Dole, Dec. 2, 1981, OA 4537, series I, Dole Files.

build up the strength of the non-party organizations which contributed significantly to their initial election victory."[61]

Blackwell was out of step with prevailing administration thinking. The
more conventional view acknowledged the electoral utility of support among
cultural traditionalists, but also understood the potential danger of association with their ideas. After the 1984 elections, James Baker, the White House
chief of staff, observed that the Reagan coalition confirmed the president's
popularity but provided a fragile foundation for the GOP future. This was
because the issues that attracted evangelical Christians were different from the
economic concerns of "yuppies," a neologism of the 1980s for young, urban
professionals. "Opposition to abortion, for instance, is not an issue that is popular among most yuppies – particularly among yuppie women," he argued.[62]
Aide James Lake was more critical of the social conservatives' claims, believing that the politics of morality was incompatible with the sunny optimism at
the heart of Reagan's appeal. "No one is going to focus on how the President
has revitalized the American spirit if he is instead exhorting its soul; week
after week coming off as the stern moralizer," he wrote in March 1984.[63]

Conservative criticisms puzzled and frustrated Reagan.[64] Drafting a letter
to William F. Buckley in 1982, he defended himself against the accusation that
he had abandoned principle to focus first on economic issues by noting that the
economy had always formed a key element of his agenda and by underlining
the present importance of action on the economy. "Right now there are some
crackpots in the fiscal fireworks factory playing with matches," he wrote. "It
doesn't make much difference if they are arsonists or d––n fools they can
do a lot of damage if they aren't stopped."[65] In Reagan's mind, then, an economic crisis required his special attention in the short term. For some social
conservatives, this kind of view missed the point. According to Viguerie, for
example, "a restoration of morality is essential to the future well-being of our
country" and "as important as an economic recovery."[66]

The administration retained its principal focus on the economy and foreign policy, but thanks partly to such efforts as Blackwell's in emphasizing
the importance of social conservatives to the Republican coalition, their cause
also won action. Reagan offered a degree of support, unsuccessfully, in 1982
to a constitutional amendment to ban abortion, and he remained a passionate advocate of pro-life arguments. He appointed antiabortion people to key
positions, and his administration's spending cuts included family-planning

[61] Morton C. Blackwell to Richard C. Wirthlin, Aug. 12, 1982, OA 6391, series I, Dole Files.
[62] A. James Reichley, *The Life of the Parties: A History of American Political Parties* (New York: Free Press, 1992), 379.
[63] Jim Lake to James A. Baker, III, March 8, 1984, box 9, series I, Baker Files.
[64] Ronald Reagan, *The Reagan Diaries*, edited by Douglas Brinkley (New York: HarperCollins, 2007), 276.
[65] Ronald Reagan to William F. Buckley, Jr. (draft), n.d. [1982], box 3, series II, Presidential Handwriting File.
[66] Richard A. Viguerie, form letter, Aug. 19, 1981, OA 2903, Atwater Files.

programs among their targets.[67] Such initiatives reflected deep personal opposition to abortion, though tempered by an awareness that more Americans favored than opposed abortion rights.[68] In response to political pressures, Reagan offered similar support to a constitutional amendment to permit school prayer. Furthermore, when state laws that established moments of contemplative silence as an alternative to formal prayer faced legal challenge, administration officials assisted in defending them against attack. The defeat of such efforts was not politically problematic; Reagan, who sometimes employed biblical allusions when speaking on a host of issues, was still able to present himself to voters as the defender of social conservatism against a powerful, secularist liberalism.[69] Most important for social issues was Reagan's effort to reshape the federal judiciary. During campaigns he emphasized his intention to nominate judges with a conservative interpretation of the Constitution, and administration aides investigated potential nominees with unprecedented attention to their legal beliefs in order to implement this goal.[70]

Despite the reluctance to emphasize social conservatism in ways that might alienate other voters, the emphasis was strong enough to ease evangelicals' journey toward the Republican Party. In 1984 Reagan won four out of five white born-again Christians, and as 1988 presidential candidate George H. W. Bush won a similar share of white evangelicals and fundamentalists. During the Reagan years their Republican allegiance increased at a scale unequaled by other groups.[71] Their loyalty boosted party fortunes while complicating the coalition-building task. A 1988 Gallup poll, which looked for a typology of the contemporary electorate, reported that the party's core supporters were "Enterprisers" (16 percent of voters) and "Moralists" (14 percent). Enterprisers were wealthy, well-educated whites with economically conservative yet socially moderate attitudes. Moralists were middle-income people, often southerners and frequently born-again Christians, who were strongly conservative on social issues and foreign policy but generally favored programmatic spending. To win, a Republican candidate needed to add other groups, such as the "Upbeats" (young and optimistic) and the "Disaffected" (middle-aged and pessimistic), both Republican-leaning but independent. Maintaining the core vote of Enterprisers and Moralists was, however, challenging enough.[72] In

[67] Donald T. Critchlow, "Mobilizing Women: The 'Social' Issues," in W. Elliot Brownlee and Hugh Davis Graham, eds., *The Reagan Presidency: Pragmatic Conservatism and Its Legacies* (Lawrence: University Press of Kansas, 2003), 302–312.

[68] Peggy Noonan, *What I Saw At the Revolution: A Political Life in the Reagan Era* (1990; New York: Ivy, 1991), 164–165; Patterson, *Restless Giant*, 177.

[69] Bruce J. Dierenfield, "'A Nation under God': Ronald Reagan and the Crusade for School Prayer," in Eric J. Schmertz, Natalie Datlof, and Alexej Ugrinsky, eds., *Ronald Reagan's America*, vol. I (Westport, Conn.: Greenwood, 1997), 235–261.

[70] David M. O'Brien, "The Reagan Judges: His Most Enduring Legacy?" in Charles O. Jones, ed., *The Reagan Legacy: Promise and Performance* (Chatham, N.J.: Chatham House, 1988), 60–101.

[71] Himmelstein, *To the Right*, 122–123, 203.

[72] *Orlando Sentinel*, Jan. 10, 1988, A1.

aiming to do so, the party lost some of the advantages it had gained at the end of the 1970s. The New Right groups and the organizations of the Religious Right were no longer so powerful, while business reverted partly to its earlier political pragmatism by distributing contributions more even-handedly among Republicans and Democrats (especially incumbents), though still on balance favoring the former.[73] Furthermore, Republican fundraising advances encouraged improvements within the Democratic Party, so that the Republican edge became smaller during the 1980s.[74]

According to conventional measures of a president's party leadership, Ronald Reagan was notably, unusually dedicated to the Republican cause. He was an energetic fundraiser and campaigner for party candidates, although, unlike Nixon, he relied on managers and aides to deal with not only the detail of electoral strategy but also its larger design.[75] However, especially as measured by Republican fortunes in Congress – a key indicator of the party's success in seeking a majority – the consequences of Reagan's dedication to the cause were disappointing. Throughout the Reagan years the party failed to make real gains in the House, where incumbency seemed much more significant than presidential popularity in explaining results; in 1986, despite the president's wide-ranging efforts to defend the GOP majority there, Republicans lost the Senate.

The disappointment was all the greater because during the administration's first year there were high hopes that the 1980 victories would lead to more secure control of the Senate and to the capture of the House, together with state-level gains – all part of a realignment. Although the goal to win a Republican House in 1982 was a very optimistic one, especially because the White House party usually suffered midterm losses, the sense of a Republican tide encouraged some leading party figures to believe that twenty gains were within reach; the defection of six conservative Democrats would then bring control.[76]

The 1982 recession helped dash these hopes. In that year Democrats made a net gain of twenty-six seats in the House – also picking up seven governorships to achieve an edge of thirty-four to sixteen over the Republicans – while the GOP Senate majority of fifty-four to forty-six remained unchanged.[77] Still, measured by the normal expectation of losses for the White House party, the results were not unusually disappointing. That fall the weakness of economic

[73] Himmelstein, *To the Right*, 200–206.
[74] Thomas Byrne Edsall, "The Reagan Legacy," in Sidney Blumenthal and Edsall, eds., *The Reagan Legacy* (New York: Pantheon, 1988), 13–14.
[75] Laurence I. Barrett, *Gambling with History: Reagan in the White House* (1983; New York: Penguin, 1984), 34; Cannon, *President Reagan*, 443–444; Critchlow, *Conservative Ascendancy*, 185–186, 204–208; Davis, *President as Party Leader*, 12.
[76] Albert R. Hunt, "National Politics and the 1982 Campaign," in Thomas E. Mann and Norman J. Ornstein, eds., *American Elections of 1982* (Washington, D.C.: American Enterprise Institute for Public Policy Research, 1983), 7–11.
[77] Hunt, "National Politics," 40.

indicators, together with low approval ratings of Reagan's presidential performance resulting from those indicators, offered weight to the claim that the relatively small scale of GOP losses was proof of the party's strength rather than decay. After all, academic models of midterm elections predicted House losses as high as sixty.[78] "Though Democrats claimed that the current recession and the 10.1 percent unemployment amounted to 'Hoovernomics,' and a rerun of Herbert Hoover and the Great Depression, the voters didn't buy it," commented one columnist.[79] Another argued that the Democrats' failure to score more extensive gains revealed their inability to offer an alternative to Reaganomics.[80] Indeed, White House polls suggested that many people were likely to blame Carter and the Democrats for the 1982 recession, rather than Reagan and the Republicans – a conclusion that administration speakers encouraged.[81] There was also optimism about the economy's future, support for Reagan's economic policies, and a willingness to be patient for their promised impact.[82] In representing a referendum on the Reagan record so far, then, the House results were fairly positive.[83] The elections' outcome was nevertheless a setback for hopes of realignment.[84]

The effectiveness of the Republicans' centralized organization, especially by contrast with the Democrats' decentralized structures, helped minimize losses. The RNC, the National Republican Congressional Committee, and the National Republican Senatorial Committee spent $19 million on 1982 House and Senate contests, compared with their Democratic counterparts' $3.4 million. Although it remained necessary for candidates to raise most of their campaign money, these central funds were an important supplement for those needing extra assistance. A further factor in the minimization of Republican losses was the recruitment of good candidates, partly thanks to the high hopes in 1981 for the party's future under Reagan.[85]

In 1984, when his own reelection was at stake, Reagan's dedication to the party faltered. The campaign consciously avoided any effort to encourage the president's non-Republican supporters to join the party. Staffer Richard Darman said that "we used the term 'Republican' ... only before Republican audiences in small rooms."[86] To justify this neglect at a time of apparently great opportunity, fellow aide Edward J. Rollins cited polls indicating that Reagan's target voters were Democrats, "who in a lot of cases wanted the

[78] Gary C. Jacobson, "Party Organization and Distribution of Campaign Resources: Republicans and Democrats in 1982," *Political Science Quarterly* 100 (1985–1986), 613, 616, 622.

[79] *Philadelphia Inquirer* clipping, Nov. 6, 1982, OA 6390, series I, Dole Files.

[80] *WP*, Nov. 8, 1982, A15.

[81] Richard B. Wirthlin to Richard Richards, June 2, 1982, box 188, Regan Papers.

[82] *New Republic*, Aug. 30, 1982, 10–11.

[83] John C. McAdams and John R. Johannes, "The Voter in the 1982 House Elections," *American Journal of Political Science* 28 (1984), 778–781.

[84] *Baltimore Sun*, Nov. 3, 1982, A14.

[85] Jacobson, "Party Organization," 609.

[86] Jonathan Moore, ed., *Campaign for President: The Managers Look at '84* (Dover, Mass.: Auburn House, 1986), 226–227.

checks-and-balances system and did not want a Republican Congress just because they wanted a Republican President."[87] Unsurprisingly, this strategy fostered Capitol Hill resentments. House minority leader Robert Michel of Illinois blamed Reagan – who "really never, in my opinion, joined that issue of what it really means to have the numbers in the House" – for the small size of the party's House gains. For political scientist Ellis Sandoz, the Reagan campaign's implications for congressional races were subtler than straight-forward neglect. According to Sandoz, the 1984 Reagan campaign amounted to a call to endorse the incumbents' record; such a campaign was powerful in mobilizing support for Reagan, but it was not helpful for Republican challeng-ers. "Reagan's coattails were prodigiously long from this angle, extending to virtually all incumbents who sought reelection to Congress," he observed.[88] The failure to articulate any clear policy agenda for the second term created problems for Reagan, too. Despite the impressive proportions of his personal victory, it did not provide much momentum toward policy goals that might have increased his presidency's achievements, therefore deepening its electoral support.[89]

Understanding Reagan's personal popularity, some Democratic incumbents moved away from their own presidential candidate to deny their Republican opponent any opportunity to benefit from this potential advantage. Frank J. Fahrenkopf, Jr., national chair, said that "we saw a lot of Democratic litera-ture with the congressional candidate in a picture with Ronald Reagan at a signing ceremony at the White House, or something of that nature."[90] Walter Mondale's taxation plans, which included an antideficit tax increase, were a proposal that many in his party were especially eager to reject. The diffi-culty of associating Democratic candidates at large with unpopular elements of the party's national agenda was a familiar one to Republican politicians. Although the parties were achieving a higher degree of ideological consistency by the 1980s, they nonetheless continued to allow considerable diversity within their ranks. This diversity was particularly visible in the Democratic Party, where many conservatives remained, especially due to its continuing tradition of southern conservatism. When voters in a district supported a Republican for the presidency but a Democrat for the House, the congressional candidate was likelier to be a conservative, sometimes one who emphasized policy agree-ments with Reagan.[91] Although the Reagan campaign was certainly reluctant to endanger the president's success among Democratic supporters through an appeal for larger party gains, therefore, the prospects of such an appeal were probably not very good anyway.

[87] Moore, *Campaign for President*, 225–226.
[88] Ellis Sandoz, "The Silent Majority Finds Its Voice," in Sandoz and Cecil V. Crabb, Jr., eds., *Election 84: Landslide Without a Mandate?* (New York: Mentor, 1985), 5.
[89] *Chicago Tribune*, Dec. 23, 1985, 13.
[90] Moore, *Campaign for President*, 228.
[91] Paul Frymer, "Ideological Consensus within Divided Party Government," *Political Science Quarterly* 109 (1994), 287–311.

Reagan's energy in support of the party returned in 1986, when the calculation was different. Reagan no longer risked the personal loss of votes, but a strong showing in the midterms potentially bolstered the authority of a lame-duck president approaching his final years in office. The White House political office created a campaign plan making extensive use of Reagan, trying to share his popularity with the party at large, presenting the message that Americans should "consider a vote for the local GOP candidates as a vote for Ronald Reagan."[92] Reagan was ready to be generous. He made fifty-four appearances in twenty-two states, traveling 24,800 miles.[93] Richard Wirthlin concluded that this activity strengthened Republican support, particularly for Senate candidates.[94] By contrast, an academic study of the House campaign suggested that this intervention had some counterproductive results; views of Reagan influenced campaign debate, but disapproval of his record apparently acted as a stronger motivation for voters than approval.[95] Meanwhile, the organizational advantages that had benefited the party in the late 1970s and early 1980s were slipping away. The Democratic National Committee was now raising more money (if still outstripped by its Republican rival in this regard) and mimicking the Brock model of service provision and candidate support.[96] In House races, Republican challengers to Democratic incumbents usually lacked experience and funding to stage an effective contest; the candidacies of Democratic challengers were better, though not enough to pose a serious threat to Republican incumbents.[97]

The key opportunity for the party remained in the South, where Republicans had still not managed to translate conservatism fully into subpresidential support. Despite Reagan's popularity, White House control did not easily become an asset locally. Republican candidates who sought to use administration connections in their favor faced the Democratic rebuttal that they were Washington-linked outsiders. In a 1981 special House election in Mississippi, Wayne Dowdy, the Democrat, neutralized Republican Liles Williams's focus on Reagan by stressing local issues and an anti-Washington message, though not by attacking the popular president; Dowdy won, even though the district had been Republican since 1972. Such a local focus was a frequently successful counterstrategy to a GOP effort to harness the popularity of the administration's conservatism.[98] When the absence of a Democratic incumbent made

[92] Mitch Daniels to Donald T. Regan, June 19, 1986, box 192, Regan Papers.

[93] Jane Mayer and Doyle McManus, *Landslide: The Unmaking of the President, 1984–1988* (1988; Glasgow, U.K.: Fontana, 1989), 404.

[94] Donald T. Regan, notes, Nov. 2, 1986, box 193, Regan Papers.

[95] Gary C. Jacobson and Samuel Kernell, "National Forces in the 1986 U.S. House Elections," *Legislative Studies Quarterly* 15 (1990), 65–87.

[96] Frank J. Sorauf and Paul Allen Beck, *Party Politics in America*, 6th ed. (Glenview, Ill.: Scott, Foresman, 1988), 144–146.

[97] Jacobson and Kernell, "National Forces," 66–68.

[98] James M. Glaser, *Race, Campaign Politics, and the Realignment in the South* (New Haven, Conn.: Yale University Press, 1996), 46–52, 130–137.

a southern district most vulnerable to a Republican gain, a "local" Democrat was dependably more successful than a "cosmopolitan" Democrat. The number of the latter was growing at the expense of the former, aiding the gradual Republican advance.[99]

In explaining the failure to make House gains, many leading Republicans emphasized incumbency and its benefits – rather than party shortcomings.[100] According to Wyoming's Representative Richard B. Cheney, writing in 1985, "the apportionment of legislative districts, PAC financing, and other incumbency advantages help to explain why the signs of a Republican electoral realignment are not being reflected in House elections."[101] For decades the average chances of an incumbent representative's return to the House were more than nine in ten. The changing political climate apparently in the Republicans' favor did not undermine incumbents' strength. Indeed, the 1986 reelection rate for House incumbents reached 98.5 percent. What further boosted these prospects was the increasing cost of House elections, because few challengers were able to raise enough funds for an effective campaign.[102]

In fact, incumbency was as advantageous for officeholding Republicans as Democrats.[103] But House Republicans were readier to sacrifice the incumbency advantage than their Democratic counterparts. They tended to retire earlier (whether to seek other office or to exit politics), an interparty disparity visible since 1954 – partly accounting for the Republicans' minority status in the House. A factor that seemed important in accounting for this pattern of retirements was the frustrations of legislative minority, the way in which opportunities for political influence were more constrained for a minority-party legislator than for a majority-party legislator.[104] What qualifies or even questions Cheney's claim is the outcome of contests for open House seats during the 1980s; Republicans won 28 percent of formerly Democratic districts, but lost 20 percent of their former districts to Democrats. Moreover, reapportionment after the 1980 census seemed to cost Republicans no more than a handful of seats at most.[105] If incumbency helped explain the slow rate of party change in the House, it did not explain the Republican failure

[99] Shafer and Johnston, *End of Southern Exceptionalism*, 147–164. This analysis classifies "locals" as those both born and educated in the state where they pursued a political career; "cosmopolitans" are all others.

[100] Lublin, *The Republican South*, 36.

[101] Zelizer, *On Capitol Hill*, 212.

[102] Alan I. Abramowitz, "Incumbency, Campaign Spending, and the Decline of Competition in U.S. House Elections," *Journal of Politics* 53 (1991), 34–56.

[103] Brad Lockerbie, "The Partisan Component to the Incumbency Advantage: 1956–1996," *Political Research Quarterly* 52 (1999), 631–646.

[104] John B. Gilmour and Paul Rothstein, "Early Republican Retirement: A Cause of Democratic Dominance in the House of Representatives," *Legislative Studies Quarterly* 18 (1993), 345–365.

[105] Gary C. Jacobson, "Meager Patrimony: The Reagan Era and Republican Representation in Congress," in Larry Berman, ed., *Looking Back on the Reagan Presidency* (Baltimore: Johns Hopkins University Press, 1990), 293.

to achieve more success in winning open seats. House results thus demonstrated the continuing power of the Democratic Party, as well as the power of incumbency.

Although House results did not reflect this increase, more Americans identified with the Republican Party during the Reagan years. The University of Michigan election study reported that 32 percent of its respondents in 1980 were Republican identifiers (compared with 52 percent Democratic and 13 percent independent), and this number reached 39 percent in 1984 (compared with 48 percent Democratic and 11 percent independent).[106] Republicans thus failed to reach a majority, but the Democrats' share of the electorate slipped significantly enough to create a more even field of interparty competition.[107]

Reagan's own popularity boosted the party's fortunes. One academic study suggested that this was worth three percentage points in the growth of the party's identifiers during the 1980s.[108] The danger of such a personalized rationale for party support was its likely instability, however.[109] If Republican support depended on Reagan, it might disappear when he was no longer president. White House aides sensed that Reagan's problems in more fully sharing his popularity with the party at large revealed more about the current nature of American politics than about the quality of his efforts in its support. Borrowing a term from political scientists who believed that a realignment, decisively leaving one of the parties as the nation's majority, was now unlikely, aide Lee Atwater said in 1986, "We are going through a period of political dealignment and I expect this process of dealignment to continue for the indefinite future." "Dealignment" implied that Americans were drifting away from affiliation with either of the parties, as opposed to a realignment, in which one party rose as the other declined. Atwater linked the phenomenon with "the transition to the communication age," thus agreeing with analysts who linked the decline of party with the rise of television. Such interpretations saw television journalism as more comfortable with personality- than institution-based coverage. More importantly, television provided candidates with a tool of direct and powerful communication with the electorate; candidates no longer needed a party's infrastructure to facilitate this communication.[110]

---

[106] Sorauf and Beck, *Party Politics*, 167. This summary counts independents closer to Democrats as Democratic identifiers and independents closer to Republicans as Republican identifiers, rather than as independents.

[107] Michael F. Meffert, Helmut Norpoth, and Anirudh V. S. Ruhil, "Realignment and Macropartisanship," *APSR* 95 (2001), 953–962.

[108] William Mishler, Marilyn Hoskin, and Roy E. Fitzgerald, "Hunting the Snark: Or Searching for Evidence of That Widely Touted but Highly Elusive Resurgence of Public Support for Conservative Parties in Britain, Canada, and the United States," in Barry Cooper, Allan Kornberg, and Mischler, eds., *The Resurgence of Conservatism in Anglo-American Democracies* (Durham, N.C.: Duke University Press, 1988), 85–86.

[109] Warren E. Miller, "A New Context for Presidential Politics: The Reagan Legacy," *Political Behavior* 9 (1987), 91–113.

[110] Reichley, *Life of the Parties*, 379–380; Norpoth and Rusk, "Partisan Dealignment in the American Electorate."

Others were less willing to accept the arrival of dealignment. Ed Rollins said that the "lasting legacy" of the 1984 campaign was the success of the party's registration drive in enrolling five million new Republican voters.[111] The claim was a response to Republican concerns that the campaign inadequately shared Reagan's popularity with the party. Efforts in 1985 to expand these gains were less successful, however, offering further support to dealignment theses. The party launched "Operation Open Door," intended to persuade voters registered as Democrats to switch to the Republicans, first focusing on Florida, Louisiana, North Carolina, and Pennsylvania. According to national chair Fahrenkopf, the project achieved its 100-day goal to win 100,000 new Republicans, but among these voters identified as interested in changing party, only about 54,000 had completed the necessary paperwork.[112] Despite the relative ineffectiveness of these efforts, some Democrats worried that their party was falling victim to a Republican tide. The Democratic Leadership Council (DLC), newly formed by "New Democrats" who wanted to shift their party from liberalism to moderation, launched a campaign to counteract "Operation Open Door." "We intend to challenge disaffected Democrats to join us in a movement to change the party rather than changing parties," said Charles S. "Chuck" Robb, Virginia governor and leading DLC member.[113]

Few officeholders switched party. One who did, in October 1981, was Eugene Atkinson, who represented a blue-collar area of Pennsylvania in the House. Reagan said that his switch offered "a loud and clear message that our party, the Republican party, stands for the working men and women of this country," marking "the beginning of a new coalition and a new era in American politics."[114] In forging the bipartisan coalition to secure passage of his 1981 economic package, Reagan told supportive Democrats that he would not campaign against them. Although he acknowledged that this position created a problem for some Republican challengers, he said, "I'd like to feel that maybe some of those Democrats are doing some soul-searching as to whether they're in the right party."[115] But not many followed Atkinson's lead. William Lucas, an obscure county-level official, joined the party to run for the Michigan governorship, while Kent Hance, who earned some intraparty controversy for cosponsoring Reagan's 1981 tax cut in the House, unsuccessfully sought the party's Texas gubernatorial nomination following his failure in 1984 to win the Democratic Senate primary.[116] A post-reelection push for converts secured about a hundred state and local officials.[117] Congressional Democrats remained reluctant to change party. The unlikelihood of Republican capture of

[111] *Boston Globe*, Nov. 8, 1984, 2.
[112] Allentown, Pa., *Morning Call*, Aug. 23, 1985, A6.
[113] Kenneth S. Baer, *Reinventing Democrats: The Politics of Liberalism from Reagan to Clinton* (Lawrence: University Press of Kansas, 2000), 75–76.
[114] Hunt, "National Politics," 1.
[115] *Fortune*, Sept. 21, 1981, 70–71.
[116] *WSJ*, May 17, 1985, 1.
[117] *Orlando Sentinel*, June 15, 1985, A19.

the House encouraged southern conservatives to conclude that they possessed more power and influence as a minority within the majority party, thanks to the seniority system and control of committees.[118] Moreover, in changing party they risked a loss of support among political allies as well as voters.[119] Many also emphasized a desire to temper the Democrats' liberalism, while perceiving distinctions between their conservatism and the Republicans'. "I want the Democrats to be a party with a social conscience but business common sense," remarked Representative Charles Stenholm of Texas in 1990, for example. "The Republicans are antigovernment. They believe that no government is the solution. I strongly disagree with that."[120] A further disincentive to conversion was a resistance to newcomers that former Democrats sometimes encountered.[121]

Even if Reagan failed to persuade many Democrats to follow him in switching party, he nevertheless left a powerful legacy that involved a longer-term, less tangible component. By the start of the twenty-first century, the party contained many politicians and activists who considered Ronald Reagan as their political inspiration.[122] In time the Reagan effect was therefore more significant as a force for mobilization rather than conversion.

Brock's efforts to revitalize the party during the Carter years encompassed attention to African Americans. Although their Democratic identification remained overwhelming, there were signs that this loyalty was slightly weakening. It was not only the growth of the black middle class that fueled optimism about potential Republican gains. Another cause was the belief among some African Americans that Democratic politicians were neglecting their concerns due to the lack of interparty competition for their vote. "We must pursue a strategy that prohibits one party from taking us for granted and another party from writing us off," the Reverend Jesse Jackson, later a contender for the Democratic presidential nomination, told an RNC meeting in 1978.

In 1980 the national committee ran a program in five Senate races promoting better communication with black voters. The results were promising. In Alabama, Florida, Georgia, Oklahoma, and Pennsylvania, the Republican candidate won more support among African Americans than Reagan did against Carter. In Oklahoma, for example, more than four out of ten African Americans voted for Don Nickles, whose overall support was 53.5 percent.[123]

The momentum created by Brock did not outlast his tenure, however.[124] The Reagan administration's record on race deepened the belief that the GOP did

[118] Nicol C. Rae, *Southern Democrats* (New York: Oxford University Press, 1994), 68–73.
[119] Lublin, *The Republican South*, 71.
[120] Rae, *Southern Democrats*, 72.
[121] *WSJ*, July 22, 1986, 1.
[122] *National Journal*, June 12, 2004, 1857; Critchlow, "Mobilizing Women," 312–313.
[123] Pearl T. Robinson, "Whither the Future of Blacks in the Republican Party?" *Political Science Quarterly* 97 (1982), 207–231.
[124] *NYT*, April 14, 1982, A20.

not take these problems seriously. Reagan articulated a color-blind philosophy that encouraged the perception that he did not grasp the reality of inequalities and intolerance. He launched his 1980 campaign at the Neshoba County Fair in Mississippi, where he talked of states' rights but not of the 1964 murder in the county of civil rights activists James Chaney, Andrew Goodman, and Michael Schwerner.[125] Reagan's lack of confidence in federal power made him uncomfortable with much action to protect and promote civil rights. It led him to oppose the denial by the Internal Revenue Service of tax exemptions to Bob Jones University, a Christian institution that forbade interracial dating and marriage, although he later insisted that he did not realize that the case involved civil rights, and revised his position to emphasize questions of the service's regulatory powers as problematic. He also favored scaling back the Voting Rights Act's reach on its renewal in 1982 until significant sentiment in Congress encouraged him to endorse it.[126]

Even leading African American Republicans were dissatisfied with the record. Having investigated the views of the Council of 100, a black Republican organization of business and professional leaders, in February 1984 aide Melvin L. Bradley reported concern about "a 'small clique' within the Administration which continues to raise issues contrary to the interest of Blacks, such as opposition to legitimate affirmative action," together with the belief that "the Administration's level of interest in economic self-sufficiency for Blacks remains inadequate, despite the President's strong business development and other statements."[127] Bradley's "small clique" notably included William Bradford Reynolds, assistant attorney general for civil rights, and Edwin Meese, III, White House counselor and later attorney general, who advocated the end of affirmative action. Political concerns led by Secretary of Labor William Brock helped inflame opposition to Reynolds and Meese among many other administration officials; policies of minority preference remained unchanged.[128] Beyond the politics of civil rights, the administration's economic agenda had a race-connected impact; African Americans were disproportionately among those adversely affected by program cutbacks and by the growing gap between rich and poor, a new inequality that structural changes in the economy as well as tax changes exacerbated.[129]

The party's critics believed that one factor that limited its policy options was a desire to seek electoral advantage in racism – to win the votes of whites

---

[125] Jeremy D. Mayer, "Reagan and Race: Prophet of Color Blindness, Baiter of the Backlash," in Kyle Longley et al., *Deconstructing Reagan: Conservative Mythology and America's Fortieth President* (Armonk, N.Y.: Sharpe, 2007), 70–89; Jeremy D. Mayer, *Running on Race: Racial Politics in Presidential Campaigns, 1960–2000* (New York: Random House, 2002), 150–172.

[126] Carter, *From George Wallace to Newt Gingrich*, 58.

[127] Melvin L. Bradley to James A. Baker, III, Feb. 14, 1984, box 10, series I, Baker Files.

[128] Hugh Davis Graham, "Civil Rights Policy," in W. Elliot Brownlee and Graham, eds., *Reagan Presidency: Pragmatic Conservatism and Its Legacies* (Lawrence: University Press of Kansas, 2003), 283–290.

[129] Carter, *From George Wallace to Newt Gingrich*, 62–64.

opposed to progress on race.[130] Once the Democratic Party's pride, the label of liberalism increasingly seemed a liability that Republicans could exploit. Its connotation of support for civil rights helped to account for the change. "To my constituents, a liberal is a person who supports the blacks, plain and simple," said one Chicago Democrat.[131] Critics also saw programs run by the national committee and state parties to promote ballot security as targeted to reduce the numbers of African Americans voting.[132]

The administration's expectations of electoral support among African Americans were low. Its 1984 target was 10 percent, about the level achieved by the Republican in every post-Goldwater presidential contest.[133] Indeed, concern about African American support often involved no serious contemplation of a meaningful increase but instead anxiety about the negative consequences of such a low figure. The growth in voter turnout among African Americans bolstered such anxiety. Advocating better communications with black Americans as the 1982 elections approached, aide Dan J. Smith advised that "the primary objective [of such activity] would be to convince black voters that Republicans do not so threaten their vital interests that blacks must turnout [sic] in record numbers to vote against us."[134] Another anxiety involved the damage among non-black Americans of the perception that the Reagan administration cared little about the problems of race or even that Ronald Reagan held bigoted views.[135] Aides recognized that efforts to win African Americans were largely limited to such symbols as appointments, but it was difficult to move beyond such a limited approach, especially in contrast to the Democrats' egalitarian commitment.[136] As head of the White House Office of Public Liaison, Elizabeth Dole concluded that symbolism was not enough, but that the administration's antigovernment priorities prevented the construction of an appeal rooted in substantive policy achievement. "The President is unlikely to make significant inroads into the Black community without abandoning his strategic commitment to federalism, further budget cuts and merit-based employment practices," she wrote in 1982.[137]

At the end of the Reagan years, a revised approach to the electoral calculation concluded that to write off black support entirely in search of white support made little strategic sense. Lee Atwater, who became RNC chair after running Bush's 1988 presidential campaign, said that the party's level of black

[130] Monte Piliawsky, "The 1984 Election's Message to Black Americans: Challenges, Choices, Prospects," *Freedomways* 25 (1985), 18–27.

[131] *In These Times*, Oct. 26–Nov. 1, 1988, 2.

[132] *In These Times*, Oct. 15–21, 1986, 6.

[133] Richard B. Wirthlin to James A. Baker, III, Michael K. Deaver, Edward J. Rollins, and Stuart Spencer, Sept. 27, 1984, box 10, series I, Baker Files.

[134] Dan J. Smith to Michael K. Deaver, Aug. 4, 1982, OA 7621, Deaver Files.

[135] Elizabeth H. Dole to James A. Baker, III (draft), Jan. 30, 1982, box 5, series I, Dole Files; *National Review*, July 8, 1983, 800.

[136] Jim Cicconi to Elizabeth H. Dole, Edward J. Rollins, Lee Atwater, and Red Caveney, April 7, 1982, box 6, series I, Dole Files.

[137] Elizabeth H. Dole to James A. Baker, III (draft), Jan. 30, 1982, box 5, series I, Dole Files.

support needed to reach 20 percent "if we want to become a majority party."[138] An overwhelmingly white party as the nation's majority was demographically implausible. Cultivation of African American voters was "a long-term political necessity and, more than that, a moral imperative," according to Atwater, known for his aggression in campaign politics, including race-conscious appeals – alluding to race-related controversies with coded language that did not explicitly mention race – to build white support.[139]

The creation of a White House special assistant on minority affairs in 1982 provided further evidence of insensitivity to group concerns, even though it represented an effort to improve matters. It failed to acknowledge the distinctiveness of different minority communities, especially that of Latino Americans, whose increased support the party coveted. Elizabeth Dole noted that Latino supporters resented the idea of single institutional responsibility for such matters, and she reported, "The strong message from grassroots Hispanic supporters is that a publicized effort to win over disaffected Blacks will intensify the erosion of support among Hispanics, who accorded the President unprecedented support in 1980."[140] Aide Michael Deaver devised an array of ideas to develop better links with prominent Latinos as a means of cultivating the larger community's support.[141] Thinking along similar lines, Dole nevertheless struggled to recruit senior administration figures to make appearances before Latino groups.[142] The family-oriented conservatism among some Latinos, a demographic group of great diversity, often became the focus for Republican cultivation – a different route to inclusivity. In south Texas, the 1984 Republican message to Latino Democrats was that their party's nomination of Mondale represented its capture by "far-out, kookie, left-wing Democrats."[143] There were Latino appointments, too, including that of Lauro F. Cavazos as education secretary in 1988, the first Latino Cabinet member.[144] This was, former political aide Lyn Nofziger later noted, "a political favor to George Bush."[145] Employing Hispanic Americans as a category, exit polling reported that a little more than one in three among them favored Reagan in 1980 and 1984 and that this proportion dropped

[138] Louis Bolce, Gerald De Maio, and Douglas Muzzio, "Blacks and the Republican Party: The 20 Percent Solution," *Political Science Quarterly* 107 (1992), 63.

[139] *American Visions*, June 1989, 16–18; Thomas Byrne Edsall with Mary D. Edsall, *Chain Reaction: The Impact of Race, Rights, and Taxes on American Politics* (New York: Norton, 1991).

[140] Elizabeth H. Dole to James A. Baker, III, April 5, 1982, box 6, series I, Dole Files.

[141] Michael Deaver to Outreach Strategy Group, June 6, 1983, OA 8546, Deaver Files.

[142] Elizabeth H. Dole to Edwin Meese, III, James A. Baker, III, and Michael Deaver, May 29, 1982, OA 5455, series I, Dole Files.

[143] Lee Atwater, report, Sept. 8, 1984, box 10, Baker Files.

[144] Francis E. Rourke and John T. Tierney, "The Setting: Changing Patterns of Presidential Politics, 1960 and 1988," in Michael Nelson, ed., *The Elections of 1988* (Washington, D.C.: CQ Press, 1989), 11.

[145] Lyn Nofziger, *Nofziger* (Washington, D.C.: Regnery Gateway, 1992), 245.

back to three in ten for Bush in 1988.[146] Lower than among most groups of the electorate, this support was nevertheless significantly higher than that of African Americans.

Pollster Louis Harris claimed in 1981 that "for President Reagan and the Republicans, the single most formidable obstacle to their becoming a majority party in the 1980s is the vote of women."[147] The appearance in 1980 of a significant "gender gap" between the parties was a surprise to many contemporaries. In earlier years the GOP had sometimes gained a greater level of support among women than men. During the 1960s and 1970s, the difference was minimal, however. By contrast, in the Carter–Reagan contest, the gap was as great as nine points according to an exit poll; Reagan secured a vote of 56 percent among men but only 47 percent among women.

Early interpretations of the gender gap tended to emphasize the party's lack of support for the Equal Rights Amendment, together with some other issues considered as particularly important to women, such as the party's association with opposition to *Roe v. Wade* abortion rights.[148] At the 1980 national convention, ERA supporters used electoral arguments as well as principle in warning fellow Republicans of the dangers of dropping the party's commitment to the amendment, urgently controversial as a result of Phyllis Schlafly's antifeminist mobilization against its ratification.[149] Conservatism was more powerful at the convention than such moderation, however. Not only did the platform omit an ERA commitment, but it included a pledge to pursue an antiabortion constitutional amendment – a reflection of the intraparty influence of culturally conservative women, rather than Republican feminists.[150] In place of the ERA, Reagan promised in his acceptance speech to encourage governors to repeal discriminatory laws and to ensure the effective implementation of federal antidiscrimination laws.[151]

The understanding of the gender gap that emphasized the party's ERA opposition was wrong, however. Conservative views on the ERA were no less common among women than men, and women were no more likely to choose a candidate on these grounds.[152] Instead, the foundation of the gender gap involved a much broader set of differences between how women and how men viewed issues and evaluated the parties. Reagan and the Republican Party

---

[146] Gerald M. Pomper, "The Presidential Election," in Pomper et al., *The Election of 1988: Reports and Interpretations* (Chatham, N.J.: Chatham House, 1989), 71; Paul J. Quirk, "The Election," in Michael Nelson, ed., *The Elections of 1988* (Washington, D.C.: CQ Press, 1989), 82.

[147] Melich, *The Republican War Against Women*, 184.

[148] Jane J. Mansbridge, "Myth and Reality: The ERA and the Gender Gap in the 1980 Election," *POQ* 49 (1985), 164–178.

[149] Bill Green, news release, July 1, 1980, box 28, ERAmerica Records.

[150] Critchlow, "Mobilizing Women."

[151] Melich, *The Republican War Against Women*, 163–164.

[152] Mansbridge, "Myth and Reality," 164–178.

advanced ideas that appealed to more men than women. Indeed, the gender gap did not represent women's rejection of the GOP or Reagan. Instead, the phenomenon involved the greater mobilization of new party support among men – especially white men in the South – as opposed to women. When the party gained strength during this period, it was therefore thanks to men; women showed no similarly new level of Republican enthusiasm.[153] This trend was particularly notable among single women, not often noticed at the time; the married were more likely to move from the Democrats and toward the Republicans.[154] The gender gap involved not only different views about issues but different ideas about their relative salience, too. A study of Reagan support in 1982, for example, found that positive views among men about the administration's policy toward the Soviet Union and negative views among women about its welfare policy accounted for much of the gender gap.[155] Another study discovered that women and men formed evaluations about the administration's economic record distinctively; women were likelier to make a political decision according to their evaluation of overall economic performance, while men were likelier to do so according to their personal situation. Women, moreover, tended to view the economic outlook with more pessimism than men.[156]

Thoughtful analyses within the administration correctly concluded that the gender gap was resistant to simple solutions.[157] But the administration only offered simple solutions, conscious of the election cycle. In his State of the Union addresses between 1982 and 1984, Reagan crafted an appeal to those women likely to be sympathetic to his economic agenda by emphasizing his support for workplace equality. His second-term addresses, by contrast, did not mention these issues.[158] Appointments similarly showed sensitivity to the campaign calendar; the proportion of women nominees to Senate-confirmed subcabinet positions reached a high of one in four in 1984, a proportion that markedly dropped in 1985.[159] Following Elizabeth Dole's advice, Reagan

---

[153] Barbara Norrander, "The Evolution of the Gender Gap," *POQ* 63 (1999), 566–576.

[154] Andrea Louise Campbell, "Parties, Electoral Participation, and Shifting Voting Blocs," in Paul Pierson and Theda Skocpol, eds., *The Transformation of American Politics: Activist Government and the Rise of Conservatism* (Princeton, N.J.: Princeton University Press, 2007), 90.

[155] Martin Gilens, "Gender and Support for Reagan: A Comprehensive Model of Presidential Approval," *American Journal of Political Science* 32 (1988), 19–49.

[156] Carole Kennedy Chaney, R. Michael Alvarez, and Jonathan Nagler, "Explaining the Gender Gap in U.S. Presidential Elections, 1980–1992," *Political Research Quarterly* 51 (1998), 311–339.

[157] See, for example, Ann Dore McLaughlin to Donald T. Regan, Nov. 5, 1982, box 58, Regan Papers; Elizabeth H. Dole to Ronald Reagan, Nov. 13, 1982, OA 6393, series I, Dole Files; Faith Ryan Whittlesey to James A. Baker, III, and Michael Deaver, May 24, 1983, box 6, series I, Baker Files; *Policy Review*, Winter 1984, 80–82.

[158] Kira Sanbonmatsu, *Democrats, Republicans, and the Politics of Women's Place* (Ann Arbor: University of Michigan Press, 2002), 137.

[159] Janet M. Martin, "An Examination of Executive Branch Appointments in the Reagan Administration by Background and Gender," *Western Political Quarterly* 44 (1991), 178–180.

established a White House Coordinating Council on Women to identify government action to help women, but the council's work lost any momentum after Dole moved to become transportation secretary in early 1983. It was, according to party activist Tanya Melich, "a campaign tool, not a commitment to further policies for women."[160] Another dominant response to the gender gap involved a desire to improve communication with women, reflecting the belief that incorrect perceptions of the administration's goals and achievements were a key problem.[161]

The gender gap was smaller in 1984, partly because the Democratic campaign downplayed efforts to mobilize women – despite the vice-presidential nomination of Geraldine Ferraro – in the belief both that this support was safe and that such efforts might alienate men.[162] By contrast, during 1983 and 1984 the Republican Party and the Reagan campaign ran advertising targeted at women. Campaign operatives attributed part of Reagan's recovery among women to the measured nature of his response to the Soviet Union's destruction of a South Korean airplane in 1983, which amended his "trigger-happy" image.[163] Though smaller, the gender gap persisted. While the margin of Reagan's victory over Mondale meant that his lower level of support among women – which still amounted to a majority – did not hurt his candidacy, the votes of women accounted for a number of Democratic victories, including the Senate seats for Illinois, Iowa, Massachusetts, and Michigan, and the Vermont gubernatorial contest.[164] Efforts to heal the gender gap were inadequate, and the gap persisted as a new aspect of the difference between the party coalitions. A 1988 exit poll gave Bush a 50–49 percent edge among women over his Democratic rival Michael Dukakis, but 57 percent of men favored Reagan's vice president.[165]

Throughout the Republican Party's long period as the nation's minority, the House of Representatives was rarely a center of debate about the majority quest.[166] The House became more central to the debate during the 1980s as a result of some members' intense frustration with minority status, their sense that too many fellow Republican officeholders complacently accepted such a fate, and their belief that a majority was within reach. This effort's leader was Newt Gingrich, elected in 1978 to represent a suburban district of Atlanta, a history professor who thought creatively if also sometimes eccentrically about

[160] Melich, *The Republican War Against Women*, 187–188 (quotation, 188).
[161] *NYT*, Dec. 3, 1982, A26.
[162] *In These Times*, Nov. 21–Dec. 4, 1984, 6.
[163] Xandra Kayden and Eddie Mahe, Jr., *The Party Goes On: The Persistence of the Two-Party System in the United States* (New York: Basic, 1985), 173.
[164] Scott Keeter, "Public Opinion in 1984," in Gerald M. Pomper et al., *The Election of 1984: Reports and Interpretations* (Chatham, N.J.: Chatham House, 1985), 101.
[165] Jean Bethke Elshtain, "Issues and Themes in the 1988 Campaign," in Michael Nelson, ed., *The Elections of 1988* (Washington, D.C.: CQ Press, 1989), 116.
[166] Connelly and Pitney, *Congress' Permanent Minority?* 24–26, 154–157.

politics. Explaining the lack of engagement among House Republicans with the minority problem, Gingrich observed that it was "easier for the minority legislator to accommodate to the system," due to benefits such as committee influence and enhanced opportunities to contribute to the development of legislation. "There are more rewards for being a good minority legislator than there are for trying to become a majority legislator," he said.[167] But a new climate was emerging, and assisting Gingrich's efforts in this regard was a new tide of partisanship that encouraged majority Democrats to eschew cross-party collaboration, as well as some minority Republicans to demand more.[168] It took time for Gingrich's initiatives to take effect, but their contribution to Republican fortunes in the following decade was important.

In diagnosing the cause of GOP problems, Gingrich emphasized the party's negative opposition to Democratic proposals and its lack of creative ideas that would provide an attractive alternative to liberalism. Gingrich, full of ideas, "may have enough energy and talent to elect a Republican House by himself," remarked a White House speechwriter.[169] He was one among other congressional Republicans who formed the Conservative Opportunity Society (COS) in 1983. According to Gingrich, Richard Nixon helped inspire its creation as a way to cast aside the "boring," low-profile nature of House Republicans. "If you really want to become the majority," Nixon advised, "you have to fill the place with ideas."[170] Gingrich later assumed control of GOPAC, an organization established in 1979 to raise funds toward the goal of a majority, and under his leadership it boosted its already-considerable efforts to develop good Republican candidates for office.[171] In *Window of Opportunity*, a book he coauthored, Gingrich gave full rein to his imagination, stressing technological change as the motor of opportunity. "Breakthroughs in computers, biology, and space make possible new jobs, new opportunities, and new hope on a scale unimagined since Christopher Columbus discovered a new world," he wrote, calling for reforms of the welfare system and government bureaucracies in order to exploit such change effectively.[172] Claiming Theodore Roosevelt as his inspiration and decrying Herbert Hoover's legacy of "a maniacal, antigovernment belief," Gingrich called for "positive, dynamic conservatism" that embraced government action to foster growth.[173]

Gingrich viewed the party's attitude toward African American support as defeatist, urging a more positive approach. Noting that many African

[167] Connelly and Pitney, *Congress' Permanent Minority?* 5.
[168] Connelly and Pitney, *Congress' Permanent Minority?* 7–8.
[169] Anthony R. Dolan to Paul Laxalt, July 25, 1984, box 26, Rusher Papers.
[170] Newt Gingrich, *Lessons Learned the Hard Way: A Personal Report* (New York: HarperCollins, 1998), 170.
[171] Douglas L. Koopman, *Hostile Takeover: The House Republican Party, 1980–1995* (Lanham, Md.: Rowman & Littlefield, 1996); Edwards, *Conservative Revolution*, 283.
[172] Newt Gingrich with David Drake and Marianne Gingrich, *Window of Opportunity: A Blueprint for the Future* (New York: Tom Doherty Associates, 1984) (quotation, xv).
[173] *NYT*, Aug. 11, 1983, A18.

Americans were conservative on some issues – "[b]lacks are anti-crime, pro-military, pro-patriotism," he said – he nevertheless acknowledged the community's faith in activist government. To tackle this support for the welfare state, he advocated the promotion of new African American leaders to teach what he called "the more powerful lessons of hard work, frugality, patience – lessons that have been learned by West Indian blacks, Korean immigrants and others who threaten to overtake blacks economically."[174] Gingrich's alternative approach seemed to lack awareness of the depth of the African American community's socioeconomic problems; the call for new leadership looked grandiosely ambitious, if not patronizing and unrealistic.

Confrontation was the essence of Gingrich's politics. He believed that Republican success depended on the communication of fundamental differences between the parties. As early as 1976 he sent Guy Vander Jagt a plan to capture a majority, emphasizing that "realigning elections are divisive, not appeasing."[175] After the passage of the 1981 economic package, he advocated an effort to promote awareness of a distinction between the Republicans as "the low interest rate, low inflation, high take-home pay and high jobs creation party" and the Democrats as "the high interest rate, high inflation, low take-home pay and low jobs creation party."[176] A later iteration of this theme, circulated by GOPAC and drawing on Gingrich's speeches, contrasted words such as "*courage, moral, children, candidly, caring, choice, passionate*" for descriptions of Republican proposals with words such as "*decay, collapse, corrupt, bizarre, self-serving, unionized bureaucracy, sensationalists* and *antiflag*" for attacks on Democrats.[177] In 1982, when the recession arrived, he privately scolded James Baker, the White House chief of staff, stating that the administration's "lack of effective leadership on behalf of the Reagan program has allowed us to take fundamental public support and lose it in the trivia of daily headlines." Among these problems, according to Gingrich, were poor communication with the public and poor coordination with Republicans in Congress.[178] For Gingrich, Reagan's politics of optimism lacked a clarity of purpose as well as the aggressive edge needed to maximize the Republican advantage. He advocated a more radical agenda for Republicans to gain control of the House.[179] Instead, they missed an opportunity, he thought. "Reagan should have prepared for [his second term in] office by forcing a polarization of the country," Gingrich said of the 1984 campaign. "He should have been running against liberals and radicals."[180] The comment echoed Richard

---

[174] *WP*, Dec. 21, 1983, A27.

[175] Mel Steely, *The Gentleman from Georgia: The Biography of Newt Gingrich* (Macon, Ga.: Mercer University Press, 2000), 74–75.

[176] Newt Gingrich, "Republican Strategy for the Fall of 1981," n.d., box 133, Regan Papers.

[177] *U.S. News & World Report*, Dec. 24, 1990, 20.

[178] Newt Gingrich to James A. Baker, III, Feb. 25, 1982, box 34, Rusher Papers.

[179] *WP*, Nov. 4, 1984, D5.

[180] Nina Easton, *Gang of Five: Leaders at the Center of the Conservative Crusade* (New York: Simon & Schuster, 2000), 159.

Nixon's emphasis on confrontation and opposition as the way to undermine Democratic success.

COS stressed interparty differences, and its members began by using "special order" speeches in the House – now televised via cable's C-SPAN – criticizing the Democratic leadership. The organization later shifted its attention to legislative discussion. But concerns about alleged ethics violations caused Gingrich to lead a clamor in 1987 and 1988 for an investigation of Representative James Wright of Texas, the speaker. COS thus retained its reputation for attack rhetoric rather than policy substance.[181] Cato, a *National Review* columnist, observed in 1988 that the society "certainly did help pressure the House Republican leadership into adopting a more aggressive, confrontational posture." But its legislative contribution was less positive than Gingrich sought. "They've had a difficult time transforming their opposition into a real program," noted political scientist Norman Ornstein.[182] Representative Vin Weber of Minnesota, one of the organization's key figures, said that even though it "encouraged greater activism among House Republicans," it devoted too much attention to "wedge issues against the Democrats, without also creating magnet issues that would attract the public," thus becoming seen "as primarily negative and confrontational."[183]

In 1988 the administration's political office made plans not only to keep the White House in Republican hands, but also to boost the numbers of Republicans in Congress and, with an eye on post-1990 reapportionment, to win state legislative chambers.[184] It again urged Reagan's extensive involvement in the campaign.[185] Reagan undertook such campaign activities, described by Ed Rollins as "the greatest baton-pass in the history of American politics." Aide Frank Donatelli counted 193 occasions in sixty-seven speeches after the end of the primaries when Reagan praised his vice president. Reagan tailored his political activities according to the Bush strategy. He thus argued that the Democrats were a risk to his administration's progress, sought to demonize liberalism as the "L word," and made appearances before targeted groups and in priority states – speaking to blue-collar ethnic Americans at Wozniak's Casino in Chicago, to United Auto Workers members in Cleveland, and to Baptists at Baylor University in Texas. The activities extended beyond help for Bush, including aid for other Republican candidates and fundraising for the party.[186] Reagan's effectiveness as a speaker underlined the distinctiveness of his political strength. Surveying the contest to succeed him in the nomination struggles, Richard Nixon wrote Reagan in praise of his public appearances: "I wish some of our candidates could

[181] Connelly and Pitney, *Congress' Permanent Minority?* 27–28, 84–86.
[182] *National Review*, June 24, 1988, 11.
[183] *Policy Review*, Spring 1990, 38.
[184] Frank J. Donatelli to Howard H. Baker, Jr., and Kenneth M. Duberstein, Feb. 24, 1988, box 3, series I, Duberstein Files.
[185] Frank J. Donatelli to Howard H. Baker, Jr., July 17, 1987, box 3, series I, Duberstein Files.
[186] Frank J. Donatelli to Kenneth M. Duberstein, Nov. 7, 1988, box 3, series I, Duberstein Files.

get that same element of passion and conviction in their speeches during this boring campaign season."[187] In addition to Reagan's campaign support for his vice president, the administration implemented policy in ways that helped Bush, postponing until after election day some unpopular decisions, and Bush's assignments included ceremonial and foreign-policy appearances designed to boost his presidential credentials.[188] Reagan and his administration's record remained popular, and this popularity benefited Bush, perhaps to a critically significant extent.[189]

Bush's acceptance speech at the national convention sought to reap the benefits of the administration's achievements; he also underscored differences with Democratic Party presidential candidate Michael Dukakis on social issues and placed emphasis on the need for "a kinder, gentler nation" of racial tolerance and concern for the needy.[190] Although he spoke of "a thousand points of light," his campaign did not manage to sustain Reagan's sunny optimism, despite presidential assistance. Most observers agreed that negativity was the campaign's defining characteristic, largely thanks to aggressive attacks on Dukakis as soft on crime – sometimes employing racially coded language and imagery – and on national defense.[191] Dukakis tried to stress instead managerial competence as a deciding issue.[192] Such an emphasis was reminiscent of Republican efforts in earlier decades to endorse socioeconomic goals similar to those of New Deal liberalism, but to claim that their party offered better management of government. It therefore demonstrated Republican success in reshaping the terms of national political debate, undermining if not destroying the Democrats' old advantage of New Deal liberalism. In significant respects that advantage endured. The economy and welfare matters involved issues that helped Democrats, whereas foreign policy and "values" issues helped Republicans.[193]

Bush defeated Dukakis by 54 to 46 percent. But Republicans remained the congressional minority. Only 9 seats changed party in the House, and Democrats made a net gain of 3 to achieve 243 seats against the Republicans' 159. Senate races were more competitive; Democrats won four seats from the Republicans and Republicans won three, leaving Republicans at a total of forty-five.[194]

[187] Richard Nixon to Ronald Reagan, Feb. 4, 1988, box 20, series II, Presidential Handwriting File.

[188] Pomper, "Presidential Election," 139.

[189] Alan I. Abramowitz and Jeffrey A. Segal, "Beyond Willie Horton and the Pledge of Allegiance: National Issues in the 1988 Elections," *Legislative Studies Quarterly* 15 (1990), 565–580; Quirk, "Election," 85.

[190] Quirk, "Election," 74.

[191] Wilson Carey McWilliams, "The Meaning of the Election," in Gerald M. Pomper et al., *The Election of 1988: Reports and Interpretations* (Chatham, N.J.: Chatham House, 1989), 177–206.

[192] Quirk, "Election," 72.

[193] McWilliams, "Meaning of the Election," 189–190; Shafer, "Notion of an Electoral Order."

[194] Gary C. Jacobson, "Congress: A Singular Continuity," in Michael Nelson, ed., *The Elections of 1988* (Washington, D.C.: CQ Press, 1989), 127–152.

The Republican Party was no longer the nation's minority. It now possessed what Richard Wirthlin called parity status. Especially promising for the party's prospects was a transformed national agenda, now friendlier to conservative concerns. Sympathetic analysts credited the Reagan administration with successes in foreign policy, leading toward the Cold War's end, and with a period of sustained economic growth.

The Republican ascent to parity status did not mean there was a level playing field for interparty competition at every level of elected office. The outcome of the 1988 elections seemed to confirm that the Republicans were the natural party of the White House. Control of the House, by contrast, seemed out of the party's grasp, while that of the Senate was clearly attainable, if more difficult to win than the presidency. This parity status had certain strategic advantages; it allowed politicians to attribute policy disappointments to their opposition. In spring 1988 Reagan replied to a supporter disappointed that the "Reagan revolution" had failed to achieve its revolutionary potential by writing of Democratic opposition to his plans. "I've had vetoes of pork barrel spending measures overturned, and our own programs buried in committee or simply killed on the floor," he wrote. "Billions of dollars have been cut from our defense budget, and some of our social programs, such as stopping runaway abortions, aren't given the light of day in the Congress." But in using the Democrats' power as a reason for his administration's shortcomings, Reagan affirmed the importance of the goal of Republican congressional control, and he turned to history to explain the limits of Republican influence over time.[195] Reagan did not mention another factor that was important – the federal bureaucracy's role in implementing policy, which permitted an influence potentially favorable to liberal goals. Interest groups also enjoyed influence, as did the federal judiciary in deciding controversies over administrative law.[196] If the quest to overcome minority status involved many challenges, the search to reshape public policy presented a new set of obstacles.

Contemporary political science offered explanations for "divided government."[197] Morris P. Fiorina, for example, observed that neither party successfully represented the center of public opinion, and that voters therefore preferred a Republican–Democratic balance, which produced policies that simultaneously sought conservative virtues of fiscal restraint and liberal virtues of humanitarian concern, without the excesses of unrestrained laissez-faire economics or similarly unrestrained big government.[198]

[195] Ronald Reagan to William W. Peaslee, April 18, 1988, box 20, series II, Presidential Handwriting File.
[196] Critchlow, *Conservative Ascendancy*, 185–191; Gareth Davies, *See Government Grow: Education Politics from Johnson to Reagan* (Lawrence: University Press of Kansas, 2007); Sidney M. Milkis, *Political Parties and Constitutional Government: Remaking American Democracy* (Baltimore: Johns Hopkins University Press, 1999).
[197] *WP*, Sept. 5, 1987, A13.
[198] Morris P. Fiorina, "The Reagan Years: Turning to the Right or Groping Toward the Middle," in Barry Cooper, Allan Kornberg, and William Mischler, eds., *Resurgence of Conservatism in Anglo-American Democracies* (Durham, N.C.: Duke University Press, 1988), 430–459.

Byron E. Shafer saw public opinion as involving two majorities, one of conservatism on social issues and foreign policy and one of liberalism on economic issues and the welfare state. Neither party managed to articulate both sets of majority views. In any election much depended on which issues became salient; debates about social issues and foreign policy facilitated Republican victory, whereas debates about economic issues and the welfare state encouraged Republican defeat. Battles for the White House more naturally involved the former and those for the House the latter, due to each institution's responsibilities; Senate contests more frequently involved a mix of concerns across these issue areas, helping to explain the Republicans' greater likelihood of winning that body. Still another view focused on the parties' internal dynamics and conceived the rise of divided government as connected especially with Democratic problems rather than Republican progress. Conflict over the party's presidential nomination, which the post-1968 reforms of the system encouraged, was an obstacle to success for a nominee.[199] The Democratic Party was more likely to suffer such conflict, as William G. Mayer, among others, concluded.[200] Nicol C. Rae further pointed out that the diversity of opinion, which led to such conflict and which impeded a presidential candidacy, was helpful at the congressional level, where it involved instead responsiveness to local conditions.[201]

The different explanations all underlined the difficulties Republicans faced in seeking to move from parity to majority status. They even suggested that dominance such as that achieved by the Democratic Party in the 1930s was unlikely to be replicated in the foreseeable future. Majority status remained a prize that was apparently out of reach.

[199] Ladd, *Where Have All the Voters Gone?* 50–73.
[200] William G. Mayer, *The Divided Democrats: Ideological Unity, Party Reform, and Presidential Elections* (Boulder, Colo.: Westview, 1996); Martin P. Wattenberg, "The Republican Presidential Advantage in the Age of Party Disunity," in Gary W. Cox and Samuel Kernell, eds., *The Politics of Divided Government* (Boulder, Colo.: Westview, 1991), 39–56.
[201] Nicol C. Rae, "Class and Culture: American Political Cleavages in the 20th Century," *Western Political Quarterly* 45 (1992), 629–650.

Conclusion

The history of the Republican Party between the Great Depression and the Reagan years reveals the persistent electoral strength of New Deal liberalism. Time and again voters demonstrated their support for this brand of government activism, which its exponents modified over time in response to changing conditions, but of which moderation was generally a defining characteristic. The Democrats' moderation usually confounded Republicans' efforts to promote what they saw as the benefits of conservatism or the shortcomings of New Deal liberalism. For much of the period the majority party displayed skill in holding together its electoral coalition and in preventing the minority from achieving a breakthrough.

More Americans consistently saw themselves as Democratic Party supporters than as Republican Party supporters, as data on party identification suggest. The GOP's greatest successes depended on defection, not conversion; these were thanks to Nixon Democrats in the late 1960s and early 1970s and Reagan Democrats in the 1980s, as well as Eisenhower Democrats in the 1950s (though contemporaries did not use this last term). Except at times of great crisis – such as the Great Depression – an individual's party identification was unlikely to change, which made the Republicans' majority-seeking mission a difficult one. Underpinning Democratic strength was the enduring dominance of concerns relating to New Deal liberalism in electoral politics and in party cleavages, even though the detail of these concerns changed over time; the Democratic Party was the party of New Deal liberalism, and the Republican Party was the party that opposed New Deal liberalism. This government activism did not maintain an equal degree of electoral power throughout the period of the Republican minority; post–Great Society political history is marked by diminished confidence in government to solve socioeconomic problems. But even this decline in New Deal liberalism's power was not significant enough to enable the Republicans to achieve majority status.

Sometimes these liberal concerns declined in salience – when foreign policy became a more important factor in electoral politics, for example – and this helped Republican prospects. The president's responsibilities as commander-in-chief meant that foreign policy was more significant in contests for the White House than in other elections; the power of foreign policy to build a majority for the party at large was more limited. This significance improved Republican prospects for the presidency, after the period of economic crisis and of noninterventionism that begins this study, even when the concerns of New Deal liberalism otherwise operated to GOP disadvantage.

The view that opposition to New Deal liberalism confirmed the party's minority status is not one that many Republicans shared. They saw matters differently, doubting New Deal liberalism's intrinsic electoral strength, intrigued with conservatism's unrealized potential at the polls. Better communication of the Republican message and better organization of Republican supporters often seemed to offer an answer to the minority problem. To be sure, when the party achieved new success in the late 1970s, good communication and good organization were crucial. But that was a time when voters were more ready to listen to the Republican message; Republicans in previous decades – John D. M. Hamilton and Ray Bliss notable among them – had shown similar attentiveness to communications and organizational problems without managing to undermine the Democrats' majority.

Of course, the minority debate did not only involve questions of practical politics. It also involved political issues and ideas. Republican responses to New Deal liberalism were either more or less accommodating – demonstrating a greater emphasis either on the need to fashion an alternative version of the Democrats' government activism or on the imperative to promote antistatist virtues. During the years of World War II's approach and the Cold War's arrival, foreign policy divided Republicans more profoundly, though this was a time when domestic matters tended to remain more electorally decisive than overseas developments. Moderate Republicans' ideas about policy, on the one hand, and conservative Republicans', on the other, were likely to lead to different analyses of and prescriptions for the party's minority problem. As early as 1936, this was visible in the distinction between Charles P. Taft and John Hamilton, both influential thinkers about this problem. Taft emphasized moderate attacks on the poor implementation of New Deal goals to win "independent" voters, whereas Hamilton employed harsher anti–New Deal rhetoric in order to mobilize grassroots enthusiasm and activism. Most famously characterized as Deweyite and Taftite, the competing visions for the GOP's future engendered over time considerable intraparty conflict – conflict that often obscured the extent to which antistatist skepticism of New Deal liberalism united Republicans, even as they disagreed about how best to pursue this agenda.

Confidence in the appeal of their alternative agenda caused some Republicans to act overoptimistically, and counterproductively, in seeking new support. If the popularity of the Democratic Party and New Deal liberalism during the "short twentieth century" primarily accounts for the Republican Party's minority status, then a secondary explanation involves the misinterpretation of mandate. On the occasions when Republicans achieved a breakthrough at the polls, they rarely consolidated the breakthrough but, instead, often squandered the opportunity. Republicans sometimes made electoral advances when New Deal liberalism's salience slipped, but it was the mistakes and misfortunes of incumbent Democrats that were primarily responsible for Republican successes in 1946, 1952, 1968, and 1980. Instead of fashioning a strategy designed to cultivate voters weary of but otherwise sympathetic toward the Democratic Party, Republicans often behaved in ways suggesting a belief that final victory was already theirs, that new voters for their party were now loyal converts rather than skeptical defectors. At each of these moments of breakthrough, leading figures within the presidential party – within the Dewey campaign and within the Eisenhower, Nixon, and Reagan administrations – all acted with more caution, with the awareness that Republican electoral success rested on shaky foundations. But the party at large often lacked such caution, instead seeing the anti-incumbent mood as a pro-Republican tide. This interpretation naturally led to rhetoric and actions that repelled rather than cultivated the newcomers to the party's coalition.

Belief in mandate among some Republicans collided with more cautious interpretations of electoral trends among others in ways that reinforced the party's problem. In the late 1940s, the misleading view that Thomas E. Dewey's low-key campaign against Harry S. Truman misunderstood a new postwar conservatism encouraged a right-wing clamor for an emphasis on conservative principles. This clamor failed to rescue the party's fortunes, but it nevertheless came close to encouraging Republicans to reject Dwight D. Eisenhower, a politician of immense, almost unparalleled, promise, in favor of Robert A. Taft, a politician with a less-than-dazzling record at the polls. Then, in the 1950s, the ambiguous achievements of Eisenhower's quest for a modern Republicanism engendered a fresh clamor for a return to conservatism, involving a remarkable grassroots as well as elite mobilization, which eventually led to Barry Goldwater's disastrous candidacy for the presidency. Nixon's thoughtful but flawed quest for a new majority in the 1970s similarly revitalized conservatism, rather than instigating a larger movement within the party toward a more moderate brand of antistatist opposition to New Deal liberalism, designed to accommodate the popular preference for limited programmatic innovation in addition to the protection of social-welfare advances.

There was thus a disinclination within the party to recognize the electoral imperative of such moderation. Instead, there was an emphasis on conservative principle – not to the detriment of concern about the minority problem but on the basis of the analysis that conservatism was a better route to party gains than moderation. This skepticism of moderation helped to stymie the majority-building efforts of Dewey, Eisenhower, and Nixon, as well as pushing the party in conservatism's direction. Matters were different for Reagan, who was the conservatives' candidate and who did not follow Dewey, Eisenhower, and Nixon in developing a project of moderate accommodation with New Deal liberalism. They were different, too, because of the clearer-cut dissatisfaction with the Democratic Party that many voters had developed. Even Reagan, however, endured conservative discontent, though this remained relatively insignificant until the 1988 nomination contest to succeed him (thus avoiding Reagan himself as a target); under George H. W. Bush as president, discontent with the perceived shortcomings of the Republican record in office then turned active. Because of such perceptions, the 1990s became a turbulent decade for the Republican Party, although it was also the decade when the party finally made lasting gains at the congressional level.

Misinformation partly explains Republican misinterpretations of mandate. The 1936 *Literary Digest* poll, which forecast a Landon victory, most infamously exemplifies the technological obstacles to accurate information about the electorate during the early years of the Republican minority. But many contemporaries recognized that the poll was wrong. A better example of misinformation is Rogers Dunn's analyses of the electorate, which encouraged Republicans to perceive the existence of a hidden vote during the 1950s, as well as to believe in the significance of the bought vote during the 1930s and 1940s. Dubious methodology underpinned Dunn's work, but he found a receptive audience among Republicans who looked for evidence in support of their instinct that New Deal liberalism's popularity was an illusion. Belief in the bought vote discouraged serious discussion of the minority problem during the 1930s, whereas in the 1950s belief in the hidden vote fostered conservative opposition to modern Republicanism, leading toward Goldwater's 1964 candidacy. Some Republicans embraced and believed Dunn's analysis because it supported their preferred strategy for the party; it downplayed the electoral power of the Democrats' ideas.

Such analysis furthermore made sense to many Republicans. Their own political observations and experiences suggested the existence of deeper reservoirs of conservative faith than polls and elections revealed. One factor that distorted Republican analysis of the minority problem and distracted attention from engagement with it was the personal political success of individual politicians. In the 1940s Senator Raymond E. Baldwin pointed out that the party's dominant voices were those from safe Republican areas, where the minority problem was not a locally pressing one, and where constituents consistently demonstrated a preference for a conservative alternative to New Deal liberalism. Misinformation therefore muddied Republican analysis of the minority problem, but it did not remain crucial to misperceptions of the electoral situation.

The later part of this period was a time of sophisticated analysis of public opinion. There seemed to be few reasons for any persistence of misinformation in an era of extensive polling, together with rigorous methodology through which to understand poll results. The Nixon and Reagan administrations were avid consumers of pollsters' offerings, and part of the national committee's revitalization that William Brock engineered during the 1970s involved the systematic use of polling. Still, poll-informed engagement with the minority problem was not necessarily more constructive than non-poll-informed engagement. On the one hand, poll results were open to misinterpretation. On the other, successful implementation of poll-informed analysis was likely to encounter a variety of obstacles, as the travails of Nixon's majority quest demonstrate. In 1970, for example, poll-informed confidence in Richard Scammon and Ben Wattenberg's Social Issue encouraged the development of a negative message that failed to maximize Republican gains or to create a solid foundation for further party growth. Misinformation, then, was problematic for the Republican Party. But better information did not offer a complete solution to the Republican problem.

The pluralistic, as well as ideological and programmatic, dimension of New Deal liberalism attracted Republican criticism. After suspicions in the 1930s that Democrats relied on the bought vote to secure victory, many Republicans subsequently attacked their opponents for responsiveness to interest groups rather than the larger national interest. Labor's role in supporting Democratic candidates especially invited Republican concern and spurred counterorganization. During the minority period, Republicans lacked similar allies; though considered the party friendly to business, until the 1970s they did not view business as a source of support that counterbalanced labor. The party coalition's narrowness had implications for the nature of Republican engagement with the minority problem, especially notable with respect to race; the GOP's whiteness obstructed the likelihood of success in rebuilding African American support.

A study of public opinion in 1964 led Lloyd A. Free and Hadley Cantril to argue that Americans were "ideological conservatives" but "operational liberals." For Free and Cantril, this insight helped explain both the Republican perception of support for Barry Goldwater and the reality of overwhelming victory for Lyndon Johnson. According to their analysis, Republicans were right to notice that antistatist values of individualism and self-reliance shaped a majority's political worldview. But these values coexisted with the necessarily statist acceptance of the need for government action to tackle the nation's social and economic problems. This operational liberalism qualified the electoral potential of ideological conservatism.

Investigation of the Republican Party's engagement with its minority problem between Hoover and Reagan encourages the conclusion that Free and Cantril's observation has relevance far beyond 1964. During the era of New Deal liberalism's dominance, there remained much confidence among Americans in its programmatic ambitions, moderated and qualified by belief in conservative virtues of small government and individual endeavor. Until liberal critiques of the Great Society's reliance on "opportunity" liberalism gained currency within the Democratic Party, awareness of this antistatist impulse usually informed its politicians' initiatives. This moderation constrained any Republican effort to characterize persuasively these initiatives as dangerous and hostile to national ideals, though many Republicans viewed them in exactly this way. And Republicans were right to perceive that many Americans shared their antistatist suspicion of a powerful federal government.

The challenge that the party faced was to work out how to persuade voters of their view that the Democrats' agenda was a threat to conservative virtues, but that the Republicans' agenda did not turn away from active, constructive concern with the socioeconomic problems of the day. It was a challenge that Republicans failed inasmuch as the Democrats' agenda remained more attractive to more Americans than theirs did.

Creativity characterized the Republican response to the party's minority status. This creativity often showed a grasp of the dilemma that, in speaking to the electorate's ideological conservatism, the party should not neglect the operational liberalism among a majority. More frequently, however, conservative principle reinforced a tendency to overlook operational liberalism, an oversight that did not minimize but instead maximized the Democrats' advantage during the era of New Deal liberalism.

Archival Sources

Abilene, Kansas: Dwight D. Eisenhower Library.

Dwight D. Eisenhower Papers as President of the United States: Administration Series;
    Ann Whitman Diary Series; Campaign Series; DDE Diary Series; Name Series.
Dwight D. Eisenhower Records as President, White House Central Files: Official File.
Stephen H. Hess Records.
Robert Humphreys Papers.
Howard Pyle Records.
Republican National Committee, Office of the Chairman (Leonard W. Hall) Records.
Bernard Shanley Diaries.
Thomas E. Stephens Records.

Ann Arbor, Michigan: Bentley Historical Library, University of Michigan.

Walter De Vries Papers.

Ann Arbor, Michigan: Gerald R. Ford Library.

John T. Calkins Files.
Richard B. Cheney Files.
Dorothy E. Downton Files.
Gerald R. Ford Congressional Papers.
Robert T. Hartmann Papers.
Jerry J. Jones Files.
A. James Reichley Interviews.
Robert Teeter Papers.
Agnes M. Waldron Files.

Bloomington, Indiana: The Lilly Library, Indiana University.

Charles Abraham Halleck Papers.
U.S. History Manuscripts.
Wendell Lewis Willkie Papers.
Willkie Clubs Papers.

*Charlottesville, Virginia: Albert and Shirley Small Special Collections
Library, University of Virginia.*

Hugh Scott Papers.

College Park, Maryland: National Archives.

General Records of the Department of Labor, Office of the Secretary (RG 174):
    Records of George P. Shultz, 1969–1970.

College Park, Maryland: Special Collections, University of Maryland Libraries.

Spiro T. Agnew Papers.

Edinburgh, Scotland: Edinburgh University Library.

BBC Press Cuttings Collection.

*New York, New York: Herbert H. Lehman Suite and Papers,
Columbia University.*

Frank Altschul Papers.

Pocantico Hills, New York: Rockefeller Archive Center.

Rockefeller Family Archives: Record Group 4 (Nelson A. Rockefeller Personal Papers);
    Record Group 13 (Public Relations).

*Rochester, New York: Department of Rare Books and Special Collections,
Rush Rhees Library.*

Democrats-For-Willkie Papers.
Thomas E. Dewey Papers.

*Simi Valley, California: Ronald Reagan Presidential
Library.*

Lee Atwater Files.
James A. Baker, III, Files.
Michael K. Deaver Files.
Elizabeth Dole Files.
Kenneth M. Duberstein Files.
Presidential Handwriting File.

St. Paul, Minnesota: Minnesota Historical Society.

Minnesota Republican State Central Committee Records.
Harold Stassen Papers.

Stony Brook, New York: Special Collections and University Archives, Frank Melville, Jr. Memorial Library, Stony Brook University.

Jacob K. Javits Papers.

Tempe, Arizona: Arizona Historical Foundation, Hayden Library, Arizona State University.

Barry Goldwater Papers.
Theodore Humes Papers.

Topeka, Kansas: Kansas State Historical Society.

Alfred M. Landon Papers.

Washington, D.C.: Manuscript Division, Library of Congress.

Henry Justin Allen Papers.
Joseph and Stewart Alsop Papers.
William Edgar Borah Papers.
Henry Brandon Papers.
Raymond Leslie Buell Papers.
Harold H. Burton Papers.
Raymond Clapper Papers.
James Couzens Papers.
Bronson M. Cutting Papers.
Russell Wheeler Davenport Papers.
ERAmerica Records.
James Aloysius Farley Papers.
Henry Prather Fletcher Papers.
John D. M. Hamilton Papers.
Hanna–McCormick Family Papers.
Lewis Graham Hines Papers.
Roy Wilson Howard Papers.
Harold L. Ickes Papers.
Frank Knox Papers.
Ernest Irving Lewis Papers.
Katie Louchheim Papers.
Clare Boothe Luce Papers.
Charles Linza McNary Papers.
Ogden Livingston Mills Papers.
National Association for the Advancement of Colored People Records.
George W. Norris Papers.
John Callan O'Laughlin Papers.
Gifford Pinchot Papers.
Donald T. Regan Papers.
Donald R. Richberg Papers.
Jackie Robinson Papers.

Theodore Roosevelt Papers.
William A. Rusher Papers.
William Safire Papers.
Everett Sanders Papers.
Charles P. Taft Papers.
Robert Taft Papers.
Robert A. Taft Papers.
James Wadsworth Family Papers.
Wallace H. White Papers.
William Allen White Papers.

West Branch, Iowa: Herbert Hoover Presidential Library.

Rogers C. Dunn Papers.
James P. Goodrich Papers.
Bourke B. Hickenlooper Papers.
Herbert Hoover Papers.
Theodore G. Joslin Papers.
Robert H. Lucas Papers.
Nathan William MacChesney Papers.
James H. MacLafferty Papers.
Bradley DeLamater Nash Papers.
Gerald P. Nye Papers.
Edgar Rickard Collection.
Vincent Starzinger Papers.
Lewis L. Strauss Papers.
Edgar French Strother Papers.
Walter N. Thayer, III, Papers.

Yorba Linda, California: Richard Nixon Presidential Library and Museum.

Richard M. Nixon Pre-Presidential Papers.
Richard Nixon Pre-Presidential Speech File.
Richard Nixon Vice Presidential Collection.
Small Deeded Collections.
White House Central Files – Subject Files: BE Business-Economics.
White House Special Files – Central Files (Confidential Files).
White House Special Files – Staff Member and Office Files: Patrick J. Buchanan;
    Dwight L. Chapin; Charles W. Colson; Harry Dent; John D. Ehrlichman; H. R.
    Haldeman; President's Office Files; President's Personal Files.

Index

Abortion, 233, 235, 236, 249, 256, 260–261, 273, 280

Abrahams, A. E., 205

Activist government, 4, 183, 277; and the Hoover administration, 32, 33; and the New Deal, 41–42, 43, 45, 51; popularity of, 1–2, 41–42, 43, 195, 204, 282; and Republicans before the Great Depression, 15–16; and Richard Nixon, 216–217, 218–220, 231. *See also* New Deal liberalism

Activists and activism, 19, 26, 31, 54, 62, 75, 102, 109, 135, 164, 205, 283–284; and Barry Goldwater, 182, 187, 189, 191–194, 196, 201–202, 207; Barry Goldwater's views of, 163; and Citizens for Eisenhower, 165–168, 186; compared with British activism, 72–73; in 1952, 144; and "modern Republicanism," 161–162; and responses to the 1948 campaign, 126; and Richard Nixon, 214, 230; and Ronald Reagan, 259–260; and the Willkie campaign, 85, 96, 102; women as activists 28–29, 74, 75, 170–171

Adams, Julius J., 138

Adams, Sherman, 152, 168

Adamy, Clancy, 168

Affirmative action, 270

African Americans, 14–15, 42, 185, 213, 220, 286; during the Eisenhower years, 174–176, 180; during the Truman years, 137–139; and Herbert Hoover, 19–20, 29–30; and the New Deal years, 51, 64–66, 67, 68, 69–70, 74; and the 1946 elections, 114; and the 1952 elections, 146; and the 1964 elections, 182, 193,

20–203; and the 1976 elections, 244; and the Reagan era, 269–273, 276–277; and Richard Nixon, 225; and the Republican National Committee, 109; and Wendell Willkie, 88, 93–94, 102; and World War II, 105, 106

Agnew, Spiro T., 214, 227–228, 239–241

Agricultural Adjustment Act (1933), 45, 56

Agriculture. *See* Farmers and farm issues

Aiken, George, 138

Alabama, 180, 202, 269

Alaska, 82

Alexander v. Holmes County Board of Education (1969), 224

Allen, Henry J., 18, 38, 64, 110

Alsop, Stewart, 160

Altschul, Frank, 71, 76

Amalgamated Clothing Workers of America, 107

"Amateurs," 84–85, 167, 168, 194

American (as Republican self-characterization), 15, 36, 63, 131

American Conservative Union (ACU), 206, 241

American Enterprise Institute, 255

American Federation of Labor (AFL), 67, 107; Labor's League for Political Education of, 125

American Federation of Labor and Congress of Industrial Organizations (AFL–CIO), 169, 197, 198, 233. *See also* Committee on Political Education

American Independent Party, 242

American Labor Party, 129

American Legion, 58

American Liberty League, 58, 63, 68

American Motors, 186

Americans for Democratic Action (ADA), 198, 206
Anderson, John B., 247
Anticommunism, 6, 58, 89–90, 107, 131; during the Cold War, 113, 123–124, 128, 131–133, 136, 154, 201, 217, 219
Antifeminism, 256–257, 273
Antigovernment sentiment. *See* antistatism
Anti-internationalism, 151–152
Anti-interventionism, 79–80, 83, 92, 97–100, 110
Antistatism, 5, 12, 16, 121, 184, 269, 283–284, 286–287; and Barry Goldwater, 163, 192, 194; and civil rights, 138, 176; and Dwight Eisenhower, 143; and the Fair Deal, 114–116, 125, 129–130; and the Hoover administration, 33, 35; and "modern Republicanism," 154–155, 160; and the New Deal, 44, 46, 52, 70, 77; and Newt Gignrich, 276; and 1970s conservative revitalization, 244, 252–253, 256; and Ronald Reagan, 243, 248–249, 251, 259; and Wendell Willkie, 101
Arizona, 85, 86, 163, 189, 199, 202
Arkansas, 212
Arnold, Thurman, 80
Ashbrook, John M., 206, 241
Associated Willkie Clubs. *See* Willkie clubs
Atkinson, Eugene, 268
Atlanta, Georgia, 180
Attack politics, 158, 272; and the Fair Deal, 128; and the Hoover administration, 31–32, 36; and the New Deal years, 52, 62, 63; and Newt Gingrich, 277–278; and Richard Nixon, 136–137, 157–158, 216, 235, 237
Atwater, Lee, 267, 271–272

"Backlash," 195–198, 203
Baker, Howard H., Jr., 249
Baker, James A., III, 260, 277
"Balance of power" argument, 30, 65, 93–94, 139, 225
Baldwin, Raymond E., 117, 285
Banks and banking, 26, 32–33, 45, 91, 119, 123, 144
Baptists, 278
Barkley, Alben W., 132
Barnett, Ross, 189
Barton, Bruce, 60
Beall, John Glenn, Jr., 229
Bean, Louis, 114
Beck, James M., 36

Beedy, Carroll L., 21, 48
Bell, Jeffrey, 241
Benham, Thomas W., 211
Bennet, William S., 65
Big government, 5, 91, 143, 155, 160, 199, 209, 213, 280; as anti-Democratic rhetoric, 80, 157
Bipartisanship. *See* Cold War bipartisanship
"Black and tan" Republicans, 19, 29, 65
Blackburn, Ben, 230
Blackmun, Harry, 224
Blackwell, Morton C., 259–260
Bliss, Ray C., 184, 207, 254, 283
Bob Jones University, 270
Bohlen, Charles, 151
Boise, Idaho, 92
Bonus Expeditionary Force ("Bonus Army"), 34, 36
Borah, William E., 20, 26, 38, 52, 53, 54–55
"Bought vote," 49–52, 88, 95, 105–106, 134–136, 285–286
Bradley, Melvin L., 270
Brewster, Owen, 141
Bricker amendment, 151–152
Bricker, John W., 106, 151–152
Brinkley, David, 201
Brock, William E., III, 229, 253–254, 256, 265, 269–270, 285
Broder, David S., 119, 217
Brogan, D. W., 117
Brooke, Edward W., 212
Brown, Clarence J., 115
Brown, Edmund G. "Pat," 188, 212
Brown, Katharine Kennedy, 187
Brown v. Board of Education (1954 and 1955), 174, 197, 224
Brownell, Herbert, Jr., 108, 138
Bruce, Donald C., 206–207
Bruner, Jerome S., 103
Buchanan, Patrick J., 222, 231, 235, 237, 241
Buckley, James L., 227, 229
Buckley, William F., Jr., 162, 207, 241, 251, 260
Budgets and budget deficits, 33; and Dwight Eisenhower, 157, 159, 190; and the Fair Deal, 113, 117, 126; and Richard Nixon, 216, 230–232; and Ronald Reagan, 257–259
Buell, Raymond L., 85, 89, 90, 94, 97–98
Buffalo, New York, 196, 252
"Bull Moose" Party. *See* Progressive Party (of 1912)
Bull, Stephen, 233
Bunche, Ralph J., 66, 70

Burch, Dean, 195, 199, 207
Burger, Warren, 224
Burnham, Walter Dean, 203
Bush, George H. W., 261, 271–273, 275, 278–279, 285
Business, 32, 33, 186; and active support for Republicans, 71, 144, 168–169, 185, 192, 255, 262, 286; as Republican constituency, 12, 14–15, 39, 48, 52, 61, 98; and Republican policy, 17, 26, 161, 220; and Wendell Willkie, 81, 90, 91, 101, 102
Busing, 197–198, 218, 223–224, 256
Butler, Hugh, 113
Byrd, Harry F., Jr., 227, 247

Caddell, Patrick H., 244
California, 75, 115, 136, 161, 188, 193, 197, 199, 212, 253
Cambodia, 233
Campaign finance, 27, 67, 86, 107, 245–246, 263, 266
Campaigns. *See* elections and campaigns
Campbell, Phil, 36
Candidate-centered politics, 9, 10, 86, 96, 168, 173–174, 245–246
Candidate quality, 140, 153, 185, 229, 245, 263
Cantril, Hadley, 194–195, 251, 286
Capehart, Homer E., 127
Capper, Arthur, 21, 25, 37, 53
Cargo, David F., 225
Carlson, Frank, 89
Carson, John J., 11
Carswell, G. Harrold, 224
Carter administration, 249
Carter, Jimmy, 243–244, 247, 250, 254, 263, 269
Case, Clifford, 152–153
Castro, Fidel, 180
Catholics: and the Democratic Party, 11, 15, 42, 67, 180, 244; support for Republican Party among, 89, 133, 146, 190, 203, 233–235, 239, 244, 256–257
Cato (*National Review* columnist), 278
Cavazos, Lauro F., 272
Chaney, James, 270
Changing Sources of Power (Dutton), 236
Chapin, Dwight L., 228
Charlottesville, Virginia, 88, 167
Chase, Stuart, 80
Cheney, Richard B., 266
Chiang Kai-shek, 128
Chicago, 198

Chicago Tribune, 119
China, 128, 206, 232, 241
Choice Not an Echo (Schlafly), 191
Chotiner, Murray M., 136
Christian Voice, 256
Churchill, Winston, 112
Cincinnati, Ohio, 66, 75
CIO Political Action Committee (CIO–PAC), 106–107, 114, 116, 125, 130, 139
Cities. *See* Urban issues *and* Urban voters
Citizens for Eisenhower, 150, 165–168, 170, 181, 194, 207. *See also* National Republican Citizens Committee *and* Republican Citizens Committee of the United States
Civil liberties, 102
Civil rights, 2, 7; and the Eisenhower administration, 174, 178, 180; and Herbert Hoover, 29; and the 1960s, 182, 188, 189–191, 196, 198, 202–203, 207, 210, 212, 215; and Richard Nixon, 219; and Ronald Reagan, 270–271; and the Truman years, 122, 137–139, 167; and Wendell Willkie, 102. *See also* Race
Civil Rights Act (1964), 191, 196–197
Civil rights movement, 198, 214
Civil War, 9, 11, 14, 19, 49, 88, 99
Civil Works Administration (CWA), 47, 49, 50
Clapper, Raymond, 49, 61–62, 73, 98
Clark, D. Worth, 69
Clayton, Peter, 166, 189
Cleveland, Grover, 14
Cleveland, Ohio, 196
Cold War, 5; and anticommunism, 113, 123; and Dwight Eisenhower, 144–145, 155, 176–180; and Harry Truman, 123–124, 145; and the 1960s, 190, 192, 195, 199; and the Nixon administration, 232; and Ronald Reagan, 258, 280
Cold War bipartisanship, 110, 120, 123, 128–129, 151–152
Colorado, 22, 75, 153
Commerce, Department of, 17, 32, 225
Committee for Industrial Organization (CIO), 67. *See also* Congress of Industrial Organizations
Committee on Big City Politics (RNC), 184–185
Committee on Political Education of the AFL–CIO (COPE), 185, 206. *See also* American Federation of Labor and Congress of Industrial Organizations

Committee to Explore Political
Realignment, 141
Committee to Support Moderate
Republicans, 205–206
Commonsense, 254
Communism (as anti-Democratic theme), 36;
during the early Cold War years, 108,
112–113, 115, 119, 128–133, 136–137,
145; during the New Deal, 47, 58, 62,
63, 89–90
Communist Party, 102, 132
Congo, 180
Congressional Republicans, 134, 266; and
Democratic defections, 239; during the
80th Congress, 116–118, 120, 122, 124,
125, 126; during the Great Society years,
208–209; and the Eisenhower years,
150, 153, 156–157, 159; and Gerald Ford,
242; and the Hoover administration, 22,
26, 34; and the House policy committee,
127; and the New Deal, 46, 47, 60, 61,
68, 77–78; and the 1964 elections, 203,
206; and race, 137–138, 175, 191; and
the Reagan years, 263–264, 266–267,
275–278, 280; and Richard Nixon, 216,
229–230; and World War II, 97, 110
Congress of Industrial Organizations
(CIO), 67, 93, 106, 116, 118.
See also Committee for Industrial
Organization *and* CIO Political Action
Committee
Congress of Republican Organizations, 206
Connally, John, 237, 239, 245
Connecticut, 13
Conservatism, 3, 4, 206–207, 256, 283–285;
and the Eisenhower years, 151, 161–163;
and the Fair Deal, 141, 143; and Ford,
241–243; and Goldwater, 189, 196,
199–200, 209; and the New Deal, 45,
47; and Nixon, 232, 241; and Reagan,
259–262; and World War II, 103–104.
See also "New Right" *and* Religious
Right
Conservative coalition, 68, 70, 106,
140, 208
Conservative Democrats, 68, 69, 103,
239, 245
Conservative Opportunity Society
(COS), 276, 278
Conservative Party (of the United Kingdom),
7, 72–74, 141, 163–164, 206, 254
Conservative Party of New York State,
227, 241

Conservative Republicans, 283–285; and
Barry Goldwater, 182–183, 191, 203–
204; and Dwight Eisenhower, 150–151,
153, 155–156, 178, 187; and the New
Deal, 50, 53, 59, 61, 77; and the Nixon
administration, 222, 241; and Wendell
Willkie, 87, 91, 111
Constituency concerns, 47, 109, 117, 175, 252
Constitution as political issue, 90, 104; as
an anti-Democratic theme during the
New Deal, 43, 45, 47–48, 55–58, 62, 68;
and moderate/progressive Republicans,
52–54, 56, 59–61, 63
Consumerism, 186
Coolidge, Calvin, 22, 61, 64
Cornuelle, Richard C., 209
Corruption and ethics issues, 15, 19, 52, 112,
133, 136, 145, 154, 199–200, 278
Couzens, James J., 11, 53
Cowles, Gardner, Jr., 110
Cowles, John, 110
Cox, Tricia Nixon, 237
Cramton, Louis C., 21
Crane, Philip, 251–253
Crime, 20, 79, 198–200, 211–212, 218, 221,
228, 279. *See also* "Law and order"
Critical Issues Council, 187
Crossley polls, 138
C-SPAN, 278
Cuba, 180
Curtis, A. M., 13
Cutting, Bronson M., 26, 73

Dallas, Texas, 173
Darby, Harry, 143
Darman, Richard G., 263
Davenport, Russell, 97
Davie, May, 75
"Dealignment," 10, 244, 267–268.
See also Realignment
Deaver, Michael, 272
Defeatism as Republican characteristic,
52, 135
Deficits. *See* Budgets and budget deficits
Delaware, 13
Democracy, future of (as political concern
and issue), 30, 43, 45, 47, 54, 56–58, 61,
90, 104, 115
Democratic Leadership Council (DLC), 268
Democratic National Committee (DNC), 31,
66, 237, 265
Democratic national convention of
1932, 34

Democratic national convention of 1968, 215, 236

Democratic national convention of 1980, 257

Democratic Party, 1, 4, 7, 18, 19–20, 27, 140, 280–282, 286–287; activities during the Hoover administration of, 31–32; and African Americans, 30, 64–65, 137, 175, 269; and anticommunism, 132; association with prosperity of, 108; and attacks on the Republican Party, 158–159, 177; and "backlash," 195; and civil rights, 137, 221, 223; divisions within, 122, 190, 215, 227, 281; and the Eisenhower administration, 150, 152, 154; and European parallels, 113; and George McGovern, 236–237; and interest-group pluralism, 106; and "New Democrats," 268; 1950s strength of, 149, 159–160; and 1970 elections, 226–229; and the Nixon administration, 229–230; organizational capacity of, 73; and organized labor, 67, 164–165, 184, 254; pre–New Deal coalition of, 10, 11, 15; and presidential nomination rules, 142, 234–236, 281; and the Reagan era, 247, 249–250, 259, 262–264, 267, 271, 279; and *The Real Majority*, 218; Republican attacks on, 35, 57, 118; Republican belief in decline of, 9, 212; response to "me-too" strategy, 61; success of Republican attacks on, 113; and support for Republican Party, 68–69, 84, 87–88, 150, 153, 195, 239–240, 264, 268, 282; urban strength of, 184; and voter mobilization, 106; and women, 28, 66–67. *See also* New Deal coalition *and* Southern Democrats

Democrats for Eisenhower, 167. *See also* Citizens for Eisenhower

Democrats for Nixon, 237

Democrats-for-Willkie, 85, 87–88

Dent, Harry S., 223

Destroyers-for-bases agreement, 92

Détente, 232, 238, 241, 249, 259, 342

Devitt, Edward J., 119

Dewey, Thomas E., 73, 76–77, 96, 105, 109, 110, 283; and anticommunism, 131; antiliberal strategy of, 121–122; and civil rights, 138; on conservative Republicans, 126; and Dwight Eisenhower, 143, 145; gubernatorial background of, 120–121; and the 1942 campaign, 104; and the 1944 campaign, 107–108, 135–136; and the 1948 campaign, 117–118, 122–126; and opposition to Robert Taft, 119; on organization, 126; and polls, 97, 124; and Wendell Willkie, 100; and World War II, 79–80

"Deweyites," 118, 283

Dictatorship, 58, 62, 90, 143, 155; as anti-Democratic theme, 43, 48, 55, 61–64, 71, 88–90, 151

Dies, Martin, 89, 107

Dirksen, Everett, 191

"Divided government," 245, 264, 280–281

"Dixiecrats." *See* States' Rights Democratic Party

Dodds, Bill, 233

Dole, Elizabeth, 271–272, 274–275

Donatelli, Frank J., 278

Donnelly, Thomas C., 37–38

Douglas, Helen Gahagan, 136–137

Douglas, Paul H., 25, 152–153

Dowdy, Wayne, 265

Draft, 92, 97, 120

Drury, Allen, 230

Dukakis, Michael, 275, 279

Dulles, John Foster, 123, 128

Dunn, Rogers C., 52, 106, 134–135, 285

Dutton, Fred, 236

East, 14, 21, 23, 44, 60, 67, 77, 83, 110, 183

"Eastern establishment," 83, 119, 178, 191, 193, 240

Eastland, James, 237

Economy Act (1933), 45

Economy and economic issues: and African Americans, 175; as disadvantageous to Republicans, 158, 179, 180–181, 238; and Dwight Eisenhower 159–160; and the Hoover administration, 13, 21–23, 32–34; and the New Deal, 41, 43, 46–47, 51, 56, 61–62, 71–72, 76–77; and 1950 campaigns, 129; and 1956 campaigns, 154; and the Nixon years, 218–222, 226, 231–232; and the Reagan years, 251–253, 257–260, 262–263, 268, 270, 274, 277, 279–280; and the Republican Party before the Great Depression, 11, 17; and Wendell Willkie 80–81, 89, 91, 101, 103. *See also* "Supply-side economics"

Edge, Walter, 22

Education, 32, 117, 121, 179, 209, 221, 225, 233, 256

Edward, Marvin "Mickey," 251–253

Edwards, India, 171

Eisenhower administration, 8

Eisenhower, Dwight D., 4, 112, 283; and African Americans, 174–176; and conservative opposition, 162–163; entry into politics of, 142–144; and foreign policy, 151–152, 176–178; and Joseph McCarthy, 154; and "modern Republicanism," 155–158, 161–162; and 1952 campaigns, 144–147, 178; and political organization, 164, 170; as politician, 148–153, 158, 165–166, 169, 179, 181; postpresidential political activity of, 187–188; and the South, 173–174

Eisenhower, Milton, S., 187

Elections and campaigns of 1896, 10, 14, 156

Elections and campaigns of 1920, 16

Elections and campaigns of 1928, 12, 13, 15, 17, 20, 24, 30, and Democratic divisions, 11; and the South, 18, 173; and women, 27

Elections and campaigns of 1930, 13, 21, 24, 29, 31, 33, 37

Elections and campaigns of 1932, 13, 27, 30, 33, 35–39, 46, 57, 59, 60, 92, 156; and African Americans, 29–30, 65; and progressive Republicans, 25, 44; and Republican optimism, 18, 23, 34; and the South, 20; and women 28, 29, 66

Elections and campaigns of 1933, 47

Elections and campaigns of 1934, 41, 43, 48–49, 50, 52, 53, 57, 60, 74

Elections and campaigns of 1936, 41, 44, 58, 59, 62–67, 69, 81, 94, 134; analysis of, 51, 67; reactions to, 68, 70

Elections and campaigns of 1938, 41, 52, 69, 72, 76–77, 100, 110, 121, 122, 130

Elections and campaigns of 1940, 69, 75, 76, 81, 88–98, 101, 110, 121, 134; and the impact of World War II, 79, 80, 81, 91–92, 95, 97

Elections and campaigns of 1942, 100, 104–105, 106, 110, 121, 130, 135, 240

Elections and campaigns of 1943, 104

Elections and campaigns of 1944, 100–101, 105, 107–110, 114, 120, 121, 126, 131, 134–136, 139; and Wendell Willkie, 83, 98, 101–102

Elections and campaigns of 1946, 112, 113–116, 119, 121, 124, 128–129, 130, 216, 283; and anticommunism, 115, 119, 132, 136–137

Elections and campaigns of 1948, 116–118, 120–128, 130, 134–135, 139, 142, 145–146, 170, 284; and anticommunism, 131–132

Elections and campaigns of 1949, 128

Elections and campaigns of 1950, 112, 128, 129–131, 133, 134, 136–137

Elections and campaigns of 1952, 112, 145–148, 150, 154, 163, 178, 216, 283; and activism, 164, 166–168, 186, 191; and African Americans, 146, 175; and foreign policy, 112, 143–144, 145, 146–147, 154, 176; and the presidential nomination, 135, 143–145, 166; and the South, 144, 146, 167, 180; and the suburbs, 172–173; and women, 170–171

Elections and campaigns of 1954, 8, 148, 150, 152–153, 157–158, 164–165, 167–168, 173

Elections and campaigns of 1956, 148, 150, 153–154, 159, 162, 176, 186; and activism, 165, 166, 168; and the South and African Americans, 173–175, 180; and women, 170–171

Elections and campaigns of 1958, 148–149, 153, 158, 161, 163, 168, 174, 177, 179

Elections and campaigns of 1960, 168, 174, 176–184, 186–187, 198, 202, 212, 218

Elections and campaigns of 1961, 190

Elections and campaigns of 1962, 188, 212, 218

Elections and campaigns of 1964, 5, 182, 191–205, 209, 212, 241, 284–286

Elections and campaigns of 1966, 190, 211–212

Elections and campaigns of 1968, 212–216, 283

Elections and campaigns of 1970, 226–229, 232, 237, 245

Elections and campaigns of 1972, 228, 232, 235–241, 245

Elections and campaigns of 1973, 240

Elections and campaigns of 1974, 240, 241–242

Elections and campaigns of 1976, 242–244, 246

Elections and campaigns of 1978, 252–253

Elections and campaigns of 1980, 247, 249, 250–252, 254, 257, 262, 269–270, 272–273, 283

Elections and campaigns of 1981, 265

Elections and campaigns of 1982, 262–263, 271

Elections and campaigns of 1984, 247, 258–261, 263–264, 268, 271–272, 275, 277

Elections and campaigns of 1986, 262, 265

Elections and campaigns of 1988, 261, 271, 273, 275, 278–280, 285

Electoral realignment. *See* Realignment

Ely, Joseph B., 51

Emerging Republican Majority (Phillips), 9, 219–220, 224, 258

Engel v. Vitale (1962), 192

Environment, 216, 219, 231

Environmental Protection Agency, 231

Equal Rights Amendment (ERA), 94, 234, 249, 256, 273

Erie County, Ohio, 91

Erie, Pennsylvania, 50

Ethics. *See* Corruption and ethics issues

Ethnic Americans: and the Democratic coalition, 15, 109; Republican strategies to gain support among, 133, 185, 190, 196, 203, 214, 234, 255, 257, 278

Ethnoreligious issues, 14, 15, 20

Evangelical Christians, 255, 257, 260–261

Expansionism, 82

Extremism, 194, 207

Faction, 74, 125–126, 161, 204, 207; and anticommunism, 132; and the Citizens movement, 187; connected with individual politicians, 70–71, 75, 85, 96, 98, 117–119; and progressive Republicans, 44; and the South, 19, 139; within the Democratic Party, 122

Fahrenkopf, Frank J., Jr., 264, 268

Fair Deal, 112–113, 126, 137, 145

Falwell, Jerry, 256

Family Assistance Plan (FAP), 230–231, 236

Family issues, 28

Farley, James, 61, 62, 73

Farmers and farm issues, 89, 116, 117–118; and the Depression years, 23–24, 33, 36, 37, 45, 57, 60, 68, 91; and the 1948 elections, 123, 124

Fascism, fear of, 33, 58, 90

Federal Emergency Relief Act (1933), 45

Federal Farm Board, 24

Federal Reserve Board, 72

Ferguson, Joseph, 130, 164

Ferraro, Geraldine, 275

Fess, Simeon D., 133

Fiorina, Morris P., 280

First World War. *See* World War I

Fiscal conservatism, 220, 253, 258, 280; and Dwight Eisenhower, 155, 157, 159, 163; and Republicans during the New Deal, 57, 59, 60; and responses to the 1948 elections, 126, 127

Fish, Hamilton, 100

Fletcher, Henry P., 47–48, 49, 55

Florida, 15, 146, 173–174, 180, 212, 226, 243, 268–269

Ford, Gerald R., 208–209, 239–246, 248

Ford Motor Company, 186

Foreign aid, 119, 151–152

Foreign policy, 2, 23, 28, 79–80, 81–83, 279–283; and Barry Goldwater, 163, 192, 194–195; and Dwight Eisenhower, 143–144, 147, 150, 154, 176–180; and the 1940 presidential campaign, 91–93, 97; and the 1944 presidential campaign, 108, 110; and the 1948 presidential campaign, 123–124; and the 1950 campaigns, 129–130, 137; and the 1960 elections, 178–180; and 1970s public opinion, 249; and the 1976 elections, 243; and the Nixon administration, 222, 238, 241; and post-World War II planning, 100–101; and the Reagan administration, 258–259, 274–275, 280; Republican debate about during World War II, 98–103; and Republican differences, 119–120; and Truman administration, 128–129

"Forgotten Americans," 183, 213

"Forgotten man," 39, 42, 92

Fortune, 97, 110

France, Joseph I., 25

Frank, Glenn, 71–72

Fraser, Donald M., 236

Freedom. *See* Liberty

Free, Lloyd A., 194–195, 251, 286

Free Society Association (FSA), 207

Friedan, Betty, 235

Friedman, Milton, 231

"Frontlash," 197

Fundraising, 8, 71, 86; in 1932, 27; in 1964, 196, 204–205; in the 1970s, 254–255; and organized labor, 67; and Ronald Reagan, 262; and Republican groups, 74, 75, 207

Gabrielson, Guy George, 129, 135, 139

Gaither committee, 176

Gallup, George, 165

Gallup polls, 95, 97, 138, 161–162, 176, 247, 261; and the New Deal, 49, 58, 76, 84

Gannett, Frank E., 38, 104

Garland, Ray L., 227

Garner, John Nance, 35, 58, 89

Gender gap, 66, 248, 273–275

General Electric, 169

General Motors, 169, 186

Georgia, 139, 144, 180, 202, 269

Gingrich, Newt, 275–278

Glass-Steagall Act (1933), 45
Godwin, Mills E., Jr., 240
Goldwater, Barry, 5, 162–163, 180, 271,
    284–286; and African American voters,
    198; and civil rights, 189, 191, 196–198;
    on the Citizens movement, 187; on
    electoral politics, 182–183, 191; and
    Latino American voters, 198–199; and
    morality agenda, 200; and the 1964
    presidential campaign, 191–205; and
    Republican defections, 201; and the
    South, 185, 188–189
Goodell, Charles, 227, 229
Goodman, Andrew, 270
GOPAC, 276–277
Gorbachev, Mikhail, 258
Gore, Albert, Sr., 158, 229
Government activism. *See* Activist
    government
Government reform and reorganization, 68,
    216, 230–231
Governors. *See* Gubernatorial Republicans
Gradison, Willis D., 130
Grassroots Republican Conference (June
    1935), 56–57, 68
Great Depression, 5, 10, 44, 47, 122,
    127, 147, 263, 282; and the Hoover
    administration, 12, 16, 17, 22, 23, 26,
    28, 32–34, 39
Great Society, 3, 4, 208–211, 213, 219,
    220–221, 236, 282, 286
Greensboro, North Carolina, 167
Gubernatorial Republicans, 78, 120–122
Guyer, U. S., 39

Haldeman, H. R., 232
Hale, Frederick, 48
Hallanan, Walter S., 109
Halleck, Charles A., 158, 208
Hallett, Douglas, 238
Hall, Leonard, 168, 169, 170, 171–172,
    173, 175
Hamilton, J. G. de Roulhac, 18, 20
Hamilton, John D. M., 24, 51, 85; as RNC
    chair, 62, 64, 69, 70, 72–74, 76–77, 85,
    164, 254, 283
Hance, Kent, 268
Harding, Warren G., 16, 61, 77
Hard, William, 32, 33
Harris, Louis, 197, 273
Harris polls, 197, 249
Hatch, Carl A., 106
Hatch Act (1939), 52, 107; and 1940
    amendments ("Hatch Act II"), 86, 107
Hatfield, Mark O., 212

Hauser, Rita, 235
Hawaii, 82
Hawkes, Albert W., 141
Haynsworth, Clement, 224
Healthcare, 121, 126–127, 157, 179, 183,
    185, 204, 211, 256; and the Nixon
    administration, 216, 219, 229–231
Health, Education, and Welfare, Department
    of, 157
Hearst, William Randolph, 30, 589
Hearst group, 32
Heritage Foundation, 255
Hermann, A. B., 138, 190
Hershey, Pennsylvania, 197
Hess, Karl, 194
Hess, Stephen, 119
"Hidden majority," 4, 146, 182, 199
"Hidden vote," 144, 193, 194–196, 285
Hillman, Sidney, 107
Hinshaw, David, 17, 21, 38, 75, 85, 120
Hiss, Alger, 128, 131, 220
Historiography, 5–6, 9, 10
Hobby, Oveta Culp, 157
Hoeven, Charles B., 208
Hoover, Herbert, 61, 64, 74, 127, 143, 147,
    159, 199, 257, 263, 276; and African
    Americans, 29–30, 65; and agricultural
    issues, 23–24; Democratic attacks on,
    31–32, 35; Depression response of,
    18, 32–33, 37; and news media, public
    relations, 30–32, 37; 1928 election of,
    11, 12, 15, 17, 18, 20, 173; and the 1930
    elections, 34; and the 1932 elections,
    13, 18, 20, 25, 26, 28, 29, 33, 34, 35, 37,
    42, 46; and 1934 elections, 53; and 1936
    elections, 51; and 1940 elections, 95–96;
    on 1950 campaigns, 129; as party leader,
    12, 22–23, 24–25, 26–27; plans for
    postpresidency, 40; and postpresidential
    political activity, 70–71, 75, 79; political
    views of, 16, 33; as politician, 17–18;
    popularity of, 18; prepresidential career
    of, 16–17, 32; as progressive, 16; and
    progressives, 12, 23–26; and Prohibition,
    20, 22; responses to New Deal of, 46,
    50; and the South, 18–20, 139; as a
    symbol of Great Depression, 39; views
    of Franklin D. Roosevelt of, 34, 35; and
    women voters, 27–28, 29, 66
Hoover Institution, 255
Hollister, John B., 87
Hopkins, Harry, 49
Housing, 117, 118, 122, 157, 256
Howard, Perry W., 29
Hudson, Grand M., 21

Huie, William Bradford, 113
Humes, Theodore L., 196, 203–204
Humphrey, George, 152–153, 159
Humphrey, Hubert H., 138, 199, 214–215, 219, 228, 236
Humphreys, Robert, 165, 170, 175
Hungary, 176
Hyde, Arthur M., 24, 57

Ickes, Harold L., 25, 49, 81, 83, 84, 90
Idaho, 38, 69
Illinois, 21, 85, 86, 152–153, 167, 225, 275
Image of Republican Party, 4, 12, 39, 97, 125–126, 146–147, 205, 254; associated with depression, 108, 125, 147, 159, 181; associated with elitism, 128; associated with peace, 154, 176; and Eisenhower years, 157, 160; Kevin Phillips on, 220; and Reagan era, 250–251, 258; and *The Real Majority*, 219; and reform, 231; Ronald Reagan on, 248; and Republican label, 226–227
Immigrants and immigration, 15, 42, 109, 114, 141
Incumbency, 252, 262, 265–267
Independents for Eisenhower, 146, 167. *See also* Citizens for Eisenhower
Independent voters, 10, 59, 84, 144, 146, 244–246, 283
Indiana, 100, 121, 196
Individualism, 16, 32, 70, 200, 213
Inflation, 105, 113–114, 116, 122, 160, 231
Interest groups, 17, 72, 93, 106, 135, 140, 183, 286
Internal Revenue Service, 256, 270
Internal Security Act (1950), 132
Internationalism, 82; and the Cold War, 119–120, 144, 151–152, 154, 177–178, 192; and World War II, 79, 81, 82, 83, 98, 100–101, 110
Interventionism (and World War II), 82, 97
Iowa, 86, 275
Isolationism, 81, 97–101, 103, 119–120, 123, 143, 151, 178
Ives, Irving M., 116

Jackson, Henry M. "Scoop," 236
Jackson, Jesse, 269
Jackson, John E., 140
Jackson, Robert H., 90
Javits, Jacob K., 149, 150–151, 166, 185–186, 192–193
Jenner, William E., 134–135
Jews, 15, 67, 256
John Birch Society, 194

Johnson, Hiram, 26
Johnson, Lyndon B., 4, 150, 176, 182, 190–191, 195–197, 199–200, 202–204, 286
Johnson, Willis, 203–204
Johnson administration, 4, 218, 224, 244
Jonas, Charles A., 20
Jones, John L., 241
Joslin, Theodore G., 27
Judd, Walter, 129–130
Judis, John B., 252
Justice, Department of, 90

Kansas, 51, 60, 65
Keating, Kenneth, 202
Kelland, Clarence Budington, 109
Keller, Kent Ellsworth, 89
Kemp, Jack, 252–253
Kennedy, Edward M., 228, 237
Kennedy, John F., 149, 176, 179–180, 182, 188, 189, 190, 193, 202
Kennedy, Robert F., 201
Kennedy administration, 189
Kent, Frank R., 31, 107
Kent State University, 233
Kentucky, 146
Keynes, John Maynard, 231
Key, V. O., Jr., 8, 9, 203
Khachigian, Kenneth L., 231
Khrushchev, Nikita, 180
Kilgo, John Wesley, 139
Killen, Marcella, 129
King, Martin Luther, Jr., 174, 180, 214
Kirchhofer, A. H., 30, 31
Kirk, Claude R., Jr., 212
Kitchel, Denison, 207
Knowland, William F., 155
Knox, Frank, 39, 56, 62–63
Korean War, 112, 129–130, 132, 133, 145, 147, 154, 176
Krock, Arthur, 142

Labor, Department of, 221
Labor Non-Partisan League, 67
Labor unions. *See* Organized labor *and* Union members
Labor's League for Political Education. *See* American Federation of Labor.
Labour Party (of the United Kingdom), 112–113, 141, 163
Ladd, Everett Carll, Jr., 245
Laffer, Arthur, 252
LaFollette, Charles M., 102
La Follette, Robert, Jr., 68
Laird, Melvin R., 209, 238
Lake, James, 260

Lambertson, William P., 99
Landon, Alfred M., 68, 69, 114, 126, 143,
    207; and African Americans, 65; and the
    1936 elections, 41, 51, 59, 60–61, 73;
    and post-1936 political activities, 70–71;
    and the South, 70; views on the New
    Deal of, 56, 61–62; on Willkie, 98, 99;
    and the Willkie campaign, 87, 91–92, 94;
    and women, 66
Langlie, Arthur, 153
Larson, Arthur, 156
Latino Americans, 198–199, 225–226, 272–273
Lausche, Frank, 130, 173
"Law and order," 213, 222, 227.
    See also Crime
League of Nations, 82
League of United Latin American Citizens
    (LULAC), 225
Lehman, Herbert, 76
Lend-lease, 99
Lewis, Ernest I., 34
Lewis, John L., 93
Liberal Party (of the United Kingdom), 141
Liberty, 16, 101, 125, 143, 163, 169, 170,
    190; and criticisms of the New Deal, 43,
    45, 46, 47, 54, 63, 65, 69; "liberty versus
    socialism" theme, 112, 127–130, 145
Liberty League. *See* American Liberty League
"Lily-white" Republicans, 19, 29
Lincoln, Abraham, 7, 14, 53, 56, 64, 114,
    121, 182. *See also* "Party of Lincoln"
Lincoln Day, 64
Lindley, Alfred D., 129–130
Lindsay, John V., 186, 240
Lippmann, Walter, 81
Literary Digest, 48, 64, 285
Little Rock, Arkansas, 174
Local politics. *See* State and local politics
Localism, 32
Lodge, Henry Cabot, Jr., 143, 158, 166
Louchheim, Katie, 159
Louisiana, 144, 202, 268
Lubell, Samuel, 125, 131, 146
Lucas, Robert H., 24–25, 31, 33, 36, 131
Lucas, William, 268
Luce, Henry R., 110
Lumumba, Patrice, 180

MacArthur, Douglas, 130, 220
MacGregor, Clark, 228
Mackinac Island, Michigan, 100, 120
MacLafferty, James, 26, 35
Maddox, Lester, 242
Mahoney, George P., 214
Mahoney, J. Daniel, 241

Maine, 13, 41, 48, 161, 228
Making of the New Majority Party (Rusher),
    242, 248
Maloney, Francis T., 61
Mao Zedong, 128, 130
Marcantonio, Vito, 129, 137
Marquis, Fred. *See* Lord Woolton
Marshall, George C., 123
Marshall Plan, 120, 123
Martin, Joseph W., Jr., 86, 95, 116,
    127, 135
Maryland, 133, 196, 214
Massachusetts, 15, 202, 228, 275
Mayer, William G., 281
McCarran, Pat, 132
McCarthyism, 5, 153, 154
McCarthy, Joseph R., 131–133, 152, 154
McClellan, John, 237
McCormick, Robert R., 119
McCormick, Ruth Hanna, 21, 96
McDonald, David, 196–197
McGovern-Fraser commission, 234–235
McGovern, George, 235–238
McKay, Douglas, 153
McKinley, William, 82
McNary, Charles L., 25, 52, 53, 83
McWhorter, Charles, 184
Meany, George, 169, 233
Media. *See* News media
Meek, Joseph T., 152–153
Meese, Edwin, III, 270
Melich, Tanya, 275
Mellon, Andrew W., 16
Men, 28, 94–95, 235, 274–275
"Me too" Republicans and Republicanism,
    60–61, 62, 63, 110, 140, 204; and Barry
    Goldwater, 182, 191; as criticism of
    Dewey campaign, 125–126; as criticism
    of "modern Republicanism," 154–155,
    160; as misinterpretation of New Deal
    liberalism's strength, 134; and Wendell
    Willkie, 80, 83, 91, 101–102
Meyer, Agnes E., 66
Michel, Robert H., 264
Michelson, Charles, 31, 39, 127
Michigan, 21, 50, 164, 268, 275
Middendorf, J. William, 196
"Middle America" and "middle Americans,"
    218, 220–223, 226, 231, 233–235, 238,
    244, 248, 251
Midwest, 21, 23, 24, 26, 60, 65, 189; as
    conservative stronghold, 56–57, 77, 98,
    109, 117, 121, 161, 164, 202
Miller, William E., 185, 197–198, 199
Milliken v. Bradley (1974), 224

Mills, Ogden L., 21, 22, 34, 35, 45, 46, 48, 70, 74–75
Minneapolis, Minnesota, 129–130
Minnesota, 228
"Missile gap," 176–177
Mississippi, 29, 180, 202, 224, 265
Missouri, 89, 125
Mitchell, William D., 27
"Modern Republicanism," 150, 153–163, 175, 178, 181, 187, 194, 283, 285
Moley, Raymond, 84
Mondale, Walter F., 250, 257, 258–259, 264, 272, 275
Monopoly, 53–54
Morality as political issue, 15, 26, 199–201, 204, 211, 238, 260
Moral Majority, 256
Morhouse, L. Judson, 185
Morrow, E. Frederic, 175
Morton, Sterling, 81
Morton, Thruston B., 184, 185
Moyers, Bill, 221
Moynihan, Daniel Patrick, 221, 250
Mundt, Karl E., 140–142
Muscle Shoals, 12
Muskie, Edmund, 228, 237
Mutual Security Program. *See* Foreign aid

NAACP Legal Defense and Educational Fund, 224
Nadasby, Leonard, 190
Nation, The, 117
National Association for the Advancement of Colored People (NAACP), 29–30, 69, 93, 138, 139, 189, 198
National Citizens Political Action Committee (NC-PAC), 107–109, 114
National Federation of Republican Women, 74, 234
National Industrial Recovery Act (1933), 45, 55
National Labor Relations Act (1935), 55
National League of Women Voters, 94
National Republican Citizens Committee, 186–188. *See also* Citizens for Eisenhower *and* Republican Citizens Committee of the United States
National Republican Congressional Committee, 234, 249, 254, 263
National Republican Senatorial Committee, 263
National Review, 162, 188, 207, 241
National Women's Party, 94
National Women's Political Caucus, 234
Native Americans, 32, 94
Neal, Mills F., 167
Nebraska, 126

Negative income tax, 206, 209
Negativity (as political strategy). *See* Attack politics
Negativity (as Republican characteristic), 2, 136, 278–279, 286; conservatives on, 190, 252, 276; progressives and moderates on, 36, 117, 128, 205–206
Neoconservatives, 259
Neutrality, 79, 81, 82, 99, 101, 283
New Deal, 35, 40, 41, 209, 249; and African Americans, 64–66; popularity of, 46, 245; Republican acceptance of, 46, 59, 116, 156, 160; Republican arguments against, 42, 51, 55, 63–64, 66, 68, 72, 90–91, 113; Republican belief in weaknesses of, 50, 57, 104; Republican responses to, 43, 44–48, 56–57, 58–59, 60–64, 76–77, 90, 91–92, 101–102
New Deal coalition, 7, 42, 44; diversity of, 103, 118, 242; and Eisenhower years, 160–161; and *The Emerging Republican Majority*, 220; and the 1936 elections, 67; and the 1940 elections, 84, 92–93, 95; and the 1948 elections, 122, 124; and the 1952 elections, 146; and 1960 elections, 180–181; and 1976 elections, 244; and Richard Nixon, 234; and Ronald Reagan, 257; Republican belief in decline of, 110, 206; and turnout, 104–105; and youth, 54
New Deal liberalism, 6, 69, 129, 192, 252–253, 271, 278–279, 282–287; and Barry Goldwater, 193; conservative alternatives to, 130; decline of, 210, 247; electoral strength of, 1–2, 12, 43, 88, 108, 131, 204; and the Fair Deal, 112; and George McGovern, 236; and the Great Society, 4, 211; gubernatorial success against, 121; and Harry Truman, 137; limitations of, 3; moderation of, 44; and "modern Republicanism," 155–156; and the 1946 elections, 114–116; and the 1948 elections, 124; and 1952 elections, 145; and the 1960 elections, 179–180; and 1968, 215; and Nixon-era realignment, 219–220, 228; and Richard Nixon, 216–217; and Ronald Reagan, 257; Republican opposition to, 43–44, 70, 127, 143, 151, 161, 183; Republican responses to and interpretations of, 50, 52, 80, 85, 96, 103, 134, 136–137, 151, 158; Republican success in obstructing and challenging, 106, 116; Republican unity against, 117–119; and Wendell Willkie, 80–81, 84, 89, 91, 98, 101–102, 110

New England, 13, 41
New Hampshire, 13, 243
New Jersey, 22, 152–153
New London, Connecticut, 87
"New look," 177
New Mexico, 191, 199, 225
New parties, 25, 54, 150, 242–243.
    See also Third parties
New Republic, 77, 98, 210
"New Right," 241, 251–252, 255–257, 262
New York, 21, 74–75, 77, 177, 185, 188,
    202, 227; and Thomas Dewey, 100,
    104, 119, 138
New York City, 119, 197, 199, 233
New York Herald Tribune, 188, 201, 240
New York Times, 30, 32, 37
News media, 9, 30–32, 61, 83, 110–111,
    144–145, 200, 204, 225
Newsweek, 189
Nickles, Don, 269
Nixon–Lodge Volunteers, 168
Nixon, Richard M., 4, 276–279, 283–284,
    286; and African Americans, 214, 225;
    compared with subsequent Republicans,
    248–249, 257; and conservatives, 241;
    and domestic policy as president, 216,
    221, 226, 229–232, 235, 238; and the
    economy, 231–232, 238; and electoral
    strategy as president, 221, 224–225,
    240, 251; and foreign policy, 232–233,
    237–238; ideas about electoral politics
    of, 136–137, 158, 179, 212–213,
    216–219, 223, 226, 232, 234, 235, 238,
    245; and the 1946 elections, 115–116;
    and the 1954 elections, 157–158; and
    the 1956 election, 173; and the 1960
    elections, 149, 174, 176, 178–184, 202;
    and the 1962 election, 188; and the 1964
    elections, 201; and the 1968 elections,
    212–215; and the 1970 elections,
    226–229; and the 1972 elections, 228,
    235–239; and race, 223, 225–226;
    and the South, 224, 237–238; and the
    Vietnam War, 222, 232–233, 244; and
    women's issues and women voters,
    234–235
Nofziger, Lyn, 272
Nonvoters, 135
Norris, George W., 12, 23, 24, 25, 49, 52,
    68, 107
North Atlantic Treaty Organization (NATO),
    120, 144
North Carolina, 15, 268
North Dakota, 24, 161

Northeast, 15, 21, 65, 109, 117, 164, 189
North Korea. *See* Korean War
Nye, Gerald P., 82

Ochs, Adolph S., 30
O'Connor, John J., 69
O'Donnell, Peter, Jr., 192
Office of Minority Business Enterprise, 225
Ohio, 77, 130–131, 169
Oklahoma, 146, 269
Oklahoma City, Oklahoma, 252
O'Laughlin, John Callan, 50, 51, 55, 63, 71
"Old Guard," 14, 40, 61
Olmsted, George, 54
Omaha, Nebraska, 125
Omaha World-Herald, 125
O'Neal, Edward A., 141
One World (Willkie), 83
"Operation Dixie" (Republican National
    Committee), 173
Order of Battle (Javits), 185
Oregon, 153, 161
Organization. *See* Political organization
Organized labor, 33, 59, 63, 113, 122–123,
    124, 134, 186, 190, 255; during the
    1970s, 251; and Earl Warren, 121;
    and Goldwater, 195–197; and the
    1946 elections, 114, 116; and the
    1948 elections, 124–125; and the 1950
    elections, 129–130; and the 1960
    elections, 181; and Nixon, 233; and
    support for Democratic Party, 67, 93,
    106–107, 164–165, 168–169, 184, 215,
    233, 254, 259–260, 286. *See also* Union
    members
Ornstein, Norman, 278

Paarlberg, Don, 160
Packwood, Robert W., 234, 248
Panama Canal Zone, 243
"Parity status," 10, 248, 280
Party decline, 8–9, 10, 245, 267
Party identification, 1, 59, 84, 146, 282;
    during the 1960s, 149, 165, 172, 203,
    208, 211, 215; during the 1970s, 240,
    244, 247; and political science, 7–10,
    160; and Ronald Reagan, 267–268
Party leadership, 2, 152–153, 227, 240, 262
Party loyalty, 37
"Party of Lincoln," 19, 42, 64, 174
"Party of peace," 28, 146, 154, 176, 178
Patriotism, 190, 224, 238
Patronage, 23, 29, 139
Pearl Harbor, 81, 99, 176

Peel, Roy V., 37

Pennsylvania, 13, 49, 50, 132, 161, 202, 268–269

Percy, Charles H., 179, 186, 197

Perkins, Frances, 157

Peterson, Val, 125–126

Philadelphia, 65

Philadelphia Record, 57

Phillips, Kevin P., 9, 219–220, 224, 229, 231, 258

Pinchot, Cornelia Bryce, 59

Pinchot, Gifford, 25, 63, 64, 103, 107

Pittsburgh, Pennsylvania, 196

Political Action Committee (PAC). *See* CIO Political Action Committee *and* National Citizens Political Action Committee

Political Action Committees (PACs), 255

Political communication, 84, 190, 251, 267; and African Americans, 138, 198; as explanation for Republican problems, 97, 109, 125, 127, 277, 283; and the Hoover administration, 24, 30–32, 37, 38; and women, 275

Political independents. *See* Independent voters

Political organization, 43, 104, 108–109, 126–127, 130, 283; and African Americans, 29; and British politics, 163–164; and cities, 184–185, 190, 207; and the Eisenhower years, 150, 164–171, 184; and the Goldwater candidacy, 192, 204; and the Hoover years, 13, 27, 31; and the New Deal years, 62, 70, 72–75; and organized labor, 107–108, 126, 164–165; and Ray Bliss, 207; and the 1970s, 251, 253–256; and the Reagan years, 265; Robert Taft's views of, 144; shortcomings of, 187; and the South, 140; and turnout problem, 135; and the Willkie candidacy, 83, 86, 96; and women, 28–29

Political publicity, 27, 31–32, 38, 108–109

Political science, 8–10

Polls and polling, 18, 91, 97, 107–108, 116, 120, 133, 193, 241–242, 285–286; and *Literary Digest*, 48, 64, 285; and the New Deal, 48, 51, 58, 64; and Richard Nixon, 222, 229, 285; and Thomas Dewey, 97, 124, 138

Pomerene, Atlee, 27

Pope, James O., 69

Populism, 219–220, 255

Populist era, 10

Potter, I. Lee, 173

Powell, Lewis, 224

Presidential nomination politics, 8

Presidential strength of Republican Party, 181, 280–281

Pressure groups. *See* Interest groups

Prince Edward County, Virginia, 197

"Professionals," 84–85

Progressive era, 9, 47

Progressive Party (of 1912), 14, 22, 23

Progressive Party (of 1948), 122

Progressive Republicans, 14, 73, 89, 107, 110; decline of, 68, 77; and Herbert Hoover, 12, 23–26, 38; and the Landon candidacy, 44, 63, 64; and the New Deal, 44, 45, 46, 48, 49, 52–55

Progressivism, 14, 16

Prohibition, 11, 15, 18, 20–22, 23, 24

Protestants, 15, 67, 257. *See also* Baptists *and* Evangelical Christians

Pryor, Samuel F., 96

Public opinion, 7, 114, 195–195; and anticommunism, 133; and the Cold War, 120, 124; during the 1970s, 249; and the Goldwater candidacy, 204; and the Hoover administration, 37; and the New Deal, 41, 44, 52, 58; and the 1980 campaign, 251; problems in measuring, 18, 64; and the Reagan years, 258–259; and World War II, 97, 99, 103, 106

Public utilities, 12, 60, 80, 83–84, 91

Public Utility Holding Company Act (1935), 56

Public works, 17, 23, 32

Public Works Administration (PWA), 49

Pulliam, Eugene C., 143

Race, 4, 6, 121, 122, 236, 279, 286; during the Truman administration, 137–139; and the Goldwater candidacy, 194–195, 197, 200; and the Hoover administration, 29–30; and the New Deal years, 65; and the Nixon administration, 218–226; and Ronald Reagan, 269–272; and southern Republicans, 182, 188–189. *See also* Civil rights

Radicalism: as anti-Democratic theme, 35, 36, 46, 107, 116, 139, 158, 212, 236; as anti-Republican theme, 199, 204; as "radical liberalism," 226–229

Rae, Nicol C., 281

Randolph, A. Philip, 174

Ranney, Austin, 247, 251

Raskob, John J., 20, 31

Reagan, Ronald, 212, 242–243, 284–285; and African Americans, 269–271; and conservatives, 259–260, 285; and economic issues, 257–259, 262–263, 280; and foreign policy, 258; and Latino Americans, 272–273; and Republican revitalization, 247–249, 260–265, 267–269, 277–280; and social issues, 260–261; and women's issues and women voters, 273–275

Realignment, 9, 10; and Franklin Roosevelt, 26, 53, 103; and Newt Gingrich, 277; and Richard Nixon, 213–214, 217–220, 226, 229, 234, 239–240, 244, 246; and Ronald Reagan, 247, 249, 262–263, 267; and Strom Thurmond, 202. *See also* Committee to Explore Political Realignment *and* "Dealignment"

Real Majority (Scammon and Wattenberg), 218–219, 220, 226–229

Reapportionment, 104, 278

Reconstruction, 14, 18, 19, 88, 202

Reconstruction Finance Corporation (RFC), 27, 32–33

Reece, B. Carroll, 114

Reed, David A., 50, 74

Region, 3; and Dewey-Taft conflicts, 119, 145; and Kevin Phillips, 220; and the New Deal, 44, 54, 56, 59–60, 67, 77; and Prohibition, 21; Rehnquist, William, 224; and Wendell Willkie, 110

Reid, Ogden R., 240

Relief, 33, 49, 51, 63, 64, 65, 68, 105

Religious issues, 192, 256

Religious Right, 251, 256–257, 262

Religious Roundtable, 256

Republican Advance, 205

Republican Builders, 74–75

Republican Circles, 75

Republican Citizens Committee of the United States, 186–188. *See also* Citizens for Eisenhower *and* National Republican Citizens Committee

Republican Committee on Program and Progress, 179, 186

Republican Coordinating Committee (RCC), 207

Republican Federal Associates, 74, 75

Republican governors. *See* Gubernatorial Republicans

Republican Looks at His Party (Larson), 156

Republican National Committee (RNC), 3, 11, 127, 136, 170, 175, 211; and big cities, 183–185; and Bill Brock as national chair, 253–255, 269, 285; and Citizens for Eisenhower, 167–168; and the Goldwater campaign, 204; and the Hoover administration, 24, 26, 27, 38; and the New Deal, 46, 47, 50, 58, 65, 66, 69, 71, 74, 76; and the 1946 elections, 114–115; and the 1948 elections, 124–126; and Ray Bliss as national chair, 207; and the Reagan years, 263, 265, 271; and the South, 139–141, 173, 185; strategy committee of, 127–128; and study of communication problems, 127; and the Willkie candidacy, 88, 89, 94; and World War II, 100, 104, 109

Republican national convention of 1932, 22, 29–30

Republican national convention of 1940, 75, 81, 83, 84, 96, 207

Republican national convention of 1944, 105–106, 120

Republican national convention of 1964, 193–194

Republican national convention of 1968, 205, 212, 234

Republican national convention of 1972, 234

Republican national convention of 1976, 243

Republican national convention of 1988, 279

Republican National Finance Committee, 196

Republican Papers (Laird, ed.), 209

Republican platform of 1932, 29–30

Republican platform of 1940, 71, 94–95

Republican platform of 1948, 122

Republican platform of 1960, 178, 180, 186

Republican platform of 1980, 254

Republican Program Committee, 66, 71–72, 207

Republican progressives. *See* Progressive Republicans

Republicans for Progress, 205–206

Republicans-for-Roosevelt League, 26

Revenue Act (1935), 56

Revenue sharing, 206, 216, 230–231

Reynolds, William Bradford, 270

Rhode Island, 15

Richberg, Donald R., 167

Richmond, Virginia, 88

Rickard, Edgar, 25

Ripon Society, 195, 206

Rivers, Francis E., 94

Robb, Charles S. "Chuck," 268

Roberts, Clifford, 171

Robinson, Claude, 97, 164, 179
Robinson, Jackie, 198
Rockefeller Brothers Fund, 177
Rockefeller, Nelson A., 177–178, 180, 186, 188, 189, 193, 201, 212, 241–242
Rockefeller, Winthrop, 212
Roe v. Wade (1973), 235, 256, 273
Rollins, Edward J., 263, 268, 278
Romney, George W., 186, 189, 197, 209–210
Roosevelt, Eleanor, 138
Roosevelt, Franklin D., 7, 55, 64, 73, 112, 124, 142, 183, 257, 259; Democratic opposition to, 88; and foreign policy, 82, 91–92; and the New Deal, 44; and the 1932 elections, 13, 18, 29, 35, 36, 38, 42, 59; and the 1936 elections, 41, 67; and the 1940 elections, 80, 84, 88, 91–92, 96; and the 1944 elections, 107–108, 110; and organized labor, 93; as party leader, 40; as political strategist, 42–43; popularity of, 56, 114; progressive support for, 25, 44; and "purge" effort, 69, 152; and relationship with Republicans, 26, 48, 53; Republican responses to, 34, 35, 47, 62, 72, 76, 77, 88; response to Republican attacks of, 58; and the "second New Deal," 55–56; and Supreme Court reform, 67; views on Republican strategy of, 61
Roosevelt, Theodore, 14, 25, 82, 118, 216, 276
Roosevelt, Theodore, Jr., 35, 39, 45, 46, 53–54, 68
Root, Oren, Jr., 84, 87, 141
Roper, Elmo, 124
Rosenman, Samuel I., 103
Rosow, Jerome M., 221
Roth, William V., Jr., 252
Rovere, Richard, 148
Rubin, Carl B., 214
Rumbough, Stanley, 166
Rumford Act (California, 1963), 197
Rumsfeld, Donald, 208
Rural areas, 60, 105, 109, 134, 202. *See also* Farmers and farm issues
Rusher, William A., 162, 188–189, 192, 195, 212, 241, 242–243, 248
Russell, Richard, 142

Sanders, Everett, 46, 49
Sandoz, Ellis, 264
Santa Maria, California, 63

Scammon, Richard M., 218–220, 223, 226, 236, 286
Schlafly, Phyllis, 191, 193, 256, 273
Schlesinger, Arthur M., Jr., 99
School desegregation, 189, 197, 223, 227
School prayer, 192, 204, 261
Schwerner, Michael, 270
Scott, Hugh, 122, 125, 126, 131–132, 139, 170, 202
Scranton, William W., 193, 194
"Second New Deal," 3, 55–56
Second-wave feminism, 234–235
Second World War. *See* World War II
Seventeen Million (Mills), 70
Shafer, Byron E., 281
Shafer, George F., 24
Shouse, Jouett, 31, 68
"Silent Americans," 183
"Silent center," 213
"Silent majority," 222, 232
"Silent vote," 64, 194–195
Simms, Ruth Hanna McCormick. *See* Ruth Hanna McCormick
Simpson, Richard M., 149, 150
Sinclair, Upton, 62
Slichter, Sumner H., 93
Smith, Alfred E., 11, 12, 15, 18, 20, 24, 31, 180
Smith, Dan J., 271
Smith, Margaret Chase, 132, 170
Smith-Connally Act (1943), 106–107
Social Security, 72, 108, 118, 219, 243, 249, 253; Republican acceptance of, 91, 116, 156–157, 231
Social Security Act (1935), 55, 62, 64
Socialism: fear of, 33, 43, 140, 143, 151, 163; as anti-Democratic theme, 35, 36, 47, 48, 55, 77, 90, 101, 113, 114, 116, 135, 157–158, 169, 179; "creeping socialism" theme, 118, 141; "liberty versus socialism" theme, 112, 127–130, 145
Social issues, 211, 281; and the Goldwater campaign, 192, 199–201; and the "New Right," 251–252, 255–257; and 1970s public opinion, 249; and the 1976 campaigns, 243; in 1988, 279; and the Nixon administration, 221–222, 224–225, 226–229, 235, 236; and the Reagan administration, 259–261, 272; as "the Social Issue" (Scammon and Wattenberg), 218–219, 226–229, 286
Soldiers, 105–107. *See also* Veterans

South, 3, 6–7, 10, 21, 113, 172; during the Truman administration, 139–142; and Dwight Eisenhower, 173–174; and the Hoover administration, 18–20, 29; and moderation, 185–186, 206, 227; and the New Deal, 42, 54, 57, 60, 66, 67, 69, 70; and the 1928 presidential election, 15; in 1952, 144, 146, 167, 173, 180, 183, 220, 221; and the 1960s, 188–191, 200–202; and 1976 elections, 244; and the 1980s, 265–266, 274; and the Republican Party between the Civil War and the Great Depression, 14–15; and Richard Nixon, 224–225, 238–239; and Wendell Willkie, 88
South Carolina, 180, 198, 202
South Dakota, 161
Southern Democrats, 20, 88, 105, 137, 140–142, 191, 202, 242, 269; during the 1980s, 264–266, 269; and Dwight Eisenhower, 167, 173–174; and the New Deal, 68, 69, 88; and Richard Nixon, 227, 237–238
"Southern strategy," 188, 190, 224
Southern whites, 19–20, 66, 70, 94, 137, 173–174, 180, 182
South Korea. *See* Korean War
Soviet Union, 89, 115, 123, 128, 176–177, 179–180, 258–259, 274–275; and détente, 232, 241, 249
Spangler, Harrison E., 56, 83, 107
Spanish-American War, 82
Spending, 50, 52, 61, 65, 66, 104, 134–135, 249, 253. *See also* "Bought vote."
Spivack, Robert, 195
Springfield, Illinois, 56, 68
Sputnik, 176
Stassen, Harold, 130
State and local politics, 3, 14, 33, 44, 49, 122
State of the Union messages, 157, 159, 274; of 1954, 155; of 1971, 216, 230–231
States' rights, 57, 61, 69, 101, 139, 141, 167, 189, 190, 200
States' Rights Democratic Party ("Dixiecrats"), 122, 137, 146
Stenholm, Charles, 269
Stephens, Thomas E., 168
Stevenson, Adlai, 145, 150, 167, 172, 174, 176
Stimson, Henry L., 22
St. Lawrence Seaway Act, 157
St. Louis, Missouri, 205
STOP ERA, 256
St. Paul, Minnesota, 129–130
St. Petersburg, Florida, 173

Strikes, 36, 116
Suburbs, 172–173, 183, 184, 193, 213–214
Suez crisis, 176
Sullivan, Mark, 58, 69
Summerfield, Arthur E., 127
"Supply-side economics," 252–255, 257
Supreme Court, 102, 192, 261; and the Goldwater candidacy, 200, 211; and the New Deal, 55, 56, 58, 67–68, 69; and the Nixon administration, 223–224
Swann v. Charlotte-Mecklenburg Board of Education (1971), 223
Symington, Stuart, 157

Taft, Charles P., 51, 58–59, 61, 63, 66, 84, 166, 204–205, 283
Taft-Hartley Act (1947), 116, 125, 197
Taft, Robert, 214
Taft, Robert A., 66, 75, 77, 113, 128, 155, 161, 167; antiliberal strategy of, 121–122; on electoral politics, 135, 172; on the Fair Deal, 112; and Joseph McCarthy, 132; and the 1940 elections, 80, 97; on the 1946 elections, 114–115; and the 1948 campaign, 117–118; and the 1950 campaign, 130–131, 134, 169; and the 1952 campaigns, 143–145, 283; and opposition to Thomas Dewey, 119; on race, 137–138; and the South, 139
Taft, William Howard, 14, 51, 82
"Taftites," 118, 283
Tampa, Florida, 173
Tariff, 11, 23, 28, 49
Taxation, 104, 128, 136, 190; and the 80th Congress, 116; and the Eisenhower administration, 157; and the Hoover administration, 33; and the New Deal, 58, 60, 68, 72; and the 1970s, 252–253, 256; and the Reagan administration, 257–259, 264
Taylor, Zach, 114
Teague, Randal C., 241
Teeter, Robert M., 238, 240, 243
Television, 171–172, 267, 278
Tennessee, 15, 19, 139, 146, 229
Tennessee Valley Authority, 45
Texas, 15, 139, 144, 146, 190, 199, 268, 272
Time–Life, 110
Thayer, Walter N., 168
"Thinking voter" paradigm, 37, 39
Third parties, 14, 22, 54–55, 215, 237. *See also* New parties
Thornton, Dan, 153

Thurmond, J. Strom, 122, 124, 137, 202, 212, 223
Tower, John G., 190
Townsend, Francis E., 54
T.R.B. (*New Republic* columnist), 77
"Troubled Americans," 221
Truman administration, 199
Truman, Harry S., 107, 112, 120, 128, 142, 144, 177, 232; and anticommunism, 132; and civil rights, 137–138, 167; and 1948 election, 118, 122–125, 132, 135, 142, 145, 284; and 1952 elections, 142, 145
Turnout, 67, 103–105, 114, 130, 134–136, 140, 144–146, 163, 165, 194
Tydings, Joseph, 229
Tydings, Millard E., 133

Un-American, 45, 62
Underhill, John, 141
Unemployment, 17, 23, 71–72, 77, 90–91, 93, 113–114, 231, 249
Union members, 51, 146, 185, 208, 233–235, 251, 257, 278. *See also* Organized labor
United Auto Workers (UAW), 198, 233, 278
United Kingdom, 7, 72–73, 99, 112–113, 156, 163–164
United Kingdom general election of 1945, 112, 163
United Kingdom general election of 1951, 141, 163
United Mineworkers of America, 93
United Nations (UN), 120, 123, 129–130, 180
University of Michigan, 9, 160, 267
Urban issues, 7, 68, 184–185, 208, 210, 213–214
Urban voters, 105, 140, 186, 190, 207, 208, 213; New Deal, 42, 60, 67; and the 1928 election, 15; and the 1944 election, 108–109; and the 1946 election, 114; and the 1948 election, 123; and the 1952 election, 146, 172; and the 1976 elections, 244; and responses to the 1960 election, 183–185, 193; and the Wendell Willkie, 89
Utah, 75

Vandenberg, Arthur H., 45–46, 50, 53, 55, 80, 123, 128
Vander Jagt, Guy, 250, 277
Vermont, 13, 41, 161, 275
Veterans, 114. *See also* Soldiers
Vietnam War, 207, 210, 214–215, 222, 226–227, 229, 232–233, 244; and the

antiwar movement, 210, 218, 222, 233; and 1972 election, 236, 238
Viguerie, Richard A., 241, 260
Virginia, 15, 57, 138, 146, 167, 174, 180, 227, 240
Voorhis, Jerry, 115, 137
Voter mobilization, 37, 85, 104, 106, 126, 128, 134–135
Voter turnout. *See* Turnout
Voting Rights Act (1965), 210, 270
Vursell, Charles W., 115, 129

Wadsworth, James W., 46, 51, 55
Wagner Act. *See* National Labor Relations Act
Wagner, Robert F., 202
Wallace, George C., 196, 214–215, 219, 221, 223, 236–237
Wallace, Henry A., 89, 107, 122–124, 137
War on Poverty, 183, 210–211
Warren, Earl, 120–121, 224
Washington, 153
Washington, Val, 175
Washington Post, 176
Watergate scandal, 218, 237, 240, 243–244
Wattenberg, Ben J., 218–220, 226, 228, 236, 286
Weber, Vin, 278
Weis, Jessica McCullough, 170
Welch, Robert, 194
Welfare policy, 120, 156, 185, 216, 229–231, 241, 253, 258, 274, 281
Welker, Herman, 133
Wells, Marguerite M., 94
West, 21, 26, 75, 161, 183, 220; and conservatives, 77; and progressives, 14, 23, 44, 54, 60
West, James L., 27
West Virginia, 65
Wherry, Kenneth S., 125–126, 136
Whig Party, 9, 125
White, F. Clifton, 192
White, Wallace H., Jr., 44
White, Walter, 30, 69–70, 93–94, 102, 139
White, William Allen, 23, 34, 37, 46, 88–89
White southerners. *See* Southern whites
Whites, 67, 248, 286
Whyte, William H., 172
Wicker, Tom, 218
Wier, Roy, 129
Williams, J. Harvie, 141
Williams, Liles, 265
Willis, Charles F., 166, 168
Willkie clubs, 84–87, 92, 96, 102, 167

Willkie, Wendell L., 74, 143, 178, 186; and
  African Americans, 94, 102; Democratic
  attacks on, 84, 90, 92; Democratic
  support for, 88; and gender, 94–95; and
  goal to reshape Republican Party, 83,
  98–103, 110; and impact on Republican
  Party, 110–111; and the 1940 campaign,
  86, 89, 91–97; and the 1942 campaigns,
  104; and the 1944 campaign, 102–103;
  and organized labor, 93; political
  views and emergence of, 80–83, 86–87;
  Republican opposition to, 98–100, 103;
  Republican responses to defeat of, 95–97
Wilson, Woodrow, 14
Wilson administration, 16
Window of Opportunity (Gingrich, Drake,
  Gingrich), 276
Wirthlin, Richard, 248, 265, 280
Wisconsin, 62, 103, 133, 161, 196
Wishart, Joseph S., 126
Women in politics, 21, 28–29, 66, 75,
  170–171, 201, 234–235, 256, 273
Women voters, 27–29, 66–67, 94–95, 114,
  170, 179, 234–235, 248, 273–275

Women's issues, 27–29, 94–95, 170, 234–235,
  273–275
Women's National Republican Club, 55
Woolton, Lord, 163–164
Work, Hubert, 11, 13
Works Progress Administration (WPA), 49,
  51, 52, 105–106
World War I, 16, 34, 82
World War II, 5, 78, 99, 112; domestic
  impact of, 93; and domestic politics,
  103–104, 107–108, 110; and postwar
  reconversion, 113–114; and the
  presidential campaign of 1940, 91–92,
  97–98; and the Republican Party, 79–83
Wright, Jim, 278

Yalta Conference, 115, 128–129, 151
Yost, Lenna Lowe, 29
You and I – and Roosevelt (Taft), 58–59, 63,
  84, 204
Young Americans for Freedom, 207, 241
Young Republican National Federation, 190
Youngstown, Ohio, 251
Youth, 54, 114, 236, 248